It's easy to take good music for granted because there's so much available and because we know what we like. So we listen amidst the static of busyness and wish at least occasionally that we could listen leisurely instead of distractedly. In *It Was Good: Making Music to the Glory of God,* we are asked to pause and listen with ears made sharper with understanding. The thirty chapters need not be read in any particular order, are brief enough to fit into any schedule, and are thoughtful and accessible enough to warrant reflection and discussion. From silence to songwriting to jazz to touring to harmony to improvisation to the blues, rich layers of musical reality are unpacked so they can be appreciated for people who love music but who are not musicians. *It Was Good: Making Music to the Glory of God* is written by gifted artisans to help us know music more deeply and so be able to hear, love and enjoy it—and its Creator—with greater clarity. Please read it, and listen, and then listen some more.

—*denis* HAACK
Co-director of Ransom Fellowship
(www.ransomfellowship.org)

A book like this is a life line of hope, encouragement, and joy to a musician whose journey continues to be anything but normal after twenty-two years of worshiping Jesus through Hindi devotional music genres.

—*christopher dicran* HALE
sitarist and vocalist for Aradhna

Only slightly less understandable than the famine of sacred music we worshipers in America currently find ourselves experiencing (and after so many centuries of feasting!) is the dearth of thoughtful reflection on sacred music, its central place in the life of the Church, where it comes from, who it is for, what it does to us and within us and where it can take us. My shelves buckle under the weight of books on the liturgy in general. I find only two on the soul of nearly every profound liturgical experience known to our race—music, sweet music. Thanksgiving is due to the editor and contributors of these fine essays. May many more follow in their wake!

—*iah* SLABODA
d City Presbyterian Church
nd member of Glockenbass

As a bookseller I am   D1157903   id just the right book
that will help them relat   :allings, interests and
passions. Sometimes, in some fields, this is difficult, if there are few great books in
that field, or they are exceedingly difficult, less than theologically reliable, or poorly
written. Occasionally, though, I see a book and I want to tell everybody interested in
its topic that it is a must-read, a nearly perfect resource for their precise purposes.
Even more rare is the book I want to tell everybody everywhere to read, as a model

of creative Christian scholarship, useful, artful, beautifully designed, insightful, fun. *It Was Good: Making Music for the Glory of God* is just such a book. Everyone should be so fortunate as to have a book like this in their area of interest! Certainly for every musician, of any sort, and for anyone who likes music—or even for those who don't—this is a magnificent book, amazingly conceived and wonderfully produced. This is a truly remarkable achievement. Spread the word!

—*byron* BORGER
Hearts & Minds Bookstore

Musicians will be encouraged and uplifted by the essays is this book, which seeks to put into words our shared wonder and gratitude for the gift of music in our lives.

—*karen* PERIS
The Innocence Mission

Lively, engaging and eminently readable—this book shows that it is still possible to write about music in a way that enriches our experience of it. Above all, it will renew your gratitude to God for making such an art possible.

—*jeremy* BEGBIE
Duke University, author of Resounding Truth:
Christian Wisdom in the World of Music

Is it possible to fully elucidate the spiritual, emotional, intellectual, even physical experiences of music making? Perhaps the best way to go about it is to gather a choir of voices. *It Was Good: Making Music to the Glory of God* offers a rich resource of perspectives, each working to share some aspect or moment in the experience of that mercurial characteristic of human being we call music and its place in the life of faith.

—*dave* PERKINS
*Associate Director of the Religion in the Arts and Contemporary Culture
program at The Divinity School of Vanderbilt University*

Making music to the glory of God is both a calling and a delight. Dialoguing with other artists who embrace the same vocation is a source of particular joy for me, and this collection of thoughtful essays invites readers into reflections and conversations that will nourish and inspire. The diverse voices represented in *It Was Good: Making Music to the Glory of God* weave together rich harmony with subtle dissonance. If you listen carefully, you may just hear the answering voices of saints and angels in heavenly counterpoint.

—*j.a.c.* REDFORD
Composer

IT was GOOD
MAKING MUSIC
to the GLORY of GOD

IT was GOOD

MAKING MUSIC

to the GLORY of

GOD

EDITED BY *ned* BUSTARD

In Christian art, the square halo identified a living person
presumed to be a saint. Square Halo Books is devoted to
publishing works that present contextually sensitive biblical studies
and practical instruction consistent with the Doctrines of the Reformation.
The goal of Square Halo Books is to provide materials
useful for encouraging and equipping the saints.

First Edition 2013

Copyright ©2013 Square Halo Books
P.O. Box 18954, Baltimore, MD 21206

ISBN 978-0-9785097-6-7

Library of Congress Control Number: 2013940012

*This book is dedicated to
Matthew Monticchio—
a dear friend and beloved brother
who has brought so much
good music into my life.*

MAKING MUSIC
soli deo gloria

Life exists for the love of music ...
—G. K. Chesterton

Music is my life.

I come by it honestly. My grandfather was a boy soprano in a professional church choir, played trumpet and piano, later was in a traveling male quartet, sang in the church choir, led singing for Christian Endeavour meetings, and led singing and wrote songs for Keswick Bible Conferences. My grandmother played piano, was a member of The South Philadelphia Girls Mandolin Band, and had an uncle who played a mean set of bagpipes. My father began with piano and then trumpet, but switched to tuba in high school, where he also played the double bass in a swing band. He graduated from college with a music education degree and led various musical groups in the church over the years. My sister cracked her head open while she and I played during a rehearsal of his group The Joyful Noise, and I remember as a young child sitting in the church pew waving my arms around wildly, trying to imitate my father as he conducted the choir. When I was in elementary school, I sang in the school choir, church youth choir, and took trumpet lessons. In high school, I sang in the school choir, a cappella choir, barbershop quartet, the church choir, took guitar lessons, and one time even fronted my friend Chris Webb's rock band. In college I sang in the choir, helped organize dances, drove miles upon miles to concerts, and perfected the art of making mix tapes. After college, I was the assistant manager of a music store,

store, served as the art director for the alternative music publication *Notebored Magazine,* and even DJ'ed a dance club once.

After all that investment in music . . . I ended up becoming a visual artist. It was inevitable since when I wasn't making music, I was drawing. But when I was young, I struggled to have a good understanding of what it meant to be an artist and a Christian. I couldn't see how the visual arts could be glorifying to God. But it was obvious to me that as Christians we are called to make music since there are a profusion of references in the Bible to making music. We read about amateur and professional music, music in daily life and worship, as well as instrumental and vocal music. And if there is any doubt about the centrality of music to the Faith, simply open to the middle of Bible. What do you find? A hymnal complete with music dictation throughout for harp, tambourine, trumpet, timbrel, lute, strings, pipes, and clashing cymbals. And in the midst of all of the instructions given in Scripture we have immense freedom of expression, as Tim Keller reminds us:

> . . . there is a great deal of freedom in how these absolutes are expressed and take form within a particular culture. For example, the Bible directs Christians to unite in acts of musical praise, but it doesn't prescribe the meter, rhythm, level of emotional expressiveness, or instrumentation—all this is left to be culturally expressed in a variety of ways.[1]

The variety of music found in the Bible is delightful. According to Job 38:7, at the beginning of Time the morning stars sang together. Jubal, the father of all those who play the lyre and pipe, was making music in the fourth chapter of Genesis. Paul encouraged the Ephesians to sing to each other psalms, hymns, and spiritual songs, and David called for 288 professional musicians to work in the temple. But worship is not the only place for music specified by the Bible. There is singing after going through the Red Sea. The Israelites had work songs for harvest time and sang while digging wells. There were songs for serving your time as a watchman on the walls, and there was music for war or tearing down city walls. There was music used for calming deranged Kings. And in Zephaniah 3:17, we are comforted to know that God rejoices over us with gladness and exults over us with loud singing. Also, in the gospels we learn that Jesus sang with his disciples. Finally, we understand from Revelation that there will be an unbelievable choir at the end of Time that Christians will be part of, praising God with the heavenly hosts.

Yet throughout the Bible, our songs are mostly intended to be gifts lifted up to God in praise. For example, Psalm 96 begins:

Oh sing to the Lord a new song;
sing to the Lord, all the earth!
Sing to the Lord, bless his name;
tell of his salvation from day to day.
Declare his glory among the nations,
his marvelous works among all the peoples!

Ahh, yes, *work.* All this reflection on music in the Bible is heady stuff, but music is not something easily done. Ask any musician and they will tell you, music is work.

WORK

If there is one thing that was made clear to me after editing *It Was Good: Making Art to the Glory of God,* it is that at the core of creativity is *making,* and making is work. Much is made about "muses" and the "creative spark" and "inspiration." But my experience is that, at the end of the day, art gets made by the people who show up and do the work.

There is no way around work. As many times as I try to sit down and make art without putting in time and effort, I run right into the truth that it takes hard work to make good work. I often hope that lightning will strike and the first thing that comes out of my pencil will be brilliant. But I have found that to happen so rarely that I have been inspired to pen a proverb: *good ideas are built on top of the detritus of bad ideas.* And this is true not just for me. The band U2 was encouraged by their producer Brian Eno to look for songs in their mistakes and musings. He told them, "Honor thy error as a hidden intention."[2] It is the slow trudge through one failure after another that gets us up to the top of the mountain where the air is clear and Beauty can be clearly seen.

And that is a good thing. The hard work of making is our work. Work was our calling before the Fall, and it still is today. We were made to work and are called to work to the glory of God at whatever we are given to do. And as reborn followers of Christ we are particularly sent out in our day for "rightly ordered cultural labor, the creational task of making and remaking God's world. We are (re)made to be *makers.*"[3]

THIS BOOK

The book in your hands is the work of many. It is a book about the amazing gift of music. Mars Hill Audio's Ken Myers asserts that music is a great gift of God and that music is

> . . . a unique gift in its capacity to represent and in some way enable us to participate in the order of God's Creation. It is not merely a mode of per-

sonal expression, but a way of knowing something about objective reality. It addresses the body, the intellect, the imagination, and the emotions in a uniquely powerful way. Music is a great and powerful mystery, and something that unites heaven and earth.[4]

That is a lot of weight to give to music. And it makes the work of creating a book about music seem to be an impossible task. So for this project we have broken down music into more bite-sized portions. As with *It Was Good: Making Art to the Glory of God,* this book can be read in any order. But there is intent behind the ordering of the essays. If you read the book by following the table of contents, you will find that it begins with silence as we pause to prepare for the freedom, creativity, and delight of music (because if music isn't a delight, you're doing it wrong). Then we reflect on the calling and mission of music as we follow the journey of a particular music-making disciple of Christ. Stories like these are important because "the significance—and ultimately the quality—of the work we do is determined by our understanding of the story in which we are taking part."[5] After that, we step back to the music of childhood—a parent's perspective in raising musical children, and providing music made especially for them.

Following that pleasant excursion, it is finally time to get down to the work of *making* music. The next essays deal with rehearsing, refining, song writing, collaboration, counterpoint, harmony, listening, and participation.

In M. Edith Humphrey's *Grand Entrance: Worship on Earth as in Heaven,* we are reminded that since "in our great story of salvation, the next major act after the Creation is that of the Fall, God's people have never been strangers to the minor key."[6] Therefore it is good that we take time to reflect on music made for times of pain, and music in minor keys. This leads us naturally into the essays on the Blues, Jazz, and improvisation.

I think in my old record store we stocked World Music in the bins between Jazz and Hip hop, so I've organized things the same way here. Then this book goes to church with instruments for worship, psalms, and hymns. We struggle with making music utilizing limited resources, then finally, we return to work on Monday morning as we think about vocation, booking, touring, and the fame that may (or may not) come.

One word of warning needs to be offered before you jump into reading this book. The topic of glorifying God through music is so big and we have so many contributors that you should not be surprised to find yourself disagreeing with writers in this book. *They* even disagree with each other. It is easy to imagine that if they were all together in one room (rather than in one book) a fight or two might break out. You as the reader need to apply the advice from Paul in 1 Thessalonians 5:21—"Test everything. Hold on to the good."

Is it Real or is it Memorex?

As indicated earlier, the idea that most captured my imagination after working on the first volume in this series was that of *making*. In his book *Resounding Truth*, Jeremy Begbie declares that music is fundamentally something done. He writes, "I am proposing that music is best construed first of all not as an object or objects but as something done. So . . . we might speak of 'musicking' rather than 'music.'"[7] Therefore, music isn't primarily something on my CD shelf, in my iPod, or in my stack of hymnals—music is *making*.

I take comfort in the knowledge that nearly everyone who reads this book will skip the Preface. But for those chosen few who are actually reading this, I wish to make clear that *I am not disparaging recorded music*. I have no desire to burn my music collection and go back to the Middle Ages where I would only get to hear music at church and the occasional festival. I come from poor Irish farming stock and would never have been invited into court to hear the Handels of the day. No, I am thankful for the myriad of musical choices that are mine to experience. And I am thankful for record players, CD players, iPods, iTunes, Pandora, and whatever the next music technology will be. But the older I get, and the more concerts I attend, I have begun to feel that there are degrees of loss occurring with each step that I take away from music making.

I have come to believe that on the continuum between live performances at one end (with perhaps playing a record in a room with friends in the middle) and being plugged into an iPod on the other, there is loss. In the same way that back when I'd make mix tapes and then subsequent copies of those mix tapes, the music was degraded. I am not saying that today there is a loss in sound quality, since a track on an iPod could be light years superior to the live performance. But instead, there is a loss in the music*ness*—that is, a loss in what makes music such a powerful art form. A similar experience of loss can be found in the visual arts. I remember when I first saw Vincent van Gogh's painting *Starry Night* at the MOMA. I was shocked. The chasm between the reproductions of van Gogh's painting that I had seen in books and the actual work of art that was hanging in front of me was mind boggling.

Music vs. Musiking

Not being a competent musician myself, and being suspect of my own musings in this vein, I decided to ask writers in this book what they thought of Begbie's declaration contrasting *music* with *musiking*. Following are several of the reactions I received. Sandra McCracken was the first to respond:

> Yes, I do agree! I have been playing house concerts over the past year or two and it is remarkable how, in spite of my initial shyness in such a close environment, the reciprocation of energy in a living room, without the barrier of

microphones and speakers is much more satisfying than recording in the studio or on a distant stage. Not only does it make for a fresh experience of the music each time—even if you perform the very same songs night after night—but no two evenings are alike. The human element—different people, different cities, different moods, and circumstances—brings out variations in the performance. From funny to poignant to awkward moments, performing live music consistently presents the element of surprise.

Greg Wilbur also replied in the affirmative:

> Yes, I agree whole-heartedly . . . I can't lay my hands on it this minute, but Chesterton says that in our culture of experts we'd rather pay someone to do something instead of participating ourselves. He goes on to say that eventually no one will laugh since we'll just pay the person to laugh who laughs best. We see that in watching athletics, going to concerts, etc. The tension is, of course, between the desire for perfection versus the opportunity of being involved. However, there is no substitute for being inside a piece of music, to see and hear how your part fits in with others, to have the shared communal act of being a contributing part of something that is greater than the sum of its parts. That is part of my frustration with modern worship music and worship bands—they eliminate the vocal bass line. While the vocalists sing their upper harmonies, there is nothing for basses to sing.

Bethany Brooks affirmed the concept as well:

> Yes, yes, I love this idea. He essentially holds out an alternative to the "work concept" of music, which imagines music's truest form to be a kind of ideal that exists apart from any particular performance of a given composition. I like Begbie's affirmation that music's truest form is in performance—in particularity, in space and time.
>
> Just this morning I was thinking that one of my favorite things about my life is that I get to collaborate with incredible people, and I get to bring those incredible people together and watch them work together, making something that wasn't there before. Or the same thing can apply to bringing together performers and composers: just a couple of months ago, I hired two of the most talented, tasteful musicians I know to play electric guitar and electric bass at City Church. For the offertory, we played an excerpt of a Beethoven sonata—a combination of playing straight from the score and seamless improvisation. It was exquisite. Afterward I kept thinking, "I can't believe I got to help make that happen."

Though much of his work over the years as a record producer has been devoted to archiving music, even Charlie Peacock concurs:

> I agree with him that an act of *musicking* is enough. That the making and doing of it is, in essence, the product. If it just sort of goes out into the air, that is totally sufficient. There is function and purpose and pleasure in merely that . . .
>
> What I love about performing is that we're not as self-conscious as we are in the studio. The studio tends to produce a kind of looking-through-a-microscope kind of mentality. I just love the accidents, the tipping feeling, "We're falling, we're falling . . . no, we're not . . . we're recovering!" I mean, those moments to me are worth everything. What we tend to do in the studio is to iron all of those out. I'm learning in a fresh way how to *not* do that. Like with The Civil Wars—we record all of their performances live. In other words, when you listen to their record somebody is singing and playing a guitar, and another person is standing right there singing along. And that's it. That's what we start with. We may overdub some stuff, but we don't like lay down a guitar part to a click track and then we come back six weeks later and record the vocal. We don't do it like that. In fact, the last three or four records I've done, the whole goal was capturing performances. It doesn't mean I don't want to edit, because I do do a lot of editing. But it's about capturing the performance because we want to leave some of that humanity and stop stripping it out of the music.

Concert pianist Kendra Bigley concurred saying, "Music is meant to be shared. I tell my piano students, 'Playing by yourself: *good.* Playing for others: *better.*'" Several of the contributors in this book took issue with nuances of the music vs. musicking concept, but I think that the discussion can end with what Steve Nichols wrote to me: "You can't beat live music. Even a not-so-good cover from a live band beats a recorded version pulsing through an ear bud." Later he added, "Studio recorded music is to live music as an airbrushed model is to a true human being." Ummm . . . okay, that may be a stretch. But extreme statements always help make the point. And my point is that it is in the actual making of music (musicking) that we experience the real power of music.

MUSIC AND THE (SOCIAL) TRINITY

If that is true, then why? Why is music more "real," more of what *Music* should be when it is being played live rather than when it is being played on an iPod? The answer is because music offers a rather particular way of experiencing an aspect of who God is. We hear, feel, and emotionally connect with music. Sometimes music helps us express joy. Sometimes tears spontaneously appear as music somehow puts us in touch with some of our most profound feelings and beliefs. When we share the experience of hearing music, singing music, playing music, or writing music, we are brought closer to each other in a harmony that vaguely resembles Trinitarian harmony.

At a recent Drew Holcomb and the Neighbors/NeedtoBreathe concert, I had a profound trinitarian experience. As I was listening to the wonderful music being made, I was also seeing the musicians revel in the sheer fun of making the music, while at the same time delighting in watching my wife swept up in the bliss of it all, dancing, oblivious to my attention. I was a distinct person, my wife was a distinct person, and the musicians were distinct persons, but together we were one in the music. Later, Drew joined the NeedtoBreathe guys on stage for the encore. They are in two distinct bands, but were obviously enjoying each other as part of one group making one song. Also, my wife and I (as one flesh, but two distinct persons) were enjoying them enjoying each other, while we also enjoyed the song and enjoyed each other enjoying the event. In a similar vein (though the opposite end of the music continuum from a rock concert), I recently experienced a performance of Mozart's *Requiem*. As I was being wrapped up in the majestic music, I was also delighting in seeing my friend Rob Bigley revel in conducting the performance as if it were a full-contact sport, while at the same time delighting in watching his daughter (as part of Rob's choir) sing with delight for her father.

Like all of the good gifts God has given to us, music—if used in the way that He intended—points us towards Him. As when a man and his wife are joining together in their marriage bed, they are reflecting the mystery of Christ and the Church, so too music mirrors the perfect harmony and mutual love between the Father, Son, and Spirit.

Seeking to describe this mysterious harmony in the Trinity, the Athanasian Creed declares that

> . . . we worship one God in Trinity, and Trinity in Unity; Neither confounding the persons nor dividing the substance. For there is one person of the Father, another of the Son, and another of the Holy Spirit. But the Godhead of the Father, of the Son, and of the Holy Spirit is all one, the glory equal, the majesty coeternal.

The creed goes on later to state that the Trinity is incomprehensible, which is comforting as I wax poetic in these heady heights. Although we are finite and our understanding will forever be limited on this side of Heaven, I believe we receive experiential knowledge of the truth of who or what the Trinity is through music. Perhaps that is why music resonates in us so deeply.

In his essay on the Sistine Chapel in *It Was Good: Making Art to the Glory of*

God, Dr. James Romaine asserted that we reflect God's glory in our creativity. In addition to that, I think that we can reflect the glory of the social aspect of the Trinity in the making of music. I've seen this worked out in a jazz trio my friend Matthew Monticchio is in called The Go Particle. As it says in the Athanasian Creed, "none is afore or after another; none is greater or less than another." In this jazz trinity of piano, bass, and drums, they love and serve each other, submitting one to the other. They weave together so well that they are one musical entity with three voices. Only recently have I come to appreciate the depth of mutual submission in the group. This happened after the trio's drummer, George Yellak, came on staff as our church's chief musician. I've learned that George isn't just an excellent drummer but is instead a multi-talented artist, adept at many instruments. Yet I never knew that before because in the jazz trio he shares the spotlight so that the three may become one. The music they make becomes a sort of aural diagram of the interwoven sociality of the Trinity in a similar way that the *Scutum Fidei* (Shield of the Trinity) diagram is a visual representation of the same mystery.

SDG

Regardless of what music ultimately is, and what aspect of God's glory it particularly reflects, ultimately this book is about the glory of God. "[T]he angels sing, we sing, because of the life and love that God has showered upon us."[8] We were made to sing to the glory of God. He deserves glory from us due to his majesty as well as his kindness to us. Some see an obligation to glorify God as a burden or limitation. But this is simply not the case. Living lives to the glory of God makes us more of who we are. It is the difference between merely existing in black and white and taking in all of life in full technicolor. Steve Nichols elaborates on this as he writes:

> An emphasis on God and his glory does not clip wings. Instead, an emphasis on God and his glory lets us unfurl our wings to the fullest.
>
> . . . Christ doesn't say lose your life and you'll never find it again. He doesn't say it's gone. He says we lose our lives and we find them. We stop holding onto them with all of our might and we will gain them.
>
> By enjoying God's world as God's gift, by enjoying the God-given relationships we have, by enjoying the work of our hands, by developing our God-given abilities, we are living for God and his glory.
>
> . . . God can be at the center of our lives, he can permeate our lives, and we will find that we still have time and energy for our loved ones and for the pursuit of our talents and gifts and abilities. With God at the center, we live broadly and expansively. With ourselves at the center we live narrowly.[9]

In the end, William Edgar wraps up all of these various musings in a tidy comment he made to me: "We can make music alone, or with other musicians, and certainly with or without an audience. Though the most important audience is the one who gave us this unspeakable gift in the first place." Music can't be my life, and it can't be yours either. We need to receive music as a good gift from a good and loving Father. We also need to take that gift and make music together, pointing towards the perfect harmony in the Trinity. And finally, we need to lay the music we've made at God's feet as a gift of glory back to our Creator.

Endnotes
1   Timothy Keller, *The Reason for God: Belief in an Age of Skepticism* (New York: Dutton, 2008), 44.
2   Steve Turner, *Imagine: A Vision for Christians in the Arts* (IVP Books, 2001), 107.
3   James K. A. Smith, *Imagining the Kingdom: How Worship Works* (Baker Academic: Grand Rapids, 2013), 5-6.
4   Ken Myers, *Music Practice*, a lecture for the Society for Classical Learning, June 2012.
5   Wendell Berry, *Sex, Economy, Freedom & Community: Eight Essays* (Pantheon, 1994), 109.
6   Edith M. Humphrey, *Grand Entrance: Worship on Earth as in Heaven* (Grand Rapids: Brazos Press, 2011), 191.
7   Jeremy S. Begbie, *Resounding Truth: Christian Wisdom in the World of Music* (Grand Rapids: Baker Academic, 2007), 39.
8   Edith M. Humphrey, *Grand Entrance: Worship on Earth as in Heaven* (Grand Rapids: Brazos Press, 2011), 191.
9   Stephen J. Nichols, *Welcome to The Story: Reading, Loving, and Living God's Word* (Wheaton: Crossway, 2011), 114-115.

OUT OF
the Silence

On August 29, 1952, David Tudor gave a recital of contemporary piano music in Woodstock, New York. One of the pieces he performed that night had never been played before. It confused and disturbed the audience, sending a shock wave throughout the classical music community and well beyond. The piece was 4'33", composed by John Cage.

Consisting of three movements, the piece can be "played" on any instrument, as the musician does not actually strike a single note. For four minutes and thirty three seconds the musician just sits there. There is nothing but silence.

Of course, for John Cage, there is much more happening here. Music is being made; we just need to shift our understanding of what music is. However, in order to shift our understanding of what music is, we need to shift our understanding of what silence is.

Like so many of his artistic contemporaries in the twentieth century, John Cage pushed the limits as far as possible. In his search for silence, the composer went to the quietest place that he could find. In his collection of essays and lectures on silence Cage writes:

> For certain engineering purposes, it is desirable to have as silent a situation as possible. Such a room is called an anechoic chamber, its six walls made of special material, a room without echoes. I entered one at Harvard University several years ago and heard two sounds, one high and one low. When I described them to the engineer in charge, he informed me that the high one was my nervous system in operation, the low one my blood

in circulation. Until I die there will be sounds. And they will continue following my death. One need not fear about the future of music.[1]

A student of Zen Buddhism, the composer came to understand music as
nothing but a collection of sounds. In other words, the ambient sounds that surround you as you read this book are music. Maybe you're playing music in the
background while you read this. Maybe you're in a library and all you can recognize are faint whispers in the background. Either way, John Cage would say that
you are surrounded by music; you simply need to listen. But for Cage, while he
enjoyed the sounds, they did not point to a greater meaning or purpose. While he
found the silence to be full, he also found it to be empty.

As a follower of Jesus Christ, I too find the silence to be full of sound. But,
unlike Cage, I find the silence to be full of meaning. I believe that the silence
contains the very presence of God.

THE SILENCE OF GOD

God's presence in the silence can be understood in at least two ways. First,
God speaks to us in the silence. On the afternoon of July 24, 2008, my brother-
in-law, Brian Storer, was killed in an airplane accident. He was 24 years old. His
father, Mark Storer, was the pilot and was also killed. My sister was left a widow
and her two little boys were left without a father. On the day after the accident
I went out to the crash site with the rest of the family. The plane had crashed in
a wooded area and many of the trees were still smoldering when we arrived. Yet
the area had been thoroughly cleared and the wreckage from the debris had been
almost completely removed.

As we walked towards ground zero I became numb. I didn't know what to do.
We all stood there in stunned silence. I remember looking down at the ground,
at the very place where the breath was sucked out of my brother-in-law and his
father. This was the place where life turned into death. There was nothing there. I
felt nothing. It was almost as if we were standing at the threshold of a black hole.

The German theologian Karl Barth wrote, "It is a terrible thing when God
keeps silence, and by keeping silence speaks."[2] I didn't hear God speaking that
afternoon. In fact, I wondered if God was there at all. It wasn't until some time
later, during a reading of 1 Kings 19:11–33, that I came to a new understanding.
The prophet Elijah was on the run and his life was in danger. He headed to the
mountains and hid in a cave. Then the word of the Lord came to Elijah.

> [The Lord] said, "Go out and stand on the mountain before the Lord, for
> the Lord is about to pass by." Now there was a great wind, so strong that
> it was splitting mountains and breaking rocks in pieces before the Lord,
> but the Lord was not in the wind; and after the wind an earthquake, but

the Lord was not in the earthquake; and after the earthquake a fire, but the Lord was not in the fire; and after the fire a sound of sheer silence. When Elijah heard it, he wrapped his face in his mantle and went out and stood at the entrance of the cave. Then there came a voice to him that said, "What are you doing here, Elijah?"—1 Kings 19:11–13 (NRSV)

God did not speak to Elijah in the wind, the earthquake, or the fire. Instead, God spoke to Elijah in the midst of "sheer silence." As I reflected on these verses I realized that I had witnessed something similar. The crash site was not an empty pit of nothingness. It was full of God's presence. I didn't need to go back to know that this was true. As I entered into times of silent meditation I could sense God in ways that I had not before. I knew that He was near. I believe that God still speaks to us in this way if we would but quiet ourselves and listen.

God speaks to us in the silence, but there is a second way in which God is present in the quiet. God listens to us in the silence. Revelation 8:1 (NIV) reads, "When he opened the seventh seal, there was silence in heaven for about half an hour." Why is there silence in heaven when the seventh seal is opened? When we read this verse in its context we realize that here God is listening to the prayers of the saints in the midst of the silence. In the midst of the revelation of Jesus Christ, heaven goes silent and listens for the prayers of God's people.

Prayer is often understood as a dialogue between humans and God. But there is another kind of prayer, a silent prayer, in which God listens to us and we listen to God. One of my favorite examples of this comes from a Dan Rather interview with Mother Teresa. He asked her, "What do you say to God when you pray?" She replied, "I listen." At this Rather responded, "Well, then, what does God say?" Mother Teresa smiled and said, "He listens."[3]

In silence, we can both hear God speaking to us and know that God hears us when we pray. This only ever happens by the grace of Jesus Christ, the very one who "was oppressed and afflicted, yet he did not open his mouth; he was led like a lamb to the slaughter, and as a sheep before her shearers is silent, so he did not open his mouth."—Isaiah 53:7 (NIV)

THE REST OF GOD

This basic understanding of God and silence reverberates into our understanding of music and silence. Christian tradition teaches that God created the world *ex nihilo* (out of nothing). Another way to say this is that God wrote the music of creation out of a kind of silence. Without silence, there can be no music. Human beings do not create music in an *ex nihilo* kind of way; only God can do that. We create music out of rest.

Our music begins with rest. In Genesis 1, we encounter the six-fold creation rhythm of "there was *evening* and there was *morning*." This rhythm serves as a signpost to the Hebrew understanding of rest. For Jewish people still, the Sabbath begins with sundown. This observance of the Sabbath points to the fact that God is active and at work even when we are sleeping and at rest. God is at work before we begin our work. Within the Christian understanding of the Lord's Day, we too begin the day in the light of Jesus Christ, whose resurrection precedes our awakening. We must make every effort to enter into this rest.

STOP

One of the first lessons I learned as a young pianist was to take a deep breath before I started to play. As a child, I would regularly barrel right into the next phrase or song or idea. It was all one continuous wave of sound. My fingers were tight. My back was hunched over. I was, for all intents and purposes, disengaged. I just wanted to get started and the idea of stopping before starting didn't make any sense to me.

"Stop. Breathe. Now . . . play." Over and over and over, this lesson was engrained into my psyche. I had been making noise, but it was not until I learned to breathe first—that music begins with rest—that I started to make music. Greg Wolfe writes, "Silence is not something we experience very often today. We live in a society of noise and endless distraction. Artists have always understood and respected that the creative act emerges out of silence."[4] This is the rhythm that God invites all of us into.

If the first lesson is that music begins with rest, then a second lesson is that musicians often speak the loudest through the notes they don't play. When Ken Kesey eulogized Jerry Garcia he wrote, "It was the false notes you didn't play that kept that lead line so golden pure. It was the words you didn't sing."[5] Why was Miles Davis so incredibly popular? There are many answers to this question, but one answer has to be that he knew what notes not to play. Where does the pocket come from in funk? By not playing where you shouldn't be playing. And the same can be said for all music.

REST

When I first started writing songs from the piano I wanted the songs to sound as full as if an entire band were playing with me. This made me a very busy piano player. When I moved from high school to college I started to play more jazz. The bass player in the trio I worked with threatened to cut off my left hand if I didn't get out of his space. Eventually he would just hit my left hand if I got too busy on the low end. I eventually learned my lesson. When I made my first full band recording of music in my early twenties I once again realized just how busy my piano playing really was. It was like my piece of the musical puzzle was much too big and bulky to fit with any of the other pieces. In music, less is often more.

Understanding music in this way is more than a *via negativa* (understanding what something is by studying what it is not) approach. Understanding music in this way is the starting point. Silence is not the enemy of music in the same way that silence is not the enemy of the Word, Jesus Christ. On the contrary, it is only through silence that we can actually listen for Jesus Christ. Saint Augustine provides the coda for my argument, "In the beginning was the Word. Only wordlessly can one come to a perception of this; it is not made apparent by the agency of human words."[6]

If I were to go on, I feel that I would defeat the very purpose of this chapter on silence. Instead, I invite you into a space of silent prayer and reflection. Take the next couple of minutes (why not make it four minutes and thirty three seconds) and pray in silence. Remember that God speaks to us in the silence. Remember that God listens for us in the silence. Remember that, in music, we must rest before we can make music.

Endnotes

1   John Cage, *Silence: Lectures and Writings* (Middletown: Wesleyan University Press, 1961), 8.
2   Karl Barth, *Evangelical Theology: An Introduction* (Grand Rapids: Eerdmans Publishing, 1963), 136.
3   Timothy Jones, *The Art of Prayer: A Simple Guide to Conversation with God* (Colorado Springs: Waterbrook Press, 2005), 118-119.
4   Gregory Wolfe, *Intruding Upon the Timeless: Meditations on Art, Faith, and Mystery* (Baltimore: Square Halo, 2003), 26.
5   Ken Kesey, "The False Notes He Never Played," *The New York Times Magazine,* Dec. 31, 1995.
6   Hans Urs von Balthasar, *Explorations in Theology: The Word Made Flesh* (San Francisco: Ignatius Press, 1964), 134.

THE BEST THING
in life is free

A friend of mine once spoke to me about what he called the "existential hum, the uneasiness which keeps us moving, which never allows us to feel entirely at ease. He had tried heroin once. He said he understood at once the seductiveness of that narcotic. For the first time in his life, he was not annoyed by the existential hum."
—Kurt Vonnegut, *Palm Sunday,* 185

Jesus said, "If you continue in my words, you are really my disciples. Then you will know the truth, and the truth will set you free."
—John 8:31

When we listen to music we love, we feel free, unencumbered, more like ourselves. Certain pieces can so utterly engage us that we're not just hearing with our ears, but with our whole selves: our emotions, reason, intuition, memory, and nearly every part of our physiology, as well. When this happens, something tangible changes inside. We move. We resonate. Music opens us up. It puts us in a state of mind where we feel more confident, more capable of coping with things that hold us down, that leave us feeling powerless, resentful, ashamed, hopeless.

At the same time, I wonder whether music can do anything more than merely produce feelings, especially when it comes to freedom. Can music actually help people become free? Outwardly? Inwardly? Or is it simply a very effective way to drown out the existential hum? I ask because I've noticed that most people put more effort into feeling free than actually becoming free, and I also know that music can play an enabling role. As John Calvin said,

Now among the other things proper to recreate man and give him pleasure, music is either the first or one of the principal, and we must think of it as a gift of God deputed to that purpose. For which reason we must be the more careful not to abuse it, for fear of soiling and contaminating it, converting it to our condemnation when it has been dedicated to our profit and welfare." (Calvin, *Preface to the Geneva Psalter*)

As I see it, the connection between music and freedom hinges on two things: music's power to affect our outlook and its ability to tell the truth. Depending on how we listen, and what we do in response, music can either make us freer or more constrained. I'll show how in three sections. First, I'll show how certain built-in abilities of music can soothe the effects of oppression while offering courage to change habits and attitudes. Next, I'll show how all of this might go south, especially when we use music to reinforce only the "truths" we want to believe. And finally, for those of us committed to the ongoing process of respond-ing to the Gospel, I'll show how music can play a role in the process of shifting alliances from the kingdom of this world to the kingdom of God.

THE LIBERATING POWER OF MUSIC

Mozart's music always sounds unburdened, effortless, light. This is why it unburdens, releases, and liberates us.
—Karl Barth, *Wolfgang Amadeus Mozart*, 47

Freedom is directly mentioned in far too many songs to count. "Freedom's just another word for nothing left to lose." (Kris Kristofferson, "Me And Bobby McGee") "Freedom comes when you learn to let go." (Madonna, "Power Of Goodbye") "Freedom, well, that's just some people talking. Your prison is walk-ing through this world all alone." (The Eagles, "Desperado") "What you thought was freedom was just greed." (U2, "Gone") "Before you ask some girl for her hand now, keep your freedom for as long as you can now. My Mama told me, you better shop around. (Smokey Robinson, "Shop Around") People of all times and cultures have not only used music to describe and define freedom, we've used music to cry out for it. Think of negro spirituals. Think of protest songs. And it's not just a song's lyrics that convey freedom; something in the music itself helps us imagine freedom. Musical imagination happens when notes, rhythms, and chords begin to inhabit us (or we inhabit them?) such that we begin to sense what freedom feels like in our limbs, hands, feet, chest, neck, and shoulders; it hijacks our heartbeat and infiltrates our breathing; it broods in the gut and challenges the throat; it infiltrates those hard-to-locate "spiritual" parts of us we call heart and soul; it clarifies thinking. As T.S. Eliot put it, "We become the music while the music lasts." Once music gets inside, we immediately "know" what it's like to live unfettered, unburdened by fear, resentment, loss, and failure—whether or not the lyrics mention freedom directly.

Freedom is actually a subtext of all music because its very materials resist the effects of oppression. The simple fact that music starts, keeps going, then finishes is a testimony to perseverance, instilling confidence to those of us who feel weak, disoriented, unappreciated. That it does so with grace and elegance reminds us of the dignity we may have lost or forgotten. That a melody can walk, jump, skip, stoop, lean, lounge, or fly feels like permission to go where we want to go, as quickly or slowly as we please. The simple fact that in music, shorter phrases add up to something beautiful, grand, and meaningful ennobles the drudgery of repetitive, seemingly pointless work. The simple fact that music always knows where it's going, that it rarely seems trapped, gives us hope. That music is so frequently playful awakens something childlike within us. The simple fact that music "makes us" tap our toes, bob our heads, sway, or get up and shake our booties challenges self-conscious notions about the body. The simple fact that we find musical patterns intriguing, delightful, fun, and intelligent offers a stark alternative to the calloused outlook we acquire when we feel beaten down. The simple fact that music never questions its own authority, that it just steps up and says what it says—sings—feels especially heroic to downtrodden folk who have lost their voice. And the simple fact that notes, rhythms, and chords can capture and express emotion, solely through the ways that they move, grants us full per-mission to feel.

At the same time, not every "simple fact" correlation will hit all people equally. A lot depends on one's experience with oppression: where it originates, its inten-sity, whether it's seasonal or perpetual, whether it's limited to one area of life or feels pervasive, whether it's shared with others or unique to ourselves. This might explain a bit of what we commonly chalk up to "taste." Perhaps we're drawn to particular songs, styles, or artists in part because of the specific ways they liberate our thoughts, feelings, or bodies. After all, each musical style and genre is created by amplifying some musical aspects while muting others. One guy irons his shirts to Vivaldi. Could it be that the precision in this music helps him overcome his fear that he's not very good at the task? His neighbor does her dusting to indie folk. Could it be that the rough edges in the music help her avoid stressing over what her mother would think?

And then certain musical genres seem to harbor freedom at their very core. A negro spiritual's rhythms and groans simultaneously capture physical degrada-tion and inner triumph, with melodies that brood, percolate, pierce the heart, and soar to heaven. Jazz improvisation thrives on spontaneity, yet actually depends on a strict underlying structure—a paradox that gets to the very nature of freedom, something that philosophers and political scientists have been telling us for mil-lennia: that liberty requires boundaries. Ethnomusicologists Charles Keil and Steven Feld point out that "Any good composer tries to give some spontaneity to his forms, and conversely, any good improviser tries to give some form to his spontaneity." (*Music Grooves,* 55) This is not limited to instrumentalists. What else demonstrates freedom like Ray Charles' rendition of "America the Beautiful," which flagrantly and gracefully refuses to let even a single note land where it's "supposed to?" Or explore the other side of the equation, listening closely for what might make Mozart's music seem so "light and effortless" to Karl Barth. Or if not Mozart, try Beethoven, who just a few decades later used essentially the same materials to create deep, sudden, emotional shifts and contrasts—an entirely different musical exercise in freedom.

Let's see how some of the features I've mentioned might play out in a single song. In "Fire and Rain," James Taylor sings about his friend Suzanne, a woman he'd met in drug rehab. Her suicide, combined with Taylor's own struggles with drugs and loneliness, make for pretty bleak lyrics. The music, however, testifies to something deeper than his pain: hope. The guitar introduction is subtle, airy, even optimistic. Rather than just strumming out straight chords, Taylor playfully twists and bends individual notes, adding "grace notes" (the technical term for this sort of ornamentation is apt here, especially because despairing people are hardly prone to putting up cheerful decorations). Then right before Taylor begins to sing, he hones in on one note—repeating it while bearing down on it lightly, building anticipation. This short introduction opens space to breathe for those coping with grief, and for the rest of us, makes the story we're about to hear more bearable.

As Taylor describes learning of Suzanne's death, he sounds somewhat matter of fact, even a bit numb. The relatively low-energy verse allows the chorus, when it arrives, to take speak authoritatively without having to flaunt itself.

> Just yesterday morning they let me know you were gone.
> Suzanne the plans they made put an end to you.
> I walked out this morning and I wrote down this song,
> I just can't remember who to send it to.

> (*Chorus*) I've seen fire and I've seen rain.
> I've seen sunny days that I thought would never end.
> I've seen lonely times when I could not find a friend,
> But I always thought that I'd see you again.

At the chorus, the confident, descending bass line helps make the declaration about "fire and rain" feel unambiguous. It's curious, I think, that these words have been taken to mean so many things—purification; trouble; warmth and cleansing; light and darkness; happiness and tears; testing and baptism; suffering and rebirth—and yet we still get exactly what Taylor means. Each word receives a different type of harmonic support. There's tension on the word "fire," which releases entirely on the word "rain." Roughly the same scheme of tension and release is replayed over the next two lines, although, rather than getting tired and overly familiar, the music actually gains fortitude. Suffering ain't gonna win here, even in the face of dashed hope: "I always thought that I'd see you again."

The specific note Taylor hits on "again" is typical for the ending of a big section or an entire piece. Its technical names are "the tonic" or "the keynote." It's a note that typically sounds final. ("Oh, come let us adore him, Christ the Lord." "There's a land that I heard of, once in a lullaby." "From every mountainside, let freedom ring.") But in "Fire and Rain," this final tonic note is accompanied by a long, forcefully strummed, unresolved chord, giving it a sudden surge of energy that's hard to categorize: Anxious? Buoyant? Foreboding? Defiant? What's more, Taylor holds this chord for twice as long as any other chord in the song. Something's definitely up. No groveling, no bitterness, no sentimentality—just Taylor, through music, resisting the finality of death.

At this point, we see how music can do more than just make us feel free. It can offer comfort, hope, confidence, and dignity—all in short supply to the oppressed. It can both point the way toward such things, and help us experience them within ourselves. What we do with those insights and sensations make all the difference between simply feeling free or actually becoming free.

Music's Truth-Telling Ability

> None are so hopelessly enslaved as those who falsely believe they are free.
> —Goethe

Try a little experiment. Sing the time—"It's 12:07"—two different ways: first quickly in a high voice and a major key, then slowly in a low voice and a minor key. In music, facts matter, but not nearly as much as how we feel about them. I like how Leeland Ryken puts this: "Art is not about things as they are, but things as they matter."

Music has three basic approaches to truth. A musician can tell it like it is (focusing on experience). A musician can tell it like he or she wants it to be (focusing on desire). Or a musician can tell it like it ought to be (focusing on belief).

In "Fire and Rain," Taylor doesn't shrink back from the facts of his experience. Themes of addiction, institutional abuse, loneliness, fear, disorientation, and suicide are present and accounted for. Nor is he shy about being totally honest about his feelings about these issues and how they naturally intersect with his beliefs. The shared focus on facts, feelings, and faith is a big part of what makes the song seem so true. It's the music, though, that gives him a way to express all of this in the context of hope, a truth deeper than mere experience, desire, or even statements of belief.

Taylor's multi-dimensional approach to truth-telling stands in contrast to so many songs that take a much narrower focus. When a song simply says, "Here's what happened to me, and now you know why I'm so happy, pissed, lonely, cynical, or worn out," that doesn't give a song truth that "matters." A one-dimensional approach to truth leads to one-dimensional living, where conclusions about ourselves, others, and God are linear, thin, brittle, and incapable of connecting diverse aspects of the real world in meaningful ways. No freeing power there.

Consider the song "I've Got a Feeling" by the Black-Eyed Peas, a very catchy exercise in positive thinking. There's something both exciting and cool about the introduction. We hear regular groups of repeated chords over a sustained bass. That the chords are staccato gives them energy, even a little sparkle. That they pump at a tempo much faster than the average resting rate for a human heart communicates anticipation. Yet this kept in check by the relatively subdued volume, and the fact that the bass is just behind the beat. This is what it feels like when cool people get excited about something. At the same time, it seems that the volume and energy are set to give the impression of hearing dance music while walking up to a club.

After a half minute, lead singer will.i.am sets forth his thesis with an utterly confident, wry happiness: "I've got a feeling, [pause] that tonight's gonna be a good night." Repeating the last phrase several more times makes it feel inevitable, right, true, especially as the music picks up a little, and he adds "woo-hoo." But how is he so sure? What's going to make tonight so good? Actually, nobody needs to ask; it's evident from the music. It's party time! A little dancing, some time to catch up with friends, some weekend freedom from the pressures felt at work, right? How can that be wrong? But the song is not about simple relaxation. The music and the lyrics flaunt a distinct type of "partying"—hedonistic freedom—front and center as the reason for living. To the partier, all other endeavors are either to be tolerated as an means to an end (no money, no party), or simply an impingement on the freedom to snatch whatever we desire.

> Tonight's the night, Let's live it up
> I got my money, Let's spend it up
> Go out and smash it, Like oh my God
> Jump off that sofa, Let's get, get off
> I know that we'll have a ball
>
> If we get down and go out and just lose it all
> I feel stressed out, I wanna let it go
> Let's go way out spaced out, And losing all control
>
> Fill up my cup, mazel tov
> Look at her dancing, Just take it off
> Let's paint the town, We'll shut it down
> Let's burn the roof, And then we'll do it again
>
> Let's do it, Let's do it, Let's do it,
> Let's do it, And do it and do it,

Let's live it up, And do it and do it
And do it, do it, do it, Let's do it, let's do it,

Let's do it Monday, Tuesday, Wednesday, and Thursday
Friday, Saturday, Saturday to Sunday

Get get get get get with us, You know what we say
Party every day, pa pa pa party every day

Embedded in this song is the simplest slogan of freedom in our culture: "Just
do it." Why is it that we feel especially free when we let go of inhibitions and
gratify desires? Because oppressed people don't have that option? Is this why we
sometimes use "free time" for something "naughty"—something we don't normally
allow ourselves to splurge on—a shopping spree, pigging out, playing video games
for far too long, or watching a racy or stupid film? Recognizing this impulse helps
us see why "I've Got a Feeling" is true for all of us, not just the party crowd.

But it's not the whole truth. Not even close. The Master taught us that humility, thankfulness, and obedience set us free. Indulgence enslaves. Now to be clear,
parties are commanded as part of the way we live out our faith together—the
Feast of the Firstfruits, Commemoration of the Ten Commandments, the Feast
of the Trumpets, the Feast of the Tabernacles, the year of Jubilee, the Passover
(with its four cups of wine). We might also include Jesus' turning of water to
wine—top quality wine—at a wedding. It's impossible to say that God is a fuddy-
duddy when it comes to celebrations. But while the objective of God's parties is
to remember, the objective of hedonistic partying is to forget. His way of truth is
incredibly hard; a narrow road leading to the eye of a needle. Narrow, but hardly
one-dimensional. Wouldn't the one who is himself the Truth attend the Black-
Eyed Peas' party? We can get a good sense of what he might have said to people
there by reading the stories of gatherings he went to back in his day.

What I'm less certain about is what he might say to followers who don't seem
to see a difference between feeling free and becoming free. How many Christians
have constructed a theology that prioritizes happiness? For example, a Christian
artist who goes by the name "Rawsrvnt" has made a cover of "I've Got a Feeling."
Most of the song is essentially identical to the original, except that he replaces
the morally questionable words with a (weakened) paraphrase of the Shema
(Deuteronomy 6).

Jesus we're livin for your name
We'll never be ashamed of you
All Praise and all we are today
Take take take it all, Take take take it all.

I give you my heart, my Lord, I give you my heart
I give you my soul my Lord, I give you my soul
I give you my mind my Lord, I give you my mind

I give you my strength my Lord, For you, My God,
I only ever give my all

Can substituting a few words transform the focus from hedonism to worship? Perhaps. (Many have been quick to note that Martin Luther substituted sacred lyrics in "drinking songs" of his day, except that it turns out that the popular songs he baptized had nothing to do with drinking or carousing). But here, Rawsrvnt's insipid words don't begin to capture the sense of the Shema, which calls for overt God-love—fervent service—the opposite of passive surrender. Nothing in the music engenders anything close to devotion, either. Instead of redirecting the party attitude in the original song, Rawsrvnt adds a kick drum right at the start to ramp up mindless anticipation.

On one hand, it's common for people to "ignore" lyrics and just groove with a song's easy-going, motivational beat and catchy tune. As I pointed out in the first section, so many built-in aspects of music can undo effects of oppression. Maybe this is a valid way to listen to either version of "I've Got a Feeling" (and other similar songs)?

But if truth matters, and if we owe it to a musician to take his or her work seriously (respect it), then we can't merely slough off the implications of their music. Music is fellowship. It's a way of discovering God through encountering each other in meaningful ways.

Are we free to use music in any way we wish? Isn't it better to recognize that music ought to open us up to something bigger than the feelings we get while listening to it? Here, we might compare music to any other blessings given to us by our Father God. Every good gift that God has provided is capable of enriching our lives when we receive it as he intends. Food, vocation, wine, sex—all wonderful, all meant to be enjoyed in the context of covenant and community. But going straight for the good feelings out of context will cheapen and distort everything. Compare, "Hey Jed, wanna go for a beer and have a talk?" and "Hey Jed, wanna go get drunk?" The deep emotions that arise from thorough truth-telling within music are most able to liberate. But when we choose music because it tells only truths we want to hear (or brings feelings we want to feel), we turn music into a vehicle for worshipping idols of our own making.

FREE INDEED

Music helps you find the truths you must bring into the rest of your life.
—Alanis Morissette

The Lord is my strength and my song. He has become my salvation.
—Exodus 15.2

Freedom is a step-by-step process; something to grow into throughout our lives. "If you continue in my words . . . you will know the truth, and the truth will set you free." Continuing is necessary because the ramifications of the Gospel are too far-reaching to manage in one dose. Yet at the same time, everything the Master says is utterly simple. Start today; understand as you go. Practice peace. Practice joy. Practice loving our neighbor. The best music helps us believe that "I can do this thing." It gives clues for where to start continuing, as it lets us test drive the victorious feelings we long for. The worst music lets us off the hook, agrees with the impossibility of the situation, and nudges us to snatch the instant rewards we think we deserve.

Freedom depends on obedience. That seems like an oxymoron until we realize that what most people long for the most is to be free from failure—our inability to do what we know is right. After countless attempts to improve ourselves, we settle. And we secretly resist anyone who suggests we start over again, try a little harder, or even consider something new.

But that's the great thing about music. It undoes all of our excuses. It opens doors that have been slammed shut. A song can wriggle in where a pastor, a counselor, or even the scripture itself isn't welcome. One day we hear the simplest little tune, and it starts to work on us, saying "C'mon, you know this is right." We can't argue, because the music disarms us. Thoughts and feelings become intermeshed. Music helps us "know" things—deeply, kinetically—things impossible to convey through words alone: the very substance and content of love, joy, grief, resolve, mercy, awe, value, justice, beauty, hope, and freedom. Music rekindles the imagination in ways that make belief in an unseen world seem both vivid and plausible. Music feeds and enables faith.

For too many people, this is where the music stops. Rather than turning whatever has been awakened inside us into a prayer or impetus for action, we let the thoughts and feelings fade away with the final notes, even though songs are designed to be memorable, re-singable, and re-playable. A song is as close as our breath, and as intimate. Whatever truth, comfort, and inspiration it offers can ultimately direct us back to God. We grab hold of the Gospel as it grabs hold of us.

My students seem to get this. Halfway through a course I teach, I ask them to write about following question: "How does a song you love help shape who you are at this point in your life?" Their choices have ranged from country, to Chopin, to Kid CuDi. They're surprised to find that what initially attracted them to their song happens to be areas where God is challenging or healing them.

Kristi wrote, "I listen to this song whenever I'm feeling helpless or powerless. I listen to it when I feel like my voice isn't being heard. I listen to it on days when it seems the real me wasn't present." Alex found that his song "helps me realize the connection and the gap between who I currently am, and who I want to be." Segun explains how a song helped him "break the curse of trying to buy everything I longed for just to fit in with the crowd." Nathan finds that "This piece makes me reconsider my relationships with people—people I love, people who frustrate me, people who I don't know well, and think about how I can give them my love in a deeper and more meaningful way. It also reminds me that I ought to cry out for love when I am in pain."

Over time, I become more and more convinced that God intends music to open our hearts, minds, and bodies to his Spirit so that our affections, thoughts, speech, and actions might be re-formed and re-energized to align with his purposes in our lives and his coming kingdom. Music opens us up, changes our outlook, and renews our hope by making us both more vulnerable and more determined. Every time this happens, we have an opportunity "do business with God": to remember his word and his ways, to reflect on our own sinfulness, to renew our commitment to follow, and to let him remind us that we belong to him. To be free.

FINGERPAINTING
and plumbers

Human life begins with a primordial calling. Our Maker orders our days, knows their number, shape, and scope. And he calls us out from the womb exactly when he means to. In that secret place, over the span of about forty weeks, he forms and weaves our DNA, the map that organizes our personality and our essence.

God is a master designer. His fashion sense is perfect and unchanging. He doesn't need to modify the form of what he makes from year to year, because it is so excellent as it is. The human body is, and has always been, universally gorgeous.

He doesn't need to change the color palate of springtime wildflowers, or the Swiss Alps, or the African plains, because their beauty is never tired. His aesthetic is flawless, and it never needs to be re-imagined. He makes beautiful things that surprise our senses, things with exceptional form and function.

I think about the simple skill and beauty of my hands typing on the keyboard. I think about the bounty of Katy's urban, vegetable garden on her front lawn. Or the stunning interplay of words and music of Paul Simon's *Graceland* album. Or the everyday miracle that my dear friends were surprised by twins after a dark season of infertility and illness. These are glimpses of a creator God. He delights in vivid color and surprise, in subtle fragrances and lavish feasting. These things remind us that we were made for a fullness of life that is more than just breath and blood.

Genesis declares that man and woman are made in God's image. This implies a profound calling for us as his image bearers. His generous invitation to us to be co-creators with him is a great honor, that the ultimate Designer would let us share this with him. We reflect and imitate his glory in this way, and he gives us the ability to make and remake, build and rebuild. This practice is our primary calling. This is the way by which we glorify and enjoy him forever.

Early in life, children thrive on "making things." Building a fort, making up a song, baking cookies, role-playing as super heroes, finger-painting; it is a child's full time work to play. Tiny humans know how to practice the art of creativity without much prodding. They are simply obeying the creative mandate that is encoded in their very being. When we grow up and move out into the "real world," we replace these practices with jobs and responsibilities. But can't we do both?

Why do we compartmentalize imagination into weekends and vacation? Are there ways we are already applying creativity, but don't recognize it as art in the everyday? I have learned much about the intersection of art in the everyday by standing on the shoulders of so many before me like Francis Schaffer, G.K. Chesterton, and C.S. Lewis. These are not new ideas. In his book *Imagine,* Steve Turner (paraphrasing Francis Schaffer) says

> Evangelical Christians traditionally take redemption as the starting point to everything. But if creation is the starting point—everyone was made in God's image and is blessed with artistic gifts, able to display that original image in some way.

As a musician and a songwriter by trade, I have the fortune of contemplating these ideas at length. But art is not just for career artists. As I interact with other writers, caregivers, teachers, engineers, doctors, neighbors, yoga instructors, bus drivers, and every other kind of person I meet, I have been convinced that everyone who has been made in God's image (which is everybody) is alive to this same creative mandate.

I had a busted water pipe underground this winter. Our line was gushing water to some unknown cavern below my house, which only revealed itself in the numeric digits of my water bill. I was nine months pregnant at the time, with a fevered one year old, and a traveling husband. I was at my wits end with the stress of not knowing anything about who to call or what to do about it when God sent me a plumber who had skill, trustworthiness, and creativity to know where and how to dig, to repair the pipes, and patch up the front yard. Problem solving with a particular set of skills and experience is art. And it takes all of us to create the larger narrative; mine and yours and the guy next door's. According to Ranald Macaulay and Jerram Barrs in their book *Being Human,* "Every person is an artist. The whole of life is a creative act. The warp and woof of each life is equivalent to the artist's paint or the musician's sounds."

The strands of calling, work, and creativity function best when they're wound together into one strong rope. By good work and imagination in our everyday rhythms, we glimpse a microcosm of Genesis' opening scene. It's as if we each have a little square plot of soil to work with. We can cultivate order, beauty, joy, and fruitfulness in the life plot we have been given. In it we can grow food, shade, bright flowers, and a place for our relationships to thrive.

> LORD, you have assigned me my portion and my cup; you have made my lot secure. The boundary lines have fallen for me in pleasant places; surely I have a delightful inheritance. Psalm 16:5–6

In my own story, I have experienced calling and creativity in layers. Over my thirty-one years of life, I have been called to be a daughter, a sister, a musician, a student, a wife, a mother, a friend, a caregiver, a neighbor, and a writer. These different roles will sometimes war and reconcile with each other. They take center stage in rotating and overlapping intervals like acts of a play.

In my early twenties, I was primarily a student. I worked two jobs, formed life relationships. I went to church. But my priority for that season was to be a student. Since my husband and I met in 2000, we have been vocationally called to spend our creative energies touring our music. For the present season, I spend my days teaching and diapering and nurturing two babies from morning to night (or through the night, I should say). And once every year or two (so far, even with children in tow) I am called and inspired to distill my life experiences into words and melodies and to record these songs in an album.

As you might imagine, these life-roles each require different skills, but not one is more lofty or one less spiritual. In my most ordinary days of mopping the kitchen floor when I am desperate need of a shower and a double espresso, I am doing caregiving work that is no less in value to performing songs in front of a few hundred people under lights and applause. And I have to preach this truth to myself at both ends of that spectrum. I cannot get by with ego as a performer nor self-pity as a mother. They both answer to the same value system—the finished work of Jesus. Under this measurement I always come up short, and under this same measurement I always have exceedingly more than I could ask for.

Bleary-eyed nights when I am rocking a tearful baby, learning just how to hold her to calm her nerves, I am literally practicing a form of art. No one might be there to affirm me or to write poems about it, but it is an exhilarating and tangible faith exercise.

Domesticity is a good example of a calling that reveals the social hierarchy in our culture. The classic party question cuts to the core, "So, what do *you* do?" Most people still passively consider full time parenting marginal and less specialized work, at best. It might garner you a polite smile and pat on the back, with an upgrade in status if a mother can juggle both career and children. We measure each other first by occupation. The more your salary and visibility, the more power and currency you have to spend socially. And this socio-economic hierarchy probably defines us more than the sacred, secular debate.

G.K. Chesterton in his essay "What is Wrong with the World?" examines the values of those who would consider domesticity to be a small and trivial task.

> How can it be a large career to tell other people's children about the Rule of Three, and a small career to tell one's own children about the universe? How can it be broad to be the same thing to everyone, and narrow to be everything to someone? A woman's function is laborious, but because it is gigantic not because it is minute.

In my growing experience in caregiving, the skill and creativity it requires to help a child understand something and everything about their world for the first time is a vast responsibility, and one that brings regular opportunities for imagination, innovation, and creativity, whether or not anyone is watching. Yesterday I wrote a song for my infant daughter to quiet her as I gave her a bath. It was a beautiful melody, with a simple lyric about baby toes and other mother-ease rhymes. Now, I realize that this song will never be recorded or sung or sold, but it brought such beauty and tranquility to that fleeting moment of her childhood for us both. And I have no doubt that the Master Creator was pleased. This is what it means to make art in the everyday. And for a songwriter, living life makes better art. Creativity is a muscle that is toned and maintained across all areas, not just when I sit down to write a song.

In my own story, I sometimes feel divided by so many different kinds of creative work and callings. But I am finding that each enhances the other. I am a clearer communicator after eight years of marriage. I am a more animated storyteller for knowing my children. I am a becoming more of peacemaker in conflict because of my neighbors. I understand more about spiritual life by growing tomatoes in my backyard or pulling up weeds.

Let me frame it another way:

In 1972 Betty met Jesus. In 1977 her fifth child was born, and she names her Sandra. Betty taught her daughter hymns and scripture from a young age. In 1984, Mrs. Dare, whose own kids were grown, loaned Sandra a piano so that she could learn to play. In 1989, Sandra wrote her first song for a middle school ensemble that was performed at their graduation. Sandra later goes to college in Nashville to study music. Skip ahead to 2000 . . . Sandra meets Derek at a coffee shop in Franklin, Tennesee, by way of Kenny the guitar player. Kenny's wife Susie, seven years later, as a skilled midwife, delivers both of the Webb babies. And Tony, the plumber, repairs the broken water pipe so that Sandra can get back to work on this essay. You get the idea. You have a story just like this one.

There is not one path to calling or vocation, as a musician or otherwise.

Finding the steps of your path is as unique as the double helix of your DNA. It is not about meeting the right people, or being the most talented, or the smartest one in the class. It is life by the Spirit. With the Spirit, your failings will point you to new strengths. With the Spirit, you can stay the course when it doesn't make a profit. With the Spirit, you can learn when to trust your instincts and when your heart is deceiving you. With the Spirit, you can find strength to choose a path that feels like death to you, but is really obedience.

Becoming who you were made to be more often comes by way of our weaknesses and our failures, pointing us to a deeper art and a more beautiful story—the story of Jesus. Jesus calls us to be more fully human and more honestly broken, so that we can be our true selves and invite one another to do the same. Like the brilliant line in the thought-provoking film *I ❤ Huckabees*, asking "How am I not myself? How am I not myself?"

Jesus life, death, and resurrection has secured our freedom to ask ourselves that question. He has made us to find glory in our humanity, and in our unique gifts and callings. Not to make us mindless, zombies of sameness, but vibrant, bold participants who have been given particular tasks and abilities here in this life. My husband always paraphrases Paul, saying, "We're diverse members of one body." It has become a mantra that has shaped these paragraphs you are reading.

Each of us is like a brick, interweaving to build one big house. The house is the place where our gifts, resources, opportunities, and callings come into being. Jesus called this house the Kingdom. Many members, one body. Many parts, one whole. Many branches, one tree. It is the restoring, renewing work of the Kingdom of God. The being made right of all things. God is the builder and the architect. One day, we will view the whole picture. The whole house. But most days, we just see one ordinary red brick.

At the moment, Derek is recording a new album. Susie is delivering babies. Kenny is playing guitar some and mostly doing carpentry work. Betty is using her retirement years to nurture and encourage women in the gospel. Tony is work-ing days at Metro Water. My son, Rhodes, is finger-painting and learning about colors. And for now, I am rocking a baby and writing this essay. All these bricks form one tiny square of God's great narrative. God's art making is as vast as the Texas sky, but it can be squeezed into a tiny grain of sand, and then multiplied out by the millions. This is the significance of each hour, each breath, each human being. Who could ever tire of the smell of Earth on your hands? The brilliance of a sunrise? The kiss of a husband? The first cry of a newborn child? The hush of the crowd after Handel's *Messiah* in a symphony hall? It is so little, and yet it is too much. May God give us the grace to take it in, and the grace to spend ourselves making and remaking all things for his glory.

THE DISCIPLINE
of delight

Bad 1st sentences!

With this essay, I want to provoke Christians to take delight in music. More specifically, I hope to move believers to pursue pleasure in the sensory experience of creating and hearing music. Really, this is an essay about experiencing beauty in any of its physical forms (including ones bound up with invisible yet physical waves of sound), and much of what I want to say could be said just as easily about enjoying the beauty of a painting, of the wood grain of an old wardrobe, of the shape of a lover's hand. As such, this isn't an essay that tries to settle questions about the nature of art, and I won't give much attention to the relative merits of understanding music aesthetically or expressively or cosmologically. I simply want to consider the pleasure we derive from beauty that is mediated to us by other human beings or that we ourselves have a hand in creating. Music is this sort of creation, and for me, it is the one that has been the keenest and most constant source of delight. Elaine Scarry writes, "Beauty always takes place in the particular,"[1] so I write about the particular pleasure of music.

The injunction to pursue delight seems counter-intuitive. Isn't true delight an unaffected, spontaneous experience, something that can't be coerced or solicited? If delight can be sought, don't we feel a nagging hesitation that, even if it's permissible to receive delight when it turns up, perhaps it's unseemly to chase after it? While true that we can't conjure up delight by the force of will, the obstacles to delight are legion in our world, and overthrowing these obstacles can clear the paths by which delight will find us. This is a serious matter for Christians because our experiences of delight in God's world are intimately bound up with our vision of his new creation and of God himself. To those around us, our unabashed delight in beauty can bear witness to our coming redemption and coming Redeemer. It matters that Christians delight in beauty. But alas, the very words 'beauty' and 'delight' have a problematic reception; this is the first obstacle we must address.

BEAUTY AND DELIGHT

Philosopher Etienne Gilson writes,

> We call beautiful. . . what causes admiration and holds the eyes. It is of the essence of the beautiful in art, even from the simple point of view of its nominal definition, that it be given in a sensible perception whose apprehension is desirable in itself and for itself.[2]

Perhaps surprisingly, some artists and beholders reject beauty as an ideal for artistic creation. One category of reasons are those Scarry labels "the political complaints against beauty,"[3] and I'll touch on these concerns in a later section. Other objectors feel that beauty is an insufficient and trivial category for art in a world that is full of ugliness. The brokenness of the world does shade our experience of beauty—again, I'll discuss this later—but for now I offer Gilson's qualification that "natural ugliness becomes compatible with artistic beauty when an artist makes it serve the end of his art."[4] We are drawn to the resonance we experience in Shakespeare's tragedies, Prokofiev's War Sonatas, and Wilco's *Yankee Hotel Foxtrot* no less because of their violence and dissonance. According to the ancients, the constituent quality of the beautiful which catches our eye or ear is radiance, or *claritas*, which Gilson takes to represent a diversity of sense qualities: "Gray landscapes, dull tones, muffled sounds, and words spoken in a low voice have as much or more effectiveness on our sensitivity than brilliance properly so called. Qualities of this kind share the same power to attract and hold our attention, as under a spell."[5]

As beauty shows up in an infinite variety of shapes and shades, so does the pleasure it provokes. I don't use the word delight to prescribe a particular emotional response to music, least of all one that's unfailingly chipper or saccharine; rather, I take the liberty of allowing delight to represent a spectrum of effects. The words of Gilson that I've quoted point to several facets of aesthetic experience: attraction, admiration, captivation, and desire. Apprehending beauty is a kind of love. But is it properly a love that rests, contented, or is it heart-sick love: desire, which for T.S. Eliot is love in an unfulfilled state?

> Desire itself is movement
> Not in itself desirable;
> Love is unmoving,

> Only the cause and end of movement,
> Timeless, and undesiring
> Except in the aspect of time
> Caught in the form of limitation
> Between un-being and being.[6]

Scarry portrays beauty's pleasure in terms of desire, almost restlessness, as beauty incites the act of replication:

> Beauty brings copies of itself into being. It makes us draw it, take photographs of it, or describe it to other people... The generation is unceasing. Beauty, as both Plato's Symposium and everyday life confirm, prompts the begetting of children: when the eyes see someone beautiful, the whole body wants to reproduce the person.[7]

C.S. Lewis's early encounters with literary beauty awakened desire in him, and he names this effect Joy, "an unsatisfied desire which is itself more desirable than any other satisfaction."[8] He posits that Joy is distinct from—and superior to—Happiness and Pleasure.

Certainly, music awakens in us wistful desire. It is a temporal art, and the experience it offers us is inherently fleeting. I don't dismiss the appeal of Joy's painful stabs, which are perhaps distinct from a radiant, satisfying pleasure. But the two need not compete with each other, and I stand by the language of delight. Longing and fulfillment may be more intermingled in the believer's present experience than we often suppose.

Allowing that beauty is the quality by which music captivates us and that delight is an acceptable name for its pleasure, our next task is to ask how these forces play out in our experience. We taste glimmers of delight in music, even moments of overwhelming pleasure. But afterward, we may wonder, Why not more? Why not more often? What are the obstacles to delight?

MERCENARY OBSTACLES TO DELIGHT IN MUSIC

We might expect that those most immersed in musical beauty are the most attuned to the delight it brings. A close look at many musicians and aspiring musicians, however, gives the impression not so much that we love music but that we desire to be good at our art, to be better than others, to achieve fame and success, not to fail. Ego is at stake, resulting in arrogance or insecurity or both. This is hardly surprising, considering the public nature of performance and the idolization of the musical personality for the past two centuries. A musician driven by ego and competition may still find pleasure in music's beauty for its own sake, but the 'mercenary' motivations (as Lewis would call them in "The Weight of Glory") diminish and distract from musical delight.

Mercenary treatment of music, which seeks not the proper rewards of beauty and delight but rewards that have no 'natural connection' with music, isn't a vice unique to performers. Listeners, too, may derive a sense of status from their ability to 'appreciate' certain kinds of music. This is evident in popular discussions of highbrow/lowbrow music, especially in America during the first half of the 20th century. In a 1939 volume of *Harper's Magazine,* Dickson Skinner posits, "[I]n general it seems to be agreed that symphonic music is within the category of the superior and that fondness for it is a mark of discriminating taste."[9] Skinner's article, "Music Goes into Mass Production," touts the role of radio in propelling America to cultural maturity, ready to take over from a fading Europe. Skinner tells of letters from listeners to 'The Music Shop,' an early morning radio program of classical and semi-classical music, couched with commentary by an announcer, broadcast from Ames, Iowa:

> The greater part of them are from women—mothers whose children hear the program at breakfast before school, housekeepers who listen while they work. "The more I hear good music, such as you give us, the more I love it, and the more I hear that kind the more I dislike the other kind."[10]

Writing around the same time, Theodor Adorno blasts NBC's Music Appreciation Hour for failing to bring listeners into a real relationship with music but leading them instead "to a fetishism of ownership of musical knowledge by rote." Referring to a 'musical spelling bee,' Adorno writes, "By influencing the pupils to recognize The Established, the principle of fun, supposedly a principle based upon the listeners' own needs and own spontaneity, is implicitly superseded by the desire for prestige attaching to recognition of the socially recognized."[11] According to Adorno, such programs obscure music's beauty by inserting concerns about erudition into the middle of the aesthetic experience.

Since the second half of the 20th century, as modernity's hierarchical ideas of culture have given way to the relativizing tribalism of post-modernity, the sense of status derived from appreciation for 'superior' music has largely morphed into a sense of identity derived from allegiance to a particular musical subculture. The effect is the same, as the chosen style of music becomes a tool for forging the listener's identity, which is reinforced by dismissing or despising other styles of music, shutting off any delight they may offer. This tendency is taken to an extreme in subcultures that refuse to find enjoyment in whatever was deemed most enjoyable last week (more on hipsters in the next section). The point is, in all of these cases, we employ music as a means of belonging, accepting only what conforms to our preconceptions of what we like.

I'm being a little unfair. There's nothing wrong with having tastes, with specializing in certain kinds of music. Familiarity—with Brahms' Fourth Symphony or the compositional techniques of Steve Reich or the playing of Lonnie Johnson or the genre of Afro-Cuban drumming—enables new kinds of hearing, bringing new kinds of pleasures and serving the cause of delight. But perhaps in an effort to justify the directions in which we turn our finite attention, we can become preoccupied with an image of our musical selves, leaving only enough attention for superficial listening, lacking an open-handed readiness to receive aesthetic pleasure however it may come.

Paradoxically, expert listening can be as much of an impediment to musical delight as superficial listening. As I've said, knowing more allows us to hear more, multiplying the avenues for pleasure: the subtle shades of tone color; a chord progression fulfilling or confounding the expectations of conventional harmony; a singer's style bearing the traces of a particular folk tradition. But the same knowledge exposes deficiencies in the craft and performance of the music we hear or play, and once again, those whose expertise should afford the most delight in music sometimes enjoy it the least. I wager that I'm not the only musician who has cringed through a musical experience—in a concert hall or church sanctuary—that others found wonderful and moving. This is a difficult matter for those concerned with musical delight; it seems inevitable that some kinds of enjoyment must be sacrificed to enable others. A deeper problem arises from a musical culture that fosters posturing and self-promotion, in which musicians habitually listen for deficiencies rather than pleasure and assert their musical superiority by refusing to express delight. During a rehearsal with an older student in my early days of graduate school, I said that I found a section of a piece satisfying. "Be careful," the violinist cautioned, "you won't last long saying that kind of thing around here." If we're honest, most musicians can recall giving a deliberately cool response to music performed by ourselves or others, not merely as a reflection of our judgment but in an effort not to 'lower' ourselves.

When trained musicians are reluctant to express enjoyment of music, amateur listeners come to second-guess their delight as well. Once, after I played a movement of a Prokofiev sonata as a prelude to a church service, several friends expressed how much they enjoyed it then quickly made the disclaimer that they didn't know much about music. These friends were members of an excellent choir but they didn't feel qualified to make a judgment, and they devalued their own appreciation.

At the heart of these obstacles to delight, of these mercenary uses of music, lies self-idolatry, our failure to love our neighbor and, ultimately, our failure to love God. Our addiction to self-aggrandizement turns our imagination from the music to ourselves, interrupting beauty's approach with attempts to bolster our shaky supremacy or allay our haunting fears.

DELIGHT IN A BROKEN WORLD

Sometimes, though, musicians lack delight not because of a critical attitude but because of burnout. One woman shared a story of hearing the student orchestra of one of the world's finest music colleges then running into the conductor in the park the next day. She told me, "I said something that was probably very stupid: I said what fun it must be to conduct such talented musicians." The conductor's response was a swift shut-down of her glowing sentiment, telling her that rehearsing the students was hard work. As ungracious as his reply may have been, it contains a valid point: even in a pursuit as delightful as music, work is cursed in our fallen world, and we experience frustration when we toil for results that fall short of our intentions. David Brooks, commentator on American life, speaks of the keenness of this dissatisfaction in a culture propelled by achievement and self-improvement:

> As anybody who looks at meritocratic life knows, this creed is not easy on its disciples. There is no rest. Expectations don't sleep. . . whatever you are doing, you should never be merely as good tomorrow as you are today... Capacities are there to be cultivated, heading toward some never achieved perfection.[12]

Such dissatisfaction is especially potent in a field where we hunger to realize the beauty we imagine and fear that artistic opportunities will dry up if we deliver a poor audition or botched solo.

Burnout also looms because life is difficult for those trying to support themselves through a music career (perhaps excluding the aforementioned conductor!). Most musicians have stories of driving to a rehearsal in a snow-storm or performing with a high fever because the concert had to go on. Some grow weary of days on the road, of working with temperamental musicians, of the stress of erratic or insufficient income. As years go by, bitterness can crowd out even the memory of the delight that first drew them to music. My piano tuner tells of a client, an experienced accompanist, who views her own playing like typing on a typewriter. After a lifetime of pouring themselves into their art, some musicians continue simply because they feel unqualified to do anything else.

Listeners, too, find that brokenness and decay in the world sap their pleasure in music: the distraction of a coughing audience member, the pain of a headache, preoccupation with a quarrel at home, the lingering misery of a disappointing career. The song that moved us during a tumultuous college semester now sounds stale or stilted. There are times when the solace and comfort we expect from music—the muted cousins of delight—do not come through for us. If the vanity of life—the inevitable

... cold friction of expiring sense
Without enchantment, offering no promise
But bitter tastelessness of shadow fruit
As body and soul begin to fall asunder[13]

becomes the lens through which we view of the world, we may approach aesthetic experience with an attitude of detachment.

Irony is one form this detachment can take, particularly when hipness is at stake. Rather than commit to any beauty whose shelf life is as short as its undiscovered-ness, the "ironic figure" dallies with ambiguous enjoyment. In a passage that reads like a description of the prototypical hipster, Kierkegaard writes,

> There is something seductive about every beginning because the subject is still free, and this is the satisfaction the ironist longs for. At such moments actuality loses its validity for him; he is free and above it.[14]

Kierkegaard offers historical examples in which "one was conscious both of the majesty of life and the reality of glory, yet at the same time ironically above it," then later concludes, "With irony . . . when everything else becomes vain, subjectivity becomes free . . . Whereas everything else becomes vain, the ironic subject does not himself become vain but saves his own vanity."[15] Irony may allow for moments of droll amusement, but as a habitual mode of reception, it does not lead to full-throated delight. For performers and listeners, sincere and ironic alike, the experience of music is not immune from all the sorrows and vanity that plague life in a fallen world. By itself, music can guarantee neither redemption nor escape.

ETHICAL OBJECTIONS TO AESTHETIC DELIGHT

Even in our moments of enjoying music with ease, at peace and well-fed, conscientious humans remember that the brokenness of the rest of the world has not ceased. Ethical concerns about pleasure and hunger, beauty and injustice put a more deliberate check on delight. This is true for both Christians and non-Christians, with some variations.

Pursuing musical pleasure can seem like an inexcusable, selfish use of attention and resources in the face of poverty, abuse, hunger, and genocide. How often have I sent away my little neighbor girl, hungry for interest and attention, in order to practice piano? Some fear that aesthetic experience hardens us toward the needs of others. "Do the identifications with fictions. . . somehow immunize us against the humbler, less formed, but actual claims of suffering and of need in our surroundings? Does the cry in the tragic play muffle, even blot out, the cry in the street? (I confess to finding this an obsessive, almost maddening question)," writes George Steiner, survivor of the Nazi occupation of Europe.[16] Particularly within the academy, as noted by apologist William Edgar, the suspicion lurks that, beyond the individual's response to aesthetic delight and human misery, institutional notions of greatness and beauty in art are complicit in oppressing the powerless and furthering injustice.[17] Elaine Scarry spends much of her treatise *On Beauty and Being Just* addressing claims that attention to beauty distracts us from injustice and engages us in oppressive reification.

The twentieth century Christian variation of this "is a pragmatism, which argues that evangelism is prior to cultural pursuits."[18] In light of the desperate situation of those who don't yet know Christ's redemption, it may seem inexcusable for people who have tasted the gospel to spend time and energy on their own musical pleasure. From this point of view, music need not be excluded but is only worth pursuing in avenues that correspond overtly to prescribed spiritual outcomes, its beauty subjugated to the achievement of those outcomes. Charlie Peacock observes,

> If music is indeed the powerful tool many say it is, they can't leave it idle when there's a job to do. If something powerful is not accomplishing its powerful purpose, then its power is being wasted. If they feel strongly about the waste, they're likely to feel anger, regret, grief, or frustration . . . In similar fashion, those who believe that the musical energies of God's people should be spent on praise and worship, evangelism, and discipleship with very few exceptions will likely be angered and frustrated when that energy is redirected.[19]

Such concerns lead us to shun the pursuit of delight in music as inappropriate or superfluous to our calling in the world.

PIOUS FEARS ABOUT AESTHETIC DELIGHT

The suspicion that cuts closest to the heart of musical delight is that it entails debauchery and idolatry. Physical pleasures and sensory delights have a way of becoming addictive, swaying our hearts and minds and taking over our lives. Is it coincidental that the subcultures surrounding many music scenes feature other sensual habits that clash with holiness and self-control? A bass player I know, a recovering alcoholic, said that he would never encourage his child to pursue music, because he may as well hand him a bong.

We idolize not only sensual musical experience but the people who are vehicles of our musical pleasure. How many of us, after being undone by an extraordinary performance, have found ourselves seized with a longing to know, to emulate, perhaps to collaborate with the performer? For a moment, at least, our ordinary callings—to love the people in our lives, to serve faithfully in our professions, to emulate the humility of Christ—seem pale and tiresome.

Augustine was one Christian who saw an inherent captivating tendency in the pleasures of sound: "I used to be much more fascinated by the pleasures of sound than the pleasures of smell. I was enthralled by them, but you broke my bonds and set me free. I admit that I still find some enjoyment in the music of hymns... but I do not enjoy it so much that I cannot tear myself away."[20] He continues,

> So I waver between the danger that lies in gratifying the senses and the benefits which, as I know from experience, can accrue from singing. Without committing myself to an irrevocable opinion, I am inclined to approve of the custom of singing in church, in order that by indulging the ears weaker spirits may be inspired with feelings of devotion. Yet when I find the singing itself more moving than the truth which it conveys, I confess that this is a grievous sin, and at those times I would prefer not to hear the singer.[21]

When we, like Augustine, suspect that created, sensory things compete with God for our affections, we might conclude that competition is the default relationship between gift and giver, and that the safest solution is to hold the gift at arm's length. From this perspective, musical delight is not merely elusive or superfluous but dangerous, a potential enemy of our souls.

SUSPECTING SUSPICION

Yet whatever our qualms and hindrances, most of us sense a measure of goodness and innocence in our purest musical pleasures. Instinctively, we know that Christians ought not to shun all musical delight, and experiences scattered throughout a life of devotion confirm this hunch. One clue is that biblical imagery is rich with sensual references. Psalm 133 describes the unity of God's people as being like an outpouring of precious oil on the head, down the beard, and into the collar of the robes of the high priest. Scripture employs very sensual language when describing the future consummation of God's purposes, from the savor of rich food and well-aged wine of Isaiah's messianic banquet (Isaiah 25:6) to the sounds and sights of Revelation: voices like trumpets and harps, a King with flaming eyes and a crown-covered head, a city radiant as jasper, a flowing river bright as crystal (Revelation 4:1, 14:2, 19:12, 21:11, 22:1).

Language like this assumes that we have a rich experience of the senses. The biblical authors harness this experience to heighten our sense of the beauty of unseen—or not yet seen—realities. This method is made explicit in Proverbs 24:13-14:

> My son, eat thou honey, because it is good;
> and the honeycomb, which is sweet to thy taste:
> so shall the knowledge of wisdom be unto thy soul:
> when thou has found it, then there shall be a reward,
> and thy expectation shall not be cut off.

Jonathan Edwards adopts this text as the basis for his sermon, "The Pleasantness of Religion." He sidesteps the directness of the Proverb, suggesting that "eat thou honey" is not so much a command as a concession that the reader does eat honey—why then the imperative case?—but he concludes,

> God has given us of his redundant bounty many things for the delight of our senses, for our pleasure and gratification. . . Religion allows us to take the full comfort of our meat and drink, all reasonable pleasures that are to be enjoyed in conversation or recreation; allows of the gratification of all our natural appetites. And there are none of the five senses but what we are allowed to please and gratify."[22]

If not commanding that we take pleasure in the beauty we currently taste, feel, hear, and see, the Biblical writers certainly assume that we will do so, and they marshal that pleasure to allure our hearts toward future glory. Notice what is lost if we seek a short-cut to the spiritual principle, bypassing the physical experience; the effectiveness of the metaphors requires that we have first had our hearts kindled by the sensual enjoyment of physical creation.

THE GIFT AS AN ARTIFACT OF THE GIVER

If the first hint that delight has a place in the life of the Christian is the sensual language of scripture, the next is the way our delight in music is increased by our apprehension of the beauty and generosity of God and in turn feeds this apprehension. Enjoyment of a gift and enjoyment of the giver do not form a zero-sum equation, and competition need not define their relationship.

A beautiful God creates beauty; a generous God gives it to us to enjoy. In the words of Edwards, "The earthly comforts of the Christian are also very much sweetened by the consideration of the love of God, that God is their Father and friend and gives them these blessings from love to them, and because he delights in them."[23] In human relationships, our enjoyment of a gift is enhanced when it comes from someone we love, whose love we desire. This is especially true when the gift represents something of the character or creativity of the giver; perhaps this is why we feel compelled to knit scarves and write poems for those we love. Jeremy Begbie writes that Karl Barth embraced Mozart's music

> as part of a good, physical creation giving God praise; a creation testifying to God, magnifying God, but as finite and transient—created, not divine. It is sometimes said that Barth was captivated by Mozart's music; it is probably more accurate to say he was captivated by God's goodness through Mozart's music and without needing to escape the created sounds in the process.[24]

To experience musical delight in the context of the love of God does not detract from the enjoyment of beauty as beauty because the character of the gift reveals the nature of the One who gives it.

Our grasp of God's goodness in his created gifts communicates volumes to those around us. The physical and aesthetic pleasures of music—the timbre of an English horn or of a telecaster run through a vintage effect pedal, the charming rhythmic games of Brahms or the easy groove of Allen Toussaint's New Orleans piano—are the same for believers and unbelievers alike. If we hesitate to share in innocent enjoyment of musical pleasures, we portray a false image of God and fail to testify to his creative generosity. Instead, we should take delight a step further as we fellowship with the source of beauty. C.S. Lewis writes,

> We do not want merely to see beauty, though, God knows, even that is bounty enough. We want something else which can hardly be put into words—to be united with the beauty we see, to pass into it, to receive it into ourselves, to bathe in it, to become part of it.[25]

By our delight in music as a gift from our loving Father, we offer to those around us a glimpse of what it means to be united to beauty Himself.

THE WISDOM OF HUMILITY

Our delight in sensory beauty connects not only to our view of God but of ourselves. The call to this delight is fitting in the believer's life as it calls us to submit to our physical creaturely existence. Etienne Gilson quotes historian Lucien Febvre in the *Encyclopédie Française*: "Assuredly, art is a kind of knowledge." Gilson counters,

> [A]rt is *not* a kind of knowledge or, in other words. . . it is not a manner of knowing. On the contrary, art belongs to an order other than that of knowledge, namely, in the order of making or, as they say, in that of "factivity."[26]

In the realm of faith, Nicholas Wolterstorff warns that dismissing art's physicality in order to discern its spiritual significance amounts to a dismissal of the incarnation:

> The practice, in one's contemplation of a work of art, of looking only for the message and of fixing only on the world projected, of taking no delight in the artifact which bears the message and presents the world, might be called a "docetic" approach to the arts—on analogy to an early Christian heresy that denied the genuine bodily nature of Christ.[27]

Wolterstorff reminds us that "the fundamental fact about the artist is that he or she is a worker in stone, in bronze, in clay, in paint, in acid and plates, in words, in sounds and instruments, in states of affairs."[28] Though some attempt to use music to transcend an earth-bound existence, like builders of an aesthetic tower of Babel, an honest encounter with music's material embeddedness affirms our creaturely existence.

Similarly, music calls us to submit to and rejoice in our temporality. In the words of Jeremy Begbie, "Music, in a very concentrated way, tells us that something can take time *and* be good. Music takes time to be what it is, and as such can be glorious."[29] That said, submitting to music's claim on our time requires a kind of humility:

> Music says to us: "There are things you will learn only by passing through this process, by being caught up in this series of relations and transformations." Music requires my time, my flesh, and my blood for its performance and enjoyment, and this means going at *its* speed.[30]

In an age that values control, efficiency, and the instantaneous, listening to music, like praying, stands against our addiction to productivity and a sense of our own power.

In essence, materiality and temporality force us to reckon with our own finite particularity rather than be seduced by what Kierkegaard terms the "world-historical."[31] Begbie picks up on Rowan Williams' description of music as a "moral event":

> (Music) can remind us that we are not in control of the world, that we do not have the overview, that we are *in* the narrative of the world's history and never above it. . . .In short, we are liberated from the destructive illusion that we are supposed to be God.[32]

Music doesn't preclude the infinite or the timeless but, again, points us toward the incarnation, which T.S. Eliot characterizes as the intersection of the timeless with time:

> Men's curiosity searches past and future
> And clings to that dimension. But to apprehend
> The point of intersection of the timeless
> With time, is an occupation for the saint—
> No occupation either, but something given
> And taken, in a lifetime's death in love,
> Ardour and selflessness and self-surrender.[33]

In the humility of embracing our own particularity, we begin to answer the ethical and evangelistic objections to delight, objections that stem from a sense of responsibility to discern the ultimate and ignore all else. Banishing beauty in pursuit of evangelism or justice reveals a false understanding of our make-up as human beings. In a refutation of Maslow's hierarchy, music doesn't stop in settings of suffering and injustice; slave songs, battle songs, and exile songs warn us against a reductionistic approach. Dismissing beauty for ethical concerns also reveals a false view of God. In the words of composer Mark Hijleh, "God's economy is not like our economy. He wants great symphonies to be written *and* all his children to be fed." The story of the Bible reminds us that, for all of human history, God has chosen to speak into the vulnerability of our physicality, temporality, and particularity. We go astray when we seek ultimate ends while ignoring the kinds of creatures he's made us to be and the ways in which he communicates himself to us.

THE HOPE OF NEW CREATION

Of great help here are the categories of ultimate and penultimate which Dietrich Bonhoeffer employs in *Ethics*. For Bonhoeffer, the ultimate is justification, the final word of God that breaks into the darkness and sin of human life to bring forgiveness, salvation, and fellowship. To the penultimate, or things before the last, belongs the whole realm of human understanding and action, all that precedes this final word of God. In seeking to understand the relation of the ultimate to the penultimate, Bonhoeffer rejects the "radical" solution which would claim that

> [u]ltimate and penultimate are . . . mutually exclusive contraries. Christ is the destroyer and enemy of everything penultimate, and everything penultimate is enmity towards Christ. Christ is the sign that the world is ripe for burning.[34]

He also rejects the "compromise" solution, in which

> [t]he world and life within it have to be protected against this encroachment [of justification of the sinner by grace alone] on their territory . . . The ultimate has no voice in determining the form of life in the world. Even the raising of the question of the ultimate, even the endeavor to give effect to God's word in its authority for life in the world, is now accounted radicalism and apathy or antipathy towards the established orders of the world and towards the men who are subject to these orders.[35]

Only in Jesus can the ultimate and the penultimate find right relation:

> In Jesus Christ we have faith in the incarnate, crucified, and risen God. In the incarnation we learn the love of God for His creation; in the crucifixion we learn of the judgment of God upon all flesh; and in the resurrection we learn of God's will for a new world. There could be no greater error than to tear these three elements apart; for each of them comprises the whole.[36]

The Christian life, then, means "neither a destruction nor a sanctioning of the penultimate."[37] Rather, the penultimate prepares the way for the ultimate. It is not a "method" that guarantees attainment of the ultimate, for

> only the coming Lord Himself can make ready the way for His coming ... Christ alone brings us the ultimate, the justification of our lives before God, and yet in spite of this, or rather just because of this, the penultimate is not taken from us but is spared. The penultimate is swallowed up in the ultimate, and yet it is still necessary and it retains its right so long as the earth continues.[38]

Bonhoeffer speaks of the penultimate in regard to the ethical, but I think the category may fairly be extended to our understanding of beauty, as well as goodness, within the world. Bonhoeffer's treatment of the penultimate accords with God's revelation through creation and redemptive history and his establishment of physical sacraments. When God delivered Israel from their Egyptian oppressors, he rescued a particular people at a particular time. It was a penultimate deliverance, for the generation that had been delivered from slavery rebelled against God and died in the wilderness. Yet this event and the commemorative feast God appointed derive real significance from their relation to the ultimate as physical signs that find fulfillment in the greater exodus accomplished by Jesus, our Paschal Lamb. We keep his feast not as an end in itself but to prepare the way, in anticipation of the day when we'll dine with him, eating real food in his physical presence. Similarly, our baptism in water reminds us of God's rescue of Israel through the Red Sea and joins us to the resurrection of Jesus, a physical, historic event that points to the future resurrection of those who are his.

From these, we learn to delight in God's other gifts of grace, including music, as signposts of a reality yet to come (the ultimate) while preserving the validity of the experiences themselves (the penultimate). We sing songs that matter in a broken world—both cries of lament and anthems of joy—because we were made for a whole world and because our creator has not abandoned us. Music can't bear the inordinate burden of being our salvation, but we will escape disillusionment as we see music rightly, as a gift from the One who is bringing salvation, even in the moments when the brokenness of our lives overshadows its beauty. In this way, we will be ready to welcome delight when it finds us again.

THE NEW CREATION ALREADY BEGUN

Finally, delight in music befits the Christian because it increases as we abandon mercenary, self-centered ways of using music. Elaine Scarry elaborates on Simone Weil's notion that a vision of beauty undermines self-centeredness:

> At the moment we see something beautiful, we undergo a radical decentering. Beauty, according to Weil, requires us "to give up our imaginary

> position as the center"....When we come upon beautiful things—the tiny mauve-orange-blue moth on the brick, Augustine's cake, a sentence about innocence in Hampshire—they act like small tears in the surface of the world that pull us through to some vaster space; or they form "ladders reaching toward the beauty of the world," or they lift us (as though by the air currents of someone else's sweeping), letting the ground rotate beneath us several inches, so that when we land, we find we are standing in a different relation to the world than we were a moment before. It is not that we cease to stand at the center of the world, for we never stood there. It is that we cease to stand even at the center of our own world. We willingly cede our ground to the thing that stands before us.[39]

Believers ought not to assume that we embrace the decentering qualities of beauty better than unbelievers; each person contains her own peculiar mix of brokenness and grace. Because of lingering suspicions of the physical and sensual in some Christian traditions, we may have more to learn than our unbelieving friends about letting beauty sweep us off of the ground. But as the Spirit breaks our addiction to self-promotion and brings to life the new creation in us, we find new freedom to soak in musical beauty without concern for our identity, expert reputation, or professional status.

This unembarrassed enjoyment will work its way into our communication with performers, colleagues, listeners, students, and friends as fellow-recipients of beauty. Scarry describes how decentering in the face of beauty alters our relationships:

> [A]t the moments when we believe we are conducting ourselves with equality, we are usually instead conducting ourselves as the central figure in our own private story; and when we feel ourselves to be merely adjacent, or lateral (or even subordinate), we are probably more closely approaching a state of equality... A beautiful thing is not the only thing in the world that can make us feel adjacent; nor is it the only thing in the world that brings a state of acute pleasure. But it appears to be one of the few phenomena in the world that brings about both simultaneously: it permits us to be adjacent while also permitting us to experience extreme pleasure, thereby creating the sense that it is our own adjacency that is pleasure-bearing.[40]

The gospel goes beyond 'adjacency' to love and servanthood, seeking the good of the other in self-sacrificial ways. How can we—I speak particularly to fellow-musicians—let the decentering qualities of music spill into love for others? A few (convicting) ideas to stir the imagination:

- Be ready to delight in music made by colleagues; be quick to express this delight in their gifts.
- Enable students to experience musical delight by playing with and for them and by articulating pleasure in their musicality; model vocabulary that helps them to conceive of music-making as a joy to themselves and a gift to others.
- Engage in rich preparation for performance, aiming to create an experience of delight for audience members; communicate with audiences in ways that help them take hold of the music and free them to express enjoyment.

These acts are self-sacrificial in that they require us to stop wielding music for ego and superiority but they don't diminish our own musical delight. Wolterstorff writes,

> [W]e must. . . insist on the. . . point, so often denied in the contemporary arts—namely, that one can find joy in carrying out one's responsibilities to one's fellows. Indeed, is it not true here too that he who loses himself will find himself? And is it not precisely the artist narcissistically concerned to find himself who will at last discover that he has irretrievably lost himself? The Byzantine artist placed himself humbly at the service of the church, invoking the presence of the departed saints by depicting them, so that the liturgy could take place in their presence as well as in the presence of men on earth. Is it likely that he found less joy in his work than does the contemporary artist who sets himself his own problems in the hope that in solving them he will find joy?[41]

Aesthetic delight, then, should not only run rampant in individual believers but should pervade our experience of community.

DELIGHT AND THE WAY OF THE CROSS

And yet. So many of the cautions and qualms about delight are terribly important, and I don't want to dismiss the questions they raise. Musical delight must not be our only or highest goal. There are times when obedience to our calling—to care for a child, to show hospitality to a stranger, to gather with the body of Christ—leaves us with less time to practice, to sit and listen, to indulge in our own musical pleasure. The command to show generosity to those in need may mean less money for concert tickets or new musical equipment. If we find ourselves being consumed by a musical obsession—a genre or a performer or a vision of musical success—it may be wise to enter a time of fasting from it, as we fast from the good and necessary and delightful gift of food, to remind ourselves and confess to God that our only good is in him. Such situations require thoughtful consideration, prayer, and wisdom from others. We need patience and humility,

resisting a default posture that would push us either toward or away from musical pursuits.

But we ought not to skirt these decisions by dismissing delight. The pre-
emptive sacrifice of something God has not required is a move of self-protection
rather than faith, and suspicion of his gifts is a distraction from the real nature of
cross-bearing. Richard Gaffin writes,

> Christian suffering, the sufferings of Christ, do not have to be sought; they
> are not, at least in the first place, an imperative to be obeyed... Suffering
> with Christ... is not a condition to be fulfilled in order to earn adoption,
> but a condition or circumstance given with our adoption.[42]

Gaffin surveys the full scope of suffering experienced by Christ and his followers
in a broken world and concludes,

> Where existence in creation under the curse on sin and in the mortal body
> is not simply borne, be it stoically or in whatever other sinfully self-cen-
> tered, rebellious way, but borne for Christ and lived in his service, there,
> comprehensively, is "the fellowship of his sufferings."[43]

Believers affirm that every square inch of creation belongs under the kingship of
Christ yet insist that, for now, every square inch of creation is

> groaning in anxious longing for the revelation of the sons of God. And in
> the meantime, until that revelation at Jesus' coming, these adopted sons,
> under the power of the Spirit... also groan, not in isolation from creation
> or by withdrawing from everyday life and responsibilities, but they groan
> with creation; they groan out of their deep, concreted solidarity with the
> rest of creation. They groan by entering fully and with hope for the entire
> creation... into the realities of daily living and cultural involvement, know-
> ing all along that for the present time these are all subject to futility and
> decay, knowing full well too, even though it so often proves elusive and
> difficult to maintain, the balance to which they are called, that peculiarly
> balanced life-style demanded of them... [44]

Pursuing delight in music as a good gift from God, a hint of the new creation—in
the very places where the brokenness of the world makes such delight elusive and
tenuous—is a way of sharing in the sufferings of Christ that honors the generosity of God.

As we've seen, heightening delight in music requires that we abandon our
selfish ambition and vain conceit, receiving God's gifts with humility and wonder.
(Is it surprising that Paul breaks into song in Philippians 2, as he urges us to imitate Christ in his humiliation and glory?) In our sanctification we find the same

spectacular coexistence of suffering and delight, for the Spirit by whom we put to death the deeds of the flesh is the same Spirit who assures us that God is our Father and that glory awaits (Romans 8). Edwards muses on this paradox:

> [T]hough it be a deep sorrow for sin that God requires as necessary to salvation, yet the very nature of it necessarily implies delight. Repentance of sin is a sorrow arising from the sight of God's excellency and mercy, but the apprehension of excellency or mercy must necessarily and unavoidably beget pleasure in the mind of the beholder. 'Tis impossible that anyone should see anything that appears to him excellent and not behold it with pleasure, and it's impossible to be affected with the mercy and love of God, and his willingness to be merciful to us and love us, and not be affected with pleasure at the thoughts of [it]; but this is the very affection that begets true repentance. How much soever of a paradox it may seem it is true that repentance is a sweet sorrow, so that the more of this sorrow, the more pleasure.[45]

In the discipline of receiving aesthetic delight, we taste this reality. What a sweet way to learn, over and over again, how to take up the cross of a Savior whose yoke is easy and whose burden is light.

God's loving-kindness is always the final word in the life of the believer. When he grants us the enjoyment of sensual gifts, such as music, we ought to receive it with open hands, eager to teach our wayward hearts about his dizzying generosity. This way, when we find ourselves enduring seasons of pain or following him down pathways that seem dark and frightening, we can walk forward with the assurance that He has promised us himself and that, in him, we will find hope and salvation, comfort and love, beauty and delight.

Endnotes

1   Elaine Scarry, *On Beauty and Being Just* (Princeton: Princeton University Press, 1999), p. 18.
2   Etienne Gilson, *The Arts of the Beautiful* (New York: Scribner, 1965), pp. 22–23.
3   Scarry, *On Beauty and Being Just*, p. 57.
4   Gilson, *The Arts of the Beautiful*, p. 43.
5   *Ibid.*, p. 32.
6   T. S. Eliot, *Four Quartets* (New York: Harcourt Brace & Company, 1971), p. 20.
7   Scarry, *On Beauty and Being Just*, pp. 3, 4.
8   C.S. Lewis, *Surprised by Joy: the Shape of My Early Life* (New York: Harcourt, Inc., 1955), pp. 17–18.
9   Dickson Skinner, "Music Goes into Mass Production," in *Harper's Magazine* 178 (April 1939), p. 485.
10   *Ibid.*, p. 487.
11   Theodor Adorno,"Analytical Study of the NBC Music Appreciation Hour," in *Musical Quarterly* 78.2 (1994), pp. 352–53.
12   David Brooks, *On Paradise Drive: How We Live Now (and Always Have) in the Future Tense* (New York: Simon & Schuster, 2004), p. 149.

13 Eliot, p. 54.

14 Søren Kierkegaard, *The Concept of Irony*, tr. by Lee M. Capel (New York: Harper & Row, Publishers, 1965), p. 270.

15 *Ibid.*, pp. 270, 275.

16 George Steiner, *Real Presences* (Chicago: University of Chicago, 1989), p. 144.

17 William Edgar, "Beauty Avenged, Apologetics Enriched," in *Westminster Theological Journal* 63 (2001), pp. 108-109.

18 *Ibid.*, p. 108.

19 Charlie Peacock, *At the Crossroads: an Insider's Look at the Past, Present, and Future of Contemporary Christian Music* (Nashville: Broadman & Holman, 1999), p. 86.

20 Augustine, *Confessions*, tr. by R. S. Pine-Coffin (Harmondsworth, Middlesex, England: Penguin, 1961), p. 238.

21 *Ibid.*, p. 239.

22 Jonathan Edwards, *The Sermons of Jonathan Edwards: a Reader*, ed. by Wilson H. Kimnach, Kenneth P. Minkema, and Douglas A. Sweeney (New Haven: Yale University Press, 1999), pp. 15-16. See also: Stephen Nichols, *Heaven on Earth: Capturing Jonathan Edwards's Vision of Living in Between* (Wheaton: Crossway Books, 2006).

23 Edwards, *The Sermons of Jonathan Edwards*, pp. 17-18.

24 Jeremy S. Begbie, *Resounding Truth: Christian Wisdom in the World of Music* (Grand Rapids: Baker Academic, 2007), p. 219.

25 C. S. Lewis, "The Weight of Glory", p. 8.

26 Gilson, *The Arts of the Beautiful*, p. 9.

27 Nicholas Wolterstorff, *Art in Action: Toward a Christian Aesthetic* (Grand Rapids: Eerdmans, 1980), pp. 82-83.

28 *Ibid.*, p. 91.

29 Begbie, *Resounding Truth*, p. 222.

30 *Ibid.*, p. 222.

31 Søren Kierkegaard, *Concluding Unscientific Postscript to Philosophical Fragments, Vol. I*, tr. by Howard V. Hong and Edna H. Hong (Princeton: Princeton University Press, 1992), p. 135.

32 Begbie, *Resounding Truth*, p. 223.

33 Eliot, *Four Quartets*, p. 44.

34 Dietrich Bonhoeffer, *Ethics*, tr. by Neville Horton Smith (New York: Touchstone Book, 1995), pp. 126-7.

35 *Ibid.*, p. 129.

36 *Ibid.*, p. 130.

37 *Ibid.*, p. 132.

38 *Ibid.*, p. 140

39 Scarry, *On Beauty and Being Just*, pp. 111-12.

40 *Ibid.*, pp. 113-14.

41 Wolterstorff, *Art in Action*, p. 83.

42 Richard B. Gaffin, Jr., "The Usefulness of the Cross," in *Westminster Theological Journal* 41.2 (1979).

43 *Ibid.*

44 *Ibid.*

45 Edwards, *The Sermons of Jonathan Edwards*, pp. 18-19.

MESSAGE BOY:
mission remix

In the first volume of this series, *It Was Good: Making Art to the Glory of God,* I wrote on the theme of *mission.* I had thought that what I wrote was clear enough, but then after that book came out I spoke at a conference of CIVA (Christians in the Visual Arts) and found that I needed to unpack the ideas in my essay a bit more for people. So in this volume I will do a "remix" of sorts, revisiting some of the ideas in the first essay, and sharing my story in hopes of illustrating my thoughts in a way that is easier to understand.

First things first: I want to tell you, my brother and sister musicians, that you've chosen a noble vocation. Or, perhaps music has chosen you? That's even better. An invitation is preferable to a cold call. In your vocation you must at all times and in all ways relentlessly pursue success. That is, as long as success is defined as increased skill and ability, imagination, humility, generosity of spirit, good humor, gratitude, innovation, love, and empathy, and becoming more like Jesus, not less. Your life as a musician is an invitation to become one kind of person in the world and not another, while leaving the world a better place than when you first arrived. It is a unique calling to live a seamless, integrated, creative life before God and the world, cultivating and enjoying the gift of music. Take it seriously—at the same level of seriousness you hope surgeons and airline pilots take their work.

Music involves many things, and not the least of these is the work of story-telling and storied living after the pattern of Jesus. Your songs and performances will tell stories, as will your life. Make sure both of them are true and winsome. In imaginative ways, shape your work to be inescapably connected to the Father's business in the world. Ask yourself how your musical life might cooperate with

God in restoring rightness, doing justice, and showing mercy. Wonder out loud how music might remove impairments to healthy functioning. See your musical life as one faithful way to care for God's creativity—people and place, and all of creation. Be in perpetual dream mode about how music might exist for the good of people and to proclaim God's excellence as Creator.

As I already said, this essay is a "remix" of a previous essay on mission. It is a 12-inch single filled with loops and samples drawn from my life expereinces. Let me tell you my story, as I shared it with some friends recently, as a simple way to see how God wove His Kingdom work into my life:

CONVERSING WITH MERCY

I was born in Yuba City, California into a musical family—my father was a musician, trumpeter, educator. I think the first thing to understand is that the place and the people that you are born into are not neutral. It makes you one kind of a person and not another. And so being born into a musical family gave me the opportunity to watch a musician work. And then as I was able to develop questions and articulate them, I could ask my father. "How do you write out the rhythm pattern *dah-de-dah-de-de-dah-dah-dah-dah-dah-de-dah?*" And then he would show me how to tap the subdivisions with a pencil. And he just taught me the tiniest little nuances of what it meant to put music together.

In the beginning I told my father I wanted to be a drummer, so he bought me a practice pad. And I said, "That's not a drum set." He said, "That's right. You have to learn to play all of the sticking on the practice pad and if you get good enough at it, I'll buy you a drum set." I said, "That's no fun." So I said, "I want to learn to play tenor saxophone." So he got me a clarinet. I said, "Why did you get me a clarinet?" He said, "Because you are just a little guy and you can't hold that tenor saxophone yet. It's going to take a great deal of air to blow through it. You need to learn on the clarinet first. You'll be fine, just play." So I played it for a week and I put it down. Then I said, "I want to play the trumpet." So he bought me a cornet. I said, "Why did you buy me a cornet?" He says, "Because you're a little guy and it's just a little instrument and you can hold it and you don't have to push as much air through it, and you can learn on it. Because you have to develop your embouchure." What is an embouchure? "Well, it's really developing your lips and the way that you pass the air through the horn and you develop the sound and the tone and so on and so forth." So, I finally decided that I wasn't going to ask my dad to get me any more instruments. We had a piano already, so I taught myself to play the piano. And of course along the way I learned to play a little bit of clarinet, a little bit of drums, a little bit of trumpet. But it was really the piano that set me free. And a big reason for that was because I could see the orchestra. I could see it in front of me. The keys, all of them. I could go all the way down with the contra bass and the tympani. I could go all the way up the top with the piccolos and the triangles and all that sound up there. I could live in the middle, right where my voice was. I could find the same notes where my voice was. And so, I taught myself to play piano based a lot on seeing the music unfold. And of course I had to develop technique, and get my digits to go where I wanted them to go. But a lot of it was just a matter of discovery.

But it wasn't happening in a vacuum, it was happening inside of a musical family where you could ask questions, where you could observe. And then my father was a teacher too. So I spent a lot of time around students. I went with him to every marching band appearance that he conducted or stage band or any of that. I was there, I was Bill Ashworth's little boy. And I was there watching him teach others and make music.

Another significant thing is that we lived in a very little farm town. In our town there was a really interesting character. His name was Drew Sallee and he had a band called Drusalee & The Dead. They drove around in a hearse and every little kid in our town thought Drusalee & The Dead were the most amazing thing. They only put out one single in northern California, but they were such a big deal. They started every show with Drew Sallee lying down in a coffin. And then he would rise up playing his tenor saxophone. One time, my dad was supposed to go over to the gym when Drusalee & The Dead were playing and he was the teacher that was designated that week to go to the gym and collect the money and put it away for the kids who had paid to go to the dance. And I got to see their opening, and it was like my life was changed forever. My dad said, "Ah, that's crap." And I said, "I don't think so." We had a lot in common in terms of our love of jazz and great singers like Ella and Tony Bennett, and people like that that my parents listened to. But we were definitely at a divide with Drusalee & The Dead.

That divide was never more apparent than when we moved out to the country and there was another musical family that lived right behind us. Their son played blues harp, guitar, and ocarina. There was a song at that time by The Troggs called "Wild Thing" that had an ocarina solo in it. So every kid back then wanted to buy an ocarina and learn how to play that. And I was no different. The first time I went over to visit Ralph's house I saw Ralph's whole bedroom was devoted to music. He taught me how to tune in Wolfman Jack and this LA radio station late at night. Ralph said, "If you stay up until 1:00 in the morning you can tune him in." I was sure these were the secrets of the universe. But that's the way you learn, you learn from other musicians. And he would just sit and listen to records. He was the first person that I ever saw that just sat and listened to records. And the whole time you'd be listening to them he'd be saying, "You hear that? You hear that? That's amazing!" It would get you so excited about music.

My dad's whole thing was about accuracy. So it was all about pitch and tuning. Tuning was super important to my dad. If you played something on your instrument, he would go "flat, flat, no up, up, up, up, stop, alright, next." He had an unbelievable ear and of course that's what I have to do in the studio now. I learned that from him. As a record producer, I'm checking tuning all the time! So I remember this one time when Ralph was playing his guitar my dad went out in the backyard and jumped up on the fence and yelled, "Tune that $@#&% guitar!" I'll never forget that. And again, you see, there is something of value that I've taken: it's good to be in tune. But it's also good to be Ralph. It's good to have that passion for music and that desire to just uncover everything and celebrate it. I learned so much as a boy just by watching and listening.

The first legit band that I was in was called Blind Horse. It was a horn band, and so I played trumpet in it and farfisa organ. We played Santana songs, Chicago, Blood, Sweat, and Tears—and all that kind of stuff. So, you start your first band. What are you learning? You are learning how to communicate, how to talk to each other. You learn that people need a lot of direction. Maybe *you're* the person that needs a lot of direction. Or maybe you're the person that's frustrated by the lack of direction. I was the kid saying, "Come on guys, come on guys. Hey let's rehearse it again, let's run through it again." Or "Hey let's rehearse from the second verse on out, because that's really the only part we need to rehearse." I had seen my dad do that so many times when he was conducting the orchestra or stage band. He'd hit that baton on the music stand and they would do four bars of rehearsal just over and over again until they've ironed out the problems. So that's what I brought into playing in rock bands. I was the guy saying, "Hey, let's don't just keep playing it wrong every time, that's ridiculous."

ANDI BEAT GOES ON

The next phase of making music is going from playing other people's material to playing your own. I remember when I was 14 years old, I was in love with the girl I would eventually marry. Andi was an older woman, 15. I was writing my first songs. I had the inspiration of this beautiful young girl that I was in love with, and I remember these two songs in particular that I wrote. One of them was called "Hey Lady Love." Fortunately in our high school was a senior who played drums in the high school band (but also was a DJ on the local top 40 radio station) who offered to record me. We met at this raggedy old house in the middle of a peach orchard with a bunch of hippie dudes living in it and he recorded my little song, "Hey Lady Love." I was 14 years old.

That summer we went on a family vacation to Morro Bay. And I was thinking, "We are so close to Los Angeles, wouldn't it be amazing if I could go to Asylum Records and give my tapes to David Geffen?" I asked my dad, "Could you take me to Los Angeles so I can give them my songs?" And in a rare moment of magical whimsy he said, "Yes, I'll do that." And so he drove three hours into the heart of Hollywood. I remember the smog was so bad that I felt I would be sick. I had my cassettes (the original cassettes—it wasn't like I knew enough to make a copy or anything) in this little brown bag, and I walked into Asylum Records. The receptionist was very sweet and she was like, "Well, how can I help you?" There were gold and platinum records all over the walls and I said, "Well, I've got some tapes here for Mr. Geffen . . . that I would like for him to hear . . . some songs that I've written." And she said, "I'll see that he gets them." Then my dad and I got back in the car and we went and got a hamburger and then drove back to Morro Bay. And that was my first interaction with the music business. Several months later I got a very kind letter from Asylum Records saying, "While we're not able to use any of your music at this time, or do anything to help you, the door is always open to you, please submit again." That was very kind. I thought, "Well, Okay, yeah, let's do it again!" I was on my way.

In high school, all I wanted was just to make music. At that time I was in bands that were more commercially oriented—because we had to function in our culture. We were always playing for parties or playing for dances, and during that time people danced a lot and so you had to play music that people danced to. But I think what happens, at least for somebody who is creating their own music but having to play someone else's is eventually you come to a crossroads and say, "Look, I'm either going to be on this track for the rest of my life, playing other people's music, or I have to risk something and try to play my own music." I left high school when I was sixteen, after my junior year. I came to believe I needed to be playing my own music exclusively probably when I was around nineteen or twenty years old. As a result, I didn't stay in college very long either. I dropped out of Cal State Sacramento in 1976 I believe.

I was married by that time and working as a professional musician. Then I did what so many musicians have done before me: I became a fry cook. After two weeks of that I said to myself, "As God is my witness I shall never be a fry cook again." And I got really, really serious. I buckled down and practiced and practiced and practiced as an instrumentalist. And the cultivation of skill and ability created new opportunities for me which introduced me to new people and new music. More fusion-oriented music—a hybrid of different forms of music, which was a huge thing when I was growing up. In northern California it was really a hot bed of ecclectism, which we don't really understand that much anymore because we're all so oriented to our niche. Nowadays it's like, "I'm really into Americana Folk Music," or "I'm really into Jazz," or "I'm really into Alternative Rock." But when I was growing up, all those same people would all be on the same bill. A fellow by the name of Bill Graham (who later became my manager) was really the architect of that kind of concert promotion during that time. And the culture loved it. People celebrated ecclectism, innovation, and people being different. That was the whole point of the '60s and '70s. People really experimenting to be a different kind of human being, to love and celebrate different things.

I then joined a band called The Runners—which was a very popular kind of experimental funk band in Sacramento, California. That was my first experience of regional touring. These people were playing their own music, and as was typical of the day, they all lived in the same house together. And also typical of what I was starting to experience was, these were people who had kind of gone before me. In other words, one of the fellows had been involved with Jefferson Airplane before, and one of the fellows had already made a record for a major label. You start to spend time around people who had already been there and done that, and hear their stories. Either like they deflate you or they get you even more excited about what the future might hold. That is what happened with The Runners.

After playing with The Runners, I could see, "Well, oh, that's how you do it." So I started a band called The Planets. In those days, it was very entrepreneurial. If you weren't entrepreneurial, you had to get a manager, and you weren't going to get a manager unless you were already successful. So some part of you had to be entrepreneurial enough to get it going. And I found out about myself that I could be entrepreneurial. That was an important aspect of my success and something that I believe that God used ultimately.

DOWN IN THE LOWLANDS

Around that same time, I gained enough facility that I had my working, sort of rock/pop group, and then I would also play jazz with a trio or quintet on the weekends. But then I got into a little bit of financial trouble. I remember I had to go back out on the road and play in a top 40 band called Sister Rose. We were playing up and down California, performing other people's songs. I had to sing "Do You Think I'm Sexy" by Rod Stewart, which was probably the lowest moment for me. And like several times before, I remember saying, "God, if You are witnessing this, as You are my witness, I will never do this again." I went back to Sacramento after that and I told my friend Steve Holsapple (the person I would credit with first discovering and mentoring me) that I was ready to commit myself entirely to my own music. He knew a fellow Maurice Read who owned a Bohemian-intellectual-political watering hole called Maurice's American Bar. They had a little raggedy upright piano and I started playing there on Monday nights doing all my own songs. And then I got popular enough to be moved to Tuesday, then to Wednesday, then to Thursday, and then they started giving me the whole week-end. That's when Chuck Ashworth became Charlie Peacock.

Then I met a fellow named Sal Valentino, best known as lead singer of The Beau Brummels. He hired me to play keyboards on tour with him. He had helped get Ricki Lee Jones signed to Warner Brothers and he said, "I want to take you to Warner Brothers. I think you're amazing. I want to take you around to all the record company people I know." Now I'm back in LA, but I'm back there under completely different circumstances. I'm not showing up in David Geffen's office with my brown bag, but I'm showing up with an advocate who wants to tell my story for me. That's how I first got integrated with record labels. By 1980 I recorded for A&M Records the first time. A producer named David Kershenbaum signed me to a development deal there. Tommy Boyce and Bobby Hart—two of the guys who wrote a lot of songs for The Monkees—bought my first song that I ever sold. It was called "You're So Attractive." It went something like this: *You're so attractive baby/You're so attractive/You're so attractive baby/You're so attractive.* I didn't end up making a record at that time, but it was a start, and eventually "Lie Down on the Grass" was released by A&M Records in early 1985.

BIG MAN'S HAT

By 1982, as an independent artist I was supporting my family, and in my music from that period you hear me starting to ask questions or making statements to show that I was a spiritual seeker. I'd moved past the "You're so attractive baby" to "I'm looking for a mind of the spiritual kind" (from "What They Like," the B-side of "No Magazines"—a single that Tower Records released). I began to see the role of the artist as something that was deeper and more expansive. But I didn't own it yet. In many ways I was still a little boy. It's like I'm wearing a hat that I hadn't grown into yet. I may have been married and loving a woman, but I was a boy. I had the mind of a boy. I had the interests of a boy.

Around that time everything shifted for me. It's like I started to grow up and started to believe that I needed to have something to say. Right about that time I really started to attract producers and record labels and people who wanted to invest in me. And also I had really changed my lifestyle a lot. I was a real seeker, reading and praying to the God-of-the-Bible. I'd get up every morning and pray to the God-of-the-Bible to stay clean and sober that day. In the evening I would thank the God-of-the-Bible. There wasn't a Christian around me. Then God sent a saxophonist to tell me the Story that would match up and meet up with what was happening inside my heart and mind. From there it wasn't about me anymore. My self-pursuits were replaced by a much nobler, grander vision for artistry which would be not service of self, but care of the planet, service and love of people. To do things that might be experimental or challenging in order to bring humanity a little bit more forward, to open up hearts and minds to experience life more fully. Big ideas became my nutrition and that just changed the way I looked at everything. Looking back I see it was the Holy Spirit giving me a reason to live, redefining and rewiring my whole intentions.

Then, interestingly enough, Christians began to come out of the woodwork. I'd be playing at the club and somebody would walk by and they'd say: "I'm praying for you, brother." I'm like: "Who are these people?" I remember one time I was walking to this club and these two young women were standing there and they said: "Are you going in to perform?" and I said: "Yeah, yeah. You guys coming in?" and they're like: "Can we pray for you first?" and I was like: "Uh ... well, yeah, okay." I remember standing out there in the alley and they were praying this beautiful, sincere prayer for me. Then it became really natural for me to be a person of faith, just mixing it up out in the world. Whenever we would play we would be back in the kitchen before the gig and have a big time of prayer.

Back in early 80s my band was fairly popular in northern California night clubs and as a young Christian it could be confusing. Not everyone was supportive - some people thought I should be playing in churches. Personally, I wasn't completely sure either, but I prayed about it, asking God to help me. I said: "I know, You can provide me with any job you want. But until You provide me with another job, this is my job. Right?" I made one immediate concession. I gave up my 10% of the bar. I was popular enough that I got 100% of the door and 10% of the bar. But I knew a lot of people coming to abuse alcohol and I decided that I wasn't going to profit from that.

WHOLE LOT DIFFERENT, WHOLE LOT THE SAME

There were a lot of things like that to think about in the beginning. It was a challenge. There weren't very many professing Christians doing that because, basically, the *modus operandi* was that you should stop playing bars if you were a Christian. Instead, for me, it became the place that I learned to write those songs that have come to be known as my Christian songs. I learned very early on that it's one thing to sit in a room and say, "Do you know that Jesus Christ is your personal Savior?" and it is quite another to develop a language, melody, and presentation that is winsome enough that the whole world might want to sing along, and develop a great curiosity for the love of God, people and planet, and more specifically the story of how God is making all things new through Jesus—"thy kingdom come, thy will be done"—and all that.

In 1984 I released my debut album, *Lie Down in the Grass* on Exit Records distributed through Word Records. I learned a lot of things from that experience. I learned that Christians can be very uptight people. But at the time I didn't know that in Christian music there are "gate keepers" all the way along. I didn't know anything about their agenda. I just wanted to be a great artist for Christ's sake. So when we made *Lie Down in the Grass* we just made things we thought were cool, what we liked, and what we wanted to listen to ourselves. No one ever said "Make this more Christian" or "Where's Jesus in this?" It was just like be who God made you to be. I never for once even thought, "I wonder what Christian radio stations will think of this?" So I can't communicate how completely surprised I was when we turned in the cover and it was rejected outright! "Those are pagan symbols, people are going to freak out on this." I literally had no idea of what was happening to me and why people were so worked up. But I quickly found out.

Whenever I would meet the craziness of the Christian subculture, I was always felt God would somehow increase my humility by little by little revealing my own craziness. He would convict me of my own sin and ridiculousness and the give me a commensurate amount of love and grace for people. I'm so grateful for that. I know many musical people who have a lot of bitterness toward the Church and/or Christian music. I'm not one of those people. I'm a generally happy person without grudges. I'm grateful to have experienced what I went through during the short time I was in the thick of it in what I suppose is best described as a form of commercial Christian music. If it was from the hand of God, then I am grateful for it.

Lie Down in the Grass was leased to A&M through a series of deals that Word had in process. At that time Amy Grant was at the top of the heap, and so they made this multi-tiered deal with the label. Exit Records got a college radio push and we got product people assigned to us. Then I got a call from a big gruff man from New York City and he said, "Hey, you want to go out on tour with The Fixx next week?" I was like, "Well, *yeah.*" So I signed with a couple of fellows named John Huie and Ian Copeland (his brother Stewart played for The Police) through a booking agency called Frontier Booking International, and then I was out on the road. I was out touring with The Fixx, Let's Active, General Public, Missing Persons, and the Red Hot Chili Peppers. I never played at a church.

I WILL NEED YOUR HELP

Then it was time for me to make another record. We didn't like our relationship with A&M, and through a record executive named Lou Maglia we ended meeting a kind of legendary figure in the music business, Chris Blackwell. We set up in our church and played for Chris, and the next thing I knew The 77s and I were on Island Records. I started traveling internationally and I started doing records over in London. I was touring all the time and also playing jazz in an electric improvisational band called Emperor Norton with Brent Bourgeois, Larry Tagg, Bongo Bob Smith, Henry Robinett, and Aaron Smith.

Nigel Gray, who produced The Police and Siouxsie & The Banshees, co-produced my Island Records release with me and Brent Bourgeois. I'd already done some producing inside of the little imprint of Exit Records. I had produced The 77s and Steve Scott. And I was also a songwriter for CBS, under contract to them, so I used the studio all the time. To put it in perspective, before I ever had a major label record deal, I had recorded probably sixty songs on my own and had put in thousands of hours in the studio already. But it was at that moment when I had the confidence or the faith to believe that record producing might be something for me.

Then my phone started ringing.

People started finding out about me. "Hey, there's this guy who is a Christian in mainstream pop music." I played at the Cornerstone, Creation, and Greenbelt Festivals. I met Amy Grant for the first time at Greenbelt Festival and I had just started finding some music created by Christians that I liked. I remember the first time I heard "Lead Me On" by Amy, I was like: "Wow! This is a real record. These are real substantive songs of real merit and have really done well."

By 1988 we had moved on from Island Records and I had another epiphany: "I don't need a major label to affirm whether I can make music or not." So we went back into the studio and we started making music, compiling some of these sixty demos that I had, and just starting putting out these cassettes on our own. As a result of that, we kept touring. We went to Cornerstone Festival in the summer of 1989 and sold about $12,000 worth of cassettes. Jimmy Abegg, Vince Ebo, and I formed a trio that people really enjoyed. We did that for about three years pretty steadily, touring all over Europe and the United States.

HIRING A WORKER

I then did showcases for all the major labels, and I thought Atlantic was going to sign me, but I think God closed the door for reasons that have since unfolded. Then Peter York and Bill Hearn from Sparrow Records came out to see me play live at this club called The Wild Blue. (In those days we played for three hours nonstop. Our thought was that if you didn't leave our gig thinking you have had the greatest night of your life, we had failed.) We poured it on thick that night and Peter and Bill loved it. They offered me a record deal and promised to bend over backwards to create as much work for me in Nashville as they could. And they did that. We moved to Nashville where I recorded *The Secret of Time*, *Love Life*, and *Everything That's On My Mind*. I probably produced fifty albums for other artists, wrote hundreds of songs, and it was very good and very fun. Until it wasn't. At the point that it wasn't, I started the re:think label. I signed Sarah Masen and Switchfoot. I headed back to my original vision to be about God's people everywhere and in everything. The glass of water called Christian music was just too small. I needed an ocean of possibilities. I did that, and most people know that the Switchfoot story culminated in selling well over two million records on *The Beautiful Letdown* alone.

The next step of my career was, of course—*to write a book?* Why I thought I would have the authority to write a book, I have no idea. But I literally took a year off. I look back on it and I think it's because I love the church. I love the church and I want people to be set free. I believe that the Gospel sets people free and what I could see around me was a general lack of freedom, personally and artistically. The intention behind Christian music is very good because they want people to be safe and sound from the negative and hurtful influences of the world. But what it doesn't do is prepare God's people to be God's kind of person everywhere and in everything. The overriding premise of my book was that there is something flawed about the system. It doesn't mean that we shouldn't have Christian music. It was never about discounting the work of Christian music or trying to say that there's something specifically wrong with it. In fact, I tried very hard not to write that kind of book. I'm not a person who rags on Christian music. If your son or daughter would grow up and say, "You know what, I love the church with all my heart. What

I want to do for my vocation is to make music out of love for the church, to serve the church." I would say, "I'm one hundred percent with you—how can I help you do that?" What I wanted to do was to help people see that the possibilities for the music Christians can make are so much richer, grander, more beautiful, wide, and deep than a genre of music. The whole ideology of a genre is to make things smaller and more categorizable. And what I was saying was that no, in fact, we want to go the opposite way. We want to go so far in the opposite way that we go in to the mystery of where God works.

Music is one way of loving God with your whole being and loving your neighbor with the same love and care you desire. Good music can actually be a means of doing for others what God has so graciously done for you. Sing over people, mend their hearts, and open them up to a renewed life. Be the wonder and surprise they need and for which they hope.

IS THE BRIGHTNESS STILL IN ME

I've been trying to make that little riff on wonder and hope sing true for thirty plus years. It doesn't matter whether I'm the artist or I'm producing another—this is my focus. Music is a gift you give back. That's the business I'm in. But, it's a gift that comes in many shapes for many reasons. There's nothing predictable about it. In my own artistic life I've tried to be about surprise. Every recording I do is different from the last. I generally set out to make something I haven't made before. So I'm not the artist you turn to for a consistent sound. The difference between my jazz recording *Love Press Ex-Curio* and my folky, Americana record *No Man's Land* could not be greater. But there are commonalities if you look for them and certainly the canon of American music is one of them. Still, I do work with many artists who are committed to a consistency in their sound. The Civil Wars EP that had the song "Poison and Wine" on it pointed the way to the full length *Barton Hollow* and we kept the sound very consistent. With the second, self-titled full length, we kept the consistent performance sound but added new flavors, showing the diversity and growth of the band—letting people know they weren't a one trick pony. Sometimes the sound is shaped and directed by the performance (as is the case with The Civil Wars), and sometimes it's about the artist imagining new music for each outing (which is the case with me). When my wife Andi and I began the non-profit Art House America, our dream was to inspire people to a diverse, imaginative, creative life—one that would dream good dreams for the world at large and for the Christian church that we love and count ourselves a part of. The music I create and produce is a reflection of that vision. This includes music specific to serving the Church (Keith & Kristyn Getty); music in the tradition and family of country legend Hank Williams (grand-daughter Holly Williams), a blend of jazz piano and South African Zulu choral music (Ladysmith Black Mambazo), and Top 40 pop hits with Switchfoot and Amy Grant. My goal is always richer, grander, deeper, wider, more beautiful, and reflective of God's diverse creation.

THIS IS HOW THE WORK GETS DONE

As you are developing, wind your way up through the circles of affirmation that are family, friends, school, church, city, region, state, province, and country. Do all that well, and then you just might find yourself making a few musical trips to stages in such dreamy places as London, Amsterdam, Koln, Berlin, Sydney, and Shanghai. Make sure you take the phrase "if only" out of your vocabulary (as in, "if only I had a 1953 Fender Telecaster"). Great tools are nice to have, but they are no substitute for great and astonishing ideas. I would venture to say that music is everywhere and in everything. If you must have some tool to discover it, then it's likely you don't even know what you're looking for yet. Confused?

Do this. Put away everything you own that is traditionally considered a musical instrument or tool. Now, for eight to twelve hours each day, work to gain total and complete independence in the fingers of both your hands. For example, tap 4/4 quarter notes with your forefinger on your right hand while tapping 3/4 quarter notes with your middle finger—put a new emphasis on one with each bar of three. Add eight note triplets in 4/4 time with your little finger. With your left hand, tap out the rhythm pattern of a dotted quarter note followed by an eighth note. Let your left thumb tap out two eighth notes followed by a quarter note until a bar of 7/4 time is complete. You now have several independent rhythms going on, as well as three independent time signatures. Imagine working through every possible variation of rhythm, time signature, and tempo with each individual finger and gaining mastery in this. Imagine working on it every day for five years! Once you can do anything you imagine, pick up a guitar and change the world.

For all the talk about how bad the music business is, I offer this: Sing songs, not business. Get your music on, not your mogul. And remember, there is no limit to the creativity of God and no knowable end or limit to the imagination of those who bear his image. The music of God's people is only truly faithful to the degree that it trusts in and reflects this.

For example, my friend Brooke Waggoner is an excellent songwriter, but more than that, she's a fully-orbed, imaginative musician. Her engine runs on surprise and wonder. I know that any new music from her will take me places I haven't gone before. And I'm not scared either—she knows how to create an enjoyable journey full of unexpected but delightful twists and turns. Ruby Amanfu, another dear friend who worked with Brooke in Jack White's band, has THE voice. Not many people get a truly unique voice, but Ruby did, and so that's how she changes the world—Joy Williams too. All these dear women have to do is open their mouths and sing!

And then there is Zach Williams of The Lone Bellow. He has passion on stun.

Zach shows the world what it means to be committed to an idea—in this case a song. He doesn't sell it. He embodies the song. Zach and the song become one and you better either listen or leave the room. That's a world-changing gift—both keeping people in a room mesmerized, or driving them into the street, simply because they can't deal with the level of commitment you bring to your art and life.

I also think of my friends Ricky Skaggs, Andy Leftwich, and Bryan Sutton from the bluegrass world. These players are some of the greatest musicians the world has ever known. Highly intuitive, well studied but not in a stuffy academic way. They make real, emotive music that also serves to keep the bar high on what musicians can do if they serve God, people, and planet in selfless ways—that is, putting in the crazy amount of hours it takes to get as good as they are. Then there's Jon Foreman and Sara Groves, two of the greatest lyricists I've ever had the privilege of working with. They tell stories that move people to change and to greatness. There are so many people I could mention who do the very real work of imagining for the music of our time. These friends, and many more like them, are trying to do their small part in cooperating with God as he so graciously lifts the perceived limits of imagination and draws the willing into new and timely ways of creating a better, more beautiful world.

Here's the deal: Business ebbs and flows, but the music is not going anywhere. The artists and songwriters may change with every generation, but the music is not going anywhere. The economy may contract and expand, but the music is not going anywhere. Music lives in rarified, protected air.

No Place Closer To Heaven

Hopefully all this story-telling, hard-knocks wisdom, and reflections on the music business mixed together to help you imagine what it might be like to see your life serve for the good of people and to proclaim God's excellence as Creator.

Above all, we can never, ever forget that the life, death, and resurrection of one man—Jesus Christ—inspired the greatest body of music and art the world has ever known. The music of God's people is not going anywhere but forward to the new heavens and the new earth where all God's people will sing together:

Worthy is the Lamb, who was slain,
to receive power and wealth and
wisdom and strength
and honor and glory and praise!

To him who sits on the throne and to the Lamb
be praise and honor and glory and power,
for ever and ever!

So learn the art, find pleasure in your privilege, imagine and love well, learn to read a contract (or at least get a good lawyer), be kind and generous, keep your hands clean, read books, watch films, and listen to lots and lots of music. Finally, if at all possible, learn the secret of making music—not sacred, secular, Christian, or otherwise, but true music, just the right sounds and meaning at the right time in history for the good of people and planet.

RAISING
rockstars

Jan reached over and took my hand, placing it on her bulging tummy. It was a provocative gesture for a young couple sitting near the front of the formal sanctuary. Her belly felt alive, like Leviathan writhing up from the deep.

"It's the pipe organ," she whispered with a grin, as the bellowing pipes rumbled our wooden pew. "The baby always moves when the organ begins," she assured me.

Jan, a classically trained organist herself, then leaned back with contentment.

Mother and child were responding to the auditory beauty around them. So began the musical life of our son, Jon.

Our son's spontaneous, prenatal expression came without formal training or practice; this mirrored our own inexperience at parenting. We were twenty-five years young, full of excitement and terribly nervous about beginning our new family. Little did we realize this journey of procreation would lead us to see God's creation afresh through a child's eyes.

Along the way, we made several discoveries about raising creative children. These insights interwove themes of childhood development, spirituality, mission, and creativity. But as naive parents, there was no predetermined point on the horizon toward which we were headed. We especially had no idea that our two sons would grow up to be professional rock musicians—with the character, spirituality, and creativity that is now associated with the band Switchfoot.

RE-CREATING OUR OWN CREATIVITY

When our first son, Jon, finally made his dramatic entrance, arriving two weeks late, an unspoken question arose: Now what? Leaving the hospital, we gently cradled our almost nine pound, blond-haired Viking to the car and pensively drove up the winding mountain road to our tiny cabin home. Our lessons in parenting were just as circuitous and only beginning.

Many parents are like we were: unaware and inexperienced. Yet gradually, most of us find our footing and settle into a parenting style. At a minimum, many of us simply repeat the patterns of our own parents, who were only imitating their parents. Family traits are too easily recycled. Unfortunately, this haphazard approach is perhaps the most common style of parenting. Of course, it only works well with parents who have come from perfect families!

In our broken world, intergenerational family dysfunction can climb uninvited through the windows of any new family. Thankfully, many parents recognize its unwelcome presence, and realize they must deliberately change the habits from their childhood home. They must establish their own crisp, new parental map. The creative home begins here: Believing that God can re-create your own life and those whom you love!

The learning curve can also be steep concerning our knowledge of childhood development. Of course, we want to give these fresh baby minds every advantage, but what is appropriate—and when? On this point, it was helpful for us to admit our ignorance and find the right tools. We became students again, and learned all we could about the bio-psycho-social needs of our little prince. We quickly discovered that play is the child's work. So we combed the marketplace for fresh ideas on how to make our home user-friendly for our young explorer. These insightful materials helped us break new ground in our family, and move away from familiar, but unhelpful, patterns. (One important tool was a subscription to *Growing Child.* This newsletter arrived monthly, and highlighted the developmental benchmarks that each parent could encourage.)

Jan and I belong to the TV tray generation. Yet we questioned this focal point for meals after reading about the negative effects of staring at the hypnotizing tube. So we broke with our traditions and postponed having a television until our children were eight and ten years old. By that age, their creative legs were strong, and they chose more active pursuits.

Recent research has confirmed our suspicions. In the book, *Thinking and Literacy: The Mind at Work*, the authors present solid research linking hours spent in front of the TV to decreased academic performance in all subject areas. Additionally, the October 2007 *Pediatrics* magazine, writes, "Consistent, heavy television viewing (more than two hours a day) throughout early childhood can cause behavior, sleep and attention problems." Jane Healy, a leading authority on education, wrote in *New Horizons for Learning,* "A brain which is actively involved and curious is likely to develop stronger connections than one which is merely a passive recipient of learning."

That is why less is more when it comes to establishing a creative home. If we are engulfed in sound bites and engaging visuals, we can grow numb to the subtle whispers of honest, raw creative moments. *Anhedonia* is the inability to gain pleasure from normally pleasurable experiences. The child who is over stimulated by battery noise and flashy images may struggle to appreciate the quieter joys of digging in the sand, singing to himself in the silence.

What drives us to fill every space with activity and noise? Why do we complicate our lives with the clutter of consumerism? When was the last time you flew a kite, or turned off the television and made up a story, or built a fort? Young minds need room to breathe, a place to hear their own imaginative voice. You can lead your child down the path of inspiration, rather than the path of least resistance.

A CREATIVE GENETIC CODE

Responsible parents quickly discover their vital role to love, nurture, and instill confidence in their children, thus encouraging the child's own responsibility. These are the lofty goals of parenting. Without these qualities, our children will flounder. When the fledgling child finally spreads her wings to fly, every parent hopes they have done their job well, and are not releasing an insecure, immature, or irresponsible adult onto society. When the baton is passed from one generation to the next, we hope to have placed it well in our child's hands.

Yet parents who believe in a personal God can have even higher aspirations. We understand that we must hold onto our child's hand until he is firmly grasping God's larger hand. We want to nurture within our child an understanding of God's wonderful nature, so they will make their own decision to believe in and enthusiastically follow Christ.

But there is an aspect of this spiritual goal that is often neglected: We must also inspire our children to be creative. Why do we often ignore this essential component, even in our educational systems? Our common excuse might be that we, as parents, are not artistic. Consequently, we lower the bar and expect little artistry from our children. But is not creativity a vital aspect of the nature of God, whom we want our children to know and love?

The Master Sculptor of heaven and earth has made us in His image. When we encourage our children to become artistic creators, they discover the authentic image of God. Even as we carry God's rational and moral image into culture, we also carry a deposit of God's brilliant creativity. He *is* the Creator!

Because our sons are musicians, Jan and I are often asked if we are musical. When we reply that we do enjoy music or play instruments, the response is often, "So that's where they got it!" The assumption is made that musical talent is simply passed on by genetics. Putting too much weight on *nature* or genetics may cause us to neglect the greater role that *nurture* plays in developing artistic children.

Is creative talent inherited by nature—and not by nurture? The answer is both yes and no. We have God's creative DNA. Therefore, we are all predisposed to display His talent; it is our *nature*. This goes beyond any parent's ability to play the banjo or sing on key. All God's children are creative. But not all are encouraged in its expression. How can we foster an environment in which creativity will thrive?

THE CREATIVE SPACE: A GARDEN OF CHOICE

As infants, Jon and Tim were eager to stuff every object in their little mouths. It was as if they were saying, "I want to know all I can about this world, engaging every single sense!" The more they could touch and taste, the more they would learn. Our task as parents was to help our children discriminate between dirt and donuts, without killing their insatiable appetites to learn.

Discovery and *choice* are key elements in raising young artisans. Discovery involves *choice*. Each object that a child inspects is both a choice and a moment of insight. This sense of wonder and curiosity should never be lost. Of course, an adult who puts everything in her mouth would be intolerable. But a persona of any age with an appetite to grow, learn, and taste all of life is a creative individual.

There are two important aspects of discovery: breadth and depth. Depth should follow breadth. Diverse experiences in a wide variety of subjects will create a broad platform from which the child may freely explore. Then the child's curiosity will lead to digging deeper in specific interests. Parents have the fun assignment of offering these assorted moments of discovery. The child's understanding and appreciation for all things will naturally multiply: Looking at insects deepens an awareness of design; watching a play can teach movement and timing; drawing a spaceship inspires imagination and story.

These stimulating exercises are both spiritual and creative. Sampling the full pallet of creation increases a child's appreciation of his Maker. It also inspires confidence in one's own creativity.

A cautious parent might be tempted to over-censor these discovery moments. After all, a parent *is* the child's primary gatekeeper. A parent can function as a brake or accelerator in a child's life. Perhaps our main concern is for safety because, certainly, parents are Protectors. But we must also to be the enthusiastic Pushers of learning and wonder. We can give our children a broad brush, loaded with colors. We have a heavenly Father who will walk us through all of life, exploring its caves, meadows, and mountains. Our God brings both safety and discovery.

God created everything and saw that it was good. The first couple was encouraged to eat from every tree in the garden, except one. There was only a single tree, not many trees, which were forbidden. The garden experience was a rich, life tasting experience of fragrance, flavors, sounds, and textures. Artistry runs free in an environment of discovery and choice. Creative space is indeed space: a wide place that allows the child to grow.

Our children's garden space included an entire closet of odds and ends. There were the usual craft essentials of construction paper, glue, and scissors. But there were also some surprises to challenge the imagination: empty spools, random sized boxes, pieces of cloth with various textures, buttons, pipe cleaners, and seeds. And all of this could be anything one wished!

When our son Tim was not quite five, he wanted to learn piano from watching his brother play. Then in fourth grade, he showed an interest in guitar, so we enrolled him in a local class, still continuing the piano. At ten, he asked to join the school band and try out the saxophone, along with practicing the piano. When Tim was eleven, his brother Jon needed a bass player for his band, so he also leaned into this new opportunity. Now Tim plays the bass professionally. But I wonder if Tim's interest in music would have continued without this freedom to explore? And he still enjoys the piano!

DIGGING DEEPER: CULTIVATING A SPECIFIC GIFT

Parents are like anthropologists who have moved in with an aboriginal tribe to discover their culture. Young children leave clues about their interests and future aspirations. Before he could walk, our son, Jon, would pull himself up next to the stereo console and bounce, anticipating the songs. He would repeat one of his very first words, which was "mooney" for "music," demanding another record. Daily, he would spread out all the pots and pans on the floor and experiment with sounds. Later he constructed "music machines" and made up tunes with words. When he was in kindergarten, he dressed up as *Psalty the Singing Songbook* and serenaded his classmates. He volunteered to sing "Away In a Manger" when he was barely five, in front of our entire church. He was dropping hints and we began to catch them.

This is why it is important to expose children to a variety of interests: You never know what will stick. But when we, as parents, notice a pattern in those interests, we can gently encourage those passions. What activity does the child return to, again and again? Why is this pastime so enjoyable to him or her? How can I deepen this interest, without narrowing the choices or quenching their own motivation? Is there a related activity that might expand their interests?

Our son, Tim, loved to role-play and would often dress in different costumes throughout the day. We encouraged this fun by creating a costume chest, but we also took him to see children's plays. This related adventure allowed him to experience both actors and costumes in the context of a story. Tim was later inspired to land several leading roles in his elementary school productions, and to write several original plays.

He is still a gifted writer, now using this story telling ability in songs—and he is still comfortable on stage!

It is helpful to keep a journal of your child's milestones and preferences. Over time, you will see the dots connect, and the unique trajectory of their life. This also allows our children to tell us who they truly are, as opposed to who we might want them to be. We are merely discovering what is already there, responding to the creative impulses that were instilled by God Himself.

Jan has taught art classes to home school children. The most challenging moment for a child is to face the large white paper lying on the table before them. As the child stares at this blank sheet, you can almost hear their mental wheels turning as they imagine what could be drawn on that paper. This is the most important moment in the entire art experience, digging deep into the imagination.

But this is also the most challenging moment for parents who stay behind to watch. The emptiness of that pure white paper often becomes unbearable after several minutes with no activity. A few well-meaning parents sometimes pull up a chair and offer suggestions for the picture. Or others second-guess what the child had begun to draw: "Is that the right color for a tree?" Of course, this completely short-circuits the child's own creative process.

Helping our children dig deeper does not mean that we take the crayons out of their hands. It simply means that we find new opportunities for them to explore in areas of interest. And we offer many encouraging words about their creative offerings.

Our encouragement must not be a qualitative judgment about the child personally. Rather than, "You are such a good artist," we can comment, "I like the colors you chose and the way you drew that plant," or, "You've really practiced and now you play that piece beautifully!" Always remember: Criticism should be saved for adult professionals, and not thrown at the sensitive child artist!

Depth also includes discipline. Our son, Jon, has likened songwriting to an archeological dig. I assume this means long hours combing through soil in the hot sun to find a real treasure. True genius never lies waiting on the surface, but our disciplined passion will keep us digging.

Music lessons can be a blend of passion and persistence. Our sons wanted to learn the piano quite young, so our encouragement to practice needed to be age appropriate. Chubby five-year-old hands are connected to a very squirmy body, and we wanted to keep the overall tone positive.

When older, we held a set time each day of at least 30 minutes, 5 days a week, for practice. There were numerous protests along the way. Yet because they had chosen their instruments, and had pre-agreed to finish the course, we would simply remind them of their commitment. Practice time could be moved about in the day, but it was non-negotiable. The old adage, "You will thank me later for this!" has certainly proven true. Finding the right teacher was also critical; we were happy to finally find one who would encourage Jon's desire to write and play his own music.

Recently, two sailors were rescued several miles off the coast of San Francisco.

Late at night, in high seas, their small craft had capsized. Fortunately, they were experienced, and had spent weeks in physical training for this race. Immediately they knew what to do: find the radio, which they had sealed in a waterproof bag. After their miraculous rescue, the captain attributed the hours of practice and training to saving their lives.

Your child's training in artistic skill may not save them from a near-death experience. But our son, Tim, has shared that the long hours of practicing piano were ultimately useful as a life skill. Mastering a difficult piece gave him the courage and stamina to press through other difficult experiences in life, as well as in his musical career. As parents, we also need courage to press through any momentary resistance to the greater good. If we take the long view, our children will also share that vision.

THE POWER OF EXAMPLE

Thankfully and fearfully, our children will follow us, like ducklings waddling behind their mother. They intuitively want to be who we are, and do everything we can do. *Imitation* is the primary vehicle for learning. We falsely assume we can adopt the philosophy of, "Do as I say, not as I do." It is the tacit knowledge of who we actually are that will shape our children.

This means the entire human package is potentially transferable: the smile and the stubbornness, the candor and the criticism, the humor and the hypocrisy. So the greater question is, how many of *me* do I want? This is the primary way our children learn: They simply imitate us.

Perhaps the first responsibility of any parent is to personally grow up. My life task is to become the person God created me to be. The child will largely follow that example. We must be transformed before we can be transformers. Essentially, creative people beget creative little people. Am I open to change in my own life? Am I curious for the unknown? What am I learning right now? If I am leaning into the new and challenging, my children will naturally inherit this creative confidence. Curiosity is contagious!

We know that children of parents who enjoy reading will also be avid readers. Perhaps it is time for us as parents to dust off the easel, take piano lessons, or write that poem. Our children will see this open door and follow us into the room of creativity.

Personal taste can also be taught by example. We frown on parents who ruin a child's appetite with junk food, but do we stuff young minds with empty activities? We can settle for the flat taste of popular culture, or we can develop a more discerning palate by sampling the genius of artists throughout the centuries. We visited art museums, toured historic buildings that were wonders of architecture, and attended live symphony concerts. Developing good taste is like carving a path in the woods, which we reinforce and deepen over time.

THE ART OF BEING

Several years ago, Jan and I were privileged to stand in awe at the base of Michelangelo's towering statue of David in Florence, Italy. The Apostle Paul declares that *we are God's masterpiece* (Eph 2:10 NLT). The term is *poiema*—his poem, his work of art. God uses the creative process to write His character and plan on our hearts. God wants to paint my life with his love and truth. This daily experience of transformation is the art of becoming, in every dimension, who we are designed *to be*.

It is fascinating that most religions are focused on practices or *doing*. We learn to attend services, what Bible translation to read, how much we should tithe, which songs to sing, what small group to join, and how to tell others about our faith. All of these positive activities are inadequate in themselves; we must *become* the person God has called us to *be*.

Likewise, it is not *what* we want our children to become but *who*. One focuses on *doing*, the other considers *being*. A wise president of my alma mater told visiting parents, "Choose a college based on who you want your student to be—not based on what occupation you want them to do."

We are shaped by our closest relationships. Our *being* is practiced through spending time together. During these critical close encounters, our children will observe and absorb our values. The parent must continually ask, as Switchfoot has sung, "Are you who you want to be?" Whoever I am is who they are becoming.

I began to learn this difficult lesson when I noticed my son, Jon, acting more obstinate. An observing friend shrugged, "He's just a two year old." But my wife knew better. Jon didn't need another "time out"—he needed more time with daddy. This was not something I had experienced much growing up, so I had no model for spending quality time with my son.

Fortunately, I found some wonderful guidebooks to lead me through this unfamiliar territory. Joseph Campbell, in *How to Really Love Your Child,* suggests that there are three ways to show genuine love to your child: Eye contact, physical contact, and focused attention. As we practice these three languages of love, we are filling up their very receptive love tanks. The effect is almost instantaneous, eliminating many future disciplinary confrontations.

THE ART OF BEING TOGETHER

We all know the frustration of scrounging through our car or pockets for coins to feed an expired parking meter. We are often out of time. But what our children crave is spending more time together. Carving out these moments became a high point of the day for me. After work, from the moment I walked through the door, we would hit the carpet and wrestle. It was great exercise, too, because our boys had so much pent up energy, coupled with the inner drive to be loved. As we rolled on the floor, laughing and struggling, their love tanks were filled. In a language they could understand, I expressed to them their value—they were worth my gaze, my touch, my attention.

Reading became another wonderful way to share a moment with our kids. Our evening book time often found us in the pages of Narnia. These were magical years, with Jon on one leg and Tim on the other. We imagined our way through the seven Chronicles, three times. Not only was this quality daddy time, but Jon and Tim were introduced to the character of Aslan, the Christ-like figure.

Two other unexpected benefits emerged from these hours. Since Lewis was a master of a well-told story, the rich narrative of Narnia was subconsciously planted in my sons' open minds. They learned the art of storytelling and its place within the great story of redemption. Secondly, God used these stories to make my own closed, adult mind more childlike. I was fresh out of graduate school, and rigidly locked into my own mental constructs. The magic of Lewis breathed imagination and childlike wonder into my own rigid soul. In a creative space, no one, not even the parent, is safe from renewal!

Jan's together time with the boys was often more visual, with colorful paper, paints, or pencils. She taught them basic lessons on drawing, encouraging them to find their own artistic style. When the focus is on spending time together, the pressure to be precise is thankfully removed. Whatever is drawn is just right because the process was the greater good. The journey became the destination, and the media truly is the message that will linger.

Our home held many musical memories, from playing Bach in the background, to freeform family band experiments—with lots of singing! But Jan and I were wary of being our children's formal tutors. We preferred being the fun parents who enjoyed our children's progress, as opposed to being the taskmasters. I remembered from my own youthful piano lessons that this was not the sort of together time I wanted!

If we fast-forward past the stuffed animal and storybook years, we reach the steep climb of adolescence. Every parent must make a deliberate, all out run to scale these heights. In our family, this challenge was met with two passions: surfing and rock 'n' roll. Sitting on either surfboards or amplifiers was a great bonding opportunity for all of us.

Unpacking the lyrics of the Beatles and Led Zeppelin was not always easy, but it did prepare them for the culture they were about to invade. I valued the opportunity of being their native guide into this strange world rather than simply entrusting this task to their peers. There could be no substitute for the investment of hours we spent, and still spend, together. Parenting in love is spelled "T-I-M-E"—a commodity often spent *for* children, but rarely *with* them.

THE PLEASURE OF YOUR COMPANY

Every family develops unique ways to express the joy of simply being together. For me, it was pressing my forehead against my son's and saying, "I love you." We called these spontaneous bursts of appreciation, "free hugs." One often overlooked ingredient that releases creative freedom is the simple enjoyment of our children. It is not hard to discern whether a parent truly enjoys their child, and how much. A parent who delights in their child will lose track of time, instead of checking their watch. This pleasure breathes value and confidence into every little human.

How much do we truly enjoy our kids for who they are? Do we pause to imagine the thought patterns behind those incessant questions? Do we get past the mess to climb into their world of make-believe? As we wipe off the crumbs, do we appreciate all those freckles? We know that scripture teaches that children are a gift. But often as busy parents, we are too stretched or frustrated to appreciate the package.

A child's demand for attention is usually inconvenient, so it is easier to brush the small person aside. But whenever I avoid or enjoy my child, I am giving a lesson about their value. Indirectly, the avoided child is also learning to disrespect and create distance from the ignoring parent. But the child who sees delight reflected back from a parent's eyes will naturally long to be like and be with the engaging parent.

Adults must keep pace in a world of standards and constant evaluation. But a parent who only appreciates the *doing* side of life, while ignoring the *being*, will raise children who perform for love. Their hearts will long to be loved for who they *are*, but they will redirect this drive into being loved for what they *do*. We want to authentically fill the love tanks of our children, which means we must love them simply as little persons, just as our Heavenly Father loves us. The *doing* will come, along with those esteemed parental values of excellence and proficiency, but only after the security of *being*.

From this place of esteem, a child can venture out into the world of artistic self-expression. This world has many critics as well as fans, but this foundation of being enjoyed apart from performance will allow the young artist to weather the variable winds of opinion.

TRUTH THAT CAN BE TOUCHED: ENJOYING GOD

Form must always follow substance. In the spiritual realm, this means that family prayers and devotions must adapt to the life and pace of the family. The reverse usually ends with an undesired forced feeding of religion. Yet most parents of faith want to establish some form of family devotions.

For our busy young family, only Saturday mornings were available. We planned a short and simple "Jesus Time" in which we celebrated in songs, read a picture Bible story, and prayed for each other. Our young children looked forward to this family ritual every week. And this is the larger goal: to give children a hunger and delight to know God. "Jesus Time" was a happy time! But this spiritual pattern changed when our kids became involved sports. Evening prayers then became a warm and significant pause at the end of the day. But for the rest of the waking hours, our children learned their spiritual lessons on the run.

We followed the advice of the *Shema* in Deuteronomy 6:4–9

> Hear, O Israel: The LORD our God, the LORD is one. Love the LORD your
> God with all your heart and with all your soul and with all your strength.
> These commandments that I give you today are to be upon your hearts.
> Impress them on your children. Talk about them when you sit at home
> and when you walk along the road, when you lie down and when you get
> up. Tie them as symbols on your hands and bind them on your foreheads.
> Write them on the doorframes of your houses and on your gates.

Moses tells every parent that the most important life lesson is to love God. We
are to teach this truth to our children in every setting: at home, while traveling, at
school—not just at church. The best way to learn a language is on the streets, not
in the classroom. So the best way to learn a life of love for God is through daily
activities—not just in formal settings.

This is particularly true for a child's creative growth. We can practice life with
God during our bedtime talks, on the way to a soccer game, just sitting on surfboards, or while learning some new guitar riffs. God is infinite, and can be found
in all of life. As parents, we are merely the tour guides.

Your child will grow out of chord books and dance lessons. But this ability to
enjoy God in His creation is always age appropriate and can never be outgrown.
I am grateful we still have long, significant talks with our adult children, and the
content covers a wide spectrum of subjects, from the philosophy of Kierkegaard, to
musical arrangements, to buying a home, or riding waves, and raising children. All
are spiritual discussions, and Christ's mind and presence want to be in each one.

A CREATIVE COMMUNITY EXPANDS THE HORIZON

Traveling minstrels still roam the countryside. Musicians, including songwriters, were frequent guests in our home. Artists always seem to find one another.
We have also had the privilege of hosting musicians who were performing at our
church. All styles of artists, from folk, jazz, classical, bluegrass, or rock, would sit
around our table. This immersion in a musical community has a profound impact
on the watchful eyes and ears of young children. It puts music within reach.

Our sons were given impromptu guitar lessons, taught the basics of recording,
and overheard many conversations about songwriting. Even their first demo tape
was hand delivered to a record label by one of these artistic friends. Again, the
multiplied power of example shaped our children's own early interests.

Unfortunately, our early congregational experiences did not initially promote
the visual arts very well. But my wife, Jan, is an artist, so she filled this need by
teaching the basics of line, color, and composition. Looking back, I believe the

church should be the initiator of all the arts in every community. It is our rich heritage, and this influence needs to be reclaimed.

As the promoter of art in the community, the church can provide the creative space for young minds to experiment and grow. The message of Christ touches all areas of life, so our local church body can become that full expression of Jesus' life. Our artistic voice is needed to communicate the full story of redemption.

The rich fabric of this creative community can also improve the young artist's ability to relate well to other people. An artist's EQ (emotional quotient) can be almost as enhancing to their career as their musical IQ. A rude off-stage remark to a fan can travel far away to influential places. Similarly, a good story about treating the club personnel with respect can reach a wider audience than the music itself.

When Switchfoot was just beginning to tour, they played a show in a well-known Los Angeles club. A short time later, they learned that the venue's owner had put their music on the club's answering machine. The reason? Her crew could not stop talking about how well they were treated by this new band.

The caricature of the Prima Donna artist does not lead to a fulfilling life, let alone artistic career. Real musicianship requires cooperation with other artists, and the humility to realize you are part of a much larger picture. A young artist can gain this perspective by belonging to a creative community.

THE ARTIST AS MISSIONARY

"Be safe," is often a parent's final word to a child venturing out the front door. Yet wise parenting does not simply mean protecting children from harmful beliefs or behavior. Safety and protection are too minimal as goals. Yet many Christian parents have only this one defensive strategy, without an offense. They choose schools, sports, and friends that will incubate their child from the dangers of mainstream culture. But true spiritual nurture must go beyond simply keeping the kids safe.

What is our parental strategy for raising a spiritually confident child who will artistically and spiritually impact their world? A posture that leans into the opportunities is really the best defense. This means encouraging our precious children to be authentic followers of Jesus, wherever He may lead. The children who are personally transformed by their Savior will in turn transform others in their world with the love and truth they have found.

When Jon began kindergarten in public school, he invited a new friend to church, promising, "We have pizza with God!" He had misunderstood last week's sermon title, "Having Peace with God." In spite of the miscommunication, Jon was simply catching the bigger picture of including others in God's family. And they did come to church the next week!

Instilling this confidence to invade and influence culture does not happen accidentally. It involves intentional exposure to society in every shape and form. Though fallen, it is still the world God "so loves."

When Jon was just one week old, we drove down the mountain to take his first baby pictures. The camera in the delivery room had broken the day he was born! Also, the 21-hour labor had given Jon a cone-shaped head, so he was much more photogenic a week later. We arrived at the photographer's on Halloween afternoon. The studio was next to a costume shop, and folks were being fitted and photographed for their evening of trick or treat. A long line of witches and goblins were standing outside on the sidewalk. We wove our way to the door through the ghoulish crowd, nervously clutching our innocent newborn.

We later realized this was an important metaphor for the future role of our children. Though innocent, they would go into the dark places of this world with the light of our Lord. Little did we realize this would literally happen as they entered into the heart of a lost world with their music.

The first missionary/artist was Jesus of Nazareth. As God, the Creator, he now came to transform the canvas on which he had first painted. Mission is restorative art. It involves understanding the intent of the Original Artist, recreating the original colors and medium, so that the painting is restored to its original beauty.

It is vital for parents of creative children to breathe into them this kingdom theology. The calling of every believer on earth is to first be transformed by the Creator/Redeemer King. Then we can transform our spheres of influence with his love, truth, and beauty. Jesus invaded this world and he calls us to do the same. This global and outward focus will shape our approach to music and the arts. It will instill passion in our children that goes beyond playing an instrument or drawing well.

The church is now waking from a long sleep, during which she withdrew from culture and society. Like a castle with high walls, drawbridge and moat, she has tried to defend her people, doctrine, and lifestyle from the evils of society. But she has not succeeded in protecting them at all. The most current moral statistics that compare believers with unbelievers are flat: We are the same. And through protectionism, the church has tragically withdrawn from her great purpose to be salt and light to our culture.

This is my Father's world, must be her song.

THE INTEGRITY OF THE ARTIST

To truly engage our children in Jesus' dynamic work of redemption, we cannot simply be utilitarian in our approach. We cannot see human beings as merely potential converts, but unique persons whom we must know, befriend, and love. Then our artistic expression will follow, and not simply be utilitarian either. Music written and performed by believers cannot be only evangelistic in words. Our visual art cannot be limited to a Bible story illustration. True art is honest.

We must allow and encourage this honest expression in our children. The believing artist, who is true to herself, her art form, and to culture, will write music that is seamlessly authentic. Love and truth will kiss, and salt and light will do their powerful work. If the music is dishonest, the listener will sense the disparity and quickly turn away.

Our homes can be a wide, open space for all types of music and art. Some forms will be blatantly religious in declaring worship or an evangelistic message. Some forms will be more subtle, or pre-evangelistic, in wrestling with important issues from a Christian worldview. And some art is simply describing the heart of the artist as he authentically interacts with God, society and creation. We can celebrate all the forms our budding artists might use to express their gifts.

Our goal is not to raise good religious citizens. A child raised in the church culture can easily become desensitized to the mission: To bring the kingdom of God to this world. It is also easy for churched kids to be reclusive and distant from culture. The goal is not to raise good church kids, but courageous kingdom kids. This higher goal will raise confident, responsible children who will creatively bring Christ to their culture.

How can we practically do this? We can encourage our children to enter culture by walking with them through all facets of life. We must introduce our children to both the beautiful and beastly sides of culture. This means not only field trips to the opera or museum, but also serving on a bread line or visiting an orphanage. It can include short-term mission trips to the developing world to plant gardens, or feed malnourished children after school.

Without this practical interface with the messiness of life, a child's faith will be theoretical, and inwardly focused. Their own spiritual disciplines will make much more sense once they realize the challenges that await them. As we allow our children to be stretched beyond their familiar comforts, they will grow.

Raising children who are both creative and missions minded are really two sides of the same coin. Children who are confident in their own emerging talent can be equally confident of the creative, redeeming love of God for this world.

CREATIVE SPACE DEFINED: A GARDEN WITH WALLS

Every well-tended garden has a fence. The challenge for parents is to strike the balance between adventurous risk-taking while encouraging absolute surrender to the will of God. These are not mutually exclusive objectives. In fact, radical discipleship is a lifetime adventure. Faith is always stepping past the known into God only knows what.

Too often, parents can misinterpret the moral will of God as a small confined space of limited choices. Actually, God's moral lines guarantee lasting freedom in all areas. But the parent's own interpretation of God's will can be quite narrow, and only a small garden space remains.

Similarly, the young artist can misinterpret God's will as too restrictive and therefore rebel against the false belief that creativity only thrives outside of God's lines. And isn't this the age-old problem, going back to the very first garden? Again, this other extreme view aborts God's creative genius in the young artist as he or she wanders alone into the artistic wilderness. What a terrible burden to carry one's creative gift apart from the Gift Giver!

The parent must hand the child both of these strengths, to hold one in each hand: the permission to color outside the lines of convention, and also the humility to remain within the lines of God's good will. We find the greatest examples of creativity in God's own artwork. We are merely acknowledging His perfect ways in all things, whether in this physical creation or in the yet-to-be-creations of our own hands. Earlier civilizations wisely recognized that creative genius came from outside the person. We do know the source of all creative life. Only through realizing our dependence on Him can we truly be inspired.

Our children are comprised of dirt and deity, creations of clay who contain God's glory. The beauty of creation has already been determined. So the study of science or musical scales or drawing in perspective is really to better understand and cooperate with God's created order. We enter this garden with humility and respect.

Yet we also have a creative privilege. We dare to name animals, hum an original melody, and illustrate our imaginations on cave walls or canvas. We are allowed to be original in the truest sense, inventing what has never before existed. However, our creations are like us, made from pre-existing materials. Nothing of us is *ex nihilo*, out of nothing. The external, objective world informs the artist, and the subjective, creative artist influences the world.

Your creative child must enter into this tension between internal and external inspiration. The artist can best be viewed as a reflection or container of God's genius, because *from Him and through him and to Him are all things (Romans 11:36)*. We are not the origin and center of creation, as Descartes' influence has suggested. Instead, we are co-creators who partner with God. He alone can create out of nothing and is the Genius behind all artistic pursuits.

Our children, who hold this creative genius, can be both humbled and confident in possessing their gifts. Little artists can respond to the Artist, yielding their hearts, imaginations, and will. Like the elders of *Revelation 4*, these gifts, like golden crowns, are freely laid at the feet of our Creator. In this place of grateful surrender, we are truly able to enter the living painting of God's creative purpose.

THE KINGDOM OF GOD
(and belly buttons)

Interestingly, Jesus put a child in the centre of his disciples, "in the midst of them," in order to help them pay attention. The child, in Jesus' mind, was not an annoying distraction. The child was a last-ditch effort by God to help the disciples pay attention to the odd nature of God's kingdom. Few acts of Jesus are more radical, more countercultural, than his blessing of children.
—Stanley Hauerwas

I make music for little kids. I fell into it in the most natural way. I had moved to Nashville to make music for adults. When I wasn't touring, I babysat for the daughter of the bass player from my most recent (grown-up focused) album.

As I walked around East Nashville with a baby girl strapped to me in a carrier, I would make up little songs about belly buttons, about the sounds our mouths make, about needing a nap. Between my own musical history and the fact that I sang them for this little bit of whimsy I was carrying, the songs came out as jazz. Her parents, both musicians, took an interest in the songs, and her dad and I began to write them together. Ten years later, that bass player, Chris Donohue, and I are still writing and performing songs for kids as Coal Train Railroad.

Meanwhile, I now have a toddler, and lots of my friends have children, as well. A few of my dearest girlfriends are also among my favorite songwriters and mothers: Sandra McCracken, Flo Paris, and Ellie Holcomb. We have begun to make songs with the aim of tucking God's big story deep into the hearts of the littlest children under the name Rain for Roots.

So then, I have two musical projects created for children. One project focuses on belly buttons and snuggling. The other focuses on Jesus, the hero, king, and maker of belly buttons and snuggling. Surely there is a place in a universe with such a playful Creator for celebrating him and so many of his delightful gifts. I'm entirely convinced that both are good gifts to children.

THE STATE OF MUSIC FOR CHILDREN

Children's music is experiencing a golden age right now. Maybe it's because of our estimation of children: arguments could be made that it's either higher or lower than the preceding generations. Maybe it's because of the internet, the breakdown of the Big Music Machine and the subsequent phoenix-like resurrection of creativity in both music and music marketing. Maybe it's some other combination of factors that we'll see better in hindsight. In any case, I'd be surprised to learn that there has ever been so much music made for children before now. Let me revise that: made *commercially* for children. There are absolutely tons of the stuff, and it's gone from being primarily folk music to blues, rock, nearly anything you can imagine. (One notable exception: the symphonic world's done a bang-up job throughout musical history, with delights like Prokofiev's Peter and the Wolf and Britten's The Young Person's Guide to the Orchestra.)

One thing is clear—children's music is now considered commercially viable. People are spending money on music for children, and so money is being spent to make that music excellent, or at least commercially viable. I wonder about, but don't intend to pontificate in print on this thought: Is this the first music that's being bought by someone other than its intended listeners? What does this tell us?

The topic often comes up, though: do we even need a category for "children's music"? New parents (perhaps feeling suddenly less hip and in touch with their cultural portfolio) often cringe at the thought of listening to or proffering the stuff to their children. Madeleine L'Engle makes a wonderful point when she says that a children's book is any book that a child will read. This holds true for music as well: I love that my toddler digs Otis Redding, Ella Jenkins, and Handel's Messiah. Good music is just good music. Even so, children have a unique station in the world, with its own peculiar view, joys, and difficulties.

What are children thinking about? A quick survey includes dirt, juice, naps, snuggling, and puppies. It also includes pain, death, and the meaning of life. I once heard an offhand comment in conversation that has been defining for me: "kids are just trying to crack the code." My one year old broke her femur and spent five weeks in a cast from her armpit to her ankle. It takes two hands to count, off the top of my head, how many of our little friends have bodies with serious and chronic difficulties. Children are born straight into a broken world, and need the adults who are raising them to take that reality seriously. Children are also fantastic at enjoying and exploring the world and people before their eyes. While my one year old was in her cast, she still explored the world with an exuberance and wonder that brought tears to my eyes. As followers of Jesus, who made a point of placing children in the midst of adults in order to confound and re-orient them, we show wisdom when we think, imagine, pray, and plan about how to consider children with the same interest, respect, and fondness as Jesus does. If we believe that God is in fact interested in both art and children, this same consideration must extend to art created with them in mind.

I'm not interested in laying down laws about the details of what kind of music should be made for kids: that's just silly, and perhaps wicked. The law is, of course, love. Tempo, volume, rhythm, topic, lyrics: there are no hard and fast rules about these elements of composition. Charlie Peacock has done some wonderful talking about making art that makes people want to "stay in the room" with it. For children, this imagery gets pretty concrete, as many will literally run from the room if it hurts their ears or scares them. (As a musician, beware: you also risk the braver ones yelling, "It's too loud.") Like music for everyone else, there is abundant freedom within the boundaries of creating something loving and excellent.

Undoubtedly, though, kids have often gotten the short end of the artistic stick. Slapping on the label "children's" has been an excuse in modern popular music to market the mawkish and mediocre. This, however, does not rule out sheer playfulness for its own sake. Quite the opposite: nobody appreciates the really ridiculous like children, who are experts at free play. The distinction needed in children's music is that silly can be excellent. When adults take a low view of play and the station of children, it shows in the art they present to children: it is condescending and inane. Kids can smell it a mile away.

Conversely, I present Grammy-winning saxophonist Jeff Coffin, who has kindly graced both full-length Coal Train Railroad albums. At the top of his field and craft (he plays with Bela Fleck and Dave Matthews Band), inviting Jeff to improvise in the studio is truly akin to bringing in a brilliant child. He makes musical jokes constantly, tucking mischief betwixt the lines and making reference to jazz heroes in his melodies. He does musically what children do all the time: he stands on his tiptoes, he stands on his head. He has done his homework, he knows his art, and he remembers (has never forgotten?) how to play.

It's worth divulging here that we have a secondary, subversive mission with Coal Train Railroad. We don't just want to delight the kids, we're out to get their parents, too. A lot of adults are scared of jazz. Jazz has a reputation of being heady. Uber-cool. Intellectual. Inaccessible. It's very hard, though, to be intimidated by a song about belly buttons or superheroes when your toddler is singing along. We love to watch parents dance along with their children and just enjoy that the music's really good. They don't need to know that Chris is referencing a Charles Mingus bass line on our theme song "Coal Train." I submit that you don't have to know what's going on all the time in music (though that's another kind of fun), you just have to be willing to enjoy it.

Children are utter naturals at jazz: watch and learn. Children stop in the middle of what they're doing and stand on their heads to see things differently. They are innate and diligent improvisers. They have no pride involved in scrapping their creation and beginning again from nothing. They will try one thing from fifty angles. I'll even go so far as to say that I think that jazz musicians are trying to emulate children. While toddlers don't have a full complement of physical and verbal skills, they use those at their disposal to their utmost—reaching, stretching, exploring every nook and cranny and possibility.

In my opening quote, Stanley Hauerwas says, "The child was a last-ditch effort by God to help the disciples pay attention to the odd nature of God's kingdom." In my art and practice, the leap from jazz to children to the kingdom of God is a hop, skip, and a jump. Improvisation? When the well-to-do and influential guests RSVP in the negative in Jesus's wedding parable, the king sends out for the weak, the widows, the homeless. When He saves the world and sets the universe to rights, He does it through a newborn, for crying out loud. As my toddler notes, "Babies poop. Go wahhh." He is, to use Os Guinness's marvelous phrase, creatively subversive. He draws pictures in the dirt. He asks questions that play out like unanswerable knock-knock jokes, leaving his listeners giggling, happy children or toddlers holding their breath and having tantrums. Isn't God himself the subversive one, the playful one? Is he not the one who stands us on our heads? God who created the cosmos created belly buttons, and is effortless with the ridiculous. He is the ultimate arbiter of what is serious and silly, and seems to be at odds with us on which is which.

> He made the stars and oceans blue
> But said that none compares with you
> You are His treasure and great prize
> He knows your name, He made your eyes
> He is your Shepherd, little lamb
> The King of Heaven, the Great I Am
>   —Sally Lloyd-Jones in *Baby's Hug-A-Bible*

Author Sally Lloyd-Jones (to whose words Rain for Roots added melodies), told us that she considers herself to be an ambassador for children. I can't think of a more worthwhile calling, or a population more in need of advocates. We have a friend, a very talented and prominent pediatrician, who points out that pediatrics is not the area of medicine where you practice in order to make money. Children don't have money and influence, and parents of small children are not typically people with a lot of spare resources. Children don't get elective surgeries with high profit margins. They are inefficient in terms of our cultural priorities of power and money.

Just as we adults are getting established, are making reputations and a mark on the world, children come along and throw a wrench in the whole thing. I ran into my pastor in a coffee shop today and he noted, "Did anyone ever tell you that having kids would take so much of you?" He pointed out that having children is often an especially hard adjustment for especially busy and ambitious people. It's so true, and we are at risk of treating them as "annoying distractions." Yet, the King who holds and directs all resources directs adults to pay attention to them in order to get a sense of his kingdom. Why is this? Christians should see the glaring upside down nature of this: Jesus was adamant that children should be cared for, along with other classes of vulnerable people, like widows and the poor. He had formidable judgment for those who would harm them and lead them astray. (Matthew 18:6) Does this sound too harsh, too heavy a warning to apply to our treatment of children's music? It may be a litmus test of how seriously you take the effects of the art with which we engage. Art affects our hearts, shapes how we think about what is true and beautiful. If that isn't critical, nothing is. (Proverbs 4:23)

The influential Victorian-era educator Charlotte Mason paints the picture of spreading a smorgasbord when it comes to the art and thought we provide for children. Some aspects may be "over the heads" of some listeners. Some will eat a little, some will feast, all will be fed. We should make an effort to spread a bountiful artistic table, with something for everyone who hears, from toddlers to aficionados. For example, some little ones hear our Coal Train Railroad song "My Mouth and Me" and join in on the repeating lyrics: "I like to go ha, ha, ha, hee hee hee." Others join straight in with their own skat improvisation and are able to recognize the solos of the saxophone, drums, piano, and upright bass. Some nibble, some feast. Everyone gets nourished.

Woe to the musician performing for children who assumes that they're little idiots: they might eat you alive, but will more likely play with their toes, drink juice, or go somewhere else. In general, they're terrible at lying, and are therefore bad at being politely indifferent. It's both terrifying and refreshing to me that kids know what they like, and do not filter it through umpteen layers of baggage and misgivings. They have a relatively unformed aesthetic, neither refined nor obscured by thousands of (worthy and unworthy) voices telling them what they should consider beautiful and worthwhile. They are humble, open, un-snobbish, unafraid when it comes to their musical tastes. They can smell when they are being talked down to, something Jesus, by the way, never did to them. They are both truly humble and truly proud, and can be truly kind, but they make no pretense of being self-effacing: that's a learned behavior.

When we make music for children intended for their joy and good, we have to thread ourselves through the eye of a needle. We have to stand on our heads, have to lie on our bellies and humble ourselves to peek under doors. We have to stand on our tiptoes in hopes of glimpsing what's above our line of sight. We have to get quiet, we have to get humble, we have to forget what time it is. Jesus humbled himself and did something ridiculous, loving, and breathtaking in order to give us the kingdom of Heaven. Children remind us of this by their very existence.

PRACTICE
making Beauty

Sometimes the rehearsals stick with me more than the performances—special musical moments shared only by the players in the rehearsal room, hanging out in funky backstage spaces, arguing and laughing, eating and traveling together. The back of the house may not be as pretty as the front of the house but it's nearly always more interesting.

Then there are the thousands upon thousands of hours spent alone with the piano, working on technique, memorizing, improvising, exploring, analyzing, playing though repertoire hundreds of times. The old cliché about leaving one's best performance in the rehearsal room is true simply because of the odds.

My fondness for practice extends beyond music. Mention basketball and my mind is transported to a driveway in Virginia, shooting free throws until it was so dark I could barely see the hoop, and defeating imaginary foes with last-second shots. I played on a lot of teams, but it is the practices I remember best—joking with teammates, panting through wind sprints, and gaining my first exposure to virtuoso profanity from frustrated coaches.

In fact, my decision to pursue a career in music came in a practice room. I spent the summer following my junior year of high school at the Brevard Music Center in the mountains of western North Carolina. I'm sure that I played in a lot of concerts that summer—I still have the programs—but what I remember most are the practice rooms and the rehearsals. To be more accurate, they were rustic practice *cabins* scattered throughout the woods around the camp. I spent nearly every free moment between rehearsals, lessons, and concerts in those cabins working on new repertoire, experimenting, and thinking. It was those hours alone

with music combined with the camaraderie of other nerdy, musical teenagers at
ensemble rehearsals that convinced me that I couldn't imagine a career doing
anything else.

THE GIFT OF REHEARSAL

Timothy Keller (the pastor of Redeemer Presbyterian Church in New York
City, for whom I've had the privilege of working as music director for the past
seventeen years) tells a story about his relationship to Mozart. In college he was
required to pass a music appreciation course, and to do so he had to familiarize
himself with Mozart's symphonies and operas. He admits that he was not listening to Mozart's music for its beauty, but merely in order to pass a course so that
he could graduate from college and get a good-paying job. Or to put it bluntly, he
listened to Mozart in order to make money. But now that he has a job, the tables
have turned. He uses his money to buy Mozart recordings. What was once duty
has become pleasure.

And so it is with rehearsal. When we're young, we tend to think of practice
as the necessary preparation for the true payoff of a public performance. No
one loves to practice all the time. Sometimes it's insanely frustrating or time-con-
suming. But over time nearly every musician—especially one who has exercised
his or her craft professionally for more than a few years—comes to view this as
somewhat backwards. We eventually long for more time alone with our instruments and more time to work out musical ideas with our colleagues in relaxed
environments, without the unavoidable logistic and aesthetic constraints of performances.

For the Christian musician, who views music as a good creation of God to
be used for His glory and our delight, rehearsal is a multi-faceted gift. It is an
opportunity not only to learn music but literally to "rehearse" the disciplines of
the faith and experience the presence of God in a unique way. There are at least
five ways that I have come to see individual practice and collaborative rehearsal
as divine gifts—the pursuit of excellence, the freedom to experiment, the cultivation of discipline, the challenge of community, and the presence of God.

REHEARSAL AND THE PURSUIT OF EXCELLENCE

Rehearsal is a gift from God that allows us to pursue excellence. There is a
commonly-held view that musicians are primarily motivated by the need for
applause and the approval of audiences and colleagues. But the actual driving
force for most musicians tends to be something more internal and abstract. They
are motivated by the desire to connect with the mysteries of music itself and, for
the Christian, the Creator of those mysteries. The joy comes from making a new
musical discovery, overcoming a technical challenge, or the simple pleasure of
locking into a great groove with other players. The rehearsal room is the place

where most of those discoveries are initially made and then worked out.

For the Christian musician, the motivations to pursue excellence are numerous, beginning with the aesthetic excellence of God's creation. The "heavens declare the glory of God," (Psalm 19:1) and in particular, they reveal God's endless creativity, attention to detail, and perfect melding of form and function. He has made a world that is relentlessly beautiful, complex, and surprising. In his creation, God never sacrificed form for function. Every minute detail of each of His creations is so full of beauty that our souls can barely withstand it. As his children, formed in his image and charged with the cultivation of the earth's resources (including the ordering of sound), we should be no less concerned about aesthetics. The rehearsal room allows us to ponder over and wrestle with each aspect of our artistic expressions. In pursuing aesthetic excellence we are following in the footsteps of our Creator, and the desire for excellence naturally leads to a greater appreciation and enjoyment of the beauty of all his works—not only his creations, but his character and actions as well.

Another motivation for excellence is the direct Biblical instruction to execute our music with skill and intelligence in every context. Psalm 33:3 plainly directs us to "play skillfully." I Corinthians 14:15 describes a musical engagement of the mind that is distinct from, though not exclusive of, the spirit. "I will sing with my spirit, but I will also sing with my understanding." The Hebrew temple musicians were extensively trained and financially supported by the people of Israel. Through the examples of Jubal (Genesis 4:21), the Levitical musicians, and the musical directions found in many of the Psalms, we see that, though all people were expected to musically participate in the worship of God, the leadership and accompaniment roles were to be filled by those whose musical craft had been highly developed. All worship sacrifices were expected to come from the first, best, and purest of one's resources, and to be prepared with exactness. For the Christian musician, obedience to Scripture propels us into the practice room even (or especially) in periods of artistic dryness or disinterest. Though we will never impress God with the excellence of our artistry, it is insufficient to say that his sole desire for our musical expressions is sincerity of heart. Rather, sincerity of heart is manifested in seriousness of preparation, attention to detail, and investment of time.

Yet the greatest motivation for musical excellence is the gospel of grace. The temple and the complex sacrificial system in which the Levitical musicians worked were rendered obsolete by Jesus' death and resurrection. Yet the principle of offering our highest efforts in the worship of God—whether in the context of a church service, a rehearsal, a concert hall, or a club—has not only remained, but is supplanted, heightened, and invigorated by the unspeakable gift of grace through Jesus. We no longer need strive for excellence to impress God, or anyone else for that matter. We strive for excellence because He has already impressed us.

Grace transforms the Christian's chief end in life into an offering of worship to God. For those we love deeply, we choose gifts with thoughtfulness and joy, giving careful consideration to what will please them, and with little concern for cost. We do this not to earn their love but because we are grateful to already have their love. Music that grows out of love for God should inspire the same approach. Thus we offer the best repertoire, the most thorough preparation, the best musical execution, and the best focus of our heart—not to earn his favor, but out of endless gratitude for our adoption as his children. Through grace, the rehearsal room becomes a place of joyful and careful preparation for our musical offerings of gratitude to our gracious Creator.

REHEARSAL AND THE FREEDOM TO EXPERIMENT

Rehearsal is a gift from God that allows us to freely and safely explore and experiment with our music. When my family moved from a house in Virginia to a small apartment in New York City many years ago, I never considered that it would impact my practice habits, but the change of scenery led to two significant changes. Both changes resulted from the public nature of New York—the reality that city residents live quite literally on top of one another, with significantly less expectation of privacy than in smaller cities or suburbs.

The first change to my practice habits was simply the realization that my practice needed to be serious, extended, and intense. Walking down any almost street in New York, one hears instrumentalists and singers practicing with windows open. Sometimes these anonymous musicians are amazing, which is not surprising considering that some of them are in fact world-renowned performers. Virtuoso musicians can be found on subway platforms, parks, and street corners and, of course, in clubs and concert halls. It is truly a city filled with musical excellence. Being exposed to such virtuosity on a regular basis can drive a musician either to the practice room or to despair. For many New York musicians, it does both! So I began to put in more hours at the piano than I ever had before.

Yet the despite the benefits of increased time in the practice room, I also began to notice that something was missing in my practice. Aware that residents of neighboring apartments and others simply walking by my open windows could hear me practice, self-consciousness set in and I lost my willingness to experiment and improvise, which are great gifts of the practice room.

The practice room should be a place of frequent risk-taking, experimentation, alternate interpretations, and unreasonable tempi. It is generally a myth that spontaneity and discovery happen best on the bandstand, in front of an audience. Paradoxically, it is the disciplined musician, one who has been the most frequently and intentionally experimental in the privacy and security of the rehearsal room, who develops both the self-confidence and musical vocabulary necessary to take bold risks in performance.

Unless your last name is Coltrane, it's probably not a good idea to take an hour-long solo on a jazz tune in front of an audience. But the practice room is a place to test the outer limits of concentration, intensity, and endurance. In the operatic world, a singer's professional possibilities are strictly defined by their *fach*—their range and unique vocal timbre—which dictates their suitability for various operatic roles. But the practice room is the place to sing the "wrong" repertoire. It is the place for the jazz musician to learn Beethoven sonatas and the classical musician to experiment with chord charts. This experimentation makes us more complete and sympathetic artists.

When a transcendent musical moment is shared with an audience, it can be a marvelous experience. But there are many reasons why these moments are more likely to occur in a rehearsal room than on a stage. In rehearsal there is less self-awareness, less fear of failure, less formality, fewer constraints, and more risk taking, all of which unlock the possibilities of great music-making. Of course, the great artists are often those who are able to bring these attributes into live performances and recording situations. But imagine how great their rehearsals sound!

What is the source of this freedom, experimentation, and lack of self-consciousness? Some artists are risk-takers by temperament. But the Christian musician has a resource that goes far beyond temperament—the gift of grace. Knowing that we are fully accepted by the only Audience that matters, Christians pursue music-making unencumbered by the need for approval. Knowing that God is willing to give up everything to adopt us as his sons and daughters frees us to develop our craft unaffected by economic fears. "He who did not spare his own Son, but gave him up for us all—how will he not also, along with him, graciously give us all things?" (Romans 8:32) The experience of grace undermines our fear of failure and frees us to explore any musical avenue that our God-given creativity leads us down.

REHEARSAL AND THE CULTIVATION OF DISCIPLINE

Rehearsal is a gift of God that aids us in the cultivation of discipline in all walks of life. My son attended a unique New York City public elementary school in which all students were immersed in music and expected to practice their instruments daily, in addition to their academic homework. In fifth grade, he was interviewed at a potential middle school with a group of students from other elementary schools around the city. The interviewer asked the children to describe their after-school hours on a typical day. One by one they told of hanging out in the park, playing video games, and watching television—basically, anything to fill the hours remaining after their homework was finished. When my son was asked about his after-school hours, he gave a detailed report of homework, music studies, lessons, and recitals, with sports carefully scheduled in between. (Unsurprisingly, he was accepted into the middle school.)

Discipline in practice is the one constant attribute of successful individuals in nearly every field of endeavor. Read the biographies of sports stars, for example, and a clear theme emerges—they are always the first one in the gym and the last one to leave; they practice until the lights are turned out (then try to continue in the dark!); and they never lessen their practice disciplines when they become successful.

Musicians are often portrayed as flighty or unreliable. For most working musicians, this perception could not be further from the truth. Most professional musicians began serious, disciplined practice on their instruments at a young age and never let up. They sacrificed weekends for music classes and summers for music camps. The famous quote attributed to the pianist Jan Paderewski—"If I miss one day of practice, I notice it; if I miss two days, the critics notice it; if I miss three days, the audience notices it"—may be an exaggeration. But only a slight one. Few musicians are willing (or desire) to forego practice for more than a few days.

In most sectors of the music world there is zero tolerance for lateness, whether for rehearsal or performance. Promptness is a sign of respect for the ensemble leader and fellow musicians. Efficiency in rehearsal practice is prized by most musicians, and thorough personal preparation is the expectation before arriving at an ensemble rehearsal. If only doctors offices were run with half the commitment to promptness and efficiency as the typical symphony orchestra! (And if only musicians would make half the income of the average doctor—but that's for another article.)

Discipline in all matters is an essential element of the Christian walk. Whether the discipline of practice habits developed at a young age actually bears fruit into other areas of life varies, of course, from musician to musician. But in general, discipline begets discipline, and thus the practice room has the potential to be a great gift for all of life.

REHEARSAL AND THE CHALLENGE OF COMMUNITY

Rehearsal is a gift of God that allows us to grow in the development of meaningful community. A mysterious bond is formed between people who play music together, even when they are complete strangers. This instant bond can be a blessing allowing musicians to make friends quickly—which is especially important for a freelancer who is traveling and always working with new people. This bond can also be dangerous, quickly leading musicians into inappropriate physical and emotional relationships. But more than anything, the bond created by musicians who rehearse together presents an opportunity to grow in the teachings of Jesus—speaking the truth in love, exercising humility and deference, and upending cultural hierarchies.

For the Christian, the rehearsal room is an intensive laboratory in the application of practical, biblical principles. The New Testament is full of teachings known as the "one another" passages, which depict life in healthy Christian communities. For example, in I Corinthians 12:25, we are instructed to "have equal concern for one another." In Ephesians 4:32, we are told to "be kind and compassionate to one another." The applications of these passages to rehearsal practice are practical, immense, and capable of bringing seismic change to the musical culture of a community. Instead of being concerned about how our own music is being perceived, we proactively praise and affirm the gifts of our colleagues. Instead of confrontation, we become "patient, bearing with one another in love." (Ephesians 4:2)

In I Peter 4:9, Christians are encouraged to "offer hospitality to one another." Several years ago, my wife performed a run of shows with Hawaii Opera Theater. Following every rehearsal, rather than rushing home, all the artists and crew members remained for another hour to have a "tailgate" party behind the theater, with everyone contributing home-cooked food and drinks. This spirit of hospitality translated to unity and joy in the performances. Though not a Christian organization, it was nevertheless a beautiful application of the biblical principle of hospitality.

In Ephesians 4:15–16 we are told that a sign of Christian maturity is "speaking the truth in love." The result of doing so is that "we will grow to become in every respect the mature body of him who is the head, that is, Christ. From him the whole body, joined and held together by every supporting ligament, grows and builds itself up in love, as each part does its work." In rehearsal (or any situation), there is never true community unless we are willing to speak honestly, yet with grace. Ensembles thrive when rehearsals are marked by both openness and humility. A musician who learns to speak the truth in love will raise the level of music-making in every situation without alienating his colleagues.

Rehearsal is the space where Christians learn to exercise humility and develop a willingness to admit mistakes. It is an avenue for giving up control and allowing others to lead us into unexpected musical places. Rehearsal is a place where Christians learn to lay aside cultural hierarchies through the power of the gospel. There are no celebrities in the rehearsal room.

REHEARSAL AND THE PRESENCE OF GOD

Above all, rehearsal is another way for the Christian to experience and enjoy the presence of God. When we wrestle with assembling the raw materials of the universe—sound, space, time—into something beautiful, we are stepping onto God's turf. And sometimes in the practice of trying to make things beautiful we have moments of feeling his pleasure. As we struggle and fail in our musical efforts, we are comforted by God's love and acceptance of us—a love that emanates purely from his grace and is in no way conditioned on our performance. As we toil in rehearsal studios or alone in our practice room, wondering whether the public performances will be successes (or if performance opportunities will come at all), we take solace in knowing that we have all the applause we need from the only Audience that ultimately matters. And that's the best gift of all.

FINDING OUT
what we're
trying to say

In the beginning, God created the heavens and the earth.
—Genesis 1:1

In the very first story in the Bible, a story that most of us hear as children, we are confronted with the mystery of creativity. It's obviously a key part of God's character: it's the first thing he tells us about Himself. The story gives us insight into His omnipotence as Creator but is vague enough to leave us humbled and even confused at what we don't and can't understand. Most of the story involves the very act of creation itself, literally the bringing of substance and then order out of nothingness. But there is a moment at the end of the sixth day where God does something unexpected. He looks back over His work, evaluates it, and declares that it was very good. *The Amplified Bible* says it this way:

And God saw everything that He had made, and behold, it was very good (suitable, pleasant) and He approved it completely.—Genesis 1:31a

For those of us who spend our lives creating, doing our own best at bringing substance and meaning to a blank page, canvas or hard drive, the concept of approving our work as God does His ("completely") is foreign and to some extent even impossible to comprehend. Our response to a first draft of a story or attempt at a new piece of visual art can range from the familiar feeling of insecure uncertainty all the way to disgust. We so rarely if ever are able to approve our own work in the way that God does. Even this very essay that you are reading has been rewritten numerous times with input from a number of other, better brains.

God's creation beautifully embodies and reflects His perfection and ours always contains the markings of our own imperfection. Most of us are painfully aware of our nuanced shortcomings whether our audience recognizes them or not. We are limited and imperfect creatures but instinctively want to apply our creativity in the way that He does. Add to that the romantic myth built around creative people and specifically around the idea of inspiration—that it just "happens"—and we are understandably at times frustrated and confused. We have all heard legends of songs being written in 15 minutes, scenes in films being recorded in one take, etc., and take that as the norm rather than the exception. And when this kind of creative experience eludes us, we wonder what we're doing wrong and whether or not we have what it takes. Because it isn't the fun part of the process and because it takes great patience, there isn't a lot of practical discussion about rewriting or refining. And yet without it there will always be a ceiling on the quality of our own work.

GOD'S HEART

One way to read the Scriptures is to recognize the pattern of God's people constantly falling short of His standards, coming to terms with this through repentance, and then receiving provision from God—sometimes justice, sometimes mercy, often both—to restore the relationship. This happens over and over again throughout the Bible. In the Old Testament this required, among other things, an animal sacrifice. God commanded His people to use innocent blood to account for sin. In the New Testament Christ becomes the perfect sacrifice, covering our debt once and for all. And then the language of the New Testament evolves into new metaphors: this process of personal change becomes a "race to be run" (1 Corinthians 9:24), a goal to be sought rather than a one-time payment. Paul encourages us to "renew our minds daily" (Romans 12:2) and tells us that we are being made into the "image of Christ," changed in the "refiner's fire." Through many of his letters to young churches across the Biblical world Paul explains that God is in the process of perfecting His own creation, His people. And that through painful and slow personal change He is turning them into something beautiful and holy, His bride.

This process of becoming worthy requires sacrifice. Isaiah's lips are touched by coal in order to become clean, Paul is blinded, and some are required to lose their lives. The story of the Scriptures though is that the end-result—being made into the image of Christ—is worth it all. And God invites us to use our creativity to explore this part of Him, to get a better sense of what it means to pursue beauty and truth in a work of art as much as we are called to do it in our spiritual lives.

THE GIFT OF TENSION

Muscle mass is produced—literally—by pushing weight against the Earth's gravity. Without the tension of gravity holding us to the Earth we would have nothing to strain against and therefore be unable to build strength. Creativity works in the same way. Trying to grow the ability to be creative in a vacuum without tension (deadlines, critiques, grades, sales, or some means of measuring effectiveness) doesn't work. Of course there are instances where individual works of profound beauty and meaning grow with no practicality attached to them. But the artists who create them didn't grow that way. Creative muscles grow with regular, defined work and tension the way physical muscles do. This tension can take on any number of forms and it's worth noting that like everything else in life, there is a healthy version of this tension and an unhealthy one. The unhealthy version gets a lot of press and for good reason. Record labels, agents, publishing houses, film studios—all those who historically have held the power of deciding which works of art have "value" and which don't—have been the object of much mistrust and cynicism. What these individuals are creating isn't so much tension as obstacle. They are actually impeding and in some cases killing creativity, not enhancing it. Healthy tension from an outside and trusted source has more in common with the good gardener in John 12 who prunes his vines, helping them grow more effectively.

There is a natural and I believe God-given feeling of ecstasy and accomplishment at the act of creation. For good reason artists sometimes compare this feeling to giving birth. The act of bringing something into the world that is beautiful, true, has value, and makes the lives of others richer is a sacred thing. It is a privilege to be trusted to create, and every good artist I know at some point has experienced deep gratitude for this. More than once I have gotten a phone call from an artist at this moment and can hear the elation in their voice. They say things like, "This is the best thing I've ever written!" Even the most experienced artists feel things this dramatic when they make something new. The moment of creation is intoxicating, and I think it's by design. It's a unique experience for us as creative people and has its own rewards. Developing the skills to gain objectivity and refinement though are critical to becoming an effective artist—an artist who is constantly improving and finding better means of expression. Without this skill—without the ability to revisit a work and elevate it from something good to something exceptional—we miss a key part of creativity.

The author Ron Hansen described this tension for artists when he wrote: "The goal of writing is to be as clear and beautiful as possible, trying to produce symmetry and harmony out of chaos" (Atticus Reader's Guide). Chaos is a fair term for the state most artists are in when they create and, in some cases, an accurate assessment of a work in progress. Building clarity and beauty into that work is a challenge and those ideas can be viewed as the two poles that provide a means to examine, evaluate, and adjust creative work. Too much of the one and you have work that's well-constructed but without vitality. Too much of the other and you have something sentimental but without lasting impact.

GETTING THE WORDS RIGHT

Finding the right balance between these two poles is difficult and remains a lifetime's challenge for the best artists. It's hard to put in words exactly what it means but most of us instinctively know what side of the scale a work is on or what it's lacking when we experience it. In a 1958 interview with the *Paris Review*, the author Ernest Hemingway said this:

> Interviewer: How much rewriting do you do?
> Hemingway: It depends. I rewrote the ending of *Farewell to Arms*, the last page of it, thirty-nine times before I was satisfied.
> Interviewer: Was there some technical problem there? What was it that had stumped you?
> Hemingway: Getting the words right.

There is a reason that even legendary artists like Hemingway are reduced to describing the finishing process as "getting the words right." In some ways, to be more specific than that is to be untrue to the creative process. Even after dozens of attempts, sometimes the desired effect is still lacking. I have had the benefit of working closely with a number of successful recording artists, songwriters, and producers over the last ten years and the common thread that runs through all of their best work is this concept of the struggle to get something right. Not a meaningless, vague struggle with no goal in mind but a hopeful, intentional one. A struggle that when done well can lead to works of great beauty and a different kind of feeling of accomplishment. Even when a song or a part of a song emerges fully formed, any experienced musician knows this is an unusual gift. The reality of creating on a daily basis is a process. Learning repeatable, practical ways to refine opens doors to a deeper way to express.

THE GREATEST OF THESE

The greatest tool that an artist has is time. The emotional glow that happens at the moment a song gets written or when a short story is finished is powerful. I believe that, like Moses when he saw God's back, we get some sense of the Divine at those moments. Usually after a few hours go by or we get a good night's sleep though, the imperfections in a work start to reveal themselves and that initial euphoria can be replaced by something closer to dread or at least unsettledness. While this can make for an emotional roller-coaster ride, it is also a gift. When an artist sends me a song for feedback, I listen to it once on the day I get it and then again the next day before I respond. While initially I might only be listening for whether or not I am emotionally moved, with a few additional listens I can start to form an opinion about things like the strength or memorability of the melody; the clarity and poetry of the lyric; and the form of the song itself. Then I can begin to articulate much better what's working for me and what isn't. I need time to work through my own biases and be more objective. The atmosphere when I'm listening and my own state of mind can influence the experience so I need to time to account for that, to listen in different settings so that I separate those distractions from the work. Oftentimes the amazing experience that happens writing or hearing a song isn't repeatable. As authentic and real as it can be, it's critical to separate that from objectively great work. Letting some time go by so that the playing field is leveled is necessary and is the best way to reveal what needs to be revisited.

As is true in our spiritual lives, perseverance is rewarded. The Russian poet Yevgeny Yevtushenko said that "Time has a way of demonstrating that the most stubborn are the most intelligent." I might insert the word "productive" for "intelligent" but the same sentiment holds true. The artists in the world doing the best work have likely put in more hours than the rest of us. In his book *Outliers* author Malcolm Gladwell makes the case that very few artists become truly great at what they do until they have applied themselves to their craft for a cumulative 10,000 hours. This has absolutely been my own experience. While a young artist, writer, or producer will show occasional signs of greatness early on, they tend to be very inconsistent. Those that do high-level work on a regular basis do it as a result of developing and refining their skills and discernment over time. I have yet to meet a perfect artist. Each one has areas in which they excel and other areas in which they have blind spots. The "stubborn" ones are humble enough to take criticism about what those areas might be and dedicated enough to explore how to improve. Oftentimes this takes on the form of feedback. And that input from others—in particular from trusted peers—is another key ingredient.

THE VOICES IN MY HEAD

For years scientists who study the brain have theorized that one hemisphere of our brain is dominant in creative functions and the other is dominant in logical ones. While this is probably an over-simplification, I do think there is some truth to the idea that we tend to operate at different creative moments primarily from one sphere or the other. In *Hooah! Magazine* Switchfoot's Jon Foreman talked about the two voices he relies on when he writes songs:

"One is a creative, childlike voice that finds everything in life worthy of writing a song about," he says. "The other voice is the critical voice that's a little more aware. That's the editor. He's saying 'Oh, that's not that good' or 'You can do better.' If you only have the creative, then you write a bunch of songs that might be terrible. But if you don't have the voice of wonder then you don't write music to begin with."

We tend to over-celebrate the role of creativity in art and downplay critical analysis or rewriting. The "voice of the editor" is just as important in finding a balance between beauty and clarity. Sometimes even just having another person in the room with me who I know is listening critically to music that I'm involved with changes the way I hear music. I tend to leave the vague emotional state I'm listening in and start thinking specific things like "the tempo is too slow" or "the second verse lyric isn't as strong as the first." The editor takes over and I start making a checklist for what needs improvement. As much as I was suspicious of this practice when I started working in A&R because of my own bias toward the "purity" of inspiration, I have seen a number of examples where drastic reworking and revisions led to major success. Nichole Nordeman's Dove-award winning Song of the Year "Holy" was completely recorded and mixed two different times before being finished. Chris Tomlin's Song of the Year "Indescribable" was a last-minute addition to a record that the creative team thought was done but, after sitting with the album for a few days, had an instinct wasn't finished yet. The artists we sign to a recording contract at EMI CMG take an average of eighteen months to two years to release a record. The refining of not only the music but the artist's vision—making sure not only that the songs and record are great but that they accurately reflect who the artist is—often takes that long, sometimes even longer. Allowing someone (an A&R person, a producer, or a manager) or even multiple people to play that role in the process is key.

One thing to note is that not everyone is equipped to provide specific feedback. Sometimes artists can have their feelings crushed unnecessarily by an inaccurate or uninformed assessment of their work. This is more prevalent now than ever in the age of the internet where everyone's opinion is broadcast and preserved forever. Be careful who you give that power to! When you get criticism ask questions like: does it resonate with your own instincts about the work? Did applying the suggestion improve your work? What does this person's body of work qualify them to have an opinion on? As critical as it is to not over-rotate the other way and allow no one a chance to critique your work, not everyone is going to have something productive to say. Considering the source's experience and point of view is critical.

COLLABORATION

Closely related to having your peers review your work is collaboration. One way to get better at creating art is to find ways to work with others who are better at it than you are. When I was a jazz student at the University of Miami Music School, the legendary jazz guitarist Pat Metheny came to campus for a number of teaching clinics. He had a lot of great things to say but one particular piece of advice of his has always stayed with me: "Always be the worst player in every band you're in." If you can find a way to work on a regular basis with artists who have more experience and make better art than you do, you will be more likely to rise to their level of competence. Even when artists that I work with co-write songs that they don't end up recording, they often tell me they learned a new trick. It could be a new chord progression, a different voicing, or an unusual lyrical approach. Whatever it is, it can be a useful tool for future work.

Getting a fresh perspective is crucial for an artist. Without seeing your work in a different light, it's impossible to figure out what needs work and improve it. When I shared once with a music professor that I wasn't a Mozart fan because I found his harmonic approach simplistic compared to other music that I was listening to, he told me that I was "listening wrong." He was right. My teacher's explanation of how Mozart exploited melody and counterpoint uncovered things for me that I didn't have the maturity to recognize. Discussing and dissecting your own art and especially great works by others is a critical part of learning. Much in the same way as we develop spiritually, God has not designed a system where any one person has all of the answers. It takes stubbornness to stay committed to find them and humility to ask.

THE SEARCH

Refining your work ultimately is about making yourself more creatively articulate. The author John Updike said that "Writing and rewriting are a constant search for what it is one is saying." All of us have been given a unique viewpoint: a way of looking at the world, at life, and at God Himself that is singular. If we can find a way to express ourselves better through our art then that more potent expression is by definition more useful to the God we serve.

IMITATION
and obsession

Charles Hodge famously said that under his watch, nothing new was ever taught at Princeton Seminary. In that same spirit, I can assure you that you're not going to read anything new here—at least not anything that is original to me. These ideas were borrowed and stolen and appropriated to create a patchwork quilt of ideas and theories that have been helpful to me as a musician. That being said, this essay is a work of description, not a formula for songwriting success. I am going to offer to you, the reader, reflections on what I *think* I have done in writing sermons and poems and songs. Much of what I do in writing is intuitive and reflexive and feels more like a reaction rather than an action.

IMITATION

> Any originality in my work has come only from inability to copy well.
> —Dean Young

One of the first things I remember reading about writing—or anything targeted towards artists about how to make art—was in an essay by the poet John Woods. In that essay Woods pointed out that if one wants to write—if one wishes to make a poem or an essay or novel or song or whatever—then one must sit down. He meant that *literally:* you actually have to bend your knees and place yourself down on a chair or couch. This is what must come first. At least that's usually the case. Some people write standing up. Some people write while lying down, or while walking. But by and large, when you want to start writing—when you see a photograph of James Baldwin smoking and looking beautiful and intense, or Raymond Carver smoking and looking imposing and intense, or Bob Dylan lighting up and looking cool and intense—and you think, "I want to be a writer," the first thing you have to do (besides maybe start smoking) is sit down. You have to find a chair.

There's lots to be gained from this fact, not least of all the consolation of good company. When you sit down to write, you can draw comfort from the fact that you are doing exactly what Robbie Robertson and Eugene Peterson both did. John Calvin and Jamie Smith and Joni Mitchell and Karl Barth and Roald Dahl and Jonathan Edwards and Brian Wilson and Paul Simon all had to sit down when they wanted to write something. When you desire to pledge that sacred fraternity of songwriters or novelists, poets or preachers, you're starting off on the right foot when you actually and finally sit down. This is true not only because once you sit down that means you've stopped lots of other things you could be doing other than writing, but also when you sit down you can be sure that you're sitting just like the greats did. This is the tried and true method for writing: *sit down and write.*

But the way has been paved even more fully and farther. Once you finally sit down to write, you are not left to your own devices because you have already prepared for you a full slate of letters—if you're writing in English, twenty-six to be exact, no more, no less. You have all you need, and you need them all. And it's not as if you have to think of a way to put these letters together. That has already been done for you, too. For $2 at your local stoop sale or yard sale, you can pick up a dictionary that contains exactly how to put those letters together into words, words whose meanings and histories are pretty well established, if still moving a little bit (like an oak tree moves a little bit all the time, upwards and outwards.) All in one place, there those words are. It's all given to you, and if you want to write, you have to receive that gift, the gift of having to imitate: you sit down and you use letters that are not your own, formed into words that are not your own, arranged into the conceit of sentences and paragraphs, lines and stanzas, conceits you did not come up with.

I could keep going, of course. In music you have twelve notes, major and minor chords, and the tonal language of Western culture. The conventions of a pop song are all already set, just listen to oeuvre of Hank Williams: he wrote the same beautiful song over and over, the same song Waylon Jennings wrote twenty years later (yes, Waylon, we are sure Hank done it that way).

When we make things we are in the business of imitation, if not something akin to full-blown plagiarism. And my thesis is that this is not only a good thing, but that if any of us have any chance of making something beautiful and true, we would do well to embrace this truth and live in to it.

Here's another way of trying to say it: my friend Mike is a firefighter. If you are ever in an emergency in Grand Rapids, Michigan, it just might be that he'll be the one to come and help you, and you should thank God if it is him that comes because I can't think of anyone—truly—I'd rather see running towards me if I'm drowning or falling or failing.

Anyway, for him to be able to do that well, to save people's lives who are in trouble, he has to know the *craft* of saving the lives of people who are in trouble. That means he has to know what other people have learned about how a building burns, how people need to be lifted when they are burned, how to breathe for someone who cannot breathe on their own, how to make someone stop bleeding, etc. He can't only *want* to do those things—he can't just have a *passion* for it—he has to know how. To save someone's life you have to learn it by rote: Mike has to work out and jog three mornings a week and he has to study the literature, and he has to have the right equipment on.

Now. When the time comes for him to save your life, it's *also* going to take ingenuity and creativity and luck—or since I am a Christian, I'd say that it's going to take ingenuity, creativity, and God's Providence. When he comes to find you he'll discover that the frame of the door has collapsed in a way he's never heard of before, or he'll find that the house is old and thus the paint isn't one he's encountered before, it's burning funny. His boot might get torn off. And so he'll have to improvise.

But before the improvisation—and in service to the passion to save, to write, to create—you have to learn how to sit down and spell and how to make good sentences. You have to practice chords and learn about song structure. And before you can learn how to make a good song, you have to learn to hear one, to identify one. If you are a painter, you better like the smell of paint. And according to Flannery O'Connor, if you're going to make sentences, you better get good at it.

Become a good student of whatever you are trying to make. Learn how things work from the inside. Part of what that means in writing is reading extensively. Annie Dillard wrote, "If you ask a 21-year-old poet whose poetry he likes, he might say, unblushing, 'Nobody's.' He has not yet understood that poets like poetry, and novelists like novels; he himself likes only the role, the thought of himself in a hat."

But it will also mean—hence the title of this section—imitation. It will mean copying and emulating works of art that you want to make. Hunter S. Thompson took this to lengths that might be absurd—he actually typed out novels, word for word, that he admired. The bass player in our band, as a way of practicing, puts on the records of the Beatles and plays, note for note, the bass parts of Paul McCartney. Imitation means imitating. And so it will also mean making things that are not very good, i.e., bad aping of a style, or wooden emulation that you realize after the fact is devoid of much spirit. But that's OK.

I discovered the poems of Pulitzer Prize-winning American poet Philip Levine when I was an undergrad. Here was someone whose voice I at once recognized (he is, like me, a child of the auto factories of Detroit) but which I also perceived as deliciously fresh and life-giving, like a breeze at night in a hot room. And after I read through a few of his books—especially *What Work Is*—I started churning out hackneyed and smudged facsimiles of his poetry. I adopted his tone, his voice, and his subject matter. Somewhere in Heaven there's a stack of those poems, and because God is gracious, he's never going to show them to anyone. But I think that exercise was not one of futility, but the exact opposite. It was incredibly useful to discover which aspects of his voice could be mine, and which could not, which moves he made I was able to make, or learn to make, and which were above me or below me.

I'm stating what I fear may be painfully obvious—and isn't the obvious always painful?—to establish what I believe is of paramount importance in becoming a competent artist, that is, to be willing to apprentice yourself in the schools of good art. And this discipleship isn't just limited to the arts. At one point in time, the Church required that all her bishops have the Psalter memorized. If you wanted to be a pastor, you needed to have all 150 Psalms memorized. And the rationale of the church for this was that knowing these prayers by rote was the only way you could really learn how to pray. They believed that before you could have anything real to say, you had to learn someone else's words.

OBSESSION

In the process of imitation—of learning a craft—one is called to listen for one's own voice—or rather, to listen for the silence, to hear what is *not* being said as you internalize what has come before. As you read through the poet that speaks most directly to your heart, you diagnose the one thing that, despite his or her genius, the poet is not saying. Annie Dillard again:

> A writer looking for subjects inquires not after what he loves best, but after what he alone loves at all. Strange seizures beset us. Frank Conroy loves his yo-yo tricks, Emily Dickinson her slant of light; Richard Selzer loves the glistening peritoneum, Faulkner the muddy bottom of a little girl's drawers visible when she's up a pear tree. "Each student of the ferns," I once read, "will have his own list of plants that for some reason or another stir his emotions." Why do you never find anything written about that idiosyncratic thought you advert to, about your fascination with something no one else understands? Because it is up to you. There is something you find interesting, for a reason hard to explain. It is hard to explain because you have never read it on any page; there you begin. You were made and set here to give voice to this, your own astonishment.

Another way to talk about this is to use the taxonomy that Lewis Hyde uses in his book, *The Gift*. Hyde says that there are at least two phases in the completion of a work of art: one where the will is suspended, and one in which the will is active. It is when the will is slack that we feel moved or we are struck by an event or a turn of phrase or image. In other words, the material out of which we make something must flow before we begin to work on it. Not only is the will powerless to initiate the flow of the material, but it actually seems to interfere with that flow.

Let me give you an example of what I mean: now and again as I am out running errands, riding the subway, or walking down the street, I will get an idea for a song, usually a melody line, sometimes a chord progression. And I have found that I can sing that music over and over and over and over, seemingly searing it into my brain, certain that I will never, ever forget it. But unless I somehow get the melody recorded or down on paper, I find it impossible to recover it later in the day. I can't ever get back to that moment of effortless inspiration. When I sit down and try to recreate what I heard so easily in my head, it is like trying to reconstruct a sand castle that has been washed away, not just by time, but also by the loss of something unnameable which creates and congeals what I've found to be the best stuff that I create. Or rather, stuff that doesn't feel like I created it at all, but rather, that it arose out of me without my even trying.

I am calling this suspension of the will, "obsession." It's the place your mind goes when you're not trying to make it go anywhere. The images that come unbidden. The scenes you keep returning to. The phrase you can't quit saying. The chord changes that feel like you live there.

Your obsessions are utterly important for you to find, and it might be as difficult as it is important. It is important because if you cannot locate your obsession, then you are left with imitation—which means that you are left with someone else's obsession. Because what you and I resonate with in the work we love is where someone else has located their heart, or the portion of their heart they can express for God's glory and the world's good. Trying to sing or write someone else's obsession is sad and futile, a parading around in someone else's battle gear which is, as the young David showed us, not only ridiculous, but will also prevent you from being able to do the things God wants you to do.

It might seem not only self-evident that an artist should find their own true voice or theme, but also like the easiest thing in the world. Yet it is not easy to know what your heart has to say. The prophet Jeremiah wrote: "The heart is deceitful above all things, and desperately sick; who can understand it?" If you'd like to know the answer to that question—Who *can* understand it?—well, you're in luck because I'm a pastor and I can tell you. The answer is: *Not necessarily you, and if you finally do, it won't come easy.*

It is also difficult because what you find when you get to your heart may not be all that attractive or cool. You may not find what you were expecting to find, and you may not like what you find. If you are given the spiritual discernment to know yourself and know what is really important to you, and if you find that you are able to say the things you find in your heart in a way that is convincing and compelling (which is not the same as just *knowing* those things, by the way), you might come to find out you're not really all that interested in saying them. Obsessions might be good or bad, boring or banal. Maybe the thing that emerges from your gorgeously broken heart is a Work of Staggering Genius delivered in hip prose prized by people who matter. Or it might be that your obsession says something else.

For example, on many Sunday nights, after working all day at church, I stop by a series of stores near my block: I buy Thai food, some beer, and the *Sunday New York Times*. At the place where I buy the *Times,* they also sell lottery tickets. I end up buying maybe two or three lottery tickets per month, maybe less. But each time I pass by that store, whether I buy a ticket or not, I notice how much the jackpot is. And oftentimes when I am walking home with my Thai food and my beer and my *Times,* I fantasize about what I would do if I won the lottery.

In my fantasy of winning the lottery, I become incredibly generous. I give a lot of money away, I fund churches and missionary hospitals and I pay the bills of family members who struggle. I myself live in modest luxury, nothing too opulent. Sure, I go out to eat more, and I finally find out what the $1,000 Sushi dinner at Masa is all about. But in my lottery fantasy I mostly become a beneficent benefactor beloved by all.

I also finally have the time and the means to get a better devotional life.

At some point in the last year or so, I realized I'd been having some version of this fantasy for years. And after I (sheepishly) realized this and articulated to myself how really ridiculous it was to fantasize in this way (the ridiculousness consisting not only of the fact that this fantasy of money making me more generous and joyful and spiritually sound runs pretty much absolutely contrary to everything the Bible teaches about who God is, who I am, what I was made for, what treasure is, what blessing is, what is spiritually dangerous, etc., but also that I have dedicated my life to teaching other people these truths [!!!]), I started to think about why I engage and activate this fantasy so often. And the answers I have tentatively arrived at are not pretty:

> I fear depending on others.
> I desire to be needed and admired,
>   and even worshipped, truth be told.
> I lack faith in my good Father who has pledged
>   by the blood of his Son to take care of me.

This is just one example of what I mean by "obsession." The thing You were made and set here to give voice to ... your own astonishment. The thing you know that nobody else knows.

PARTICIPATION

So where are we?

First, the truth that almost every artist needs to apprentice herself to the craft she desires to be a part of. You need to imitate, to assemble the toolbox from which you can do the work you want to do.

Second, you have to discover the thing only you can say. After much imitation you'll get an ear for what lines don't ring true coming out of your mouth, and what lines could only ever be said with your accent. You have to dig deeply into your heart and follow it down wherever it goes.

Finally, I would say that both of these endeavors—but especially the latter—is best undertaken in the context of a community that you love and that loves you. Sometimes good art can get made by individuals in a (relative) vacuum, but I'd say it's the exception. And it's not nearly as rewarding or fun. I'm calling this art making in the context of community *participation*.

Participation means to consciously make what you make as the member of a community to which you are in some way accountable. It means that your work is, at least in some sense, *for* that community. I can't think of a better way to state what I mean by this than to describe how I've seen that happen in my life.

The sermons I write are for God's glory and they are for the good of the people of my church, Resurrection Presbyterian Church in Brooklyn, NY. My goal and my responsibility is not to *please* the people there, but it is to *feed* them. If they do not get fed, then I am not doing my job and I have failed as a preacher, as a writer of sermons. (Yes, I am aware that even my best efforts, without the power of the Holy Spirit, can do nothing but put people to sleep. And I know that my very worst sermons, aided by the Holy Spirit, can wake the dead—but we're talking about something else here.) That's what I mean by participation: the sermons I write have to be judged within the context of my community. Not necessarily *by* the community, but *in* the community.

Or consider my moonlighting gig in our band The Welcome Wagon. My goal for the songs I write, and for the playing of them, is that my wife and I, and the people we make our music with, basically sort of like the songs and think they are interesting or beautiful or whatever, and worth playing and listening to. That's the barometer.

Whenever anybody starts talking in hushed tones about the solitary and tortured genius of blues guitarist Robert Johnson or the painter Vincent van Gogh, I get the heebie-jeebies. Which is not to diminish the genius of either of those men, but I just don't think the mythos around either of them is accurate or helpful. Both of them were devoted students of their craft—their effortless genius emerged out of thousands of hours of effort. Each spent time participating in a larger community of artists. So the myth's not even true. Plus, the way of the tortured genius doesn't give us a path to take, or at least not a safely navigable path.

To make art in and for a community is to locate the pursuit of your craft within the lives of people who you love and who love you and who can help you to do what you could not do without them.

This is a good idea, I think, for lots of reasons, but one of the big ones is that there is wisdom in a multitude of counselors. If you can place your sermons or songs (and yourself) in the crucible of people who you love and trust, the work will be better.

CONCLUSION

The best way I can think to conclude this essay is to give you a case study of how some of these principles emerged in some of my work as a songwriter.

One of my favorite songwriters in the world is Daniel Smith of Danielson, and one of my favorite songs of his is called, "Sold! To the Nice Rich Man." It's a 3/4 waltz/stomp with killer lyrics recounting the perilous and beautiful narrative of a thoroughly ruined and impossibly redeemed life that might surely get redeemed (at least that's how I read it, I don't think I've ever asked Dan for his take), and an off-kilter song structure that toggles between the roaring, a-tonal verse, and a quiet, child-like and pretty chorus.

Well, because I sort of wish I was Dan Smith (I am repenting of this, help me God), when I was learning to play the guitar, I tried to learn how to play this song. But I couldn't find the chords anywhere, so I had to give it my best guess. But after lots and lots of guessing, I still was no closer. But man, I wanted to sing that song. So I sort of just approximated it, realizing as I did that I was wrong. But I played it wrong so many times, that my mistakes became canonical (to me). I kept shifting it. I played it over and over and over, listening to Dan's version in hopes of hanging on to what I loved about the song, but realizing I wasn't Dan and for better or for worse, I had a new song on my hands. The harrowing waltz became a 4/4 shuffle. The roaring verse became quiet and meandering, in part because I didn't yet have the guts to let loose in my living room, but also because I like to sing with my wife, and she sings quietly.

We played the song for our friend Sufjan as we were recording our album, and he took our quiet folksong and turned up the volume, adding a melody line on his banjo which he culled from the chords I had (re-) written. When it came time to record it, our longtime guitar player (Alex Foote) and bassist (Jay Foote) each left their fingerprints on the song. James McAllister did the same thing on drums.

While recording the demo in our living room, Monique and Sufjan and I had conceived of a little section in which we wordlessly sang ("Ooooh, oooh, ooh") through the chorus, layering harmonies on top of each other. While some people's aesthetic theory leans towards, "Less is more," Sufjan's leans/lunges towards "More is more." So we brought in a choir of friends to sing our erstwhile vocal part.

Well, just as they were finishing the last take of the song, they continued the trend of revision. Many of the choir members who were singing for us are steeped in gospel and soul, one of them said, "These 'oooh, oooh, ooohs' are great, but what about kicking off the song with a big gospel choir vocal flourish, like this: 'Whoa, whoa, whoaaaa!!!'" Well, everyone put their headphones back on, and they sang it, and it was perfect.

So, to review: Dan Smith writes and performs an apocalyptic protest song, I attempt to steal it and fundamentally alter it as I play it to death in my bedroom. Then a group of friends takes the humble cottage of a song that I've made and, to paraphrase C. S. Lewis, they throw out a new wing here, put on an extra floor there, and generally turn the thing into a mansion.

THIS IS THE WAY
love is

If there was a Mount Rushmore for Christian rock, Michael Roe's face would be carved into stone. As the lead singer of The 77s, he quickly earned a place among the genre's founding fathers when *Ping Pong Over the Abyss* was released in 1982. Five years later, the Sevens' brilliant self-titled album was released on Island Records. Unfortunately, that was same year that Island released U2's *The Joshua Tree,* an album which consumed the vast bulk of the label's resources and, many believe, caused The 77s to suffer from a lack of promotion. But Roe and his band never stopped releasing work of superior quality—including 1990's *Sticks and Stones* and 1992's *Pray Naked,* along with 2008's *Holy Ghost Building.*

In addition to his numerous solo albums, Roe has demonstrated a remarkable penchant for collaboration, must notably as a member of The Lost Dogs. The following interview stretched across two conversations. The first was on the phone following a solo concert and the second was face to face while Roe was busy breaking down his gear after a concert by The Lost Dogs.

In the chapter on collaboration in It Was Good: Making Art to the Glory of God *it says: "Collaboration calls us out of ourselves into community. The artist is no longer a specifically gifted loner, making art in a large white room, free of distraction." What have been the benefits to you artistically of making music corroboratively versus when you have recorded as a solo musician?*

That depends on whom I'm working with. Obviously, things happen when you collaborate that don't happen when you are by yourself. It's like simple elements versus chemistry—there is hydrogen and oxygen, but when you put them together you get water. So, it's that kind of thing, and it's never predictable. If you're working with people that you're familiar and comfortable with who respect your ideas, you can come up with some pretty cool things.

What did you learn about collaboration during the EXIT Records years when you were working with Vector, Steve Scott, and Charlie Peacock?

That was the one of the best times for me as far as working together with others because all of those people were super talented. We all loved each other. We were like brothers and we had a common bond and mission, so that made for a really memorable time. I learned a lot in the studio, about recording and producing. Of course, Charlie Peacock was a great inspiration to me back then. Even though he was younger than me, he had a certain way of dealing with the studio process that opened my mind to more possibilities. The main thing I learned from him was to not always do the predictable thing, but rather to try and go outside of that. A lot of times I'd play a guitar part and he would tell me, "Don't play that." And I'd say, "Why? It was perfect." And he'd say, "Yes, that's exactly why I don't want you to do it." He'd rather leave it blank than put something there that was obviously the 'right' part but stock and predictable. After working with him, I found myself beginning to think more outside the box.

Those years birthed the Scratch Band, which would later become The 77s. What did you learn about collaboration recording with The 77s?

That writing as a 'group effort' could occasionally be valuable. A lot of times we wrote as a band by jamming, recording our jams, and then incorporating parts of those into some of the songs we were already writing individually. Sometimes whole songs came out of jams. Other times, songs that began as the product of one guy's tortured vision became much better when we all combined our individual tortured visions to help strengthen it. It went all kinds of ways.

"Don't This Way" was an interesting collaboration. Mark Tootle wrote most of the middle of the song—all the words and music. The intro and outro—all that instrumental stuff—was stuff that I got from a jam that the band did. I recorded the jam, then took pieces from my solos and what the band was doing and used those to bookend the song. That combined process gave us one of our most memorable tunes.

Then there was "Caught in an Unguarded Moment." Our first drummer Mark Proctor came into a practice session with the line, "Caught in an unguarded moment"—that's it. That's all he had. And Jan had the "Oh-oh-oh, Whoa-whoa-whoa" bit that we threw on the beginning and he got credit too. It was a three-way collaboration using two really pregnant ideas and me just finishing the song. I wrote the bulk of the song, but I couldn't—wouldn't—have had the song without those ideas from Mark and Jan. To me, those are very significant contributions. I don't take them lightly because short phrases like that will write the whole song. A title can even write a whole song. Titles are very important. Of course, there are some people who come up with great titles but never get around to writing the song—like Morrissey, for instance. I love his titles, but along the way I think he forgot to make the song as good as the title. He used to write great songs all the time during The Smiths era, and even a few good ones when he first went solo. But how are you going to make a great song out of a title like "You're the One for Me, Fatty"?

"Ba-Ba-Ba-Ba" was a collaboration that went outside of the band for the other collaborators. Originally it was called "Imagine Me"—it was a sort of whiney Supertramp rip-off: "I bet you can't imagine me without my mask of tragedy . . ."

It was catchy as hell but the lyrics were duff, so I re-wrote them and begged Charlie Peacock to produce the heck out of it. He came in and turned it into an 80's power-pop dance thing (with even a little bit of surf music . . .)

It does have an infectious beat. My friends and I did a lot of dancing to that song back in the day. In 1991 you joined with Terry Scott Taylor, Gene Eugene, and Derri Daughtery to form the Lost Dogs. What did you learn about collaboration recording with them?

It bore some similarities to what I described with The 77s, only now I was confronted with three, well-known accomplished songwriters so that raised the stakes of the game. We all really felt the pressure to come up with great songs. We worked harder for and with each other—not only because we were trying to impress each other, but also because we were trying to do our very best for all of the different fan bases that were represented by each contributor to the project.

After Gene Eugene passed away, we lost our collaborative momentum and defaulted to allowing the very prolific Terry Taylor to write the bulk of the material for many albums. However, in recent years, we began to collaborate with each other once again.

Steve Hindalong (who joined the band after the death of Gene Eugene) and I recently worked together on a song called "Turn It Around." He wrote lyrics about one of The Lost Dogs' more scary excursions in our RV while on tour along Route 66. Later, when we were recording the album Old Angel, he handed me those words and I came up with the music. It was hard work grafting his words to my music, but I thought it was successful. Steve was pretty good about letting me change the words around a bit, which I appreciate because he's just so good with lyrics . . .

Dark and eerie the night we drove
Down into the shadows of Isaac's grove
Ponderin' the times when I knew I dove
Deeper than I should have gone

A true voice whispers from somewhere inside
Pleadin' with a man to do the thing that's right
Run from darkness into the light
Find the Mother Road and just drive on
The time has come, the time is now
To turn, turn, turn it around . . .

I've had a lot of fun collaborating. I need to do it more. I haven't done it in a long time. I feel bad. I haven't done my "collaborative duty" to my friends. Steve and I talk about doing it more because he's really good at it. He's got an interesting lyrical approach that's not my approach, but I like it. It's good, and we have the kind of relationship where we can be real open with each other. You wouldn't want to do it with someone that you're real uptight around—or that you thought would dominate the whole thing ... that is, unless you want them to because you're lazy or whatever, as I have been over the years.

Terry Taylor and I worked together on the song "Moses in the Desert" where he had part of the song done and I jumped in—I don't know why, I don't remember what was going on at the time—but I love how that came together because that song would have never been like that had I not jumped in. It reminded me of Peter, Paul, and Mary so I helped push it further towards that folk direction, I think. I thought it was a good way to present it.

Can you remember the first time you collaborated with another songwriter?

I had a songwriting pal back in my early 20's that I used to collaborate with all the time. It was very exciting when a song would start to come together. We were young and we didn't have the standards we do now, so it was easier to finish more tunes. Most of it was really derivative but we had fun patting ourselves on the back, blissfully ignorant of the songs' mediocrity. Later, when you have higher standards (especially lyrically), the process becomes a little more serious because there is more on the line. This is most especially true if you're a professional and have a built-in audience. You owe it to your fans to do good work.

And in that way, the audience becomes part of the collaboration?

I had never thought of it like that, but in a sense you're right—they do—if not in the composition, then in the inspiration and your drive to do it. And you're also serving them with the work. You know what they need and what they want from you. If you can, you give it to them, or at least lead them further along. Sometimes, when you're working along certain lines that are familiar and recognizable, you get excited because you know the fans are going to like it. I'm sure that's common with really popular groups who have an identifiable sound. When they do something that is a "classic" sound for them, they probably know it. Unfortunately, many of those artists perversely begin to run in the opposite direction of what they do best and instead of progressing upward, they end up destroying the very sound and style that the public fell in love with them for in the first place. It's a really tricky area because you gotta keep it growing so it won't fossilize and become stale, but if you become someone else entirely in the process, you may not be able to keep your audience. Fortunately for us, we never settled on anything so our fans never know what to expect! They actually thrive on trying to imagine what we're going to come up with next, but at the end of the day, it's all about the song. For us, that operates on the level of the lyrics particularly—knowing what people want and need from the words. When you get into areas that are real personal, you know that if you've been through something yourself first, someone else will probably relate to or benefit from that.

How is the collaborative process different based on the amount of people involved? I am thinking of contrasting your experience of creating music with The Lost Dogs vs. Kerosene Halo.
It's way easier dealing with two people, in the same way that it's easier arguing with yourself rather than with three other people. It's hard to gauge which is better. I think it's just different.

Jeremy Begbie writes in Resounding Truth, *"From the vantage point of a Christian ecology, freedom, human flourishing is found* in a responsible relation to constraints *that are worthy of respect . . . Without constraints we cannot flourish." Collaboration can be an extremely constraining experience. Have you found freedom in such constraints?*
It's hard to say. Sometimes yes, sometimes no. Again, it really depends upon whom you're working with. There are certain individuals who would cause you to clam up and others who would create a free environment to create. And that can shift around even in the same groups.

One of the best experiences I had was collaborating with Michael Pritzl (lead singer from the band The Violet Burning) on a stage show for some tandem tours we did together. I liked working with Pritzl because he allowed me to see my older material in a new light. Things that I thought were boring or locked into a certain 'style of the decade' found new life by hearing his interpretation or spin on it. And in the same way, the tunes of his that I chose for us to perform were probably not the ones that he would have expected, so we both ended up pleasantly surprised in the end.

The 77s recording Holy Ghost Building (2008) was a very orthodox album for rock n' roll. Do you see your recent interest in Reformed theology having a big impact on yourself as artist?
A big part of why I like that old-time gospel blues material is because it gets

its strength from being so rigid and so specific, and I love rubbing it in the face of my more theologically liberal colleagues. What could be more rebellious than having orthodoxy as your form of rebellion, or to be deliberately and obnoxiously conservative and evangelical . . . I love it just because it pisses people off. And if you want to take it all the way, isn't that what the Bible has always done? It has irritated people from the start. So that does appeal to certain individuals like me who like creating a ruckus. Of course, we should always use caution in trying to manipulate the Gospel towards any use other than its own, which is why most contemporary Christian music gets my back up. End of that one, because I've still got some good friends in the CCM business (laughs).

It is always a challenge for someone like me who came from a much more rigid church background because you don't ever want to box yourself in in any way. I would never want to be not open to greater clarity in my thinking and in the way that I approach writing lyrics. This is becoming more and more of a personal issue with me because there are many deep struggles I wish to express in song, but there's that part of me that's afraid to go all the way with them because some of it is so profoundly disturbing that it may be considered scandalous amongst my fan base. But then I have to ask myself—would the Bible exist if its writers were concerned about their reputations, their 'fan base' and/or 'sales'? In fact, I have often joked that if the Bible were a new book, there is no bible bookstore that would ever touch it.

The end results of my spiritual struggles haven't always led to some of the places where my peers have gone either, so that can sometimes create problems when collaborating. Imagine trying to write a fairly serious spiritual lyric with someone who holds a polar opposite viewpoint doctrinally—will the compromises and concessions you make to one another neuter the power of the statement? I tend to zigzag a lot and arrive at my answers in a more gradual roundabout way. And a lot of times, I just end up living with the contradictions. Living with the fact that something is black and white at the same time. I have spent pretty much most of my life dealing with that. In the end, what I try to do is to be heartfelt and honest in my music and get away from anything that is pandering to someone, although I suppose there's not really anyone who's completely free to say and do anything they want all the time. You have to keep your audience in mind.

Although we're discussing collaboration in a generally positive light, it isn't always pretty. Again, in It Was Good: Making Art to the Glory of God *it said, "It is important to remember that not all collaboration leaves the people surrounding the collaboration with a perfectly happy, content, successful feeling."*

Well, there is a dark side to collaboration. You have to really trust the person you're working with and vice versa. There has to be openness, a willingness not to be timid, but instead bold about the ideas. It's kind of like what I assume it would be like to visit a nudist camp. I can only imagine how open you have to be with yourself. Free, unashamed, and sort of proud—well, not proud, but confident in your ideas ... that they're valid. Even if your contribution is not good, you need to be strong about showing ideas and be emotionally prepared for someone to say, "That's not very good—you've got to change that." You have to be able to accept criticism, but you also have to have enough conviction to not give in on a certain point if you feel strongly. You have to hold your ground if something you brought to the song was really inspired. Most of the time, the conflicts and challenges work themselves out if the collaborators are respectful and patient. It's a dance, for sure.

The older I get, the more I tend toward music that is easier on my nerves because my nerves are shot. I used to wonder what was wrong with my mother's nerves, and now that I'm older, I know. Give me some cool jazz from the early 50's—give me some Chet Baker, some Dave Brubeck, Miles Davis, Monk, Stan Getz, George Shearing—that's what I listen to. And if I'm not listening to that, I'm listening to light classical stuff like Mozart, or Spanish guitar players like Segovia. This is where I live now. These are the things that inspire me and keep my nerves calm.

How do you see yourself collaborating with Monk or Chet? In some ways you are working with them since listening to them is affecting who you are now.

That's a great question. It inspires me to want to get a hold of some jazz guys and collaborate rather than working with rock people or Americana people. Maybe I do need to start seeking out jazz musicians, but not to be pretentious or to retread what Elvis Costello or Joni Mitchell have done along those lines, although I think Joni Mitchell did a good job of combining the two. Sort of working her thing into Charles Mingus' thing—I thought that was really interesting. But it isn't done often enough. I would like to see more of that adventurous collaborative spirit. I'm certain it's happening a lot more than I'm aware of, probably.

I wonder if it is a matter of the audience dictating what they want in the music?

I don't think so. It's not like I have this enormous audience pressuring me. I'm pretty much free to do whatever I want. Although I'm not going to cut my throat professionally, I don't feel a sense of audience constraint. Our fan base is too used to us jerking them around with new ideas. They expect that. What they want is the lyric, along with music that's good. So, if I suddenly came from a jazz place on a new project, I think they'd accept that as long as they knew that what I was doing was honest and heartfelt and had something they could relate to. You know, if I just go off on a 20 minute whack-fest—that isn't going to relate to the core of the people who have supported my work over the years. But if I have a four minute whack-fest with a nice trumpet solo and a lyric that talks about an honest struggle ... (laughs) **Returning to the chapter on collaboration in It Was Good: Making Art to the Glory of God *it said, "Honest humility is a difficult virtue to embody. It*** *supposes that we first know ourselves well enough to understand our true strengths and weaknesses. Once we have an accurate picture of our talents, humility calls us to act truthfully, using our strengths to support others while taking care not to feed our own pride or to make others feel smaller." How has collaboration taught you humility?*

Well, collaboration often involves subjugating your vision and ego for the greater good of the whole. In other words, you have to be pliable and fluid enough to allow other influences to come in and shape the thing as it's going, and not cling too tightly to any one idea or get too precious about it. Not that I'll back down on a point if I feel really strongly about something. But in general, it causes you to try to find grace with each other as all of the ideas come together. Sometimes that is difficult. Sometimes it can be embarrassing. There may be furious arguing involved, but it's all part of the process. In the same way as when a woman gives birth—it's messy and painful and dangerous. And you can lose the baby at any point. That, I think, is the greatest fear when you are collaborating on a project with other people—that at any point a move could be made that would ruin the effect—if not for the public, then for you. And if it ruins it for you, it ruins it for everyone else because if you can't get behind it, then you aren't going to play it or sing it with any conviction. "Snake" by The 77s is a good example of this. I never really cared for this tune (although some fans do) After we did it, we kind of went, "Why did we do that?" It was fun to try, but it didn't stick and it wasn't us so it died a natural death. I don't regret the collaboration itself. There are many things I do regret, but that isn't one of them. Making mistakes is a significant part of the collaborative process. The priority in collaboration is to work through the hard times together towards something bigger and better than one person could do by himself. Think of our salvation—even that was collaboration—the Father chose us, the Son died for us, and the Spirit renews us.

At the end of the day, what would you say is the main thing to keep in mind when collaborating?

The number one rule of collaboration is to love your neighbor more than you love the song. And the joy of following this rule is that after the dust settles, we often get to listen to some amazing, unexpected compositions.

When I couldn't find the words, you understood
When I didn't find the time, you were in no hurry
When I wouldn't make ends meet, you tied them together
When I cheated you kept to the rules
This is the way love is.

THROW BACK
the clock

> It is hard to write a beautiful song. It is harder to write several individually beautiful songs that, when sung simultaneously, sound as a more beautiful polyphonic whole. The internal structures that create each of the voices separately must contribute to the emergent structure of the polyphony, which in turn must reinforce and comment on the structures of the individual voices. The way that is accomplished in detail is..."counterpoint."
> —John Ruhn

Modern musicians generally consider counterpoint to be an antiquated practice of music in which various lines of music interact and play off of one another. Works of the high Renaissance and Baroque period fit into this category. In its simplest form, a canon, or round such as "Row, Row, Row Your Boat" or "Frere Jacques," supplies a straightforward example of simple counterpoint. However, these attitudes fail to recognize the intent, purpose, and structure behind sixteenth and seventeenth century counterpoint or why it fell out of favor in the Age of the Enlightenment. In fact, the demise of counterpoint in the history of music is more of an indication of shifting theological worldviews than musical tastes.

THE IDEA OF MUSIC PRIOR TO THE ENLIGHTENMENT

Jamie James seeks to establish what the world of music looked like prior to the Enlightenment. He writes, "There was a time when the universe was believed to cohere, when human life had a meaning and purpose. A person who devoted himself to a lifetime of study, instead of coming out at the end of it the author of a definitive treatise on the pismire, or a catalogue of the references to Norse sagas in *Finnigans Wake,* would actually have a shot at discovering the key to the universe."[1] This idea of an interconnected and structured universe found its root in the creative order of an Almighty God who made the heavens and the earth. For thousands of years, this was the dominant idea and foundation of intellectual and theological thought. Since God created an orderly world, mankind in his work and calling sought to bring order to his own sphere of influence. This is the creation mandate of Genesis 1:28 in its fullest—taking dominion over the earth and bringing order. In the arts, that included taking dominion over color, language, movement, and, with regard to music, taking dominion over sound and time.

The intentionality and orderliness inherent in the creative cosmos was a discipline for study and emulation. This was especially true in the area of music. The Music of the Spheres was the controlling concept that the order of the cosmos was analogous to the inner structure of music—in its ratios and relationships as well as in its *harmonie*. Gioseffo Zarlino writes in *Le istitutioni harmoniche* (*1558*), "But every reason persuades us to believe that the world is composed with harmony, both because its soul is a harmony (as Plato believed), and because the heavens are turned round their intelligences with harmony, as may be gathered from their revolutions, which are proportionate to each other in velocity. This harmony is known also from the distances of the celestial spheres, for these distances (as some believe) are related in harmonic proportion, which although not measured by the sense, is measured by the reason."[2]

Scholars, philosophers, theologians, and scientists such as Pythagoras, Plato, Aristotle, Confucius, Augustine, Boethius, Cassiodorus, Ptolemy, Kepler, Luther, and Newton started from this perspective of the universe. For Augustine, Boethius, Ptolemy, and Kepler this also led to the writing of books on music. Martin Luther wrote, "You will find that from the beginning of the world [music] has been instilled and implanted in all creatures, individually and collectively. For nothing is without sound or harmony...Music is a gift and largesse of God, not a human gift. Praise through word and music is a sermon in sound" (Gaines 43). The astronomer Johannes Kepler said, "The movements of the heavens are nothing except a certain everlasting polyphony, perceived by the intellect, not by the ear."[3]

As James continues to point out, "The concepts of the musical universe and the Great Chain of Being originate in the classical bedrock of our culture, flow through the Christian tradition, and remain firmly centered in the Renaissance and the Age of Reason. They are at the core of the culture. It was not until the nineteenth century that the perspective shifted decisively to the earthly, the tangible. Materialism and sensuality, qualities that had been deeply mistrusted throughout most of the Western tradition, emerged ascendant."[4] It was this change in thinking that brought about the demise of counterpoint and polyphony.

The idea and ethos of counterpoint that permeated the musical world cannot be understated. David Yearsley in his book *Bach and the Meanings of Counterpoint* gives a picture of the importance of counterpoint in the Baroque era:

> ... in the first half of the eighteenth century no set of musical practices was richer in significance than strict counterpoint. Indeed, the minute, exacting, and seemingly esoteric world of canon could match the hermeneutic resonance of the most opulent of operas. No musical endeavor generated more polemical writing and more heated opinions during Bach's lifetime than did strict counterpoint; no set of techniques inspired greater devotion from its practitioners or more spirited antipathy from its detractors. Musicians literally wrestled over coveted books of contrapuntal knowledge; some guarded troves of contrapuntal treasure with almost mythic fervor; others consigned the long traditions of contrapuntal training to useless history.[5]

BACH AND THE CREATED ORDER

The clash of worldviews and its result in the area of music can most clearly be seen in the work of J.S. Bach (1685–1750). At the time that Bach was writing some of his most eloquent musical expressions of the created order, his work was already considered to be passé and out of fashion. The fact was that Bach's intent was not to follow the fleeting fashions of his day but to seek after an aesthetic and a musical/theological worldview that transcended his own time.

In Bach's day, musical knowledge was a common and integral part of education. As James says, "It was taken for granted throughout the whole history of the West that music was a defining human activity and therefore every educated person was trained in the rudiments of music."[6] However, only a generation passed before music was not even part of the curriculum at the St. Thomas School in Leipzig, Germany where Bach had taught for more than 20 years. This is a remarkable shift considering that one of the school's founding principles had been "to guide the students through the euphony of music to the contemplation of the divine."[7] The implications of this loss are even more astounding since it was through the school that the musicians received training to provide the music for the town's churches. The loss of music in the school curriculum had a detrimental effect upon the worship of the church.

The shift of musical education out of the core curriculum hinged on what man believed about the cosmos. If there is a Creator God who made the world with a pattern and order that is manifested throughout all creation, if all things interconnect at the point of their origin in one God, if there are absolutes and objective standards for the arts, then it is the role of the artist to discern, study, and utilize the patterns and order of the cosmos with a desire to emulate the created order for the purpose of both thinking God's thoughts after Him and of gaining wisdom and understanding as to the nature and character of God. If, however, man's reason is the ultimate guide for understanding and truth, man himself becomes the arbiter and standard for the arts, and the ultimate goal becomes entertainment and pleasure rather than Godly wisdom.

As one humanist music theorist wrote in the mid-eighteenth century, "Rules are valid as long as I consider it well and sensible to abide by them. They are valid no longer than that....The rule of nature, in music, is nothing but the ear." "The critics of counterpoint were renouncing music's allegorical and cosmic nature, its claim to be a manifestation of the divine. To this generation, music was not to be written according to any higher theory or objective than that of sensual, aural pleasure."[8]

The practical results of this theological shift were staggering in the world of music composition and for church music. Firstly, compositional technique suffered as composers wrote to please audiences. Instead of leading towards wisdom, composers and audiences sought amusement—literally a•*muse* or without thought. Secondly, composers wrote music for the concert stage with a secular aesthetic rather than for the church with an ecclesiastical aesthetic. The intent of music written for a concert and for the pleasure of the audience is necessarily different than music written for a church service for the pleasure of God. This is not a critique of quality but rather of purpose. Thirdly, music shifted from the complexities of polyphony (with many equal voices joining together in counterpoint creating a united whole) to a single line of accompanied melody. There is theological significance to separate lines of music that have equal interest and "singability" that combine to create something greater than the sum of the parts. All of the voices are different but necessary with important and distinctive contributions to the whole—much like the Body of Christ. The pervasive alternative is a single line of melody which results in one music part with subservient harmonic support. This idea shifted the concept of music from multiple horizontal melodic lines with secondary harmony to vertical harmonic changes that follow one another.

This vertical harmonic progression is why in subsequent years, some of the most highly regarded art music composers (Handel, Tchaikovsky, Schubert) are known more for their melodic audience appeal rather than the depth of their compositional abilities. James Gaines goes so far as to say, "Mozart of course was the ultimate composer for the Enlightenment. A good way to break up any dinner party is to claim Bach's superiority to Mozart, but there it is: Spend any serious amount of time listening to Bach, and most of Mozart's work, however wantonly gorgeous, will seem to be...missing something."[9] Perhaps one thing the music is missing is the heartbeat of the created cosmos rooted in a strong theological foundation.

This radical shift brought Bach into conflict with Frederick the Great of Prussia. Their conflict was at the heart of the shift from a theological grounding of life to Enlightenment thought. "For Bach this new, so-called *gallant* style, with all its lovely figures and stylish grace, was full of emptiness. Bach's cosmos was one in which the planets themselves played the ultimate harmony, a tenet that had been unquestioned since the 'sacred science' of Pythagoras; composing and performing music was for him and his musical ancestors a deeply spiritual enterprise whose sole purpose, as his works were inscribed, was 'for the glory of God.' For Frederick the goal of music was simply to be 'agreeable,' an entertainment and a diversion, easy work for performer and audience alike. He despised music that, as he put it, 'smells of the church.'"[10]

Eventually, this pattern of thought led to the Romantic movement with such composers as Beethoven, Schumann, Wagner, and Mahler. As Jamie James succinctly puts it, "Romantics were concerned above all with creating the impression of being bold and original"[11]—ideas opposed to the Biblical artistic concept of craftsmanship. This desire to be larger than life was as true for the Romantic poets and artists as it was for the composers, and their resulting profligate degenerate lifestyles is perhaps further evidence of the comprehensive break with Biblical artistic standards.

MUSIC AND THE DIVINELY CREATED ORDER

That music, and especially counterpoint, was an indicator of the divinely created order was a commonly held belief in the centuries prior to the Enlightenment. James Gaines makes this point clearly: "Cosmological harmony was actually one of the few ideas on which philosopher, scientists, and theologians of Bach's time were agreed. Newton, for example, could not imagine that a world so orderly as this one could have occurred by 'natural Cause alone.' A 'powerful, ever-living Agent...governs all things,' he concluded, 'not as the soul of the world, but as Lord over all.'"[12] He continues by quoting Luther, who said "We marvel when we hear music in which one voice sings a simple melody, while three, four, or five other voices play and trip lustily around...reminding us of a heavenly dance."[13] Furthermore, Yearlsey states that, "The constant motion of the heavens is thus analogous to the perpetual revolution of the parts in a well-constructed piece of double counterpoint, whose inversions mirror the perfection of heaven and provide earthly beings with a glimpse of God's unending order, a prelude to the heavenly concert...But the relationship between these phenomena was more than simply one of likeness: the mechanics of the heavens were not simply allegorized by double counterpoint, they were manifested in its workings."[14]

The laws of music were thus intimately connected with the perceived understanding of how and why the universe worked the way it did. This view of music places great importance on the moral and theological role of harmony as opposed to the subjective and changing tastes of audiences. As such, the role of the composer was that of an artisan or craftsman who realized the potential of the raw musical materials before them in such a manner as to bring order and take dominion over those elements of creation. Bach's gifts and artistic impulses made him well suited for such a task.

As Bach scholar John Butt puts it, "all music could be the object of his own artistry, it was merely his business—perhaps, even, moral necessity—to improve and perfect the art."[15] For Bach, perfection in praise of God was more important than individual achievement.

Butt also suggests how Bach might have defined perfection when he writes, "We get the impression of a composer who believed that every theme and formal strategy brings with it a host of implications that can be realized sequentially or in combination and that the completeness or perfection of any particular piece of music lies in the satisfaction of the entire potential of a musical idea."[16] This impulse is clearly seen in Bach's later *Summa* works—compositions which are the technical and musical summation of various concepts, genres, or musical skills.

Bach's quest for perfection extended to the entirety of his art. "[His] concentrated approach to his work, to reach what was possible in art, pertained to all aspects of music, from theory to composition and from performance to physiology and the technology of instruments."[17] His goal, though ultimately humanly unattainable, was no less than striving to love God with all his heart, soul, strength, and mind.

Bach deliberately crafted musical ideas that would then dictate how they could be further developed and how the piece itself would be composed. Carl Philipp Emanuel said of his father that Bach, listening to another composer's complex piece of music with multiple melodic subjects, knew almost immediately the full range of devices and techniques which that composer could employ and ought to utilize. Carl Philipp Emanuel continued by saying that after "he had voiced his surmises to me, he would joyfully nudge me when his expectations were fulfilled."[18] Understanding the potential of a musical idea recognizes certain rules and expectations.

How Earlier Composers Still Instruct

This distinctive worldview and theological presupposition led directly to the idea of the importance of music and in the development of counterpoint as an expression of the created order. As this foundation and purpose for music changed, so did the music—irrevocably. However, the mindset of the Medieval theorists and of Church composers such as Palestrina, Josquin, Byrd, Schütz, and Bach can provide a guide for current practice and philosophy. Music is a moral force; there are standards of what is harmonious; skill, learning, and thought are necessary.

Firstly, music—even without lyrics—has a moral component inherent in its very structure and execution. Whether one believes in the connection between the created order and the resultant rules that govern harmonious music, the fact remains that a violation of those rules results in discord and not harmony—either musically or personally. The sixteenth century theorist Gioseffo Zarlino believed that "Music should be enjoyed prudently and in moderation, like wine, because it has the capacity to excite men to evil as well as good, to intoxicate, and to exclude other worthwhile occupations."[19] (Zarlino xiii). This view reflects thoughts echoed in Plato, Aristotle, Paul, Augustine, and numerous Church Fathers.

Secondly, since there is a created order that lends its structure, ratios, and relationships to create harmonious music, there is an objective standard by which music can be measured. Zarlino defended the superiority of objectively good music against the argument that new music is just unusual. He wrote, "Someone might state that such things displease not because they are poor in themselves but because our ears are unaccustomed to them. This is as much as to say that some bad, tasteless food will seem savory after it has been eaten over a long period. I do not believe that anyone accustomed to inferior food who tastes some that is superior will be unable to distinguish between them and fail to recognize that the latter is delicious and pleasing whereas the former had been poor without pleasure. Likewise I feel that even if a person were to habituate himself to such sounds, he would confess to their poverty upon hearing a well-written diatonic composition."[20] Any objective standard is rooted in the nature and character of God because true beauty is an attribute of God and is a theological issue. It is God who declares what is beautiful and true and good.

Thirdly, excellent music does not just happen but is the result of study, work, craftsmanship, and practice. As Zarlino believed, "a composer should not be satisfied with mastering his craft but should know the reason for what he does."[21] To sing and play skillfully to God's glory requires knowledge and wisdom. Just as it was necessary for God to train the people of Israel how to worship, the Church needs to continually train herself in the aspects of worship by God's standards. Part of this training is an understanding of why and how certain music works and whether it is appropriate for corporate worship.

The extension of this thought is that as the Church recognizes that some music is not suitable for worship she should simultaneously provide opportunities for other types of music to be a regular part of the life of the community. Recognizing the role of music and the distinction of how music is played in different venues is key. This can be accomplished through coffee houses with writer's nights, a concert series, guitars, fiddles, and mandolins around the campfire. Because the purpose is different, how one plays guitar on a concert stage should be different than how it is played and used in worship. The same is true for percussion and pipe organs.

THE POWER OF MUSIC

James Gaines expresses the power of music succinctly and beautifully when he says, "The beauty of music, of course, what sets it apart from virtually every other human endeavor, is that it does not need the language of ideas; it requires no explanation and offers none, as much as it may say. Perhaps that is why music coming from a world where the invisible was palpable, where great cosmic forces played their part everywhere and every day, could so deeply move audiences so far from Bach's time. Whether in the thrilling exuberance of the polyphonic

Credo or in the single voice of an unaccompanied cello, in works extravagantly expressive and as intimate as a whisper, Bach's music makes no argument that the world is more than a ticking clock, yet leaves no doubt of it."[22]

Although considered anachronistic in our day, the ideas and moral forces that shaped the development and intention of counterpoint raise significant questions as to the purpose and significance of music. Nowhere are these questions more pertinent than in the discussions of what is appropriate to offer as musical sacrifices in corporate worship. Before dismissing counterpoint as an historic relic, we should at least wrestle with the same issues that created counterpoint in the first place if only because many of the "advances" that shoved it aside originated from a decidedly non-biblical worldview. The point is not to throw back the clock for the purpose of returning to an idealized earlier age or to exalt counterpoint as a necessary part of worship, but rather to more fully understand how these artisans used their skill and knowledge to embody Biblical truth and theology through their musical compositions. As such, we can still learn a lot.

Endnotes

1   Jamie James, *The Music of the Spheres: Music, Science and the Natural Order of The Universe* (New York: Copernicus, 1993), xiv.

2   Ibid., 91–92.

3   Ibid., 149.

4   Ibid., 4.

5   David Yearsley, *Bach and the Meanings of Counterpoint* (Cambridge: The Cambridge University Press, 2002), xiii.

6   James, 56–57.

7   James R. Gaines, *Evening in the Palace of Reason: Bach Meets Frederick the Great in the Age of Enlightenment* (New York: Harper Perennial, 2005), 183.

8   Ibid., 123.

9   Ibid., 256.

10   Ibid., 7–8.

11   James, 201.

12   Gaines, 51.

13   Ibid.

14   Yearsley, 20.

15   John Butt, "Bach's metaphysics of music." Ed. John Butt, *The Cambridge Companion to Bach* (Cambridge: The Cambridge University Press, 2000), 58.

16   Ibid., 57.

17   Christoph Wolff, *Johann Sebastian Bach: The Learned Musician* (New York: W. W. Norton & Company, 2000), 339.

18   Hans T. David and Arthur Mendel, editors, Christoph Wolff, Revised and Enlarged, *The New Bach Reader: A Life of Johann Sebastian Bach in Letters and Documents* (New York: W.W. Norton & Company, 1998), 397.

19   Gioseffo Zarlino, Translated by Guy A. Marco and Claude V. Palisca, *The Art of Counterpoint: Part Three of Le Istitutioni Harmoniche, 1558* (New York: W.W. Norton and Company, 1968), xiii.

20   Ibid., 282–283.

21   Ibid., xii.

22   Gaines, 272–273.

THE RATIO
of redemption

This essay is and is not about harmony. It is not about harmony, because most of this essay concerns Saint Augustine's treatise *De Musica* (*On Music*); and in Augustine's culture, music was largely monophonic. That is to say, the music of Greek and Roman antiquity was mainly characterized by rhythm and melody, rather than the rich, multi-voiced polyphony of later Western music.[1] There were no fugues, in other words; nor were there choirs divided up into soprano, alto, tenor, and bass parts. What is more, *De Musica* isn't even directly concerned with musical tones or notes; rather, it is an extended study of musical rhythm. For these reasons, it would be inaccurate to discuss *De Musica* and then describe this essay as a consideration of "harmony."

And yet, this essay *is* about harmony. The idea of harmony pervades Augustine's treatise, although it mainly appears in words like "relationship," "measure," "proportion," and "ratio." So while he never would have heard anything remotely like Brahms—or, for that matter, The Beach Boys—Augustine nevertheless believed that *harmony* was central to the experience of music, and this was an idea he shared in common with many other ancient writers. Augustine (and again, many other ancients), thought and wrote studies of music because they believed that this musical experience of harmony was profoundly significant—not just musically and aesthetically, but also ethically, philosophically, and spiritually.

Of course, we might well ask: if Augustine's "harmony" is not the lush multi-voiced harmonies modern western listeners are familiar with—then what is it?[2] That is an important question and one to which we will return. We should begin, however, with a short overview of Augustine's *De Musica*.

AUGUSTINE'S *DE MUSICA*

De Musica is one of the first works that Augustine composed after his conversion to Christianity. It is, basically, a textbook on poetic and musical rhythm, written in the form of a dialogue between a master and his student. Most of it is also—truth be told—pretty boring reading. It is not particularly well known. One author observes that "it is not much studied nowadays, even by Augustinian specialists."[3] What is more, modern readers may be puzzled that this great Father of the church would have undertaken such a study in the first place. Why would a theologian write a treatise on musical rhythm? The Master in Augustine's dialogue offers this answer:

> We shall try and know more thoroughly by its place in this discipline *what proportion is* and *how great is its authority in all things.*[4]

Music *matters*, Augustine tells us, because it teaches us about proportion. *De Musica*'s definition of music also suggests this idea of proportion. Music, we are told, "*est scientia bene modulandi*"—to paraphrase: "music is the art and science of maintaining measure well."[5]

But perhaps all of this doesn't clarify things very much. We might ask for instance—what exactly does Augustine mean by "proportion" (or "measure")? And what does proportion have to do with music? And, finally—what does it mean to say that proportion has "authority in all things"?

MUSIC AND RATIO

The Master and student begin their study of rhythm by considering time and number. Durations of time, they agree, can be short or long. What is more, these lengths of time can be related to one another as a ratio:

> What we call "of long duration" or "not of long duration" is capable of such measurements and numbers that one motion is to another as two to one. . . . And again that one movement is to another as two to three. . . . And so it is possible to run through the rest of the numbers[6]

Here we begin to see what Augustine means by "proportion" or "ratio"[7] in music. A ratio or proportion expresses the *relationship* between two or more things, and this, the Master argues, is the essence of rhythm. Consider, to begin with, a single beat or a single rhythmic pulse. What does it mean for this beat to be "long" or "short"? Certainly not that it lasts some fixed period of time—as if a short beat were .43 seconds and a long beat 1.32 seconds, or something like that. Rather, the long-ness or shortness of a beat refers to its relationship to the beats around it. The same is true, in fact, of modern rhythmic notation. "Half note" doesn't designate a particular length of time, but rather a particular relationship or proportion: it is twice as long as a quarter note; half as long as a full measure in common time. This is the same idea that the Master draws attention to. Even the most basic element of music—a single note—functions as a long note or a short note only by virtue of its relationship to other notes around it. So, the Master will point out in the last book of the treatise: "nothing is large of itself in space and time-stretches, but [only] with respect to something shorter; and again nothing is small of itself, but [only] with respect to something larger."[8]

If proportion or relationship plays a part in determining whether a particular beat is short or long, it is even more important in establishing a *rhythm.* How, the Master asks, does a single beat become a "rhythm"? And the answer is: a beat becomes a rhythm by being related to other beats. In fact the Master observes, different rhythms are *nothing other* than various sorts of relationships between beats—two short beats followed by a long beat; two long beats followed by a short beat; four short beats, and so on. A rhythm *just is* the proportion or ratio between different beats. In the same way, different meters and different sorts of verse arise by grouping rhythms into different sorts of relationships (three groups of long-long-short; four stanzas of three groups of long-long-short, and so on).

So what sets one rhythm apart from another is not that the two are made of different "stuff." It is not, for instance, as if some rhythms are composed of beats and others are not. Similarly, what sets a pleasing or correct meter apart from a displeasing one is not that one lacks or another possesses a rhythmic pulse. All of these different patterns are composed of the same basic element—the single beat, or rhythmic pulse. What distinguishes a trochee from an iamb from an anapaest is simply *how these different beats are placed in relationship to one another.* (So, a trochee simply is the proportion "long-short;" an iamb is the proportion "short-long;" an anapaest is the proportion "short-short-long," and so on.) And again, the same is true of modern musical rhythms. Terms like "samba" or "jazz waltz" or "polka" are short-hand for a complex set of relationships; various kinds of ratios and proportions. All of this begins to get us close to what Augustine means when he speaks about proportion or ratio in music. Sounds *become music* by being in a particular sort of relationship to each other. In fact, a given rhythm or piece of music *is* a particular set of ordered relationships between sounds.

As I mentioned at the outset, Augustine's treatise is concerned with rhythm, but we could extend this same principle to melody and harmony. Consider what it means to hear a group of notes as a melody. I can begin the tune "The Old Gray Mare" on the note E, or G, or B flat—in fact, on any pitch at all. This simple act of transposition is possible because the tune "The Old Gray Mare" does not consist in a certain set of pitches, but in a certain set of relationships between tones (or degrees of the scale). When we hear a melody *as* a melody, the question our ear asks of each sound is not: "Are you an A or a C sharp?" Still less does it ask "Are you 440 cycles per second?" Instead it asks: "Where do you stand in relation to the other tones in this melody?"[9] Indeed one standard music theory textbook defines tonality as "a process of establishing the *relationship* of . . . tones."[10]

The various parts of a phrase, a melody, or a rhythm take on their meaning according to their place within a musical hierarchy—a system of relationship based upon differentiated roles, qualities, and functions.[11] Hearing sounds as music means hearing them in terms of their relationship to one another. It means discerning both the distinct parts, and how they relate to each other.

THE NUMBERS OF MUSIC

There is still another way in which Augustine discerns proportion or ratio at work in music. This kind of proportion makes itself evident when we ask how the phenomenon of music itself arises. In the last book, the Master in Augustine's dialogue considers a hymn written by Augustine's early mentor in the faith, Ambrose. Consider the hymn *Deus Creator Omnium*, the Master says. It has its own order, its own character, its own pleasing proportion of parts. But where does this order and proportion come from?

> Is it to be said these numbers are only in the sound heard, or also in the hearer's sense belonging to the ears [*sensus qui ad aures pertinet*], or also in the act of the reciter, or, because the verse is known, in our memory too?[12]

Where are the numbers of music? The hymn the Master is referring to, like all rhythms, consists of a series of "numbers"—that is to say, ratios and relationships. But where do these numbers come from?

For instance, the Master says, these ratios and patterns may originate:

> *"in the sound heard"*—that is, in the physical, acoustical properties of the music; *or*
> *in the hearer's sense*—that is, in workings of our ears and aural processing; *or*
> *in the act of the reciter*—in the way some performer controls the sound and fills it with meaning; *or*
> *in the memory because we have learned it*—in the conventions we have learned from our musical culture; *or*
> *in the judgment*—in our own active construction of musical meaning.[13]

The Master's list reads like a syllabus of alternatives from the philosophy of art! Does musical harmony reside in *sounds*, or in *us*? And if in us, does it arise from the passive response of our physical senses? Or from the active engagement of our minds? Is music a product of the physical world? Does it arise from frequency vibrations and wave forms? Or is it socially constructed—an entirely contingent arrangement of sounds learned from our culture? Is our musical sense learned or innate? Is musical harmony created or discovered? Does musical meaning come from the composer, the sound, or the listener? *In which of these do we find music?* With a simplicity which confounds all of these oppositions, the disciple responds to the Master—correctly: *"In all of them, I think."*[14]

This is the second, profound sense in which *De Musica* associates music with "harmony." For Augustine, all of these different aspects of music—physical sound, our physical perception, the conventions of a musical culture, our own active judgment of sound—they all possess "number" of some sort, and when we recite a hymn like *Deus Creator Omnium*, all of these numbers sound. In fact, the Master suggests, music not only includes all of these elements; the experience of music *depends* on holding all of these different elements together in proper ratio and relationship. Music depends on "proportion" and "ratio" at the very deepest level. Music is only possible by bringing sensation and imagination, the physical world and the social world, cultural practice and individual judgment together in relation. Remove any one of these elements and you have something other than and less than music.

It is in this way, Augustine believes, that music ushers us into the world of *ratio*—a Latin word that means both "ratio" (in the sense we use that term in contemporary English) and "reason" or "rationality" (*ratio*-nality). Music sounds out for us a world in which each thing occupies its own place, in right proportion and relation to every other thing; in which a winsome whole emerges from each part contributing its unique and distinctive voice. Music tells us that the world is this sort of place, in which relationship is possible; in which physiological reactions, social conventions, mental processes, and external physical realities can all fit together in something wonderful and tuneful.

HARMONY AS PROPORTION

This description allows us to address one of the questions we raised earlier—what does Augustine mean by "harmony"? As I mentioned earlier, although Augustine never heard an eight-voice chorale, he was deeply interested in *harmony*, understood in the sense we've been describing it here: an attractive and meaningful whole that emerges as disparate elements are drawn together. Moreover, *harmony* describes a distinctive way of being "drawn together." Harmony is not "combination" or "mixture," in which two elements merge to form some third thing. It is not "union" or "absorption," in which one element assimilates another. Nor is it "compromise" or "give and take," in which a middle ground is staked out between two elements, or in which two elements alternate. Rather, harmony is a whole which depends upon its elements remaining uniquely what they are. It is a union which allows, and indeed, demands continued distinction.

This is the ideal of "harmony" that Plato, Pythagoras, and others had in mind when they spoke of right relation between the elements of one's own person, or right relation between the various elements of society in terms of musical harmony.[15] Even more famously, these ancient writers appealed to musical consonance to describe the proportional order of the cosmos. Writing a century after Augustine, the Christian scholar Boethius articulated the idea of a "music of the spheres" (*musica mundana*):

> The orbits of the stars are joined by such a harmony that nothing so perfectly structured, so perfectly united, can be imagined. For some stars drift higher, others lower, and they are all moved with such an equal amount of energy that a fixed order of their courses is reckoned through their diverse inequalities. Thus there must be some fixed order of musical modulation (*ordo modulationis*) in this celestial motion.[16]

In speaking of harmony in this way, these writers were not suggesting that music somehow *creates* a balanced human being or a just society. Neither were they saying that music simply *illustrates* some human, social, or cosmic ideal. Rather, music offers us a genuine insight into how things are (or in some instances, into how things should be). It provides us with an unusually clear and easily grasped instance of a phenomenon—that of "harmony"—which extends beyond music. As we listen to music, we learn easily and intuitively the principles of harmony, proportion, and right relation that we might otherwise only learn painstakingly. Augustine explains this some years after the composition of *De Musica*, in a letter to Memorius:

> The powers belonging to numbers in all kinds of movements are most easily studied as they are presented in sounds, and this study furnishes a way of rising to the higher secrets of truth, by paths gradually ascending, so to speak, in which Wisdom pleasantly reveals herself, and in every step of providence meets those who love her.[17]

Music speaks to us of a world in which there is relation and order; in which an exquisite concord emerges from a multitude of elements.

Plainly, our understanding of the world is in many respects vastly different than that of Pythagoras, Plato, or Augustine. Nevertheless, many in our own time have recognized the same "unitive capacity" of music[18] praised in *De Musica*. The sociologist Tia De Nora speaks of the ability of music "as it plays in real time and as it is replayed in memory . . . to organize its users."[19] Similarly, in working with those with neurological disorders, neuroscientist Oliver Sacks has noted

> the power of music to organize—and to do this efficaciously (as well as joyfully!), when abstract or schematic forms of organization fail. Indeed it

is especially dramatic, as one would expect, precisely when no other form of organisation will work.[20]

Gesturing toward the Pythagoreans, Sacks suggests that there is indeed

a harmonic sensibility, perhaps allied to that of music. . . . One's soul is "harmonical" whatever one's IQ, and perhaps the need to find or feel some ultimate harmony or order is a universal of the mind."[21]

Philosopher Kathleen Higgins closely echoes the observations of Augustine when she points out "music's role in 'harmonizing' our powers—physical, emotional and intellectual." "Music," she observes, "enlists the entire 'self.' "[22]

These comments suggest that *De Musica's* reflections on music are not simply wild metaphysical speculation. Instead, they point to a central feature of our human experience of music, namely: harmony, proportion, ratio, and relation. This is the fundamental pulse which beats beneath all the rhythmic elaborations of *De Musica*. Musically, it is a study of how sounds stand in relation to sounds, syllables in relation to other syllables, and beats to other beats. In terms of its psychology of music, it is a reflection on how different levels of perception stand in relation to one another, depending upon, informing, judging, and completing one another. By "enlisting the entire self" in this way, music allows one an experience of order within oneself. And in addition to all of this, Augustine believes that music speaks of harmony at a cosmological and even a spiritual level.

THE RATIO OF REDEMPTION

Music, in fact, turns out to be one of the clearest ways of understanding one of Augustine's central insights. Before converting to Christianity, Augustine spent a number of years as a Manichaean. Manichaeans believed that there are two opposite and equal principles in the universe: Light, goodness, and spirit on the one side; darkness, evil, and matter on the other. One clear advantage of this Manichaean theology, from Augustine's perspective, was that it absolves God of any responsibility for any evil and suffering in the world. Is there sickness and suffering and death? These arise from the Prince of Darkness and the world of matter. If however one embraces the Christian vision of reality, then how are we to account for evil and suffering? Where does evil originate, if one says along with Genesis 1 that *all* of creation—the material as well as the immaterial world—has its origin in one good and perfect Creator?

Augustine's insight as he considered this dilemma was that evil is not a "thing" created by God, or even by some evil Prince of Darkness. Rather, evil is nothing but a disordering of what is good. Evil and suffering arise when good things are arrayed in a wrong order and relationship. Sin, for instance, is a *loss* of order:

Sin arises... only if a *disordered* fixation on lower goods draws us off from better and higher goods, and thus from the highest good of all, you, my God, your truth, your law .... They cannot match my God, who made them all, since he delights the just man, and is delight itself for those 'who keep their hearts in order'.[23]

The sins of greed or covetousness for instance, do not arise because the physical matter of silver and gold are inherently evil. These sins don't even arise from *loving* silver and gold. These material things are created by God and are beautiful! The love of silver and gold only becomes sin when that love is wrongly ordered—when we love these things more than we love God or our neighbor. So in the final book of *De Musica* the Master observes, "that soul keeps order that, with its whole self, loves Him above itself, that is, God, and fellow souls as itself. In virtue of this love it orders lower things and suffers no disorder from them." Avoiding evil, in other words, does not mean avoiding the material world. It means being "properly ordered." It means learning—perhaps even from music—*what proportion is* and *how great is its authority in all things.* It turns out that the difference between beauty and ugliness, whether in music or in the spiritual life, is not the difference between spirit and matter, but the difference between ordered or disordered relationships.

So when Augustine describes the Celestial City in his *City of God*, he describes it, above all, as a place of pleasing proportion and right relationship:

The peace of the body then consists in the duly proportioned arrangement of its parts. The peace of the irrational soul is the harmonious repose of the appetites, and that of the rational soul the harmony of knowledge and action. The peace of body and soul is the well-ordered and harmonious life and health of the living creature. Peace between man and God is the well-ordered obedience of faith to eternal law. Peace between man and man is well-ordered concord. Domestic peace is the well-ordered concord between those of the family who rule and those who obey. Civil peace is a similar concord among the citizens. The peace of the celestial city is the perfectly ordered and harmonious enjoyment of God, and of one another in God. The peace of all things is the tranquillity [sic] of order. Order is the distribution which allots things equal and unequal, each to its own place.

What will the heavenly city look like, according to Augustine? It will be a place of right relation between God and humanity; between human beings; even between the different elements of our own selves. All of these, which now jostle against one another, will be "perfectly ordered and harmonious."

Is it possible then that one reason music affects us so deeply is because it anticipates, and at least faintly, enacts the reconciliation for which all of creation is longing? Here, in music, the material and immaterial, the physical and intentional, the social and individual are brought together in harmony, in fit proportion and right ratio; for a moment at least, no longer at war with one another, but each singing its part within a universal polyphony. Perhaps in music, we hear at times an intimation of the Creation *as it will be.*

DEUS CREATOR OMNIUM

There is one thing more. According to *De Musica*, music is a matter of ratio and relation, and of maintaining right ratio between its physical, ethical, and intentional components. Relation however, is only possible in a certain kind of universe. If the universe is a grand song (as Augustine calls it in the last book of *De Musica*) there must be a conductor; a composer. There must be someone who has tuned the strings and who keeps the beat, so that it is possible for all of these elements to sing together in a pleasing harmony.

In *De Musica*, Augustine argues that our experience of music expresses— more than that—*depends upon* the harmony of (among other things) neurological structures, intentional imaginative perception, the physical stuff of musical sound, and the traditions and norms of individual cultures. How is it that in such a diverse and disparate creation—a world of visible and invisible, objective and subjective realities—such harmonies are possible? Augustine believes that our very experience of music suggests that "all things whatever and of any size are made from one beginning ... by which they are joined together in charity as one and one gift from one." This harmony, this *ratio*-nality that we experience in music, is only possible in a certain sort of universe. God, the sovereign, God, who has made all things (*Deus Creator Omnium*), is the guarantor and ground of the unity and relatedness of all creation, and as such, the ground of the possibility of music. Because "all things were created by Him and for Him," every voice in Creation sings *Deus Creator Omnium*, each part fitting together in a glittering, ineffably complex harmony.

Endnotes

1   Carl Dahlhaus, et al. "Harmony," in *Grove Music Online. Oxford Music Online*, http://www.oxford-musiconline.com/subscriber/article/grove/music/50818 (accessed May 15, 2009).

2   "In Greek music, from which derive both the concept and the appellation, 'harmony' signified the combining or juxtaposing of disparate or contrasted elements—a higher and a lower note. The combining of notes simultaneously was not a part of musical practice in classical antiquity: *harmonia* was merely a means of codifying the relationship between those notes that constituted the framework of the tonal system. In the course of history it was indeed not the meaning of the term 'harmony' that changed but the material to which it applied and the explanations given for its manifestation in music." Dalhaus, et al. *Grove Music Online*.

3   Jamie James, *The Music of the Spheres: Music, Science, and the Natural Order of the Universe* (New York: Copernicus, 1993), 71.

4   Augustine, *De Musica*, tr. R. C. Taliaferro, The Fathers of the Church: Writings of Saint Augustine,

II (New York: Cima Publishing, 1947), I, xii, 23, tr. 200. My emphasis.

5   *De Musica*, I. ii, 2. The translation of the key term *modulandi* is problematic. Commentators have variously rendered it as "measuring" (Brian Brennan "Augustine's *De Musica*," *Vigiliae Christianae* 42 (1988), 272); "mensurating" (Taliaferro, *De Musica*); or "modulating." "Measuring" has the virtue of making explicit the etymological link to "measure" which Augustine himself draws out in his text: "[*modulari*] is taken from 'measure' [*modus*], since in all things well made measure [*modus*] must be observed." The weakness of "measuring" is that it carries no sense of being a specialized musical term, which *modulandi* seems to bear in Augustine's text. I also have glossed the word as "maintaining measure" to draw out the idea that this is not a single act of taking a measurement, but an active, ongoing keeping of measure.

6   *De Musica*, I, viii, 14 , tr. 189.

7   Taliaferro observes that throughout the work, "there is a continuous play on the Latin word *ratio*, which means both ratio and reason." (*De Musica*, 194, footnote 8). Understanding the full lexical range of this word is essential to a correct interpretation of *De Musica*. This single term embraces both the concept of "reason," and that of "balance, proportion and right relation."

8   *De Musica*, VI. vii (19).

9   "What makes a melody is not properly speaking, the tones but the relations between tones.... To hear a melody is thus first of all to hear a sequence of tones which stand in specific relation to one another in respect to pitch and tones." Victor Zuckerkandl, *Man the Musician* (Princeton, N.J.: Princeton University Press, 1973), 91.

10 Walter Piston, *Harmony*, 5th Edition. , rev. and exp. Mark Devoto (New York, London: Norton, 1987), 53. Emphasis mine.

11 "The concept of the hierarchic ordering of pitch content has in one manifestation or another served as a basis for musical structure since the earliest stages in the Western tradition." Wallace Berry, *Structural Functions in Music* (New York: Dover, 1976), 27. For this same idea, see also Victor Zuckerkandl, *Sound and Symbol: Music and the External World*, tr. Willard R. Trask (Princeton, N. J. : Princeton University Press, 1973/1956), 36. as well as Roger Scruton, *The Aesthetics of Music* (Oxford: Clarendon Press, 1997); e.g. 35, 248, 249.

12 *De Musica*, VI, ii, tr. 326.

13 This fifth option is not given in the master's first statement of the problem, but emerges in the discussion which follows.

14 *De Musica*. My emphasis.

15 To name just a few of many examples, see Plato, *Republic* 443d–e, where "harmony" is used to describe the balanced relationship between the various elements of one's own person. Similarly, in *Republic* 432a, "harmony" is used to characterize right relationship between the various parts of society. And in Plato's *Timaeus*, 32a–37d, 47c–d, "harmony" and proportion characterize the diverse unity of both the cosmos and the soul.

16 Boethius, *De Institutione Musica*. Latin text at http://www.chmtl.indiana.edu/tml/6th-8th/ BOEDIM1_TEXT.html. Translation from Calvin M. Bower, *Boethius' The Principles of Music, an Introduction, Translation and Commentary* (PhD Dissertation, George Peabody College for Teachers, 1966), 44. See also *The Consolation of Philosophy*, II, viii tr. V. E. Watts (London: Penguin, 1969), 77.

17 Augustine, "Letter CI" *The Letters of St Augustine*, vol. 1 tr. R. G. Cunningham, *A Select Library of The Nicene and Post-Nicene Fathers of the Christian Faith*, ed. Philip Schaff [text on-line] (Edinburgh: T & T Clark), available at http://www.ccel.org

18 Edward Foley, *Music in Ritual*, quoted in Anthony Ruff, *Sacred Music and Liturgical Reform: Treasures and Transformations* (Chicago : Hillenbrand Books, 2007), 7.

19 Tia DeNora, *Music in Everyday Life* (Cambridge: Cambridge University Press, 2000), 7.

20 Oliver Sacks, *The Man Who Mistook his Wife for a Hat and Other Clinical Tales* (New York: Harper Perennial, 1970) 186.

21 Sacks, 207.

22 Higgins, 5.

23 Augustine, *Confessions*, tr. Gary Wills (New York: Penguin, 2002), 33. "When accordingly it is inquired, whence is evil, it must first be inquired, what is evil, which is nothing else than corruption, either of the measure, or the form, or the order, that belong to nature." Augustine, *Concerning the Nature of Good, Against the Manichæans*, chapter iv, tr. Albert Newman, in *A Select Library of The Nicene and Post-Nicene Fathers of the Christian Faith*, ed. Philip Schaff [text on-line] (Edinburgh: T & T Clark). Available at http://www.ccel.org/ccel/schaff/npnf104.iv.x.vi.html, accessed December 18, 2012.

24 Augustine, *Confessions*, 32–33.

25 Augustine, *De Musica*, VI, xiv, 46.

26 *De Musica*, I, xii, 23, tr. 200. My emphasis.

27 Augustine, *City of God Against the Pagans*, XIX, xiii, in The Select Library of The Nicene and Post-Nicene Fathers of the Christian Church, ed. Philip Schaff, Vol. II, tr. Marcus Dods. Available at CCEL http://www.ccel.org/ccel/schaff/npnf102.iv.XIX.13.html, accessed May 25, 2009.

28 *De Musica*, VI, xvii, 56, tr. 375.

LISTENING
between the lines

The books or the music in which we thought the beauty was located will
betray us if we trust to them; it was not in them, it only came through them,
and what came through them was longing. The things—the beauty, the
memory of our own past—are good images of what we really desire; but if
they are mistaken for the thing itself they turn into dumb idols, breaking
the hearts of their worshipers. For they are not the thing itself; they are
only the scent of a flower we have not found, the echo of a tune we have
not heard, news from a country we have never yet visited.
   —C.S. Lewis, *The Weight of Glory*

We squirmed and fidgeted in our seats as the sounds of a thousand "electric
insects" enveloped us and besieged our virginal ears. In and out they flew as they
screeched and screamed all around the room. The pulsating movements were
mesmerizing as much as they were disconcerting, flitting about our heads. Yet
this encounter did not stop with the entomological immersion. Primitive dance-
like percussion accompanied by a ghostly flute player, echoing fragments of a
long forgotten melody soon followed these menacing insects. People chanted in
various languages, carrying with them sinister overtones. The players plucked
their instruments and struck them in all manner of unnatural ways as allusion-
ing to music often associated with death. It was apparent to all of us in that high
school music class that we were experiencing the string quartet in an entirely different way than we had before. Never had such a cacophony of noises resonated
in our ears, at least not in any of the classical music concerts we had attended.

Yet in the midst of that chaos, within those primitive, ghostly sounds, there were moments of a mystical tranquility that shone like the sun piercing through clouds of a summer thunderstorm. The serenity imposed in those quieter moments greatly overshadowed the noise and clamor that had preceded it. It was, at times very much like God speaking out of the storm to Job.

The composer of this remarkable, unsettling, and at times sublime music knew his craft well. His understanding of instrumentation, how to pace the material, and balance disparate elements within a composition was clearly someone who had mastered the art of the composer. To my delight this was my first experience with what may be called, for lack of a better term, contemporary art music and more specifically the Avant-garde.[1] *Black Angels* was composed by the American composer George Crumb[2] and is scored for electric string quartet. I had heard other string quartets before, particularly those by Joseph Haydn and Wolfgang Amadeus Mozart. What I hadn't heard though was a traditionally classical ensemble stretched to the limits of their instruments, playing extended techniques[3] exploited to the fullest by Crumb. Alongside the multitude of techniques each instrument of the ensemble was also amplified. Given the institutionalized performance practice[4] I had been exposed to so far I never thought you could do such a thing. Such an affront to tradition would have been thought anathema, but with all that I had just experienced, this pushing of the sonic envelope had me, as a teenage fan of all things heavy metal, salivating with delight[5].

What attracted me most was that someone had the vision to step outside the box of classical music, or music in general for that matter, and approach the raw materials of music making with new ears. It was as if Crumb knew that the musical language of the common practice period[6] was insufficient for what he needed to say. He needed to create a new language out of the old.

The hurdle one must cross in listening to music that is written in a language not understood is that it requires determined attention. As a listener one cannot sit back and take a passive role. Instead one is forced to either engage in an active role as a listener or to disengage entirely from trying to comprehend the work[7]. Think of it as traveling to a foreign country where you do not speak the language. You can choose either to immerse yourself in the culture and try to negotiate the barriers imposed by the linguistic differences or to ignore them altogether because no one speaks your language.

This is, in fact, where I think we find ourselves as a culture, musically speaking. Generally, consumption of music in the West is marked more by genre classification and album sales rather than artistic sensibilities. This is one reason the parade of styles, such as country and alternative country, heavy metal and speed metal, emo and goth rock and so on, never seems to end. The problem is not necessarily with the multiple genres that can be used to classify various musics. The difficulty comes when we restrict our listening routine to a particular genre and do not venture outside it. Anything that is not in a language we are familiar with we automatically screen out. In the process of boxing ourselves in, we find we are eventually unable to discern our own aesthetic habits.

This is important because of the ability of music to act as a vehicle of discovery. We do not normally speak of music, or think of it, as a means of discovering something that can have a profound impact on the way in which we perceive the world around us. More commonly we think of music as something that should make us feel a certain way , an emotional stimulant or narcotic, or even to reinforce certain our own habitual aesthetic preferences. As Jeremy Begbie puts it,

> To speak of music as a vehicle of discovery will strike many as decidedly odd, so deeply ingrained in many of us is the idea that music can only express, confirm, or perhaps intensify what we already know or feel.

The ability of music to open up for us the wonders of creation can be quite profound. Sit down at a piano sometime and strike a single key. Listen to the sound as it changes over time. At first there is the percussive attack of the hammer. Immediately following this attack the sound starts to decay. If you listen closely you may notice subtle changes to the character of the sound. Perhaps you hear higher notes that emerge followed by lower pitched sounds or the other way around. If the piano is out of tune with itself there may be slow moving waves of sound that undulate over time or there may even be a violent beating of note against note creating a discordant clash of noise. By following this very simple experiment we can learn to approach the sound world in way in which we may not be accustomed. We are able to gain insight into the very nature and fabric of sound.

I'd like to look at several examples of how composers have explored the sound world in their own unique way in order to explore the created order. These composers, including myself, span the centuries of music history, from the Renaissance to the present day.

The first composer I will examine is Claudio Monteverdi. He was an Italian composer who lived from 1567–1643 and his musical output marks a transitional period from the Renaissance to the Baroque as he anticipated the coming stylistic changes of the seventeenth century. Monteverdi is known for his madrigals, sacred music, and more importantly the many operas he composed.

The music at hand in this discussion is one of his earliest sacred works, the *Vespro della Beata Vergine,* which borrows the introduction from his famous opera, *L'Orfeo.* This work is part of the evening vespers of the Roman Catholic Church and the movement we will consider sets the following text:

Deus, in adiutorium meum intende.
Domine, ad adiuvandum me festina.

Gloria Patri, et Filio, et Spiritui Sancto.
Sicut erat in principio, et nunc et semper, et in saecula saeculorum. Amen.
Alleluia.

O God, come to my assistance.
O Lord, make haste to help me.
Glory be to the Father, and to the Son, and to the Holy Spirit.
As it was in the beginning is now and ever shall be world without end.
Amen. Alleluia.

At the opening of the movement there is a tenor solo that intones the opening line, "Deus, in adiutorium meum intende." This solo should not be considered superfluous as just a part of church tradition at the time. In fact, it sets the tone for what is to come with the entrance of the choir and orchestra. In performance this single voice echoes the solitary prayer, seeking God for assistance. This mirrors the cries of the psalmist who often cried out to God for help, such as in Psalm 31:

Turn your ear to me,
come quickly to my rescue;
be my rock of refuge,
a strong fortress to save me.

Immediately following this lone voice, the choir and orchestra suddenly enter with all the adulation and joy they can muster. They echo this call for the Lord to come quickly with an intensity that foreshadows the great choral works of George Friedrich Handel and other Baroque masters.

Example 1: Choral entrance of "Domine ad adiuvandum"

This potent and fervent cry for help is punctuated by an instrumental ritornello[8] that is quite distinct from the choral portions. The contrast happens on several levels, all of which are striking in their placement; but for our purposes, I want to look at two of these. As can be seen on the above example, the choral music is in a straightforward meter of 2/2, meaning there are two beats in the measure and the half-note gets the beat. Think of a clock with the second hand making a regular and continual movement. This is much like what Monteverdi has done in this instance with this regular pulsation. This pulse is accentuated by the orchestral parts, especially with the trumpets echoing each other in the upper registers of their instruments.

The metrical regularity of the choral portions are then juxtaposed against the strictly instrumental portions. The instrumental portions are in a triple meter, a meter that has a lilting feel about it (think of the famous Christmas carol *What Child is This?* and you'll get the idea). Where the previous choral sections have the seemingly unstoppable drive of a train, the instrumental portions seem to take a more winsome, dance-like posture with its short-long-short-long note divisions. The triple meter ritornello can be seen in the following example.

Example 2: Instrumental ritornello

Harmonically these sections are contrasted as well. As seen in Example 1 the choral music is built on a single chord. Notice that the voices do not deviate at all from the note they start on. Contrast this with the instrumental section where there are regular chord changes on each beat giving a sense of harmonic motion or movement. This contrast gives the impression that one is listening to two completely different works. There seems to be no continuity between the two.

Yet as we arrive at the end of the work we find the genius of the composer shining through in magnificent fashion. Monteverdi takes these two disparate elements—a harmonically static, metrically regular choral section and a harmonically rich, dance-like instrumental section—and blends them into a single entity. The disjuncture of two completely dissimilar musics is brought together as the choir sings their alleluias over the rich, harmonic palette of the instrumental ritornello becoming "... a large-scale vocal and instrumental sinfonia, introducing the entire opulent vesper service with its own musical brilliance."[9] Monteverdi has taken the fundamental materials of music and exploited them in ways that draw out of them their full potential. It is as though that which was broken has now been healed, that which was apart has now been brought together.

The second composer I'd like to look at is Claude Debussy, the French Impressionist. Through his music, Debussy began to look at harmony in a new way seeking to redefine how we understand tonality or how we determine where home base is, musically speaking. This is because of the predominance of major and minor tonality in Western music where tonality is governed by a hierarchy of notes with one note serving as home base. When the music moves away from that home base there is a tension created that is not resolved until there is a return to it. Debussy wanted to think differently about how we organize notes so he experimented with scales and harmonic systems that were not conventional to Western tonal music. It was through this kind of work that Debussy was able to create the lush, esoteric harmonic landscapes that he is known for.

The work of his I'd like to explore is *L'isle joyeuse* for solo piano. But before we move on, a quick study of musical acoustics is in order. Doing so will help us understand what Debussy was after in this work.

At the root of all musical sound is what we call the overtone series. It is the most fundamental musical phenomenon we are aware of. Many of the sounds we hear are in some way related to it such as car horns, human speech, and even whale calls. The overtone series is in essence the cornerstone of all musical sound. The best way to understand the overtone series is to think of a vibrating string, as in the case of a piano or guitar. For those instruments to sound a string must vibrate either by plucking or striking so as to produce a musical pitch. As it vibrates across its full length it will produce what is called the *fundamental* pitch. This pitch is what we then identify as middle C or A or F sharp, whatever the case may be. Yet the string does not stop vibrating at that level. In fact it does so at many more levels. It vibrates at half its length (1/2), in thirds (1/3), fourths (1/4), and so on (see Example 3). This series of subsequent vibrations is called the overtone series because these are tones produced over the fundamental pitch.

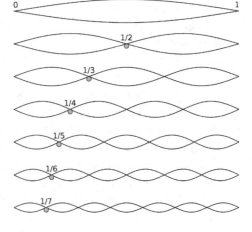

Example 3: Various ratios of a vibrating string

If one were to notate the overtone series it would look something like this:

Example 4: Notated overtone series

The series above starts on the note A with the first overtone being an A an octave higher. Following this we have an E, then another A, C–sharp, and so the series progresses. The reason this is important is that every musical tone you hear is constructed from this fundamental structure. Whether it is a piano, a guitar, or even a clarinet, you are hearing not just one note but rather a conglomeration of them. It is this collection of notes that is the root of all musical sound.

Now, you may be asking what this has to do with Debussy and actual music. As we noted above, Debussy introduced many new scales and harmonies into the vernacular that was Western music at the turn of the century. In his time it was a fairly common understanding that the entire canon of Western music was built on the foundation of certain scales, forming the concept of tonality.[10] Through his experimentation with new scales Debussy was challenging the prevailing notions of acceptable tonalities and in essence turning his back on the ensconced musical establishment. He was in no small way saying, "I want to explore new ways of hearing and playing music."

Because of this experimentation Debussy began to listen to music in different ways than he had before. This then led him to explore the overtone series as a viable means of harmonic organization. What makes this unusual is that the overtone series had not been thought of as a means controlling or organizing musical structure. In most Western music one can point to a piece and say that is in the key of C major or F minor but not so with something constructed from the overtone series. In *L'isle joyeuse* Debussy reorients our understanding of what notes are acceptable.

At the beginning of the piece there is a dizzying array of chromaticisms that blossom in the upper register of the piano, emanating from a single note, a C-sharp. Within the span of a few seconds the listener has nothing to hold onto in the sense of a harmonic or tonal center. When you hear it you cannot say you have arrived at home base because the composer has completely eliminated any sense of finding it in the morass of notes.

Example 5: First measure of *L'isle joyeuse* showing chromaticism

But after this period of confused activity there is the entrance of a musical idea that acts to calm the aural turbulence and to mark the beginning of the next section and substance of the rest of the work. To achieve this Debussy takes advantage of the first tones of the overtone series seen in the previous example, A and E. Soon afterward, a melody playfully emerges into the aural landscape, distancing us from the uncertainty that marked the beginning of the work. Upon closer examination it also appears the melody corresponds very closely to the overtone series.

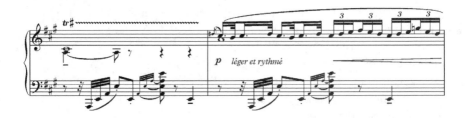

Example 6: Use of overtone series in harmony and melody

In a matter of a few seconds Debussy distances himself from the world of major and minor tonality and essentially pulls the rug out from under traditional musical practice. Yet he does not stop there, for we find that what he destroys he recreates in a new way. He displaces the traditional understanding of music's harmonic structure and replaces it with the fundamental building block of musical sound. He takes us on a journey through a landscape that is full of human creativity, one that takes the raw materials of the world and plays with them in an ingenious and joyous manner. Just as the name of the composition implies, it is a play that is full of enjoyment and is rooted in the very fabric of creation itself.

The third and final composer I'd like to look at is one that I know best, myself. This is not to laud my own work over others but rather to show how exploring and experiencing the kinds of music we have discussed have had an influence on a living composer exercising his creative calling in the contemporary landscape.

In an interesting twist, considering my early encounter with Mr. Crumb, my output as a composer began to take on a very conservative bent. I grew increasingly disenchanted with the Avant-garde and embraced with all gusto the music of Aaron Copland,[11] Samuel Barber,[12] and even more so Ralph Vaughan Williams.[13] During this time I had become an ardent critic of the Avant-garde, echoing Vaughan Williams' mantra, "What is wrong with saying something old as long as it is said at the right time?"

Yet in the midst of my conservatism, those sounds that echoed from that early experience of *Black Angels* wouldn't let go of my imagination. There was something contained in them that continued to appeal to me. And this attraction grew as other works continued to pique my interest, works like Olivier Messiaen's[14] *Quartet for the End of Time,* Charles Ives'[15] *The Unanswered Question,* Alban Berg's[16] *Altenberglieder,* and Karlheinz Stockhausen's[17] *Gesang der Jüngelinge.*

I soon found myself asking questions about how music was structured and why, in my mind, the lines of demarcation were drawn so starkly. I saw no problem with the use of traditional tonalities, but I began to realize that our use of them to the exclusion of other means of music making was unjustified. As a Christian I saw that to bypass or ignore music which does not fit within our own predetermined categories was to overlook what God has done and is doing among us. I soon saw the possibilities inherent within creation as a glorious gift from God as He has given us our imaginations for use in working with the raw materials of the universe. He hasn't given us a system that says we must do music this way or that, but rather God has given His creatures the ability to mirror Him in His own creativity. We get these building blocks and work with them in such a way as to bring order in all the diverse ways we do as people created in the image of God. We are free to create music that rings with the beauty of God's cosmos because He has endowed us with these gifts and charged us with just such a task. We get to reflect God's own creativity, or better yet, we have the privilege of imaging God in His creation.

As a Christian, theology has been an important part of my life, and how that intersects with the music I compose has been a challenge. But I found I am not alone in this endeavor. Theological reflection in music has been an interest to composers throughout history such as J. S. Bach,[18] Olivier Messiaen, and Jonathan Harvey[19] as well as others. But with this new sound world I was immersed in I was even more energized to integrate theology, faith, and music. These explorations are brought out quite deliberately in my work . . . *glass darkly. . .* for alto flute, piano, and interactive electronics.

. . . *glass darkly. . .* is a two fold meditation on the passage from I Corinthians 13. Here is how the verse reads in the King James Version that this work takes its title from—

For now we see through a glass, darkly;
but then face to face: now I know in part;
but then shall I know even as also I am known.

This verse is found at the end of one of the most famous passages in the New Testament. Chapter thirteen is an exposition of what love is: what it means to fully love someone, to be loved, and to walk and live in love and relationship with another. Paul closes this passage with the confession that at this point in our lives we cannot fully comprehend what true love looks like. We cannot live it out as it should be lived out. We are looking at love through eyes that are clouded by limitations, by the pains and shortcomings of our present lives. Yet Paul expresses great hope that one day, as Christians, we will know as we are known. That is, we will be known as intimately as one can be known by God himself and in so doing find complete satisfaction of loving and being loved.

As I think about this verse, about seeing through a glass darkly, I find that I am drawn looking for what is on the other side of the glass. "What do I see?," "What glimpses of another world would shine through?," "Can I capture a hint of what true love looks like?"

In Christian theology this true love finds its ultimate expression in the relationship between Father, Son, and Holy Spirit. It is in the Trinity that we find three distinct persons who are of one substance dwelling in perfect harmony with one another. As theologian Cornelius Plantinga says, "Each divine person harbors the others at the centre of his being. In a constant movement of overture and acceptance, each person envelops and encircles the others."[20]

As a composer these thoughts were quite intriguing in how they may influence the notes I put down on a page. How would I express these ideas musically? How would I capture in musical sounds the meaning and mystery of such ideas? This was the genesis of the work . . . *glass darkly. . .* for alto flute, piano, and interactive electronics.

The musical material, the timbres, rhythms, and harmonies themselves had to be capable of carrying the weight of just these very ideas. To put it another way, the music had to be capable of containing "the weight of glory" that is intrinsic to the theology. Therefore I knew I had to utilize a harmonic language beyond that of the standard major and minor scales. The ideas contained in this theology required something beyond tonal or even quasi-tonal pitch organization.

Just as Monteverdi exploited harmony in a new way and Debussy reoriented our ears to listen to new sonorities I needed to explore a new way of approaching the auditory world.

I chose then to take advantage of a technique championed by French composers Gerad Grisey[21] and Tristan Murail.[22] This technique is borne out of an electronic music process called *ring modulation*, a process that creates a confluence of microtones.

Before I go any further let me digress here to help in understanding this course of action. In musical terms notes are normally referred to with a particular name such as A, C-sharp, or B-flat. These notes can also be understood not just as notes but also as *frequencies*. To understand notes as frequencies it may help to think back to that vibrating string in the overtone series we discussed earlier. How fast that string vibrates determines the pitch, or frequency, of that note. This frequency is normally expressed in *hertz*. For example, a frequency of 440 hertz (Hz) is a sound wave (think vibrating string) that vibrates 440 times a second and the resultant pitch is the note A, hence the commonly used term A-440.

Ring modulation, the technique used in ... *glass darkly.* ..., is simply a process by which one multiplies two or more of these frequencies. The result is a sonority[23] that is rich with harmonic content comprised of many microtones. To understand what microtones are think of a piano keyboard. When looking at a piano you will see a pattern of alternating black and white keys. The distance between each of these keys is called a half step. Microtones are notes that find their way in between these half steps. This is very similar to the overtone series in that a ring modulated sonority is composed of many notes, most of which are not found to fit on the notes of a piano keyboard. As such, these kinds of harmonies do not fit neatly into commonly held categories such as major or minor scales.

As you can imagine the results can be quite complex so I use a computer program to help me calculate these ring modulated sonorities. One of the advantages of this program is that I can round out these frequencies to the nearest pitch I choose. This is similar to altering the overtone series to fit a particular scale. For example, if I have a pitch of 425 Hz I can round that note up to 440 Hz, the note A, or 415 Hz, the note G-sharp, if I so desire. Doing so allows me to look at, or better yet hear, a given sonority at the half step (i.e. the same as the black and white keys of the piano keyboard), the quarter step (i.e. half of a 1/2 step), and the eighth step (i.e. half of the 1/4 step). There is a fullness inherent in these types of harmonies, and I knew they had the capacity to bear the load carried within this passage from I Corinthians which is why I chose this process in creating ... *glass darkly.* ...

As I set out to finally compose this work I purposefully chose instruments whose uniqueness would allow them to express these sonorities differently. Each instrument would be able to articulate the music according to its own characteristic or identity. I took the various series of sonorities and filtered them through three different levels of resolution, the half step, quarter step, and the eighth step. This can be seen in the following example that shows how these kinds of sonorities are notated in Western notation at the 1/2 step and the 1/4 step.[24]

Example 7: Ring-modulated sonority at the 1/2 step

Example 7: Same ring-modulated sonority seen at the 1/4 step

As can be seen this is a very complex sonority made up of lots of notes. The sonority seen at the 1/2 step would be the notes the piano would play. Every note seen in this example can be found on the piano. On the other hand the flute would need to realize the notes seen at the 1/4 step as these notes do not appear on a piano keyboard, the piano is incapable of playing these without significant alteration to the instrument itself. If you compare the two examples you can see where there are similarities and divergences, given the particular resolution, with the same sonority. The process of writing actual music with this kind of material is a bit more complex than just writing these notes down on paper but notes like these are articulated throughout . . . *glass darkly*. . . such as in the following example that uses this sonority (N.B. the alto flute line is transposed):

Example 8: Excerpt from movement III of . . . *glass darkly*. . .

As each instrument plays the particular sonorities in its own unique way, what emerges is a multifaceted and multilayered representation of the given sonority. Again, the piano can only play the notes that fall on the black and white keys of the piano keyboard while the flute can more easily navigate through the microtones at the quarter step. The electronics on the other hand not only can fully realize the underlying harmonic spectrum but can also unite all three instruments through live processing.

The result is something that is sonically representational of the Corinthians passage. We are seeing, or hearing as it were, through a glass darkly, a single sonority that unites all three instruments, that binds them one to another. Yet each instrument bears its own distinct identity. Each one stands unique as it own individual and has its own role to play but yet each one is tied to the others in a relationship that is tied across the harmonic spectrum. This echos the Second Helvetic Confession of 1566 that states "... there are not three Gods, but three persons, consubstantial, coeternal, and coequal... they are joined together that they are one God; and the divine essence is common to the Father, the Son, and the Holy Spirit."

Without question there are a lot of technical challenges that must be overcome so that works like ... *glass darkly...* can exist. This kind of approach allows me to explore aspects of created reality that I could not do before. I am not limited to the confines of what I am already comfortable with but I can be stretched as a person, a musician, a Christian as to what it means to write music in light of God's own creative actions. I am able to take the most fundamental materials of musical sound and create works that have meaning beyond the novelty that is inherent in such works. I am in fact reaching into the very fabric of the created order in an attempt to draw out of it the potentialities that God has endowed it with. I want to take seriously what Gerard Manly Hopkins says about creation, that it is "charged with the Grandeur of God"[25] and therefore steward my responsibilities as well as I can as a co-creator in God's economy.

My journey as a composer is one that has taken me down many roads, having been influenced by music that stretches back centuries and through varied cultures. I have spent time with Cherokee musicians discussing the communal aspects of their music and immersed myself in the extravagant madrigals of Carlo Gesualdo. The hardcore music of bands such as DRI and The Crucified has thundered loudly in my ears as well as the lyrical Romanticism of Ralph Vaughan Williams. I have been brought low by the "Seven Last Words from the Cross" by James MacMillan and found joyful celebration in the jigs and reels of Celtic bands like Lunasa and The Chieftans. All of these musics, and many more, have fed and enriched my imagination as a musician. They all have a place in shaping how I listen to and perceive music.

The music of the West follows a similar pattern where musical trends do not

occur in isolation from one another but bear influence on subsequent generations. Our own time is unique in this history in that virtually all of the past, present, and even future of music is available at the click of a mouse. We can listen
to music that hasn't been heard in over 1,500 years while reading an interview
with a musician pioneering the use of computer technology in interactive concert
settings. This is not a time for us to shrink back into old habits of passive listening, but instead we should truly learn to listen between the lines. We are called to
engage the sound world around us and embrace the diversity afforded by God's
good creation. In doing so we recognize our roles as cultivators of creation and
assume the responsibility inherent in our call to subdue and fill the earth.

Endnotes

1   The term avant-garde refers to art that draws its inspiration from the invention and application of
    new or unconventional techniques and is therefore on the "forefront" of development in a given
    field.

2   George Crumb (1929) is an American composer of avant-garde music.

3   Extended playing techniques are the means of playing an instrument in a manner it is not usually
    associated with. For example a piano may have its strings plucked inside the instrument rather
    than by the hammers triggered by the keyboard or, as in the case of *Black Angels,* a string player
    may be called to strike the instrument with the wood of the bow as opposed to the hair of the bow.

4   Broadly speaking, performance practice refers to an approach to playing certain kinds of music
    in a manner that has been handed down from teacher to student and is informed by traditions
    inherent in a given style or genre.

5   One could easily imagine Nigel, the lead guitarist of that most fascinating of bands, Spinal Tap,
    trying to talk the first violinist into taking his amp to 11!

6   The common practice period generally denotes the practice of music making in the West from
    around 1600 to the early 1900s. Composers such as J.S. Bach, Wolfgang Amadeus Mozart, and
    Ludwig von Beethoven are clearly within this practice. Much of contemporary music in most
    genres is influenced by the tonal systems established in the common practice period.

7   Sometimes disengagement may take the form of indifference but can also be expressed by physi-
    cally walking out of a performance. Perhaps the most famous example of such extreme disen-
    gagement is the riot at Igor Stravinsky's *Le Sacre du Printemps.* This infamous moment in musical
    history is captured very well by Thomas Kelly, *First Nights; Five Musical Premiers* (New Haven, CT:
    Yale University Press, 2000).

8   A ritornello is a recurring passage of music that alternates with other contrasting material.

9   Jeffery Kurtzman, *The Monteverdi Vespers of 1610: Music, Context, and Performance* (New York:
    Oxford Press, 2000).

10 A musical scale is simply a means of putting together notes in an ascending and descending
    order. The scale is not necessarily music itself but is rather a means by which much music is
    organized and understood. There are many kinds of scales to be found in the world today but the
    most commonly used scales in Western music are the major and minor. One common concep-
    tion of the major scale is that it conveys a "happy mood" and minor scales a "sad mood" with
    the major being the most prevalent. I understand that this is a broad generalization but I do not
    think it unfair. The result of this approach, that is thinking in terms of the happy/sad contrast,
    is unfortunate as it reduces music and its organization down to only its emotive connection with
    the listener. Emotional impulses and reactions to a particular music are not wrong, but when all

music is reduced to this one common denominator, deeper levels of meaning and consideration (e.g. symbolic representations) cannot be made. Such reductionism does not take into account the myriad possibilities and implications of harmonic, rhythmic, and timbral organization. These include but are not limited to cultural trends and practices (what may mean sad in one culture may carry another meaning somewhere else), historical usage, and the presuppositions/preconditions of the listener.

11 Aaron Copland (1900-1990) was an American composer credited with establishing a distinctly American sound as opposed to one rooted in European traditions.

12 Samuel Barber (1910-1981) was a composer with roots more firmly in the European traditions but still a very distinct American voice of the twentieth century.

13 Ralph Vaughan Williams (1872-1958) was an English composer whose interest in the folk music of the British Isles did much to preserve and renew interest in those traditions.

14 Olivier Messiaen (1908-1992) was a French composer whose interests in music included theology, bird song, and the inclusion of nonwestern musical traditions in his music.

15 Charles Ives (1874-1954) was an American composer who supported himself as a successful insurance company director. He is credited as the first American to utilize contemporary avant-garde techniques.

16 Alban Berg (1885-1935) was an Austrian composer and a member of the Second Viennese School with Arnold Schoenberg, with whom he studied, and Anton Webern. The First Viennese School is usually associated with composers such a Wolfgang Amadeus Mozart, Ludwig von Beethoven, and Franz Schubert.

17 Karlheinz Stockhausen (1928-2007) was a German composer noted not only as one of the greatest visionaries of the twentieth century but he was also known for his wild eccentricities.

18 J. S. Bach (1685-1750) was a German composer of the Baroque whose work is considered some of the finest produced across all musical periods, not only musically but theologically as well. Calvin Stapert notes "[Bach's] library reveals a man with a deep and abiding interest in theology… His music shows that he applied what he learned toward achieving his goal of 'a well-appointed church music', well appointed not only musically, but also theologically." Calvin Stapert, *My Only Comfort: Death, Delieverance, and Discipleship in the music of Bach* (Grand Rapids: Eerdmans Publishing, 2000).

19 Jonathan Harvey (1935-2012) was an English composer who had been influenced by Christian, Buddhist, and Hindi theologies and philosophies.

20 Cornelius Plantiga, *Engaging God's World: A Christian Vision of Faith, Learning, and Living* (Gand Rapids, MI: Wm. B Eerdmans Publishing, 2002).

21 Gerard Grisey (1946-1988) was a French composer credited with founding the genre of "spectral music."

22 Tristan Murail (1947-) is a French composer who along with Grisey founded "spectral music." His paper "Spectra and Pixies" is an excellent introduction to spectral music. Murail, T. (1984). Spectra and Pixies. *Contemporary Music Review*, 1 (1), 157-170.

23 I prefer to use the term sonority over chord as these objects function differently than do standard chords found in common practice harmonies.

24 These processes are calculated using the program OpenMusic from IRCAM (Institut de Recherche et Coordination Acoustique/Musique). IRCAM is a French instituion founded by one of the twentieth century's most pivotal and influential musical figures Pierre Boulez.

25 Hopkins, line 1, *God's Grandeur.*

PLAYS WELL
with others

I am a performer. It seems to be in my blood. My stage premiere was at three months old when my cousins coerced me out of my mother's arms so that I could play the baby Jesus in the Christmas pageant at church. (I am told that I did a very good job and didn't cry.) As I grew older, my gifts tended toward the musical. I performed regularly in my church and small community from elementary school until I went to college, where I majored in violin (with a lot of singing thrown in).

Along the way, I mostly played classical music. This just meant that I learned to read well what was on the page. It wasn't until after college that I had friends who taught me to improvise. They would introduce a tune and ask what I wanted to play, disturbing my classical "why don't you just write something out for me" sensibilities. Eventually I was able to just jump into the mix, which widened the scope of my performance possibilities.

When I look back, I realize that I have been significantly shaped by my performative experience. My participation in various genres has altered much more than my playing or singing. My participation in music has formed my understanding and interaction with the world.

The art of playing music with others has formed me spiritually, emotionally, and intellectually. Ensemble playing has taught me to move toward others in musical space and to practice the spiritual discipline of having the eyes to see and the ears to hear. As I trained to be a theologian, music came along with me as a faithful companion, opening up theological vistas I could never have imagined on my own. Because of my experience, I teach and practice theology in such a way that I prioritize making space for others to learn, play, and sing along.

I attribute my style of teaching and doing theology to the diverse variety of ensembles that I have played in over the past decade or so. I am naturally drawn to symphonic and chamber music. However, as a church musician from a low-church tradition I have learned to play by ear and improvise from a chord chart, which has enabled me to participate in a variety of groups. In recent memory I have played everything from Brahms to Chris Tomlin to Bach to Southern Gospel music to a symphonic rendition of the music of Queen to Celtic hymns to a cover tune of Led Zeppelin's Kashmir with the band Alice in Chains. Musical experience has been 'ecumenical' for me, to say the least.

I also find that I listen to music differently than I did in the past because the more I participate the better I hear. When I listen to music, my ear searches out the depth of orchestration and the subtle contribution of the 'minor' voices. Melodies are great but I want to know what is going on in the background. This desire to hear more deeply transcends genre. I might be listening to a symphony or a string quartet but it is just as likely to be a Celtic band or even bad 80s music (was there good 80s music?). When I am actively participating in music making, I find that music speaks (or sings) and I must listen and respond. I am taken outside myself and my musical preferences are broadened and deepened. Through music making I am linked, in significant ways, to other people.

Music connects that which is deepest within our personal being to the world at large. Kathleen Marie Higgins puts it this way, "musical hearing," and I would amend this to 'musical participation,' "makes us aware of the world as a place of encounter and interaction between what is within and what is outside us."[1] No wonder we often experience music as 'spiritual'.[2] Music is a place of encounter.

In this chapter, I would like to look at (or listen to) various kinds of musicians who participate in music making, some in very unusual ways. I believe music has the power to turn us outward and connect us to others through music. Thus, I want to explore how musical participation helps us to listen better, not only to tones, but also to the people who are making music with us and for us. Through these persons and groups I hope to show the power of encounter through participation.

EVELYN GLENNIE

A number of years ago I went to hear Evelyn Glennie, one of the world's foremost percussionists, solo with the Seattle Symphony. She was amazing. She moved gracefully between the many exotic percussion instruments that spanned the front of the stage. I thought that Glennie was extremely eccentric. She was dressed casually in loose clothing so that she could move easily across the stage. She also promptly took off her shoes as she prepared to play with the orchestra. At the time I thought that she was just a free spirit making herself at home. It wasn't until years later that I found out why she removed her shoes: Evelyn Glennie is profoundly deaf. She takes off her shoes in order to 'hear' the orchestra.

It was through Thomas Riedelsheimer's documentary on Glennie, *Touch the Sound*, that I learned more about how she hears.[3] In the documentary, Glennie tells how she started going deaf at eight years old. At age eleven, when the progress of her condition became acute, she was asked what she was going to do instead of music. Her answer was that she had no intension of giving up music. It was at this point that she switched to percussion and found a very patient and extraordinary teacher.[4] She recalls how she learned to feel pitch. Her teacher started with the kettledrums and would change the pitch in varying patterns. She was soon able to identify specific pitches and intervals in different areas of her hands. Eventually she could feel pitch throughout her body. It is astounding to imagine identifying pitch through physical resonance but, as she points out in the documentary, that is how we all hear. It is just that most people feel and hear resonance through the ear. Glennie, on the other hand, hears with the whole of her physical being.

Touch the Sound follows Glennie around the world as she meets new musicians, learns about their various disciplines and then improvises with them in a variety of places. In Japan she learns the art of Japanese *taiko* drumming, which requires a disciplined practice of learning to breathe with the whole of the group. Later we see her improvising in a small café with students, as they bring out random items for her to play—plates, cans, and glasses with chopsticks as impromptu drumsticks. In New York, she is shown improvising with a tap-dancing street performer and then performing in such spaces as Grand Central Station, a high-rise rooftop, and the Guggenheim Museum. Everywhere she goes Riedelsheimer captures her interaction with the world. If Glennie feels sound, he wants the viewer to see sound.

One of the most striking parts of the film is her improvised CD project with avant-garde musician, Fred Firth.[5] For this recording project, Firth and Glennie take over an old abandoned sugar factory in Cologne, Germany, which has wide-open spaces and plenty of fun surfaces to explore. In these scenes we get a view of their playfulness.[6] They both take time to explore and interact with the space and literally play the building (and each other) like an instrument. One of my favorite scenes shows them throwing old ticker tape rolls through the air. We see and we hear the paper crinkling and popping as it falls gracefully through the open space of the factory. The whole of the building becomes an improvisatory space for Glennie and Firth's creative play and the music that they make is an exploration of the belief that sound is interaction and encounter.

THE RTO

If Glennie helps us to reimagine what it means to hear, encounter, and interact with the world, then Alexander McCall Smith and his "Really Terrible Orchestra" can teach us something of the joy of play. This group of would-be musicians

started with a single concert and has become something of an international phenomenon—CDs, concert tours, etc. What is unusual about this ensemble is that
they are not professional musicians. Well, they are not even really musicians;
they just love to participate, regardless of the sound that emanates from their
instruments.

McCall Smith teaches Medical Law at the University of Edinburgh in Scotland
and is the author of the popular *#1 Ladies Detective* series. He also happens to
play the bassoon . . . badly. As he says of his own playing, "I play the bassoon,
even if not quite the whole bassoon. I have never quite mastered C-sharp, and I
am weak on the notes above the high D."[7] Despite this lack of skill, he and a few
other friends of equal (or lesser) ability decided to start an orchestra. "Why should
real musicians—the ones who can actually play their instruments—have all the
fun?" Thus the "Really Terrible Orchestra" [RTO] was born.

Now, this is all well and good as long as they play behind closed doors with
the public ignorant of their existence; however, after a few rehearsals they began
to wonder if they should give a concert. Why not get something out of all of their
hard work? So they staged their first performance. To their surprise the "first concert was packed, and not just with friends and relations. People were intrigued
by the sheer honesty of the orchestra's name. . . They were delighted."[8] (Of course
that might have had something to do with the free wine served before the concert!)

Now they perform annually at the Edinburgh Fringe Festival to packed-out
and enthusiastic crowds. Most people love the group, but the critics are skeptical.[9]
The truth is that people come to hear them because of the sheer audacity of their
claim; they are amazingly bad musicians! But they fit into the extreme and crazy
ethos of the Edinburgh Fringe Festival. Half the shows at the Fringe are much
worse, so why not go to a known bad show that brings so much joy and humor to
those playing and attending. And what a delight to say with utmost honesty, "We
are really terrible, so come and hear us play!" The joy is found in the participation,
as McCall Smith extemporizes,

> There is now no stopping us. We have become no better, but we plow on
> regardless. This is music as therapy, and many of us feel the better for
> trying. We remain really terrible, but what fun it is. It does not matter, in
> our view, that we sound irretrievably out of tune. It does not matter that
> on more than one occasion members of the orchestra have actually been
> discovered to be playing different pieces of music, by different compos-
> ers, at the same time. I, for one, am not ashamed of those difficulties with
> C-sharp. We persist. After all, we are the Really Terrible Orchestra, and we
> shall go on and on. Amateurs arise—make a noise.[10]

As an amateur musician, I applaud the RTO for their willingness to play for the utter love of making sound. (I won't venture to say that they always make music...) I am reminded of the Psalmist's command, "Make a joyful noise unto the Lord!" Glory be to God for the ability to do something so badly that the effort alone gives joy to so many.

There were a number of letters to the *New York Times* in response to an Op-Ed piece on the RTO by McCall Smith. (They had just come to play a concert in New York...) One letter captures the essence of why this orchestra is so popular.

> As an elementary music teacher, I roundly cheer Mr. McCall Smith and his compatriots. I only wished I lived in Edinburgh so that I could enjoy and maybe even play in their group.
>
> Every day, I see the joy that music making can bring to a person's life even in the absence of talent. I see my students challenge themselves daily with singing and playing, and as long as there is effort, I feel I have done a good day's work.
>
> Miles Davis once said, "Don't worry about mistakes; there are no mistakes." In a culture that worships at the altar of "winner take all, loser be humiliated" shows like "American Idol" and its clones, it is refreshing to hear of people who are true amateurs and the audiences that appreciate their effort.
>
> After all, doesn't the word amateur mean one who does something out of love for it?[11]

I think that we all long to do something in our lives purely "out of love for it." Children so freely enter into such ventures, not worried that they are not meeting some perceived expectation of grandeur. They are simply themselves, abandoned to the moment of music making. How sad that we lose this joy of participation somewhere along the way.

I should point out here that even for groups such as the RTO, this kind of music making is not just random noise. They gather in order to learn music and play. It is this aspect of playing together that really brings joy. A group may not be very good at staying together or even reading music, but every once in a while the sheer ability to make it through a piece is a cause for celebration. I have experienced this when I sight read quartets with my friends. We often surprise each other by the number of difficult passages that we played well (or not!). So, in all of this, there is also an element of how music creates community. When we play together we have a common bond and purpose.[12]

One very negative response to McCall Smith's article points us to the other side of why this group is so necessary; although the writer of the letter, I believe, misses the point of this kind of participation.

Being married to a musician for 18 years, I fail to see... the humor in
the Really Terrible Orchestra...

I see my husband play, for truly the umpteenth time, songs every day in
order to perfect them. I also see the music industry changing where drum
machines, sequencers and the Broadway music machines put musicians
out of work; and I am insulted by the public performances and CD sales
of this orchestra.

Lest people tell me to lighten up, let them contemplate the possibility
of their job being performed badly by someone who never learned to do it
well in the first place.

That does happen...

Lightening up is not part of the prescription.[13]

I am sympathetic to the plight of struggling musicians because I believe
fiercely in the need for live musicians and live music. However, what this woman
misses is that amateur musicians are the ones who are willing to pay to hear
professional musicians. Participation leads to appreciation. The musicians in
McCall Smith's orchestra can attest to the difference between their playing and
the playing of the Scottish Chamber Orchestra and in this realization comes a
respect for the value of excellent musical craftsmanship. If orchestras and other
kinds of live ensembles are going to survive in the future, new amateur musicians
are required. As McCall Smith proclaimed: "Amateurs arise—make noise!" and
then go and hear the great musicians play.

Thus, the moral of the Really Terrible Orchestra is that these players, in all
their ineptitude and humor, are developing a new and more diverse audience
for not only their own music but for other kinds of live music as well. They are
strange evangelists for the joy of musical participation but they are also advocates
for the art of concert going. Again, we see that participation invites and facilitates
encounter.

THE FINE ART OF PARTICIPATION

McCall Smith makes a striking comment, "This is music as therapy, and
many of us feel the better for trying." This statement resonates deeply with me.
Something very wonderful happens in the very act of playing music with others.
Of course not every minute of practicing, rehearsing, or performing is magical
but there are always moments, even if fleeting, that transcend our everyday experience. After I play I often feel as if I have been taken outside of myself and, for
me, there is nothing like an evening of playing chamber music.

Chamber music is the art of playing in small groups—trios, quartets, quintets,
sextets, etc. I could call this compulsion to play in small ensembles an attempt to
be a better musician or even a better person. Chamber musicians often joke that

the world would be a much better place if everyone played chamber music. We play that we might learn and we learn so that we might live more wisely.

A quartet can be described as four soloists completely dependent upon one another in order for something meaningful to happen. In order to play with others in such an intimate setting you have to develop skill along with humility, discernment, and tact. Each player must learn to play toward one another, leaning in and handing over power and security of sound to others. It is a vulnerable and risky endeavor.

A number of years ago, I came across a wonderfully descriptive poem about quartet playing by Irish poet, Micheal O'Siadhail. In this poem, he compares the interplay and risk of the string quartet with love and marriage.

QUARTET

These players nod and gleam as if they're seeing
And hearing the other's expression, each leaning
Into the fine-nerved strings, their whole being
Vested in this interplay, this gamble on meaning.
I remember a crescendo dream. We burned and burned.
Maybe it's age. I grow in this mutual succumbing:
Bow and pluck, phrase and breath of an earned
And watchful passion, our face to face becoming.
All shall be equal we'd said. But nothing matches.
Overlaps. Voice-overs. A sudden fertile digression
Loops into our rousing silence. Something over-reaches
Equality, a lived-in music shaping my compassion.
The conversation dips and wanders and tenses again.
A shining between faces, a listening inward and open.[14]

This poem captures something of the required relationality of this kind of ensemble playing as O'Siadhail articulates the performative nature of intimacy. Relationships grow when they are lived into and out of: "their whole being/Vested in this interplay." There is a risky vulnerability to relational living and playing but it is only through this "lived-in music" that relationships can grow and flourish. Marriage and quartet playing are both a "gamble on meaning."

Recently I experienced "this gamble on meaning" in a significant way as I played a work by Ravel with a flute quintet (flute with string quartet) for a chamber music workshop. The way the piece was orchestrated demanded that we depend upon each other in every moment. In order for the flute to soar beautifully over us, the entire string quartet had to know its place: play out, hold back, emphasize one note not another, flutter indistinctly to create an almost water-like texture. In other words, we had to "nod and gleam" together, vested in each movement of breath, finger, and bow. It wasn't until we performed on Saturday afternoon that some of this "ensemble risk" finally came together. Playing our own notes well was not enough. In order to perform Ravel properly, we had to move and breath as an organism. If the soloist didn't play loud enough or with confidence then the rest felt flat and meaningless. If those with coloristic parts played with too much distinction, then it covered up the melody. We ebbed and flowed together, servants to the asymmetrical melody that unified our ensemble. Our practice and performance shaped our ensemble making—"our face to face becoming."

In a performance, one feels the intensity of the risk involved in playing together. Everything could fall apart into pieces if someone misses an entrance, skips a page of music, plays too timidly, etc. Or perhaps in this moment of vulnerability an opportunity is given; perhaps the others in the group can redeem even the worst mistakes. It is the interaction, improvisation, the moment of the playing itself that brings forth something of meaning. Sound and story unfold from this strange and fragile dependence upon one another, the risk that someone could (and most likely will) make a mistake, the possibility that the others will redeem the missteps in one's own performance by putting things back into the context of the whole. Nothing is dependent solely upon the individual player. The ensemble and the music are intertwined in time and space.

A teacher once told me that the joy of live performance could be found in the possibility of mistakes because we never really know what will happen in the moment. It is how you react in that moment that is the measure of one's musicianship. This joy of performance is often not known or understood because our day-to-day reality is more shaped by the recorded moment. We live in a mediated world of controlled and manipulated sound. Our musical world is one of re-takes, voice-overs, and digital editing. We live in a world of perfect recordings that blur the line between reality and fantasy because we can never live up to the recording. It is an unreal fantasy that live performance has the potential to deconstruct. The interplay of a string quartet takes for granted that encounter requires vulnerability between the players. To play in a string quartet is to expose oneself to the risk of failure; but perhaps the beauty of participation is the redemption of the inevitable mistake.

This vulnerable but necessary investiture in and toward others reminds me of the Christian call to be the body of Christ in and for the world. In this performative space, redemption is practiced and enacted. Music is a place of encounter between persons and it is also a place where the Holy Spirit and the work of Christ are given space to function in our lives.

THE SPIRITUAL DISCIPLINE OF PARTICIPATION

When I teach about the Holy Spirit in my classes, I often start with two general principles from British theologian, Colin Gunton.[15] First, the Holy Spirit builds bridges between persons. This means that the Spirit moves us to connect with other people and the world at large. We might say that this movement of the Spirit is about creating unity or relationship in unexpected places. Second, the Spirit maintains our individuality. Gunton points out that although we often associate the Spirit with building relationship, we rarely think about the Spirit as the one who holds our particularity in a sacred way.[16] In this theology of the Spirit, we are all individuals held by the God who calls us to be in relationship and community. This is a profoundly relational definition of spirituality.

Hence, a healthy spirituality moves us toward relationship while maintaining our individuality. This paradoxical pull between communal and individual being is a redemptive movement in life, and is a fertile space for the Holy Spirit to move and work in the world. The German theologian, Jürgen Moltmann, argues that "wherever there is a passion for life, there the Spirit of God is operating."[17] I can't help but see this pattern of passion, life, individuation, and relationship in Evelyn Glennie, The Really Terrible Orchestra, and in every chamber music ensemble in which I have ever played. Even though these examples show a more general movement of the Spirit in the world, there is something to be learned from each.

It is as if musical participation is a spiritual discipline that requires personal skill combined with a learned ability to open up to others. Much like in a string quartet, each player must be able to play her part in order for the music to take shape. There is nothing more exciting when notes, ensemble, and musicality magically come together during a performance. Everyone walks away with the thought, "So that is how Ravel should sound!"

But The Really Terrible Orchestra also teaches us something about the simple joy of participation, regardless of skill or education. It is love for the group and the journey of music making that prompts people to play and to attend their concerts. There is an open and invitational delight in this Orchestra's way of being. What is funny is that those who play in this orchestra can't help but become better musicians along the way. As many educators know, love is one of the greatest motivations for learning.

In addition to the love of making music, Evelyn Glennie has taught me a lot about the art of listening and the joy of play. Music, rhythm, and sound pulsate through her body. Her desire to encounter others from diverse musical and cultural backgrounds is inspiring. Music, it seems, has caused her to move outside of herself and transcend the boundaries of her limited senses. Her discipline of listening and of playful improvisation has guided her into a life of encounter and relationship. That her life has exceeded the expectations of that first doctor who assumed that her deafness would end her musical life is one amazing part of her story. Even more amazing is that her passionate openness has made her one of the greatest percussionists of the twentieth- and twenty-first centuries.

Thus, music is a discipline that moves us toward encounter with others. Because of this, I think of musical participation as a kind of spiritual discipline or formation. What I mean by this is that we are significantly formed (spiritually, emotionally, and physically) by the practices that we do on a regular basis. I tell my students that everything that we do is formational, so be thoughtful and intentional. We sometimes mistakenly think that there is some sort of magical spiritual practice that will fix us or make us holy. Instead it is the pursuit and the kinds of relationships in which we engage—to God, to ourselves, and to one another—that form us in the day-to-day.

Eugene Peterson once commented that there was no *one* spiritual discipline that held the secret to the Christian life. Instead the secret to spirituality was something more like, "Get bored with yourself and then get interested in something beyond yourself."[18] Even though I don't believe that music is inherently spiritual unto itself, because it does not have an attached or explicit spirituality of its own, music (especially when done with others) is one of those practices that helps us to move beyond ourselves. When we participate, we learn to listen to what is most important and we learn to tune ourselves to others. The sound of the other becomes just as important if not more important than one's own sound. In ensemble music, we practice encounter.

Music also emulates something of how the Holy Spirit works in the world. As Steve Guthrie puts it, "Sensitivity and responsiveness to the created order and to other human beings—this characterizes the Holy Spirit's work among the children of light. It is also an apt description of what happens and what is required when we sing and make music well."[19] Guthrie argues that music engages the whole of our bodies and our minds. It is strange to think of spirituality as requiring a full-bodied response to the Spirit but music moves us in this direction. Moreover, our embodied spiritual discipline connects our efforts with others and with the surrounding space.

In all of this, I am reminded of Paul's command to us that we sing with and for one another: "Speak to one another with psalms, hymns, and spiritual songs. Sing and make music in your heart to the Lord" (Ephesians 5:19). Music, in this passage, is a means of encouragement, instruction, prayer, emotive expression, and praise. It seems to be equally for the sake of the community and the individual. Singing enables the expression of the individual heart, the encouragement of fellow believers, and, overall, the praise of God. Our inner and outer lives are connected in a powerful manner through our participation in musical practice. Moreover, we are formed in significant ways as we sing and play psalms, hymns, and spiritual songs *together*, ways that we would miss if we only sang or played alone.

Our music making in the church is a purposeful place of encounter: we are not only opened up to God, we are also opened up to one another. Whether we follow through and connect with others in significant ways is another issue. All spiritual discipline must be practiced and lived into in purposeful ways; they are never ends in themselves. Just like one of my violin teachers often said to me, "You do not practice for the sake of playing for yourself in a closet, you practice so that you can perform for [and I would add 'with'] others."

There is something undeniably special about the act of playing and singing music together. Singing as a congregation allows us to participate in the kind of unity for which we were intended. Not a unity that homogenizes, erasing our individuality, but a unity that helps us practice making room for each other in love. This is the sound of God's unity as Father, Son, and Holy Spirit: the Three in One and One in Three. It is also the sound of the unity our God intended for us as the Body of Christ. When we sing in church, we come together and sing to participate in that unity, we are opened up to encounter one another and the God who is perfect Unity.

Endnotes

1   Kathleen Marie Higgins, *The Music of Our Lives*, Philadelphia: Temple University Press, 1991, 33–34. Thanks to Steve Guthrie for bringing this quote to my attention. See Steven R. Guthrie, "Singing in the Body and in the Spirit," *Journal of the Evangelical Theological Society* 46/4, 2003, 633-46.

2   Fred Firth/Evelyn Glennie, *The Sugar Factory*, Tzadik Records TZ 7623, CD, 2007.

3   *Touch the Sound: A Sound Journey with Evelyn Glennie*. DVD. Directed by Thomas Riedelsheimer. 2004; Germany, 2005.

4   See Glennie's Ted talk from February 2003 for a shorter introduction to her thoughts on listening and hearing. URL: http://youtu.be/IU3V6zNER4g (accessed December 16, 2010).

5   Fred Firth/Evelyn Glennie, The Sugar Factory, Tzadik Records TZ 7623, CD, 2007.

6   Here is a clip from the documentary. This is when Firth and Glennie first encounter the space. URL: http://youtu.be/hN7Ri50mz3k (accessed on December 16, 2010).

7   Alexander McCall Smith, "And the Band Played Badly," *New York Times*, March 9, 2008. URL: http://www.nytimes.com/2008/03/09/opinion/09mccallsmith.html (accessed March 8, 2013).

8   Ibid.

9   "'How these people presume to play in public is quite beyond me,' wrote one critic in *The Scotsman* newspaper. And another one simply said 'dire.' Well, that may be so, but we never claimed to be anything other than what we are. And we know that we are dire; there's no need to state the obvious. How jejune these critics can be!" (Ibid.)

10   Ibid.

11   Paul Beattie, "LETTERS; The 'Untalented' Concerto: An A (Flat) for Effort," New York Times, March 9, 2008. URL: http://query.nytimes.com/gst/fullpage.html?res=9B07EFDB133BF934A25750C0A96E9C8B63&scp=1&sq=alexander+mccall+smith+orchestra&st=nyt&smid=pl-share (accessed March 8, 2013).

12   This may be why ensembles are often used in cross-cultural exchanges, especially in peace-seeking endeavors. For example, the West-Eastern Divan Orchestra, started by Edward Said and Daniel Barenboim to help create a space of peace between Israeli and Arab musicians.

13   Kelly Perl, "LETTERS; The 'Untalented' Concerto: An A (Flat) for Effort," *New York Times*, March 9, 2008. URL: http://query.nytimes.com/gst/fullpage.html?res=9B07EFDB133BF934A25750C0A96E9C8B63&scp=1&sq=alexander+mccall+smith+orchestra&st=nyt&smid=pl-share (accessed March 8, 2013).

14   Micheal O'Siadhail, "Quartet," in *A Fragile City*, Newcastle, UK: Bloodaxe, 1995, 16.

15   See Colin Gunton, *The One, the Three and the Many. God, Creation and the Culture of Modernity. The 1992 Bampton Lectures*, Cambridge: Cambridge University Press, 1993, 181.

16   Ibid., 205-206.

17   As summed up by Veli-Matti Karkkainen in *Pneumatology*, Baker Academic, 2006, 126. See Jürgen Moltmann, *The Spirit of Life*, Augsburg Fortress Press, 1992.
18   Eugene Peterson in the question and answer time at his lecture for *Image Magazine's* Denise Levertov Award, Seattle, WA, May 16, 2009.
19   Steven R. Guthrie, "Singing in the Body and in the Spirit," *Journal of the Evangelical Theological Society* 46/4, 2003, 642.

SONGS OF SORROW
for healing

> By the rivers of Babylon we sat and wept when we remembered Zion.
> There on the poplars we hung our harps, for there our captors asked
> us for songs, our tormentors demanded songs of joy; they said,
> "Sing us one of the songs of Zion!" How can we sing the songs
> of the LORD while in a foreign land?
> —Psalm 137:1–4

I am not a musician. I can't read music well nor will I ever hope to compose anything worth listening to. But I know what it means to need music. I am a Sufferer.
As a Sufferer my soul needs music. Why is that? Wouldn't it be more sanctified
for me to declare my soul needs God, or prayer, or the Scriptures to ease the sufferings of life? Why yes, of course, I embrace these means of grace. But my need
for these means of grace does not diminish my need for music—especially singing. And I know that is part of God's will for me because He commands us over
one hundred times in His Word to sing to Him. Are we surprised that this is the
most recorded of all the commandments in Scriptures? In God's creative genius
He fashioned a particular gift for all His creatures to enjoy, both the Redeemed
and the Reprobate.

In this essay I would like to explore the uniqueness of music (especially singing) for worship as well as take some time to consider how music (especially
singing) relieves the soul of the Sufferer. Consider the words of this song:

My life flows on in endless song; Above earth's lamentation I hear the sweet though far off hymn That hails a new creation: Through all the tumult and the strife I hear the music ringing; It finds an echo in my soul—How can I keep from singing?

What though my joys and comforts die? The Lord my Savior liveth; What though the darkness gather round! Songs in the night He giveth: No storm can shake my inmost calm While to that refuge clinging; Since Christ is Lord of Heav'n and earth, How can I keep from singing?

I lift mine eyes; the cloud grows thin; I see the blue above it; And day by day this pathway smoothes Since first I learned to love it: The peace of Christ makes fresh my heart, A fountain ever springing: All things are mine since I am His—How can I keep from singing?

UNIQUENESS OF SINGING

How is this particular gift so different than the many others God has given us? Imagine this: it is Sunday morning and the worship leader approaches the podium. He announces that we will start our service praising God, and asks us to get out our bulletin. He encourages us to turn it over and on the back page worship God together by drawing a picture in unison, letting the different colors in our crayon box be used to express harmony. That is silly, of course. My point is God that has established singing as a universal means of worshiping Him. Singing can be a solo voice or a choir one million strong. Singing may be in unison or in intricate harmonies. However it is expressed, together we raise our voices in song to Heaven as we sing from the depths of our hearts to our Triune God. Tim Keller expressed this uniqueness well in *It Was Good: Making Art to the Glory of God* when he wrote:

> The Church needs artists to assist the body in understanding truth, but just as importantly the Church needs artists to equip the Church to praise God. We cannot praise God without art. Within the Christian Art community there is a frustration for visual artists who observe the important place of the musical arts in worship. It holds a prominent place in worship that the visual arts do not.... But there are important differences between visual and musical art that make musical art a more natural element in public worship. It is impossible to get a thousand people together to do visual arts in worship on a regular basis. A large group can appreciate a visual art display in a church setting but they cannot do it. In contrast, a thousand people can create and do musical art in a worship service and it is both musical art and worship.... We can't enjoy God without art. And even those of us who are terrible artists have to sing sometimes.

In joy or in sorrow, alone or together, someone else's lyrics and melody can fuse you to me as we share a profound moment in time and space. Music can cut across ethnicity, gender, age, and race. And somewhere in the process there are blessed saints struggling to find the perfect note or exact word to express the deepest longing in their heart so that it may find contentment in our hearts. To this we say, Amen and Amen!

To be sure, there are learned people who can explain the physical reasons why singing is different from speaking. And a virtuoso can hear the difference between a song sung on pitch and one that is not. Unlike many art forms, nearly all of us can sing. And if we feel as though we cannot sing, we can still stand with the people of God and express the depths of our soul as we contemplate the lyrics and music. Have you ever been in a time of worship where you were so overwhelmed by the song being sung that you could not utter a sound? At that time, has it ever happened that while the song was being sung, your body participated in the song? Perhaps you closed your eyes and tears streamed down your face. Perhaps you raised your hands in agreement with the song. Or maybe you lowered your head as you sang the song in your mind because you were weeping and nothing intelligible would come out of your mouth. This is the power of music invading the soul with both lyrics and melody. We need music to do this ... really we do. The uniqueness of music being sung is this: As I experience singing, this seminal moment within my suffering soul is shared by the body of Christ through the congregation singing. We can agree that this shared artistic experience is deeply profound and perhaps a bit incomprehensible.

As a Sufferer

As I said, I come as a Sufferer to you, another Sufferer. We may have many things in common or nothing at all. Yet suffering remains our common ground. The circumstances of our suffering may be vastly different. The words and music of the songs we sing make my suffering yours and your suffering mine. And as Sufferers, God gives us music to minister to the desperate pain in which we find ourselves. You and I can stand next to each other in a church pew, or stand across a continent from each other, and the music that enthralls our emotions to depths unknown becomes healing to both of us.

Brian LoPiccolo, a pastor and a gifted composer once said to me:

> Suffering . . . is a central dynamic in God's story and our story. Americans, I think, see hardship as an obstacle to our personal agendas. But the Bible presents suffering as a part of God's plan; he weaves suffering into the fabric of our redemption. If suffering is part of God's story, then we ought to consider its role.

The Gospel offers people an identity that brings us beyond our suffering. The Gospel doesn't deny or diminish our hardships—it redeems them. The Gospel unites suffering people to a God who suffered. The Gospel doesn't waste our trials—it transforms them, and gives them meaning and purpose.

God will make all things new. I wanted people to consider resurrection and restoration. The Gospel does more than redeem our suffering, it promises to end it. This is the source of hope. Now, this may sound strange to some, but the beautiful thing about suffering is that it can drive us to that hope.

None of us needs to be a virtuoso or brilliant lyricist to explain how suffering and music are linked together to bring us a measure of peace. We share the joys and heartaches of life alike, as Saint Paul sums it up for us:

> Let the peace of Christ rule in your hearts, since as members of one body you were called to peace. And be thankful. Let the word of Christ dwell in you richly as you teach and admonish one another with all wisdom, and as you sing psalms, hymns and spiritual songs with gratitude in your hearts to God. And whatever you do, whether in word or deed, do it all in the name of the Lord Jesus, giving thanks to God the Father through him.

TIMES OF SUFFERING . . . TIMES OF MUSIC

Several years ago I was made conscious of how music binds up the wounds of the broken heart. I was in the process of living through a debilitating painful crisis involving my dearest oldest daughter, Maya. Now, as I look back over those dark days, I see that the circumstances were not as insurmountable as they seemed then. In fact, what happened is common to most of us as we live out our lives in this fallen world. This particular event produced emotions in me like despair, sadness, loneliness, fear, and abandonment. It is these emotions that are the common tie between you and me. I felt confusion sweeping over me like an ocean tsunami and I thought I would drown from the full force of the tidal wave. At that time, what spoke to the emotions I was experiencing was *music*. Lyrics and melody working in concert anchored my soul amidst the flood. Music found me where I was: immobilized, fearful, defeated, confused, and feeling separated from God. But God, in His goodness and mercy to me, gave my soul music and I felt relief!

> Jesus! What a help in sorrow! While the billows o'er me roll, Even when my heart is breaking, He, my comfort, helps my soul. Hallelujah what a Saviour! Hallelujah! What a friend. Saving, helping, keeping, loving, He is with me to the end.

There I was like Jonah in the sea. . . free floating, sinking ever downward, entangled in my own emotions, circumstances, self pity, guilt, and especially unbelief. In the book of Jonah the prophet wrote, "The engulfing waters threatened me, the deep surrounded me; seaweed was wrapped around my head. To the roots of the mountains I sank down; the earth beneath barred me in forever."

What happened next was interesting. I found myself glued to our little spinet piano in our living room, plunking out the melody lines of great hymns from the *Trinity Hymnal.* I would try to sing the words as I played, but my emotions were so close to the surface that they prevented the words from coming out of my mouth. No matter. I sang the song in my heart with such sorrow and despair that I know the unuttered words of the songs and the sound of the melody from the piano became my only hope for relief and comfort. I pictured myself on a stage, and my only audience was Jesus.

O the deep, deep love of Jesus vast, unmeasured, boundless, free! Rolling as a mighty ocean in its fullness over me. Underneath me, all around me, Is the current of His love Leading onward leading homeward, To Thy glorious rest above.

The piano was God's sanctuary for me. In Medieval times, a sanctuary was a holy place—usually a Christian church—which provided immunity from the law. The Law held me captive, painfully piercing my unbelieving heart until it soared over my head. But God turned Law into Grace (unmerited and undeserved) through the music from that hymnal. The words of the hymns were my prayers and the melodies rocked me as though my own mother cradled me in her arms. My heart found consolation when everything else came crashing down around me. This song became my safety net:

O the deep, deep love of Jesus spread His praise from shore to shore. How he loveth ever loveth changeth never, never more. How He watcheth o'er His loved ones, Died to call them all His own; How for them He intercedeth, Watcheth o'er them from the throne!

Our circumstances are vastly different than Jonah's, but when all is said and done, we share his conclusion: "But you brought my life up from the pit, O LORD my God. When my life was ebbing away, I remembered you, LORD, and my prayer rose to you, to your holy temple. Those who cling to worthless idols forfeit the grace that could be theirs. But I, with a song of thanksgiving, will sacrifice to you. What I have vowed I will make good. Salvation comes from the LORD."

Indeed, God's love is like the vastness of the ocean. And that very ocean that seemed to weigh me down became the current of His love. Could Scriptures or prayer have accomplished for me the same comfort as did music? No doubt.

And yet, when life throws you overboard, the sanctuary of lyrics and melody that is music speaks differently than bare Scripture. Perhaps it is the minor key in which this song is written that tuned perfectly to my sinking soul. I don't know. Sometimes I visualize music as a very long thin needle that can be inserted into the heart where the deepest emotions of joy and heartache thrive. It is that very spot that music heals. God uses that needle to infuse His healing into us.

Another particular crisis where I, as a Sufferer, found music very healing happened as I lived through the tragic death of my mother. Psychotropic drugs had taken her to a place where no one who loved her could reach. She was stripped of her dignity, her body, her mind, and her Savior. With one breath she screamed out her hallucinations and with the very next breath she spoke words of comfort to me.

Three months before my mom died, she had a massive stroke. Her behavior had become highly erratic which caused the staff to move her from that nursing home to a private mental institution. As we waited for her transfer, music from the 30s and 40s was playing over the intercom. My mother, who was out of her mind, heard the music and began to sing. She was completely relaxed. What was left of her sanity returned to a time that was happy. Momentarily, music eased her suffering. In her mind she renewed her friendship with Tony Bennett, Frank Sinatra, Benny Goodman, and perhaps even my father who died a year earlier. What is in the essence of music to accomplish something that my mother's prescribed drugs (which could have knocked out an elephant) could not do?

The next time my sister, my mother, and I experienced music as a means of soothing suffering was three days before my mother died. She was in Hospice and had not had any food or water for days. She was unresponsive during most of that time but she did grunt and groan when we talked to her. She was actively dying. The nurses would take great care in arranging her pillows in such a way as to resemble a womb-like environment.

On that particular day, my mother began to become very agitated. She needed to say something to my sister and me. Thus far, her last words to me happened a week or so earlier. While screaming in some kind of lunatic rage she abruptly stopped, looked right into my confused eyes, and said, "Diana, don't let this trouble your heart." For me this was my mother's last words of advice and probably the most important advice she would ever give me.

So that day in Hospice, three days before my mother's death, I pulled out a collection of carefully torn pages I have been saving for my funeral. (I know this will sound odd, but for years I've been collecting songs and readings I want for my funeral, and have kept them in my purse.) Together, my sister and I sang "my" funeral songs to our mother as she lay dying. I can't even remember how we sounded. I honestly don't know if any sound even came out of my mouth. This I do know: in that moment there were three Sufferers on that death bed. Each of us had different reason for our sorrow. The music we sang was redemptive and healing. Singing together began to heal breaches between my sister and me. It softened the pain of two girls facing the death of their mother so soon after the death of their father. And music calmed my mother as we sang to her. God uses extraordinary means for ordinary people in incredible circumstances. That moment will forever be burned into my memory. In part, we sang:

> O Wondrous love that will not let me go. I cling to You with all my strength and soul. Yet if my hold should ever fail this wondrous love will never let me go. O Wondrous love that rushes over me. I can't escape this river's glorious flow. You overwhelm my days with good. Your wondrous love will never let me go.

and

> Sometimes the way is lonely and steep and filled with pain. So if your sky is dark and pours the rain, then cry to Jesus, cry to Jesus, cry to Jesus and live. And with your final heartbeat kiss the world good bye. Then go in peace and laugh on Glory's side, and fly to Jesus, fly to Jesus, fly to Jesus and live!

as well as this:

> I will not boast in anything, no gifts, no power, no wisdom: but I will boast in Jesus Christ, His death and resurrection. Why should I gain from His reward? I cannot give an answer. But this I know with all my heart, His wounds have paid my ransom.

I am convinced that you and I share heartaches. Perhaps you have never sat on your mother's deathbed singing with your only sister. But the emotions evoked by this scene you have certainly experienced. Can music heal you as it did my sister and me? Can the singing of psalms, hymns, and spiritual songs help us as God's chosen people, holy and dearly loved, to clothe ourselves with compassion, kindness, humility, gentleness, and patience to one another? Can we bear with each other and forgive as the Lord forgives whatever grievances we may have against one another as we put on love, which binds us together in perfect unity?

Another time music healed me was years later on a trip to Rome. My traveling party and I found ourselves in a small French church at the top of the Spanish Steps. It was All Saints Day—a national holiday in Italy. The church service featured novitiates dressed in white, singing the Psalms a cappella in French.

During the service the priest censed the altar with sweet aromatic incenses. The novitiates' voices were enchanting. Their voices as well as the incense floated upward until the whole church was filled with song and smoke. Slowly, the novitiates disappeared behind the altar until only the powerful fragrance remained.

That scene—coupled with the Psalms being sung—took hold of my spirit and I began to weep uncontrollably. I wondered how Isaiah felt when he wrote about that scene in Heaven where the train of God's robe filled the temple. Music and incense invaded me and I was utterly undone. I promised myself I would not utter another word for the rest of my natural life seeing that compared to this experience I had nothing more to say. As I sat there unable to move or speak or sing, I prayed for each of my children. And in those moments, I was also able to mourn the death of my parents. The singing did not just fill that church, it filled those spaces in my heart and head that needed relief from suffering. Voice, melody, lyrics, and incense provided an almost out of body experience. . . me, a cradle Calvinist! As a Sufferer, not only did music expose the deep sense of grief and frustration that clung to me, it also provided dearly needed healing.

During my mother's utter confusion, I often recited Psalm 23 to her because it was so familiar. After her brutal death the incongruity of the sixth verse bounced back and forth in my mind like a frenzied game of ping-pong. "Surely goodness and mercy will follow me all the days of my life and I will dwell in the house of the Lord forever!" My mother died writhing in chaos and confusion. How does her death even remotely resemble goodness and mercy?

Time has a way of plucking experiences from one chapter of our lives and giving that experience meaning in a subsequent chapter. The chapters may be years apart, as it was for me. It wasn't until years later, after my mother's death and after my almost mystical experience in that French church that I made sense of Psalm 23:6. I discovered a link. My mother's death bed concert and that French sanctuary filled with fragrant song helped end my mind's constant ping-pong match. If my mother's death was God's goodness and mercy following her, then the mode of her death was good. In other words, dying like an animal was, for her, good. Her death struggle came from the hand of God who promised goodness and mercy to follow His little lamb as she traveled through her valley of death. Here psalm and hymn combined to speak so uniquely:

> What e'er my God ordains is right: Here shall my stand be taken; Though sorrow, need, or death be mine, Yet am I not forsaken; My Father's care is round me there; he holds me that I shall not fall: And so to Him I leave it all.

Augustine of Hippo wisely said, "He who sings prays twice." I assert that he who sings heals twice: first with lyrics and second with melody. I invite you to allow music to help relieve your suffering in such times as I described. My best guess is there are many who can add many more personal stories to mine with accompanying songs. Dear Sufferer, what are your experiences in your suffering and how does music infuse life into your suffering heart?

WORSHIP LEADERS AS CONNECTORS

Might there be those of us who would never think of making the connection between music and suffering and how music soothes the suffering soul? While we may agree that music is an integral part of worship, the thought of music interacting on a level that is restorative may be foreign. Music may only be seen as giving glory to our Triune God. And that is correct. The chief end of man *is* to glorify God and enjoy Him forever as the *Westminster Catechism* states. Singing is part of giving glory to God. But that juncture where singing meets suffering and maladies meet music is a place of significant healing, and should not be neglected. Those responsible for planning and implementing worship will miss a big part of healing if they neglect to make the connection between music and suffering. Indeed, music adds texture as it reveals itself in layers. Some layers are soft as silk while some are stiff as tweed. Some layers may be cool like linen or warm like fleece. Use these textures when constructing worship remembering that your singers are Sufferers.

After singing *In Christ Alone* for the first time in our church, our pastor declared that we could all be dismissed without hearing his sermon because the Gospel had been perfectly proclaimed. Keith Getty and Stuart Townend put those words to sounds and an incredible song of worship with the ability to both worship God and speak to a sufferer was produced.

> In Christ alone, my hope is found, He is my light my strength, my song; This cornerstone, this solid ground, firm through the fiercest drought and storm. What heights of love, what depths of peace, when fears are stilled, when striving cease. My comforter, my all in all, here in the love of Christ I stand.

Music needs to be seen as a means of grace along with fellowship, sacraments, prayer, preaching, and the Scriptures. Indeed, before Jesus headed to His gruesome death, He and His friends ended their meal by singing a hymn. What emotions were in Peter's mind knowing that Jesus told Peter he would deny Jesus three times? How would that hymn resonate with His disciples after hearing Jesus' words we read in John 13–17? Perhaps the disciples looked back at that last hymn they sang as a precious gift; as precious to them as my mother's death bed songs have been for my sister and me.

MUSICIANS AS BURDEN BEARERS

What propels the musician's creative force to write lyrics and melodies? Perhaps the musician brushed up against a Sufferer during his moments of desperation. Perhaps the musician himself experienced the kind of suffering where his own life became bitter and hard-edged and the darkness was so pervasive that his very consciousness seemed to be surrounded by it. Perhaps in the working out of that hard-edged story, the full expression culminated in a song! Perhaps the music he produced had the ability to filter through the musician's malaise and thus helped bear our burden. Perhaps the musician's suffering produced blossoms that bloomed into lyrics and melody which then became something to be shared.

Songs can be ready-made antidotes which, upon hearing them, are able to heal our suffering souls. The musicians' work helps lift the heavy load from our shoulders as their songs bear our burdens. Brian LoPiccolo shares about the burden-bearing power of music—and its limitations:

> As a sufferer, music has been a vehicle for my grief. Some people journal their prayers, struggles, their questions, but I found great release writing songs. I was able to focus many emotions outward through writing. But the key was this: it was an expression of faith. My faith in God's goodness found its way up to God through the music. That's worship. Listening to other people's music has also touched me in grief.
>
> Of course, my wife and family, my close friends and our congregation have treated my wounds far better than music ever can. I don't want to love music as though it were a person in my life. Music will never love me back. God loves me. And he loves me through his people.
>
> Suffering impacts us, but how will we respond? Some people allow trials to hijack and define them. I saw this in Dostoyevsky's *The Brothers Karamazov*. Their souls couldn't grow beyond their childhood misfortune, and the results were tragic for them later.
>
> The Gospel offers something else. Jesus' followers have the freedom to be sanctified through trials. Why are they free? It's because they bring their sorrows and "lay them down" at Christ's feet. In Matthew 11 Jesus invites us, "Come to me, all you who are weary and burdened, and I will give you rest. Take my yoke upon you and learn from me, for I am gentle and humble in heart, and you will find rest for your souls. For my yoke is easy and my burden is light." But to take on Jesus' burden we must lay down our own. This is what the three brothers wouldn't do. But the fourth brother, Alexei, gets it! Dostoyevsky portrayed a beautiful person in Alexei Karamazov. Alexei was impacted by his trials, but they didn't rule him. He responded in faith. That's worship! I also saw that his brothers could not forgive their father. But Alexei had forgiven him, I think, and so he was free. So here's the idea behind the Dostoyevsky-inspired song "Brothers."

I close by expressing something I don't quite understand. But there are some hurts so deep that there has not been a song written to touch or heal it. In his article, "Living in Job's House" in *The Journal of Biblical Counseling* Paul Tripp calls it *Anomie*:

There is a Latin word that says it all. Anomie. This word captures those moments in life where you feel detached from meaning, detached from purpose, detached from your identity, detached from your values. Literally, if you translate this word, it means this: "There's no name for this."

For those moments look to the Cross and that glorious song sung that day. Maybe it is that song and that song alone we need to flood our souls when life's circumstances makes our heart dry as dust and no intelligent words can come out of our mouth . . . just groans. Hear the song of Redemption from those pierced hands and feet. Hear the song of Salvation from the wounded side that pours healing into our hearts. The Cross is where God became a Sufferer.

And the whole world sang *Alleluia!*

THE SHADOW
of Your wings

For many Christians, worship evokes sounds and imagery of happy people filling a happy place with happy songs. I don't for a moment think that this is untrue this side of the cross and empty grave of our ascended Lord. Of all people on the earth, the believer has reason to rejoice constantly and with all the music and vigor that they can muster. We have reasons to sing and rejoice. Our songs should be filled with the joyful news we have in the gospel: all our sins are washed away and the Father has loved us with everlasting love through the Son! No doubt we are to call one another to rejoicing at every point of our journey along the lines that the Apostle Paul drew for us: "Rejoice in the Lord always; again I will say, rejoice." (Philippians 4:4)

What about sad songs in minor keys? Surely the major key alone is fitting for this life of rejoicing we are called to. Certainly the sad tones of the minor side of composition ought to be kept from the lips of a joy-commanded people, right? That would be correct if Scripture only featured happiness and joy to be the lot of the believer on this side of heaven. That is certainly not the case, as was asserted in the previous essay. At any point of the Christian experience, loved ones are lost, tragedies occur, sufferings are endured, and tribulations break out. The same Paul who wrote "Rejoice in the Lord always" also tells us to "weep with those who weep" (Romans 12:15b). Intuitively we all know that there are themes in life that create great sadness that will not feature tones and chord progressions in the major. Jesus shares this intuition when he declares concerning his generation's refusal to respond rightly to either him or his cousin, John the Baptist:

They are like children sitting in the marketplace and calling to one another, "We played the flute for you, and you did not dance; we sang a dirge, and you did not weep." (Luke 7:32 ESV)

Dirges should be wept to. Flute-songs in times of joy should be danced to. And both "sides" to worship—rejoicing and weeping—and the music associated with them (major/minor), I believe, ought to be indispensable to the Christian's life and worship.

WORSHIP IS WIDER

The reason, I believe, that worship should include minor key songs and themes is because worship is larger than we may have believed. I would propose a wider scope for what actually designates occasion to worship and adoration. Reading through many sections of the Wisdom writings of the Old Testament will help illustrate this.

Job honored and adored the Lord while in agony. His faith and expressions of worship were at a distance from the rejoicings of the gathered throng. He was lonely and filled to the brim with sorrows and suffering. While in these places, Job offered worship to God in a most fitting manner, in cries of tear-filled trust in God: "Naked I came from my mother's womb, and naked shall I return. The LORD gave, and the LORD has taken away; blessed be the name of the LORD" (Job 1:21). Adoration will pour off the lips of a suffering child of God in a different manner than a rejoicing one. Worship in Job's harrowing experience was made of surrender and sighing. Worship in a world of cancer, car accidents, tsunamis, children dying, and churches dividing must follow this same course at many points. And I do not mean in this that minor key songs should come out only at funerals or in tragic circumstances—really, minor key songs and themes should be a part of the "regular" worship of Christ in a broken world. Consider:

> We shouldn't limit ourselves to major key songs! The Psalms reveal that much of the Christian life might be spent in a minor key, and it's time that the church became honest about this reality as well. The church needs to be able to lament together, and minor key songs help us do that. They help us to be honest about the trials and emotions that we encounter on our pilgrimage to heaven. They help give expression to our sorrowful thoughts and feelings in ways that honor God and encourage us to persevere. We neglect them to our own impoverishment.[1]

The Psalmists took similar approaches to the adoration of God through times of suffering. In Psalm 42, the writer tells us: "My tears have been my food all day and night" (v. 3), while at the same time he declares faith toward God, "Hope in

God; for I shall again praise him, my salvation and my God" (vv. 5–6). Worship must happen in the wilderness as well as at the heart of the temple's joyous service, and so many Psalms exhibit both expressions, major *and* minor key themes.

The Old Testament and in particular the Psalms are not alone in presenting us with minor key adoration of God.[2] In New Testament standards, even *after* the victorious resurrection of Jesus, believers gather to comfort one another and bring encouragement and empathy in tough times. With the reality of death and the curse comes Paul's exhortation to "encourage one another with these words" (1 Thessalonians 4:18). The comfort being the truths of Christ and his resurrection. Believers with affection and empathy know how it is to sing great hymns and songs of comfort in difficult times.

NEVER FORGET

Music is a powerful thing. As a pastor and a songwriter, I've come to find out the hard way that people will remember even a half-baked song I've written far longer than the finest of my sermons. There is something about music that drives home truth and emotion in a long-standing way. I can remember singing certain songs at specific moments of my life when God was revealing himself to me. At those times with great emotion and zeal that cannot be contained, a song takes the shape of a milestone that is looked back on and never forgotten. In a book full of essays on music being read by people who have deep appreciation for music, I'm sure this is not news.

When a melody and lyrics are married well, we will find ourselves in rapt attention:

> I believe in the kingdom come,
> Where all the colors will bleed into one, bleed into one
> But yes I'm still running
> You broke the bonds and you loosed the chains
> Carried the cross of my shame, of my shame
> You know I believe it
> But I still haven't found what I'm looking for[3]

The calling of the Christian musician and songwriter is to help marry truths worthy to be remembered with melodies and rhythms able to carry the goods. The Christian musician has something to say, and the audience or congregation needs to hear and remember it well. So which lyrics and themes are worth remembering in a minor manner of singing? If music drives home truths and emotion in ways that help to encourage and cause remembrance of Christ (Col. 3:16, Eph. 5:19), then what purpose does the minor key hold and what exactly is it helpful to drive home? Does the Lord really want us to wail our way through worship and leave with further despair and despondency with the final minor chord? There are many themes that we will find are ably carried by minor keys. Let's explore a few.

As Christians gather, we are meant to acknowledge our sinfulness and need for a Savior in prescribed ways. The Apostle John reminds us to walk in the light as he is in the light, the prescribed action being the confession of sins. Jesus teaches us to pray in the spirit of: "forgive us our debts, as we also have forgiven our debtors." Whether by prayer, confession, or by song, the Church has for millennia engaged in pursuing repentance together. Methinks a meditative minor key might bode well for songs of confession, repentance, and surrender.

Dependence on God is more than advisable. Carrying on in our own strength while neglecting to acknowledge Christ in all our ways (Prov. 3:6) is simply self-destructive. The minor key can serve wonderfully to bring home the reality that without Christ we have and can do nothing:

> Other refuge have I none, hangs my helpless soul on Thee;
> Leave, ah! leave me not alone, still support and comfort me.
> All my trust on Thee is stayed, all my help from Thee I bring;
> Cover my defenseless head with the shadow of Thy wing.[4]

Longing for Jesus in our broken lives in a fallen world is yet another theme well carried by minor keys. In the spirit of Psalm 42, the believer faces daily reminders that their lives are incomplete, and the world around them and the devil want to keep it that way:

> All my enemies surround
> And they taunt at every turn
> For they tempt my soul to say:
> "Oh where now is your God?"
> But I know my God is near
> He commands His steadfast love
> By day or night His song
> Is with me, always[5]

We can throw our hope and longings upon Jesus in and through minor keys. We acknowledge our desperate need for Him, and His exclusivity as Savior and Shelter. We confess that all is not well here on earth apart from Him, and plead that he might return soon.

These themes and many more, I propose, are ably carried by minor keys. To be most blunt: minor ain't just for funerals. We would be wise to heed the words of author Carl Trueman on this subject:

A diet of unremittingly jolly choruses and hymns inevitably creates an unrealistic horizon of expectation which sees the normative Christian life as one long triumphalist street party—a theologically incorrect and a pastorally disastrous scenario in a world of broken individuals.[6]

MINOR AT WORK

Let's get practical in the sections ahead. How does the worship leader, song writer, or Christian musician aim to make room for minor key themes in the leading of worship or the writing of songs for the gathered church and beyond? I hope that my little polemic prior to this section provided some encouragement to *why* minor keys are valuable, but how do we employ them?

Writing in Minor

There are certainly many existing songs or old hymns that are beautifully crafted in minor keys that might be tapped for worship times and performances, but I would first urge that more writing is needed for the church. It is an unfortunate reality of songwriting that too often only a few songs written by a few people end up making up the diet of most congregational worship times. The church needs more faithful songwriters at even the local level to craft effective songs in all keys, and certainly in minor keys and themes.

In writing a minor key song, whether one starts with the music or the lyrics, be thoughtful. Start with the questions like these:

- What do I want this song to accomplish?

- Where do I want people to end up after hearing this song?

- What truth and emotion am I seeking to impress through this song?

- What is the "nugget" or the kernel of this song? How should I go about supporting that kernel with lyrics/melody and arrangement?

Once you've determined a particular direction for a song, its time to simply start trying things. Try different chord progressions. Attempt using different words and rhyme schemes than you're used to using. Get out a rhyming dictionary. Maybe start with the music first (if you usually work on lyrics first) or with lyrics first (if you usually work on music first). As you are trying things be ready and willing to write and re-write a million times over until you are done. We all know that it is a rare thing that inspiration strikes in such a powerful way that a song is completed in one take. Instead we should prepare to write songs like we would write an essay for a writing class: it takes time and many edits, and yes, even the helpful critiques from others to hone them to the point of the final product.

Let's look at an example. Recently, I endeavored to write a fresh version of Charles Wesley's great hymn, *"Jesus, Lover of My Soul."* Forgive me, Charles! For me, the process of recasting this minor-key song was streamlined because the lyrics are already provided, and in the content of the lyrics the "kernel" of the song is presented clearly: our need for Christ's shelter and salvation in life. I had some choices to make, each of which can help or hurt the overall strength of the song in keeping to the kernel: did I want this to be a major key song, or minor key? Do I want this to be meditative, mid-tempo, or driving? I'm sure Wesley's words could be put to all manner of music effectively, but what made most sense to me was to keep it minor key and more on the meditative side of tempo and arrangement. Due to my musical background, a mid-tempo folk/bluegrass number dialed up as I started picking away on my acoustic guitar. Listening to it now reminds me of some of the folkier "Burlap to Cashmere" songs from the late '90s. My goal in those first few hours of hacking away at melodies and chord progressions is to find something that seems to work and exhaust it. If after two–three hours, a song seems to be emerging surrounding the arrangement and feel I happen to have discovered—then I keep writing, searching for a possible refrain/chorus, revamping the melodies and progressions, seeking to improve them. However, if after a few hours a particular line of musical thought is not emerging to a place of excitement, then I trash the idea and start from scratch. (I don't technically "trash" any idea, I tend to keep them all in some recorded format in case it may develop later, which at many points has happened.)

There is certainly no science to this, and every writer has a particular manner that they've learned and found helpful in attacking a new song. About mid-way in my process of writing music for the verses, it became evident that a major-lift chorus would be a helpful change in the song, to prevent the thing from diving too deeply into moroseness. With this major-lift, the chorus seemed to need to go to what Wesley was trying to say, and in this case, verse two seemed to fit the bill as an effective refrain/cry to God as a response to the verse lyrics. This is what I came up with:

Other refuge, I have none
Jesus, leave me not alone
Hangs my soul in helplessness
Christ, You are all faithfulness
Come cover me with the shadow of Your wings

When writing in minor, it would be helpful to consider that as with the pattern we can see in the Psalms, it shouldn't **all** be dark and morose. There is in most "minor key Psalms" a point in which the writer cries out in faith at the crux of their trial. This moment of faith becomes the refrain of the Psalmist's hope and communicates to us our only hope and rest in times of suffering and trial. We want our songs to say that which matters most: Jesus *is* alive and ruling at the right hand of the Father having paid for our sins on his cross, and now we must await his faithful deliverance while in this fallen place. Minor key songs should function in this same manner—deliver hearers to the refrain of hope as we see in the Psalms. If a minor key lacks this release to hope, whether it is found in a chorus or a tag or elsewhere in the song, I don't believe the song accurately reflects reality. The reality is always for the Christian the same: no matter how bad we have it, we have a Savior who loves us and died for us and one day returns for us! There is *always* hope as the Savior lives and rules from heaven! This musical and lyrical release should in some way seek to convey the hope we have in Christ. I would suggest in that moment of the song to both musically and lyrically deliver that hope with clarity, and maybe even with a major lift?

Much more could be said about writing songs in minor keys, but we must move on.

Leading Worship in Minor

Keeping Carl Trueman's warning in mind, the pastor, worship leader, and Christian musician alike should keep an eye out on the diet of songs they are leading the church through week after week. Take a look at the average Sunday morning or weekday small group worship time. If you were to boil down the song lists from these meetings, would a particular theme emerge? Is that theme well-rounded enough to serve all who gather in the church?

First and foremost, the songs we write and the songs we lead Christ's people through should focus on what matters most, and that is Christ himself. Christ's incarnation, his perfect life, His death and resurrection, his ascension into heaven—the gospel—should provide us with the vast majority of our lyrical and musical foci for every gathering of the church. We simply cannot sing enough about Jesus Christ and his salvation. Jesus is the central focus of the Body, and our songs must always reflect that reality.

With Christ solidly as a lyrical focus, consider also: do the songs I write or choose for worship and performance provide sufficient comfort and encouragement for the struggling saint as for those who are rejoicing and seeing Christ clearly? If our song lists boiled down show that our constant theme is: "triumph, joy, triumph!" we are not accurately reflecting the full picture that the Scriptures lead us to believe about God. We are not called to help people along in a "long triumphalist street party," rather as songsters, we can endeavor to help all of God's people to trust God through trial and minor key themes as well as rejoicing to the major ones.

I believe it behooves the believing community when our song choices provide them all with reasons to rejoice *and* trust in the Lord. For the individual who has been struggling through a massive depression for years, triumphalistic worship will seem out of place and out of reality. Yet a diet of only minor key themed songs will miss out on the joy that is set before us, and the gratefulness that should characterize our faith and worship.

May the Lord help us to bring honor to his name in all keys.

Endnotes

1   Mark Dever and Paul Alexander, *The Deliberate Church: Building Your Ministry on the Gospel* (Wheaton: Crossway Books, 2005), 123

2   We don't know the actual keys or melodies of the original tunes that the Psalms were sung to, but I am meaning the *theme* of the Psalms being minor key (examples: Ps. 28, 42, 51, 73) in our western musical tradition.

3   U2, song: "I Still Haven't Found What I'm Looking For" 9 March 1987 The Joshua Tree Island Records

4   Charles Wesley, hymn: "Jesus, Lover of My Soul"

5   Doug Plank, song: "Flowing Streams"

6   Carl R. Trueman, "The Wages of Spin: Critical Writings on Historical and Contemporary Evangelicalism" (Christian Focus: 2004), 159

BLUES
in the Garden

> The blues is an impulse to keep the painful details and episodes of a brutal
> experience alive in one's aching consciousness, to finger its jagged grain,
> and to transcend it, not by the consolation of philosophy but by squeez-
> ing from it a near-tragic, near-comic lyricism. As a form, the blues is an
> autobiographical chronicle of personal catastrophe expressed lyrically.
> —Ralph Ellison, *Living With Music: Jazz Writings*

The African American Spiritual, the root of most American music, sings of the
quest for freedom. History tells us that the Emancipation Proclamation, January
1, 1863, changed the legal status of the African prisoners of the forced labor
system in American slavery. In fact, freedom would come much later. From the
perspective of these Africans, what The Emancipation Proclamation brought was
the solemn reality of a "freed" life still tightly wrapped in oppression. This kind
of "freedom" was not the freedom for which they had hoped, fought, and prayed.

The Blues, which is the offspring of The African American Spirituals, sang of
the burden of this new "freedom." Grief, sadness, abandonment, loneliness, pain,
and suffering were the solemn reality of life. The newly liberated African was in
most cases still viewed and treated as only part human. Their skin's complexion
served as their easily identifiable passport. Life was hard. In the midst of this
struggle to endure life in a different way, the liberated slaves used their musical
instincts and gifts to create a body of music that points us to the reality of life and
struggle: the Blues.

Ain't robbed no train
Ain't done no hanging crime
Just tell 'em slave to tha blues
Even found that man of mine

Blues do tell me
Do I have to die a slave
Do you hear me screamin?
You're going to take me to my grave

If I could break these chains
And let my worried heart go free
Well it's too late now
The blues have made a slave of me

You see me raving
You hear me crying
Oh Lord
This wounded heart of mine

Folks I'm agrievin
From my head to ma shoes
I'm a goodhearted woman
But still I'm chained to tha blues
            —Ma Rainey, "Slave To The Blues"

As the forerunner to "African American Gospel" music, the Blues at first glance do not seem sacred. Once you take a deeper, longer look, however it is clear the Blues have spiritual tensions.

Let the day perish on which I was born,
and the night that said,
A man is conceived.
Let that day be darkness!
May God above not seek it,
nor light shine upon it.
Let gloom and deep darkness claim it.
Let clouds dwell upon it;
let the blackness of the day terrify it.
Why did I not die at birth,
come out from the womb and expire?

Why did the knees receive me?
Or why the breasts, that I should nurse?

For the thing that I fear comes upon me,
and what I dread befalls me.
I am not at ease, nor am I quiet;
I have no rest, but trouble comes.

The lyrics above were composed and sung by one of the great Blues singers of The Bible. They are selected verses in the third chapter of the book of Job, which theologian and jazz pianist Dr. William Edgar, calls a blues book among a few, such as Ecclesiastes (Wisdom). Job's sacred words sing truthfully about the depth of his reality, the purest form of the Blues.

While instances of the Blues can be found throughout the biblical text, some cite the profound words of Jesus on the cross as the greatest blues line uttered: "My God, My God, Why hast thou forsaken me?" (Matt. 27:46) These words reflect deep abandonment, loss, and utter despair. Jesus cries out in agony about His struggle of separation from His Father, even while enduring it.

This great Blues line was a continuation of other lines that Jesus began to sing before reaching Calvary. This song began in the garden of Gethsemane. In the garden, Jesus instructs his disciples to sit while he goes to pray. He takes Peter and the two sons of Zebedee, James and John, with Him further into the garden. He knows the last stage of His journey to the cross is very near. Peter, James, and John are the same three disciples who witnessed the glory of Jesus on the Mount of Transfiguration. Now Jesus wants these three disciples to also witness his deep anguish and deathly grief. Jesus is troubled and is overcome with a great burden of sorrow.

He communicates these feelings to the three disciples by saying, "My soul is very sorrowful, even to death; remain here, and watch with me" (Matthew 26:38). Jesus, devoid of sin, was going to experience and suffer His Father's full terrible, vengeful, all-consuming fire of wrath as punishment for our sin. Who can imagine the weight of His fear, terror, and horror of God's dreadful curse?

Jesus continues a little bit further into the garden to where His betrayal will take place a short time later. He falls on His face praying, "My Father, if it be possible, let this cup pass from me; nevertheless, not as I will, but as you will" (Matthew 26:39). This cup is the cup of suffering. Jesus cries out loud with prayers and supplications to the Only One, His Father who could save Him from death.

After a time, Jesus comes back to the three disciples and finds them sleeping. He speaks directly to Peter saying, "So, could you not watch with me one hour? Watch and pray that you may not enter into temptation. The spirit indeed is willing, but the flesh is weak." (Matthew 26:40–41). Jesus knows that his disciples, including these three, will abandon Him later when Judas with his associates in tow comes to Him bearing a betrayer's kiss.

Jesus leaves the three disciples for a second time to pray. His prays, "My Father, if this cannot pass unless I drink it, your will be done" (Matthew 26:42). He comes back to the three disciples and finds them once again sleeping because they are exhausted. There is no record of Jesus speaking to the three disciples at this point. Jesus leaves the disciples a third time to go and pray. His words remain the same, "My Father, if this cannot pass unless I drink it, your will be done" (Matthew 26:42). The cup must not and will not pass away from Him. Jesus submits to drink this cup of suffering. He is fully committed to His Father's will.

Jesus returns to the disciples and instructs them by saying, "Sleep and take your rest later on. See, the hour is at hand, and the Son of Man is betrayed into the hands of sinners. Rise, let us be going; see, my betrayer is at hand" (Matthew 26:45–46). Jesus is still talking to the disciples when Judas and his associates approach. Jesus is fully prepared to be sacrificed. He continues this last stage of the journey with obedience even unto the cross.

Jesus' determination is reflected in this African American Spiritual.

Prepare me one body,
I'll go down, I'll go down.
Prepare me one body like man;
I'll go down and die.

The man of sorrows, sinner, see
I'll go down, I'll go down,
He died for you and he died for me
I'll go down and die.
      —"Prepare Me One Body," *African American Spiritual*

In the garden Jesus shows us His true humanity. He shows us what struggle looks and feels like. He prays; He cries the Blues; He moans the Blues; and He becomes the Blues. He honors the struggle and us by allowing us to see His tensions.

Jesus, "Man of Sorrows," who is acquainted with grief is singing what W.E.B. Dubois in *Souls of Black Folk* calls the "sorrow songs." Jesus embraces the tensions; He embraces the pain; and He embraces the grief. Jesus prays in a loose version of the 16-bar Blues form.

The 16-bar Blues form has the same basic chord structure as the traditional 12-bar Blues, but with the 9th and 10th measures repeated three times. The first note of the scale is the tonic note, it is the central tone in which the other notes and chords are built upon in a song. The I^7 is the tonic chord that the song is centered on. The V^7 is the dominant chord based on the 5th of the tonic scale. The IV^7 is the subdominant chord based on the 4th step of the tonic scale.

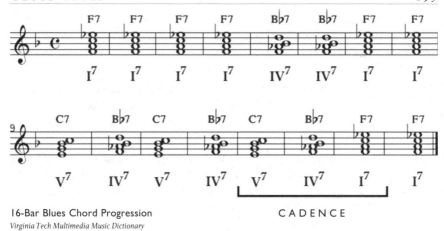

16-Bar Blues Chord Progression   CADENCE
Virginia Tech Multimedia Music Dictionary

First Phrase: Create a short phrase that will be introduced and repeated four times with the same I⁷ chord. (*Measures 1–4*)

Second Phrase: Create a second short phrase that will also be introduced and repeated twice with the same IV⁷ chord. (*Measures 5–6*)

Third Phrase: Repeat the first short phrase you created from measure 1 and repeat it twice with the I⁷ chord. (*Measure 7–8*)

Fourth Phrase: Create a short final phrase that will be introduced and repeated three times with the I⁷ chord and V⁷. (*Measures 9–14*)

Fifth Phrase: Repeat the first phrase and I⁷ chord two times. (*Measures 15–16*)

Just as there are different forms when composing Blues songs, there are also different approaches to writing their lyrics. The lyrics of a Blues song need to be authentic. Pick a theme that resonates with you and has the feel and mood of the Blues.

The Blues speak of abandonment, almost always in a romantic sense of lost love. But on a deeper level it is the loss of human connection, the loss of human touch, the loss of companionship, the loss of fellowship. Jesus knows about loss and He knows about abandonment. Right there in the garden, Jesus experiences abandonment. The same three disciples who witness the glorious scene on the Mount of Transfiguration are the same three who fall asleep and abandon Him in His time of need and struggle. Jesus is alone, while preparing to drink of this bitter cup of suffering.

The Blues give us a clear view of the struggles of life and of the relinquishment of death. Abandoned and embarked on the greatest sacrifice this world has ever known, Jesus gives us another gift—a real lesson in the area of struggle. He shows us His vulnerability through His transparency.

He asks a question familiar to most of us: "Can this pass?" What is at the root of this query? The root is the yearning to employ another method to achieve the goal. This, though, is the God of the universe, yet He is struggling to accomplish with love that which He greatly desires. Why show us His struggle? The struggle is shown to demonstrate Jesus in His humanity and, in so doing, to identify with us in ours.

Dr. William Edgar's essay, "Shadow," in *It Was Good: Making Art To The Glory of God,* asks the question, "Why is the light given to the miserable?" He tells us of the melancholy Brahms struggled with while drawing the connection between deep sorrow and deep joy. Describing Brahms' first movement in his First Symphony, Edgar states, "Throughout the piece, light battles as it were against darkness, joy against sorrow, and finally, hope emerges triumphant." It is through asking and surviving the questions of "why" that we grow to understand the deep connection of sorrow and joy. It may be in facing our shadows, and continuing to struggle that our faith is strengthened. When our faith is tested and strengthened, we can fully embrace and know that God is here for us! Jesus became the curse for us, and His strong cries and tears were heard and seen by His Father. The book of Luke tells us that His sweat were great drops of blood falling down to the ground. He drank of the bitterest cup from His Father's hands.

The Blues tell us about the hardships of this path we call life but they also ask questions, the same questions we ask our Father. Why does God allow suffering? Why do we have so much pain, sorrow, and loss? There are no ifs; we will suffer. We will have to endure loss, afflictions, and grief.

We will see the darkness approach and face the pain. We will have to endure, moan, and sing the Blues.

I hate to see the evening sun go down,
Yes, I hate to see that evening sun go down
Cause it makes me think I'm on my last go 'round
    —W.C. Handy *"St. Louis Blues"*

Did God answer His Son's prayers? The books of Luke and Hebrews tell us that an angel came and strengthened Jesus, but God did not remove the burden of the cross. What does the cross represent? It represents a mixture of beauty, ugliness, violence, truth, abandonment, fellowship, suffering, pain, endurance, hatred, love, darkness, and light.

The Blues teach us that if we embrace this life, we have to endure what this life can bring. God's word teaches us that if we embrace Christ and His cross we must also embrace what that cross represents and brings. Jesus tells us to take up our cross and follow Him. We must drink of the cup which God gives us. Jesus went before us and He recognizes the struggle to obey and the struggle to relinquish our will and way. It is the same Jesus who sends a Comforter in the garden of our Blues.

As the saying goes, you cannot have the joy of Resurrection Sunday without the darkness and pain of Good Friday.

The Blues sung mournfully in the garden teach us that through the horror of the darkest night, in the midst of the shadow of death, there is Light ever present. Joy in the midst of sorrow and hope in the midst of the Blues.

*While conversing with Bassist and Composer, John Patitucci about this book, he coined the phrase, "Blues in the Garden." Thanks John!

IT DON'T MEAN A THING
if it ain't got "le swingue"

France has always had a special fondness for jazz music. French people were among the earliest to recognize the virtues of this unique genre, often before other Europeans and even before many Americans. They welcomed it very early on in its history. James Reese Europe, one of the pioneers of early jazz (some would say proto-jazz), traveled to France with his band during World War I. His "syncopated orchestra," known as the Clef Club Band, was enthusiastically received throughout the country. In different regions of France the townspeople, sensing the music's accessibility, would give Jim Europe compositions of their own or songs about suffering in the war, and he would arrange them for orchestra, bringing new depth to these local compositions. Audiences raved. In August, 1918, the band played to packed houses at the Théâtre des Champs-Élysées and the Tuileries Gardens in Paris.

This warm reception had the effect of further convincing Jim Europe of the uniqueness of black music. When he returned to the States, he wrote, "I have come back from France more firmly convinced than ever that Negroes should write Negro music. We have our own racial feeling... We won France by playing music which was ours and not a pale imitation of others."[1] The drummer in Europe's band, Louis Mitchell, returned to France as a band leader, and played residential gigs in Parisian clubs and casinos. His Jazz Kings featured a New Orleans sound, which helped promote other musicians coming to France, including Sidney Bechet, who eventually made Paris his home. They also made some memorable recordings in 1922–23.[2]

What is it about music from African-American culture that moves not only the French, but peoples around the world? Is it about race? Or something deeper, more universal? The response to jazz in France highlights the elements of this discussion. Overall, the reception of jazz in France in these formative years is under-researched, with some exceptions. The slick, coffee table book, *The Jazz Age in France*, by Charles A. Riley II, discusses the presence of remarkable artists from all over coming to France during the 1920s, with a mention of a couple of African-American painters, but only a brief walk-on part for a couple of black jazz musicians.[3] He does point out that Gertrude Stein and Virgil Thomson cast their opera, *Four Saints in Three Acts*, entirely with black singers. Stein praised Parisians for having greater respect for artists, including African-Americans, than could be found at home.[4] The best study in English, so far, is Jeffrey H. Jackson's *Making Jazz French*, which intensely explores not only the music and musicians, but the social and political structures of France throughout the twentieth century, concentrating on the years between the two wars. And it has generous pages on the *Hot Club de France*, and role of France's greatest early jazz connoisseur, Hugues Panassié.[5] A number of excellent studies are in French. Among them we may count, Denis-Constant Martin & Olivier Roueff, *La France du jazz*; Ludovic Tournès, *New Orleans sur Seine*; and Jean-Dominique Brierre, *Le jazz français de 1900 à aujourd'hui*.[6] We will want to focus on Panassié in particular, but before we do, a little background.

THE BACKGROUND

Writing just after the Second World War, René Dumesnil argues that France's infatuation with jazz was principally a measure of desperation, wanting to be sure and embark on the right ship, the avant-garde, fearful of being left behind. Some vogues lasted longer than others. "Thus the fad of jazz lasted far longer than prognostics about the future led to believe." But jazz arrived because of a combination of enthusiasm and snobbism. It rode on the wake of various influences, "more exotic than profound," accentuating a development that would have occurred anyway, rhythmic freedom, larger orchestras, the use of rare instruments, such as the saxophone, and curiosity about world music.[7]

This is patently one-sided. I believe something far more profound than a taste for the exotic was at work. Certainly, there is something to be said for a prevalent dissatisfaction with some aspects of advanced European music and the freshness of jazz. But there was a deeper connection, one that appeared to draw French people to jazz, but also jazz musicians to France.

France was at a crossroad in the 1930s. World War I had been devastating. Some 1,400,000 Frenchmen lost their lives; and more than 1,000,000 had been gassed or disfigured and left permanently invalid. Women and children suffered more, if possible, and longer, than the men. In the 1920s and 30s much of the female population was in *"le grand deuil,"* or *"le demi deuil."* The population of

France grew only 3% between 1900 and 1939, and that mainly because of immi-
gration. This compares to Germany's 36%, Italy's 33% and Great Britain's 23%.
Moving from terrible economic downturn and unemployment in the 1920s, to a
temporary surge in 1930, then a huge depression beginning in 1932, the result
in 1935 was that an astonishing 1,000,000 were unemployed and the country
plunged into debt.

Jean-Louis Loubet Del Bayle, in his study of *Les non-conformistes des années
30*, explains both the anxiety and the hopes within the political realm during the
1930s.[8] Paul Valéry in 1932 had declared that France did not know where it
was going, impotent as it was because of prodigious knowledge and accelerated
change, but without a compass. Because of the cruel awakening which dispelled
the dreams of peace cultivated after 1918, the years from 1932 on saw many
things crumble.[9] At the same time, in the arts there was a drift from novels or
memoirs, often involving psychological preoccupations, to much more social
engagement. Whereas the Surrealists often belonged to the Communist Party,
and dialectical materialism was in the atmosphere, suddenly France was strongly
attracted to Charles Péguy, Bernanos, Céline, Malraux, and Saint-Exupéry. This
added a measure of gravitas to the more sparkling, unconstrained spirit of the
previous decade. As Del Bayle puts it, after the joy of the former group, "we saw
the sky be covered with clouds and we lifted our heads to see the first lightning
[of the storm]." Joy was replaced by risk, experience by engagement, he adds.[10]

ANXIETY

A kind of quest in the 1930s, fairly ephemeral, grouped together much of
the youth of its time, which was looking almost in vain for cultural renewal.
It focused on two symptoms considered especially nefarious for the world.
Ironically, the first was America! In the June 1930 issue of *Revue des Deux
Mondes*, André Chaumeix counted no fewer than a dozen books appraising the
United States, a minority of them admiring and the rest sharply critical. Many
youth movements of the day were drawn to the latter. For example, Robert Aron
and Arnaud Dandieu wrote of *Le cancer américain*, which was spreading far
from the war zones, using a shelter provided by modern technology. A special
issue of *Rédaction* was dedicated to "America on trial." These works did not simply denounce the mechanization of the world, for they admitted a certain role for
technology. But they worried about a society in which "man appears as a machine
for consumerism and productivity without any other reason for existing, any
other happiness, and other destiny."[11] This was, among other things, a critique of
advanced capitalism.

The second negative indicator was European nihilism. For many younger
people, Nietzsche was the emblem of the times. Nietzsche regretted nihilism, but
saw no way around it as long as people held on to the vestiges of Christianity and

Platonism. According to him, humans, having hoped to surpass their own reality, fell back into non-being; having hoped to attain the supreme wisdom of being, they managed to attain only the desperate solitude of the fool.[12] Eugen Weber's study of France in the 1930s, *The Hollow Years*, reminds us that fifteen different cabinets were formed under the presidency of the Protestant Gaston Doumergue, 1924–31, three of them in the eleven months just before the murder of his successor, President Paul Doumer, in 1932.[13] Then there were another seventeen under Albert Lebrun, 1932–40. The right and the left resembled two different countries in a France that some, like the historian Jean-Baptiste Duroselle, considered un-governable.[14] While Hitler was tightening his grip and Mussolini was expanding Italian power into Africa, most French leaders could only stand by and complain. Strikes and demonstrations throughout France expressed the frustration of the many against unemployment and ineffective leadership. A slim socialist victory in 1936 could not stave off the discontent. Despite slight improvements for workers, the general picture did not improve. While Spain entered a revolution, France exercised prudence. Despite evidence for the bombing of Guernica by the Germans, so powerfully captured by Picasso's best-known painting, which were inspired by photographs he saw in *Ce soir* and other French papers, the right-wing press managed to convince the French that the Basques themselves had perpetrated the devastation. And although France could probably have withstood Hitler, or even brought him down in 1936, by September of 1938, when the Munich capitulation was signed, most French people greeted the agreement with enthusiasm, while the government attempted to negotiate a non-aggression treaty with Germany (which was signed November 22).

HOPES

Yet into this vacuum came a certain amount of expectation. Into this dark context did come considerable cultural renewal. Despite Weber's negative title, he helpfully points out that France knew both serious times of trouble and yet also quite a significant degree of cultural rekindling in the decades between the two World Wars. Education under the Third Republic had been little different from previous eras, with its strict discipline, and the rigorous inculcation of Greek, Latin, ancient history, and the classics. But after the Great War, this would change. For example, philosophy now stressed Pascal and Bergson. Henri Bergson (1859–1941) was the great antidote to nineteenth century materialism, stressing liberty and the vital spirit. "Didactic philosophy, avant-garde science, school textbooks, and the inchoate yearnings of young and not-so-young people searching for beliefs coincided, and coincided further with the contemporary Catholic quest for up-to-date justifications."[15] Like the cinema, philosophy showed that time and space were interconnected. "Like art, philosophy suggested that experience could plumb intuition, instinct, or the unconscious, in a kind of sensual divination."[16]

Three youth movements also characterized this period, *La jeune droite, l'Ordre nouveau,* and *Esprit.* Space forbids any analysis of these groups, save to say that while they diverged considerably one from the other, there were at least two commonalities. The first was a sense that humanity had fallen into a pure rationalism. (This is why the Surrealist movement was attractive to so many at the time. It appeared to refuse this reduction.) The other was an attempt at being socially engaged while recognizing the need to nurture the human spirit.

The depression apparently affected artists much less than other professionals. For one reason, their works were considered more durable and secure than stocks or bonds. For another, American money, private or institutional, was being spent in generous amounts on the arts. But perhaps more importantly there was a sense of renewal and freshness in the arts not known in the economic or political realms. France in this age is an astonishing seedbed for the visual arts, particularly as they tried to connect with people without slouching into Socialist realism. Raoul Dufy (1877–1953) was original though underrated. He and Matisse moved from their prewar *fauvisme* to more decorative styles, including tapestries, in an attempt to revive a dying trade, one supported by the Front Populaire. Edouard Pignon (b. 1905) remembers the link between modern art and revolution, trying to connect abstraction to the people, who struggled to welcome it. This required new departures if it was to succeed.

HUGUES PANASSIÉ

Enter American music in general. And enter jazz. A great deal could be said about the way jazz was received by the French. Each of the above feelings, the anxiety and the hopes, found their foil in the coming of jazz to France. For convenience, and also because he is such an intriguing, not to say important, figure, let us concentrate on a unique early jazz critic, Hugues Panassié (1912–1975). No one better embodies one typical kind of French attitude in this cultural moment than Panassié. He was prolific, dogmatic, humorous, entrepreneurial, and arguably one of the major reasons for the popularity of jazz in France in the years between the two World Wars. Panassié fell in love with jazz as a young man. He had inherited enough money to be able to live independently and to kick off a number of initiatives. In 1932 he founded the Hot Club de France, and acted as its president until his death. In 1933 he attended a concert of the Duke Ellington orchestra at the Salle Pleyel. Only twenty one, he went backstage and interviewed a number of the band members, including Cootie Williams and Barney Bigard. An excellent writer, he prolifically recorded his ventures into the world of jazz.[17]

Among the fascinating aspects of his life, he used jazz records as a way to defy the Nazis who had occupied France during World War II. The Nazis hated jazz, mostly because it was produced by blacks, but also because it seemed (and was!) subversive of socialist doctrine. In *Really the Blues*, Milton "Mezz" Mezzrow describes Panassié's approach:

> The Nazi censor was shown a record labeled *La Tristesse de St Louis*, and Hugues explained helpfully that it was a sad song written about poor Louie (*sic.*) the Fourteenth, lousy with that old French tradition. What the Kultur-hound didn't know was that underneath the phony label was a genuine Victor one, giving Louis Armstrong as the recording artist and stating the real name of the number—"St Louis Blues."[18]

Panassié was a subversive, in the best sense. And he loved life. All those who knew him testify to his humor, his love of French wines, his encyclopedic knowledge of just about everything, and, of course, his strongly held opinions about just about everything!

Although most historians recognize his role, few interact with his views in any depth, and even fewer try to understand him in the context of French social and cultural history. A possible exception is Whitney Balliett, who describes him in an article originally published in *The New Yorker*. There he notes that besides the erratic "Aux Frontières du Jazz," by the Belgian Robert Goffin, Panassié's *Le Jazz Hot*, published in 1934,[19] was the first book of jazz criticism, "and put jazz on the map in Europe and in its own country" as well as to America. He adds, wryly, that the French are old hands at introducing other cultures to themselves.[20] The book was a revolutionary celebration, he says, exulting relatively unknown current musicians such as Duke Ellington, Art Tatum, and Bix Beiderbecke. At the same time, Panassié stumbled over several facts. Among them, according to Balliett, his absurd obsession with Milton Mezz Mezzrow and Tommy Ladnier. He did "correct himself" somewhat in his next book, *La véritable musique de jazz*,[21] but fell into more difficulties, because this time he rejected just about everything that was white (still with the exception of Mezz and Tommy) with a *mea culpa* about his lack of proper education in the real jazz of black people. Finally, Balliett discusses Panassié's complete aversion to bebop or "progressive jazz," as he calls it. But besides a brief outline, we don't learn a great deal about Panassié's fundamental aesthetic commitments, nor his reasons for rejecting bebop, from Balliett.

Panassié was drawn to the very conservative Roman Catholic renewal groups. The royalist *Action française* was banned by the Vatican, permitting Catholics to embrace the wider views of Jacques Maritain and, especially, of Léon Bloy. It might stretch things to attribute Panassié's love of jazz to this renewal. We do not exactly know how far he may have been drawn to one or more of the three movements mentioned above. Yet we do know of his affinities to various aspects of them, whatever his connections might have been.

For example, Léon Bloy (1846–1917) was Panassié's all-time favorite prose author. From a Free Mason and Voltairian skeptical family in Périgueux, he moved to Paris in 1867 and came under the sway of Julien Barbey d'Aurevilly, who influenced him to become a Roman Catholic. He became a prolific writer, whose fame spread after the publication of *Le Salut par les Juifs* (1892). A fierce critic of the middle class (the bourgeoisie), Bloy's conservative Catholicism combined a sense of the need to find authenticity through suffering and poverty with a bow to Cabalism. He believed history to be an immense liturgical text where the tiniest parts have as much significance as the chapters and verses. A melancholy man, he thought that honest persons must admit they will never know who they are. Panassié discovered Bloy when ill as a child. It changed his life, he admits, and led him to discover a Catholicism "hitherto unsuspected, because L.B. spent his time excoriating, particularly, [of] Catholics, priests, bishops, even the Pope."[22] Thanks to Léon Bloy Panassié identified what they believed to be the hypocrisy of official Catholicism, together with the "sniveling sentimentalism" of much of 20th century religious culture, but also, as they saw it, the beauty of deeper spirituality and the virtues of religious writings not generally popular, from the Church Fathers down to the present.

I believe this spiritual commitment in the style of Léon Bloy is an important part of Panassié's aesthetic principles. His views on jazz are curiously anti-bourgeois, as he understands that, and at the same time touting a canonical list of names and acceptable principles. One need not read extensively into Panassié before encountering his fierce polemic against critics who fail to discern the right kind of jazz from the wrong kind. He was merciless of anyone who confused the very white Paul Whiteman or the British Jack Hylton with true jazz.[23] He has detailed accounts of critical reviews by Americans and French people who confuse hot improvisation for carelessness.

As mentioned, new departures were in the air. One of them was the Surrealist movement, which burst on the scene with the *Manifeste Dada* (1918) by Tristan Tzara, followed six years later by André Breton's *Le Manifeste du Surréalisme* (1924), in which he declared that thought should be freed from any control by reason or any aesthetic or mental preoccupations. Curiously, perhaps, Hugues Panassié was quite fond of the Surrealists. He enjoyed André Breton. His favorite poet was, and remained, Pierre Reverdy, who had affinities with Surrealism, but also with the Catholic Church. This unique figure, born in Narbonne 1889, of a family of sculptors, lived for 16 years in the Bateau-Lavoir of Monmartre. He was friends with Aragon, Apollinaire, Picasso, Braque, Matisse, the sculptor Pablo Garballo, and many others. Without officially belonging to the movement, he associated with Surrealism, and became one of its principal poets. André Breton praised him as having a unique rhythmic gift, and as putting a halo over ordinary events of life. In 1926 Reverdy had a religious conversion and spent the rest of his life in the abbey of Solesme, writing what many consider to be his most inspired works, including, "Sources du Vent," "Ferraille," and "Le Chant des Morts." He was a solitary figure and his poems are full of suffering, yet they also project hope, and celebrate the intricacies of the social and natural world. He died in 1960.

Panassié praised Reverdy extravagantly, calling him the greatest theoretician as well as poet of modern times. Though they met and had long discussions, the subject of jazz was seldom brought up. Once, though, Panassié played some music for him, and it elicited the following remark, which Panassié dubbed the best statement ever made by an outsider: "The superiority of music over words is in its precision. It is absolutely impossible not to be taken in by the truth of black music. For the unflawed white person the black person has an answer for everything our civilization has made us lose. We cannot keep going around in circles as we have been, we must move ahead or leap."[24]

Panassié certainly does not represent the entire consensus of French reception of jazz. But his views and judgments do reflect the many cross-currents of the times. Above all, they represent at least one form of the "hopes and fears" of Europeans during the early twentieth century. As such they connected with something deeply significant about the music called jazz. But before we explore this connection further, a rather important parenthesis must be opened.

WHITHER BEBOP?

Panassié's most violent polemics were over the move from traditional jazz to bebop, or what he called *le jazz progressiste*. Appropriately labeled a revolution, the bebop movement was a reaction, though with some continuity, to the jazz of the 1930s. The so-called swing era featured big bands, highly synchronized jazz, meant for dancing. At its best it reflected the creativity of jazz. It also reflected the roots of African-American music, going back to spirituals, blues, and ragtime. For example, Fletcher Henderson's orchestra, formed in 1922, resided first at the Club Alabam then at the Roseland, in New York. It was a seedbed of great musicians and creativity. Louis Armstrong, Don Redman, Benny Carter, and Coleman Hawkins, mentioned above, as well as many other jazz luminaries, played with the band. Yet soon, white imitations were able to rise to prominence, particularly because they had access to economic power. While black celebrities like Armstrong, Ellington, Bill Robinson, Bert Williams, could hold their own, most blacks had little access to the economic power and success the white bands did.

A fascinating case in point is Coleman Hawkins (1904–1969). At the turn of the decade the swing craze either died down, or became too sweet. Hawkins found that his introverted personality and detached style lent itself better to a new way of playing. He abandoned the large orchestra in favor of the small combo. After his stint with Hylton he went to New York City where he met some talented younger musicians. In 1939, he recorded a version of "Body and Soul" that would literally change the face of jazz music. Featuring Teddy Wilson on piano and Louis Bellson on drums, the piece was laid back, inventive, meditative, all within the parameters of jazz's swing. Hawkins became the model for a generation of saxophone players, including Charlie ("Yardbird") Parker (1920–1955). Parker's breathtaking improvisations, his innovations in melody, harmony, and rhythm, would be at the heart of the bebop revolution.

Though one could hardly find a "typical" bebop artist, since there were so many different personalities, yet at least three features emerge which are in conscious dissonance with swing music. (1) Bebop is distinctly African American, and from New York. Not that there was racial exclusion, but this music was more clearly rooted in the uncomfortable realities of race in America.[25] The term itself likely comes from being beaten, or "bopped." The musicians were experimenters, trying to see how to push harmonies to new levels. They also played around with the beat, not following the usual hierarchy of strong and weak beats. Solos were long. "Blues notes" like the flatted fifth were prominent. (2) Most of the pioneers were young in 1942, in their teens or twenties, and were thus formed by the boom and bust cycle of the swing era, including the great depression and the outbreak of World War II. In many ways, the status quo was undermined. (3) At the same time, and this point is often forgotten, the beboppers were committed to careers as commercial dance musicians. They were about creating a good artistic product. So they weren't the negative, disgruntled musicians reacting to sentimental swing, as they were often portrayed, but were more often than not just frustrated that things hadn't worked out.

Bebop was developed in the school of the jam session. Late at night, musicians would experiment with new rhythms and "changes" (chord progressions). Often they would take standards and mess around with them. For example, "How High the Moon" would become "Ornithology," using the same chords but sped-up and enriched. Though at first the jam session was an in-house experimentation, it eventually became a symbol of alienation. There was a plea for authenticity. Real jazz could only be played away from the marketplace. It became "avant-garde" not because isolated, nor the romantic outsider, the "beatnik" savant that some whites wanted it to be, but as a feeder for new ideas.

ANTI JAZZ?

Now, for Panassié, this revolution was completely problematic. It was a departure from the great, traditional classic jazz, exemplified in New Orleans or in Duke Ellington's artistry. In a word, for him, it was "anti jazz." According to Panassié, though bebop claimed to evolve into newer, more creative forms, in fact it was a concession to the worst features of modernity. Panassié lumps Charlie Parker together with Arnold Schoenberg (1874–1951) the twelve-tone composer who changed so many rules in classical music, and considers the entire "progressive jazz" phenomenon to be a rupture with the mainstream. Whereas Schoenberg leapt into atonality, the new jazz left behind swing and everything that made up the black experience.

Naturally, personal factors were involved. His disagreeable break with Charles Delauney, his earlier colleague and co-founder of the Hot Club, is a tale in itself. They questioned each other's judgment and taste, they battled it out for the right to direct the publications coming out of the Hot Club. There were questions of authority and accountability. But mostly, Panassié's polemic against the newer jazz was an aesthetic question. In his discussions of Charlie Parker, whose music he disdains, he takes great delight in quoting him in an aside, where he "admitted" that bebop was not jazz. He found such a quote by Parker from a *Downbeat* interview, which goes on to say that bop had no roots in jazz. Panassié used it throughout his polemics against critics who accepted bebop. Who is to know exactly what Parker might have meant by this? He likely was criticizing the so-called jazz of the commercial swing bands. And there is something inconsistent here in that Panassié had earlier agreed with Duke Ellington that jazz was not a helpful label.[26] It's the same for Dizzy Gillespie, the great trumpet innovator associated with bebop. Panassié opines that he is "a most skilled trumpeter who started out inspired by Roy Eldridge [but who] then sought to express himself in an original style, abandoning the musical tradition of his own race in order to use instrumental techniques and harmonic intervals drawn from a study of European music." According to Panassié's historiography, these musicians, including Dizzy Gillespie and Charlie Parker had begun as jazz artists, then, becoming "European," they broke with the form.[27]

Of bebop itself, Panassié states, with no nuance, that it simply is not jazz. He gives several reasons for this view. (1) Bebop musicians abandoned black instrumental tradition, and adopted white ways of playing, with no inflections or vibrato or phrasing with lots of contrasts. (2) The rhythm section lacks swing, and instead uses "pseudo-Spanish figures imported from Cuba and certain Latin American countries." (3) Boppers systematically use chords and intervals drawn from European modern music, thus destroying the harmonic climate of jazz.[28] Panassié considers that one cannot dance to bebop music, despite the setting for much of the music which was meant precisely to restore the true dance element in jazz.

PRESUPPOSITIONS

Again following his mentor Léon Bloy, Panassié rails against the notion of progress. In his vehement book *La bataille du jazz*, he launches a sustained critique of the whole notion that modern jazz is a positive evolution from traditional jazz. He sternly opposes another French critic, André Hodeir, whose notion of jazz is summed up in the word "evolution." He quotes Baudelaire's invective against the idea of progress, in which he attacks such a fatuous idea as progress, along with the French obsession with American industrial society, which have nothing to do with the moral world or the supernatural world.[29]

As we know, there was considerable anti-American sentiment in France in the years between the wars, and even afterwards. Panassié was certainly not anti-American, but his attachment to the African-American race was so strong that he lumped together the evils of mechanization and bad music with white America. For example, he severely denounced Benny Goodman's music as white, mechanical, and rigid, without the sensibility of blacks. Any redeeming factor is there because of Goodman's collaboration with Teddy Wilson and Lionel Hampton, black musicians, as well as his use of Fletcher Henderson's arrangements. I personally have sympathies with some of his judgments about the music, though not his essentialism. But most seriously, he was often quite blind to many of the beauties of the more contemporary music. Miles Davis, for him, was just a sell-out to white culture. Exceptions to bebop did exist. In fact for Panassié, being "modern" is not a fault, as long as it is in continuity with the roots. Thus, musicians like Erroll Garner, Ray Bryant, Jacki Byard, and many others, were carrying on the trend of true jazz (le vrai jazz). They are more-or-less clandestine travelers and must believe that true jazz is not at an impasse (note the curiously evolutionary language!).[30]

There is surely a lot going on in this polemic. Some of it is no doubt aesthetic. A good deal of it seems to me to be rooted in issues of authority. Without being able to prove such a connection empirically, I have come to believe there is a strong analogy between Panassié's conservative (intégriste) Roman Catholicism and his authoritarian views on jazz. Just as in the church there are lists of doctrines and saints, so in jazz criticism there is a proper aesthetic and a proper list of acceptable musicians. In his historiography of decline, there is a sort of nostalgia for an Edenic, pre-fallen natural human, found in the black race. The Mass can only be in Latin, and Vatican II had destroyed the liturgy of Pius X, thus severing the true continuity of the Church from the time of Saint Peter. The analogy of "true jazz" to Catholic conservatism is patent.

One of the sadder results of these positions was that Panassié became more and more isolated from mainstream journals and critics. The Bulletin which he had founded, and which contained so many helpful reviews of disks, increasingly became the voicepiece for these anti-progressive polemics. Today, long after Panassié has been gone, the periodical seems to sustain itself principally as the opposition to much of regular jazz. It is almost co-dependent on forms that it rejects. Dare we say that the spirit of outsider opposition does particularly well in France, whether in government or in other areas of life.

JAZZ AND GOOD SUBVERSION

What can we learn about this unique man, and his views of jazz from the Christian point of view? First, jazz is indeed subversive in the best sense. It is an agent for renewal, even in the most difficult circumstances. Here is how it worked. Despite the horrors of slavery, hope and renewal were sewn into the African community. The sheer numbers accounting for slavery are astonishing. By 1786 the number of slaves in the British colonies of America and the West Indies added to 2,130,000. This figure represents only half, or less, of those who were uprooted from their homelands, since they either died in mid-passage or were so "unfit" upon arrival that they were exterminated by their captors. But numbers do not come close to conveying all that was suffered by enslaved Africans. The decimation of families, the paternalism, the brutality of the working conditions, these were at the heart of the experience of slavery.

Yet into this sad story, another was overlaid. The gospel of Christ came into the lives of many slaves. Whether during the two great awakenings, or more quietly, thousands of enslaved Africans came to faith. One could not miss the irony here. Black slaves embraced the religion of their oppressors, without endorsing their oppressive practices. And from thence, very simply, biblical faith became the mainstay of slaves, and then African Americans. As Sylvia Frey and Betty Wood put it:

> The passage from traditional religions to Christianity was arguably the single most significant event in African American history. It created a community of faith and provided a body of values and a religious commitment that became in time the principal solvent of ethnic differences and the primary source of cultural identity. It provided African-Americans with an ideology of resistance and the means to absorb the cultural norms that turned Africans into African Americans. The churches Afro-Christians founded formed the institutional bases for these developments and served as the main training ground for the men and women who were to lead the community out of slavery and into a new identity as free African American Christians.[31]

How is this related to subversion? Very simply, the gospel allowed Africans not only to survive, but often to get the better of their circumstances, transforming them into opportunity.

Let us take two examples, the case of worship, then of the dance. Plantation owners did not often welcome the conversion of their slaves. Often the new believers would have to worship in secret. They built "praise houses" far away from the plantation and brought blankets and sheets, hanging them on the walls and then dousing them with water, producing insulation against any who would hear their music and preaching. The sounds were extraordinary, by all accounts. Chroniclers record that worship and singing were fresh, passionate, and full of vitality. One witness said, "Everybody's heart was in tune, and when they called on God they made Heaven ring." She adds, "[My old plantation would] make the dense old woods, for miles around, reverberate with their wild notes. These notes were not always merry because they were wild. On the contrary, they were mostly of a plaintive cast, and told a tale of grief and sorrow. In the most boisterous outbursts of rapturous sentiment, there was ever a tinge of deep melancholy."[32]

This pattern of hiding and then creating new life is typical of the earliest Christian experience of the enslaved Africans. Because of the gospel, suppression, followed by reemergence, was the way not only to survive but even to flourish under persecution.

A second example is the dance. This one is fascinating. One set of impediments to Africans dancing came from a series of laws, known as the black codes, in various states. Many legal issues revolved around whether or not a slave was fully human, and thus could have certain rights. The legal tradition inherited from the European background meant the rational idea of the equality of every human before the law. This took on a new significance when labor power became more and more of a commodity. But in the South, drawing partly on ancient communal and feudal law, it was critical to treat slaves as property. Thus a kind of contradiction was built into the legal system, not to say the mentalities. At any rate, various codes were written which tried to balance these two opposites. Some of them disallowed the same kind of education for slaves as for white children, yet provided for certain forms of learning. Murder laws began to be written which had some consequence when a white killed a black, often by excessive discipline, but yet enforcement was not guaranteed.

In many cases dancing was prohibited in the black codes. Slave dancing was often frowned upon especially when using the drums. Among the reasons cited were the appearance of lewdness, and the possibility of leading to a riot.[33] But the converted slaves adjusted to these prohibitions in a creative way. Of course, drums were somewhat a concealable Africanism, since you really do not always need the actual instrument in order to achieve the requisite level of percussion. Handclapping and "Patting juba" were techniques using just the body to produce rhythmic sounds.

But there are other interesting ways in which suppression and reemergence occurred over the issue of dancing. For example, when dancing was forbidden in Congo Square, New Orleans, the black leadership went to the town fathers and asked them to define the dance. They did. After deliberation it was determined that dancing meant crossing your feet![34] So, instead of dancing, technically, black people invented several non-dance movements. For example, such movement was known as the ring shout. Participants would form concentric circles and jump up and down. Often there was a small group standing still, clapping hands and swaying, encircled by a larger group moving in a ring. All were singing, often antiphonally, and keeping time. But they would never cross their feet! Just watch a black choir move up to the altar: they're moving but not dancing!

The name of the movement, *shout*, is likely from the Afro-Arabic word, *saut*, to dance around the Kabaa in Mecca. When this rite was carried into North America it took on both a subversive and a religious signification. It became a "dance," and biblical precedents were often cited, as in occasions where the Israelites were known "to dance before the tabernacle." The word *shout* understandably was associated with the biblical injunction to "clap your hands... and shout before the Lord." (Ps. 47:1)[35] This kind of renewal is at the heart of African-American music.

Many times the reemergence was full of satire and mischief. For example, at the formal dances held on plantations, there could be parody by blacks who on the surface were full of respect, but underneath were able to mock their oppressors. According to Morgan p. 586: "Us slaves watched white folks' parties where the guests danced a minuet and then paraded in a grand march... Then we'd do it too, but we used to mock 'em, every step." Slaves were inventive, open to white influences but always accepting them on their own terms, often parodying what they saw.[36] The music known as the blues derives from this kind of spirit.

Other examples include the use of double meanings. Consider the expression "get happy," associated with the popular jazz tune of the same name. It's really an expression about spiritual renewal. For example, in the spiritual, we find these lyrics: "I went to the valley and I didn't go to pray; but my soul got happy and I stayed all day."[37] Of course we know the recently popular gospel song "Oh Happy Day." And it is well-known that the spirituals were often loaded with such double meanings, to be used as signals to alert the slaves. For example, "Wade in the water, children," an allusion to Joshua stepping into the Jordan, was used to alert the fugitive slaves that their pursuers were using bloodhounds, and it was best to flee in the river, to ward off the scent. Or, "I'm on my way to Canaan land," was code for fleeing to Canada, where slavery was forbidden. These and many other example show how the Christian faith gave courage and vitality to an oppressed community.

It seems that Panassié and the Hot Club were fully aware of the good subversion afforded by jazz music. They may not have been fully aware of the extent to which African Americans were able to liberate many parts of social life, including worship. Indeed, they may not have emphasized enough the importance of Christian faith as a worldview in the background of jazz, though they certainly recognized it. Yet, they did understand the gift of renewal in the midst of a troubled world, no doubt because this so paralleled the needs in their own context.

Two addenda might be noted. First, this pattern of subversion is not restricted to African American music, nor to slavery. The French Huguenots used music for very much the same purposes in their resistance against attempts to rope them in through centralization in France. Music is something of an ideal instrument of opposition. Second, jazz had had a similar role in various contexts outside of France. One notable example is its function within the Soviet Union. There, the situation was intensified owing to the contradiction between the ideology of populism and the racist practices of the communist system.[38]

AUTHENTICITY

Second, as we have seen, Panassié and his colleagues had strong opinions on what represented true jazz and what did not. Friendships and institutions were fractured over which musicians and which trends were the real thing. What explains this great zeal, not to say dogmatism? We saw a parallel between this quest for orthodoxy and the conservative Roman Catholicism practiced by many of these early French jazz critics. I do think there is some reason for this quest for truth, the concern for authentic jazz vs. imitations, woven into its the history, making this unique American music a natural foil for France's own yearnings after authenticity at the time of its reception.

While many of us do not share all of Panassié's particular opinions, especially his judgments on so-called progressive jazz, the issue of authenticity is indeed crucial when discussing jazz music. We should note in fairness that while some of his views seem quaint to us today, homage is due before a great deal that Panassié got right, and that he did for the success of jazz in France. The Hot Club was truly one of the first outfits to recognize the beauties of jazz, well before others. It sponsored groups and organized concerts and achieved a few recordings, many of which helped jazz to achieve its reputation outside of America. Panassié was a warm and generous man whose life was spent supporting musicians and their music. We need to honor that, while closely scrutinizing views that were idiosyncratic at best.[39]

But more deeply, authenticity does matter in music, whether in jazz or other genres. There is plausibility for arguments which note a more pure beginning, and then a degree of compromise, whether through commercialization or some other kind of worldliness. I would argue that one of the reasons for the freshness of jazz is its church connection. Is it not the case that the sufferings of slavery, and the hope of the gospel, gave this music something of a quality of depth not always found in the surrounding culture? Can it not be said that much of this wonderful music was hopeful without being nostalgic, because, through the gospel, it had come through the valley of darkness, and then to the banquet table?

Panassié was not alone in celebrating the authenticity of the earliest jazz, which he believed was most deeply rooted in the African-American culture. Hans Rookmaaker (1922–1977), another European, was particularly enamored with early jazz, and spent much of his life exploring it. For him the New Orleans sounds of musicians such as Joe "King" Oliver was an apex. Rookmaaker praises Oliver for a number of qualities. First, his band was not a collection of soloists, but an ensemble of musicians always working together.[40] He compares their sound not to later swing music, but to Bach's *Brandenburg Concerti*, with their polyphony, and also their joy, serenity, and "the same lack of any romanticism or rhetoric" as baroque music.[41] Second, the band was black. And also (going much further than Panassié), the music was the fruit of black Christian culture. "We can typify many aspects of this black culture as early Christian; these people stood alone, with their faith in their hearts and the Bible in their hands, just as the churches in Ephesus or Corinth to whom St Paul wrote."[42]

Later, this original integrity would be broken, Rookmaaker argued. Oliver played jazz in the West, but his music did not belong to the West of Paul Klee or Piet Mondrian. Later, however, the modern West would creep in. First, solos took on a modernist individualism. Louis Armstrong "blew New Orleans jazz apart by his individualistic, improvisational, fierce interpretations... He was the big man and the band permitted to accompany him was much weaker."[43] Swing music replaced New Orleans. With it came "the abandonment of the real Negro elements in jazz for the benefit of white elements... " Duke Ellington's music is "more Western in spirit." Worse, "The music itself fails to move us after we have heard it a few times. It lacks depth and authenticity, which we need, it leaves a void."[44] From there everything goes further downhill. Modern jazz is as lifeless as the photographs in the exhibit, *The Family of Man*, which basically says, life goes on, but with no particular overarching meaning.[45]

While Rookmaaker dates "the fall" earlier than does Panassié, on the whole he attributes to the original jazz more overtly Christian qualities than does Panassié. He defended jazz against its detractors, warning his readers not to associate jazz with negative things such as the primitive, the barbaric, the unchristian, etc. Instead, of earlier jazz especially, he says, "Let us be fair in our judgment; black music, in its many varieties, is certainly worthwhile and sometimes is a clearer fruit of Christian civilization than a lot of Western music is."[46] The major point is that both authors care deeply about authenticity. This, I take it, was a concern during the years when jazz first came to Europe. This concern led many to advocate for a music, as well as a life, that was real, rooted in something genuine.

In my own view this is right. While I do not share either Panassié's or Rookmaaker's historiographies, particularly the "state of nature" vs. "the fall" (things are more complex in the world of jazz as it developed), I do share in their view that when it burst onto the scene, the music was fresh, rooted in something better than some of the arts from decadent European culture. Naturally, other elements are mixed in. There was something exotic about this music from such a different culture. Many of the best jazz scholars have been white people, and surely part of that is because the music seems unsullied, singularly different from the dominant Western music. Perhaps is was their chance to get free from their own rather more complex and alienating way of life. The temptation becomes strong, then, to form opinions about the music which justify it and canonize it. Much like the "early music" movement, which tended to justify the purest sounds of period instruments and performance techniques, the love of early jazz was a quest for the real thing.

In our own time various critics and artists are encouraging research into authentic jazz. There is a back-to-the-roots movement which on the whole is doing a great deal for the perpetuation of jazz music. It is certainly a mixed bag. Authenticity has many names. Consider, for example, the work of trumpeter Wynton Marsalis. Not only his teaching, but his performing are "conservative," in the sense that they seek to identify the deepest roots of jazz with the social and cultural environment which gave them birth. In his album *From the Plantation to the Penitentiary* he makes a musical statement about the way things are in New Orleans and America after Hurricane Katrina. A number of the songs are a commentary on the problem of slouching away from the roots. Although generally Marsalis does not care for rap music, there is a hip-hop tune on this album called "Where Y'all At," which uses a blues-like gospel background, with call-and-response, taking a bow toward the church tradition of New Orleans music. He rails against the faux trendy leaders of today:

> All you '60s radicals and world beaters/
>   Righteous revolutionaries and Camus readers
> Liberal students and equal rights pleaders/
>   What's goin' on now that y'all are the leaders
> All you patriots, compatriots and true blue believers/
>   Brilliant thinkers and overachievers
> All you when I was young we were so naïve'ers/
>   Y'all started like Eldridge and now you're like Beaver

Like many African Americans, Marsalis is crying out for true leadership in the world. He misses the authenticity of the black experience when there were such mentors as W. E. B. Du Bois, Booker T. Washington, and others.

My own conviction, as I draw this to a conclusion, is that jazz does have something authentic about it, and must constantly be defended against counterfeits. But we will not correctly identify its true source unless we recognize that it owes a great deal to its roots in the Christian worldview of enslaved Africans. The music has had its ups and downs, and many trends and counter-trends have marked its history. Different jazz connoisseurs assign different degrees of Christian influence or none at all to jazz in its various eras. The French in particular and

Europeans in general responded to jazz in part because it represented something subversive in a good way, and something fresh and authentic. Not always fully aware of the force of the gospel in this music, still, the attraction of it in a time of great upheaval, between the two wars and beyond, is undeniably connected to its Christian roots. In order to do greater justice to this remarkable ancestry, however, critics and scholars will have to recognize more fully the spiritual background for the music we call jazz. The French were really onto something!

Endnotes

1   From the *Literary Digest*, April 26, 1919, cited in Eileen Southern: *The Music of Black Americans: A History* (New York: W.W.Norton, 1971), p. 349.

2   See http://www.redhotjazz.com/mitchellsjk.html.

3   (New York: Harry Abrams, 2004). Josephine Baker is cited prominently. Riley also notes the interest that American expatriates took in black music. For example, Gerald Murphy became quite an expert in the Negro spiritual, returning to Hollywood as the music consultant for *Hallelujah!*

4   Ibid., p. 91.

5   Jeffrey H. Jackson, *Making Jazz French: Music and Modern Life in Interwar Paris* (Durham & London: Duke University Press, 2003).

6   Denis-Constant Martin & Olivier Roueff, *La France du jazz, Musique modernité et identité dans la première moitié du XXe siècle* (Marseille : Eds Parenthèses, 1998. Lodovic Tournès, *New Orleans sur Seine, Histoire du jazz en France* (Paris : Fayard, 1999). Jean-Dominique Brierre, *Le jazz français de 1900 à aujourd'hui* (Paris : Hors collection, 2000).

7   René Dumesnil, *La musique en France entre les deux guerres 1919–1939* (Paris: Milieu du Monde, 1946), pp. 53–4.

8   (Paris: Seuil, 1969).

9   As Pierre Brossolette would write, in *Notre Temps*, 2–9 juillet 1933, p. 634.

10   Op. cit., p. 23–4.

11   T. Maulnier, *La crise est dans l'homme*, p. 14 ; See Del Bayle, Op. cit., p. 255.

12   See "The Improvers of Mankind," in Friedrich Nietzsche: *Twilight of the Idols*, R. J. Hollingdale, transl. (London: Penguin Classics, 1990; orig. 1889).

13   (New York: W. W. Norton, 1994).

14   See his *Le Drame de l'Europe de 1919 à nos jours* (Paris: Imprimerie nationale, 1969).

15   *The Hollow Years*, Op cit., p. 209.

16   Ibid.

17   See "Ellington Defends His Music," *The Duke Ellington Reader*, Mark Tucker, ed. (Oxford; New York: Oxford University Press, 1995), chapter 17,

18   Milton Mezzrow & Bernard Wolfe, *Really the Blues* (New York: Citadel, 1990), p. 211. Original edition, 1946.

19   (Éditions Corréa).

20   "Panassié, Delauney et Cie," *The New Yorker*, Feb. 14, 1977, pp. 43ff., reproduced in Whitney Balliett: *American Musicians: 56 Portraits in Jazz* (Oxford, NY: Oxford University Press, 1986), p. 3.

21   First published in English, as, *The Real Jazz*, in 1942, then in French (Robert Laffont, 1945).

22   *Monsieur jazz* (Paris: Stock, 1975), p. 29.

23   Although, interestingly, Coleman Hawkins, the greatest black tenor saxophonist of the era, came over to work with Jack Hylton for five years. True jazz may have been African-American, but there was more admixture of races than Panassié often admitted.

24 *Monsieur Jazz*, Op. cit., p. 52.

25 Scott DeVeaux, *The Birth of Bebop: A Social and Musical History* (Berkeley: University of California Press, 1997), p. 169.

26 In various places Duke said that he wished the label jazz were not used to describe his music. He would prefer their being only two kinds of music, he once quipped, good music and the other kind!

27 *La bataille du jazz* (Paris: Albin Michel, 1965), ad loc.

28 "Be Bop" in *Le Dictionnaire du jazz*, Hugues Panassié with Madeleine Gauthier (Paris: Albin Michel, 1971, 1980), pp. 37–8.

29 The quote is from Baudelaire's *Curiosités esthétiques* (1855), *La bataille du jazz*, Op. cit., p. 93.

30 Ibid., p. 190.

31 *Come Shouting to Zion: African American Protestantism in the American South and British Caribbean to 1830* (Chapel Hill: The University of North Carolina Press, 1998), p. 1.

32 Gwendolyn Sims Warren, *Every Time I Feel the Spirit* (New York: Henry Holt, 1997), p. 15.

33 Mary Turner, *Slaves and Missionaries: The Disintegration of Jamaican Slave Society, 1787–1834* (Barbados, etc.: Press University of the West Indies, 1998), p. 75.

34 Art Rosenbaum, "We Never Did Let It Go By," in Daryl C. Dance, ed.: *From My People* (New York: Norton, 2002), pp. 535 ff.; John Storm Roberts: *Black Music of Two Worlds* (New York: Schirmer, 1998), p. 49; Albert Raboteau, *Slave Religion: The "Invisible Institution" in the Antebellum South* (Oxford, etc.: Oxford University Press), 1978, pp. 68 ff.

35 John Storm Roberts, Op. cit., p. 162. See also Art Rosenbaum: Op. cit., p. 535.

36 William D. Morgan, *Slave Counterpoint* (Chapel Hill: University of North Carolina Press, 1998), pp. 590 ff.

37 Ibid., p. 166.

38 See the fascinating S. Frederick Starr, *Red Hot: The Fate of Jazz in the Soviet Union* (New York, etc.: Oxford university Press, 1983).

39 P.S. I am often asked whether Panassié was of any influence in Great Britain, or even Holland and Germany, where American jazz musicians like Duke Ellington received great adulation in the 1930s. My educated guess is that he wasn't. Neither did Rookmaaker, discussed below, seem to know much about him. Panassié in particular and the French in general were not well-listened to outside of France. There were parallel phenomena at work, noticed by similar critics, the subject of another study on another day.

40 Hans R. Rookmaaker, *Jazz, Blues, Spirituals*, G. Bromiley, E. Reitsma & A. L. Sewell, transl., in *the Complete Works of Hans Rookmaaker*, vol. 2 (Carlisle: Piquant, 2002), p. 212.

41 Ibid., p. 214.

42 Ibid., p. 215.

43 Ibid., pp. 242–3.

44 Ibid., p. 253.

45 Ibid., p. 295.

46 Ibid., p. 303.

CAUGHT UP
in the Present

Iron sharpens iron, and one man sharpens another.
— Proverbs 27:17

I have been involved in music, playing in groups that improvise and ones that don't for most of my life. I have often felt the closest to God and his Spirit in a very tangible way on stage, when the connection, communication between the musicians with each other and the audience is weightless and free. These are the moments when unexpected divine intervention happens and the beauty is absolutely other in nature, beyond and above what we can explain. When an improvising musician who has worked all their life to gain the skills necessary on their chosen instrument to break free of the constraints of the technical/ theoretical aspects of music, becomes honest, transparent, and selfless with the musicians they are playing with, the inexplicable can happen. The group that travels together—living in hotels, airports, concert venues, in places throughout the world—is a family and a microcosm of community that can be a fruitful vessel for the improvisations of the God who spoke everything into existence. I am challenged to work with and love all kinds of people in a creative and selfless way with the inherent struggles and suffering that can result. It is an earthy spirituality when people deal with such drastic highs and lows together. James 1:2 reminds us to "count it all joy, my brothers, when you meet trials of various kinds..." The artistic heights on stage are balanced by the rigors and dangers of modern day travel, the emotional and spiritual challenges of being away from spouses and children, and the physical wear and tear of decades of being a nomad.

IT'S NOT ABOUT YOU

The individual in this group environment learns that the truly transcendent musical experiences only occur through true community and by being present in each moment. I feel it is the highest level of listening and understanding that I have ever experienced. Each person in the group has to also let go of any control issues in order for the music to flourish, letting go of preconceived and contrived modes of expression, struggle and be daring enough to co-create without a safety net. Saint Paul speaks to this working out in church life in 1 Corinthians 12:

> As it is, there are many parts, yet one body. The eye cannot say to the hand, "I have no need of you," nor again the head to the feet, "I have no need of you." On the contrary, the parts of the body that seem to be weaker are indispensable, and on those parts of the body that we think less honorable we bestow the greater honor, and our unpresentable parts are treated with greater modesty, which our more presentable parts do not require. But God has so composed the body, giving greater honor to the part that lacked it, that there may be no division in the body, but that the members may have the same care for one another. If one member suffers, all suffer together; if one member is honored, all rejoice together.

In addition, I often encounter fellow musicians from other countries, cultures, and religions, with very different styles of music. When we are open to learning from each other with a variety of approaches, we become even more flexible as artists. In fact, this is parallel to what I experience as I try to live a life of faith. I am challenged to let go of my agenda, my pre-conceptions about God, my faith, my life, and my family. I am constantly challenged to live in the present moment and not get bogged down in the past or obsess about the future. Or as Jesus put it, "Therefore do not be anxious about tomorrow, for tomorrow will be anxious for itself. Sufficient for the day is its own trouble."

Two things you see coming out of collaboration, especially the hothouse of touring are humility and idolatry. They are two sides of the same coin. It is a great challenge for us all to be authentic and not put forth a false sense of humility, only to wind up with a thinly veiled ego-driven agenda that we worship to cover up our insecurities. This always gets in the way of communication and meaningful community. I like what noted pastor/author Tim Keller says about humility: "Humility is not thinking less of yourself, but rather, thinking of yourself less." C.S. Lewis discusses this in *The Screwtape Letters* where he reminds us that humility is not "pretty women trying to believe they are ugly and clever men trying to believe they are fools." Lewis continues to state that it is God's will for a Christian "to be so free from any bias in his own favor that he can rejoice in his own talents as frankly and gratefully as in his neighbor's talents—or in a sunrise, an elephant, or a waterfall." But we want people to validate us, think we are talented, clever, creative. This can be an idol that is extremely destructive to any art form as well as spiritual growth. In a musical setting it can manifest itself when the musician is tethered to patterns, worked out "licks" and device-laden playing that is completely non-interactive and acts as a safety net, keeping the others at arms length so the musician can remain in control. Making music that is snug and sheltered or lazy is not glorifying to God or loving to your neighbor. For people who are familiar with improvised music like Jazz, it is easy to tell when someone really isn't improvising at all and it comes off like what Saint Paul calls "a clanging cymbal."

PLAYING IN A GROUP AS DISCIPLESHIP

There is also the challenge of prioritizing wisdom, fostering empathy, mentoring and investment in human relationships over knowledge, technology, material things, wealth and individual/isolated achievement. In the world of music, a young musician can get caught up in the acquisition of technique, mastery of the mechanical aspects of playing their instrument and again, focus inward instead of learning the empathy of interaction and outward focus towards the others in the group. Nowadays, there is also the preoccupation with technology and marketing, often before the young artist has anything of substance or depth to share. This is also a result of priority placed on the individual as opposed to the group.

Agents and managers often push talented young artists to perform with their own groups very early on as opposed to spending some years working with older, more established musicians. This kind of mentality is a short sighted approach that often backfires after the initial excitement about the young artist wanes and they begin to be judged by same high standards as the elders. In addition, the "young lions"miss out on the valuable experience of learning other peoples' compositions and being flexible enough to create within another composer's boundaries. The essential self- editing process that we learn from our elders is also lost when there are no years of apprenticeship. In the same fashion, in our desire to grow as Christians, we must also be humble enough to seek wisdom from our elders in close personal relationships where we open our hearts to embrace discipleship with transparency about all of our struggles.

The writer of Hebrews urges us to "lay aside every weight, and sin which clings so closely, and let us run with endurance the race that is set before us." Tools and technology—whether it is a new loop machine for the musician or a glitzy new study bible for the Christian—are not sinful things in themselves but they may be good things that are adding weight and must still be set aside to see real growth occur.

There is a practical and historically well-documented way to combat this isolationism. Throughout the history of music and especially in African culture, the AURAL/ORAL tradition of mentoring by the elders is a beautiful, community-oriented way to nurture the young artist. It teaches respect for the elder master musicians and the music is passed down in a highly personal and interactive way. Traditions, music, and culture are taught by the elders through singing, playing to, for and with the younger musicians. The information doesn't get written down as much as it is taught and memorized through repetition, experientially, in community. Trust becomes key as lives are intertwined and links of history are forged between generations.

The kind of community model we just looked at is a lot like the church and true Christian community when they are at their best. I know the value and richness of a home group setting where families are knit together as they share joys and sorrows in an intimate way, without pretense. When this happens, the Spirit has an opening to work without hindrance. Just as on the bandstand, when the musicians dare to let go of predetermined ideas and inward focus and interact based on the spirit they share with each other, they also have the opportunity to feel more connected to the elders that came before them and paved the way for them. This gives them the awareness not to fall into the youthful traps of pride, arrogance, and the magical thinking that they are "reinventing the wheel," so to speak.

I know personally from my own youthful folly (and now, middle aged folly) that maturity and discernment can only come through trial, error, mentoring, and the nurture of a community environment. My elders shaped me, were patient with me in my youthful arrogance, encouraged me, and taught me to focus outward and be empathetic, interactive, and "think of myself less." It has been the same process in my Christian walk. Of course, this measured and more patient approach is not easy. It involves suffering, coming to grips with limitations and failings, and goes against the grain of our modern society. Nowadays there is so much isolation through technology that young people sit next to each other and text instead of talking. This is completely counterproductive and counter intuitive to the things of the Spirit in life and in music.

Touring the world in a group that becomes a family is another part of this experience that gives it great depth of meaning. When you are subject to the rigors of travel, experience a particularly scary flight or some dangerous near misses on the ground, help each other when you are emotionally or physically drained etc., you build powerful and lasting bonds. When you encourage one another's personal and artistic dreams, share a wonderful meal, have an uplifting concert together where everything goes right, or a concert where you are frustrated, see some sights in an unusual part of the world that inspire you, plan future projects, share new compositions or recordings with each other, again, you establish connections that are eternal and deeply spiritual. You learn to love and accept each other in the unguarded moments when you are spent and cranky, when you are joyous, introspective and need space, or just joking around and killing time in an airport. As the years pass, you come to know each other on a very deep level. You have had years to discuss everything from the lightest discussion about sports to the loss of a loved one. All of these experiences come out in the music. When people build up that kind of trust with each other in life, the music is so much more meaningful, full of colors and emotions that have had years to distill into something special and uncommon in the world today.

Sometimes, some of the members of the group I have been working with for the last ten years, The Wayne Shorter Quartet, and myself, teach seminars at universities and conservatories around the world. Many times the young musicians want to know "How can I find my individual and distinctive voice on my instrument?" I find it very interesting that if you look at any artist in Jazz music who really shaped the music and changed it, they came from a community of musicians, be it linked to a certain city, a seminal group, or a movement of musicians that extended the tradition. They were mentored by older players and often apprenticed for years with an older established bandleader. The music they played told stories of who they were culturally, where they were coming from stylistically (you can hear who influenced them in their sound and phrasing), and they built upon their awareness of the history of the music. That is why the really significant breakthroughs involved groups that everyone talks and writes about—The Duke Ellington Orchestra, Charlie Parker and Dizzy Gillespie's groundbreaking groups in the 1940s, Miles Davis's famous Quintet in the 1950s and his famous Quartet of the 1960s as well as John Coltrane's amazing Quartet in the 1960s. These are just a few examples. The point is that each of those groups had an original sound, born out of the empathetic synergy that developed between the players. In the process, all of those groups contained artists, which as individuals were very distinctive and often recorded as leaders on their own solo recordings. The educated listener can identify Duke, Miles, Bird, Dizzy, and Trane etc. in a few notes! So, once again, the community facilitated great artistic and very spirited music, which changed the course of music in the entire world. It is very easy to see the parallel between this community environment and a body of believers. Oftentimes they intersect anyway, as many of the musicians I work with are believers.

HEAVEN IN A JAZZ CLUB

Another thought I had is how Jesus and the disciples and their "small ensemble" is another metaphor: their relationship through community enabled them to experience the highest highs and survive the hellish lows of the Gospel story. There is definitely something deep and lasting about learning together as a group of musicians that functions as a family. You learn patience, forbearance, kindness, and selflessness when dealing with traveling around the world in a way that is, in reality, not like most people think. A music tour is not a sightseeing tour. You are away from loved ones, spending many days just getting to somewhere, only to see the airport, hotel, and concert venue, then sleep a few hours and move on. You have the feeling like you are constantly at the mercy of people and circumstances that you cannot control. This is obviously not as extreme as the life the apostles, but there are some similarities that can teach us valuable spiritual lessons. There are also the wonderful, uplifting times when the music reaches inside us all, musicians and audience members alike. In these moments, you know why you go through the rigors of travel to share the music with people you don't even know! God visits the place and the presence of his Spirit is palpable and undeniable. Once again, the lows and highs in the musician's life can't truly be compared with the things the apostles experienced. What could be more incredible than to experience the Transfiguration and Resurrection of Christ? At the same, what could be worse than witnessing Jesus' crucifixion, death, and, in Peter's case, the outright denial of his Lord? It is almost impossible to imagine making it through all of that and then going on to write their accounts and even for some to be martyred for their faith. When I think about the experience that the disciples had in their time with Jesus, every day they had to improvise and adapt to the new challenges that the savior put before them. The trust that they put in Jesus, to leave everything and just simply follow is so inspiring.

I would like to speak about focus, the ability to bring all one's energy to bear in a singular fashion, to be intent on each moment, with regard to music and life. I play the bass and I feel that the viewpoint of the bassist in music is interesting because of the unique position we occupy in most, if not all, musics. As bassists we stand at the crossroads of rhythm, harmony, melody. In Jazz music, we must constantly compose, improvising a foundation for all of the musicians to draw upon, usually without ceasing because we are in the rhythm section, the engine room of the group. The interesting "view from the bottom" of the music is very stimulating but requires unswerving focus, humility (being always concerned for the whole picture, not just one's individual part), and the flexibility to react quickly to the others and create a vibrant, buoyant atmosphere. In my years with Wayne Shorter (one of the most important composers and saxophonists in Jazz history), he has inspired and encouraged me to constantly expand my role as bassist and be an equal voice in the melodic counterpoint as a soloist or duet partner with him, during the course of the improvisations within the music we make. This is living on the edge and not in the moment, it is by the millisecond! As a result of this kind of communal musical experience, I am learning with time to savor and be thankful for all of the experiences that I have as a musician, one note at a time! I truly am dependent on God for the strength to focus and create each and every note I play. In the same way, as I depend on God to help me focus, be present, and not take others in my life for granted, I can grow in service to the body of Christ and be creative.

I am also in awe of how I perceive God's hand in all of the interaction within the music, and the joy we experience in the family/community of the group whether we are on or off the bandstand. Of course, this experience is all bound up in my walk of faith. It really isn't a parallel, it is all directly connected. When the audience is open to experiencing this blended community, they become engaged, get caught up in the present, fuel the musicians with their emotional responses, and the community is expanded. Unfortunately, this is not always the case, and I don't want to present a rose-colored, utopian fantasy. We still live in a fallen world and there are many challenges and failures for us all; however, I have experienced this blessing enough times to know that it can happen.

And ultimately, isn't this how the church should work? We see it happen in a jazz club through Common Grace and in Acts 2 we see it as the disciples of Christ were all swept up in the awe of God's power exhibited through his Holy Spirit:

> Now when they heard this they were cut to the heart, and said to Peter and the rest of the apostles, "Brothers, what shall we do?" And Peter said to them, "Repent and be baptized every one of you in the name of Jesus Christ for the forgiveness of your sins, and you will receive the gift of the Holy Spirit. For the promise is for you and for your children and for all who are far off, everyone whom the Lord our God calls to himself." And with many other words he bore witness and continued to exhort them, saying, "Save yourselves from this crooked generation." So those who received his word were baptized, and there were added that day about three thousand souls.

Perhaps a jazz group is God's elect preaching like St. Peter and the audience are the fields white for harvest. We musicians collaborate together to make beautiful music. Done right, we all get swept up into the glory of it all. And some, in the end, turn and go back to thank Jesus for the miracles he has done in our lives.

Is Music
a universal language?

When I travel and play music as a singer-songwriter, people learn about my life through story and song. I tell them about how I grew up in a non-western culture as a missionary kid. They also learn about my continuing interest in crossing cultures, Bible translation, and languages. And after my concerts they often say something along the lines of, "Oh, you can use music in missions, right? Music is a universal language!" But although they mean well, I think the way that statement is generally intended is actually more false than true. I'll try to explain what I mean. The three words to consider here are *music, universal,* and *language.* Since definitions of both *music* and *language* are likely to be more difficult to pin down, let's first try to get at what people mean by *universal* in connection with music.

If you get the chance to look at pictures from the Hubble telescope, do it. In case you were worried that the universe is too small, it will ease your mind. I am continually blown away by those images. Most people when they use the word "universal" are not thinking on that grand of a scale, but that's really what it means. It carries the sense of all-encompassing, which is how it seems to be intended to modify the word 'language.' So is music really a 'language' that is all-encompassing and therefore able to communicate to all people everywhere?

As Keith Getty points out (in another entry in this volume), to some degree the answer is "Yes": music is universal in the sense that it exists in all cultures. However, does every culture have the same music? Is a single piece of music universal in how it communicates to people in another culture, that is, is it universally understood to 'mean' the same thing? The obvious answer to each of these questions is "No."

These answers bring to light assumptions and presuppositions about music that are ethnocentric—rooted in a single (western) culture without a complete awareness of the role and reality of music in other cultures. It's not a bad place to start, it just happens to be somewhat uninformed. In fact, it is only when you straddle the music of two different cultures with an insider's view of each (a sort of bi-musical-ism), that you can appreciate the connection between music and culture, and create a new kind of music to bridge the two cultures. As others in this volume note, what we call 'music' is actually an over arching term for many different 'musics' that each have their own way of speaking and articulating and communicating. A musician who learns more than one kind of music is actually learning another dialect or language.

Detractors at this point may clamor and raise the point that particular pieces of music evoke strong emotional responses from people of many different cultures and are popular around the world. Getty discusses his fear that world music is homogenizing due to a strong desire for western songs. Hold those thoughts for a minute, as we consider language and then how music acts in similar ways to language.

MUSIC AND LANGUAGE

There are over 6,000 languages in the world today and when God started speaking to Abraham and his progeny there were likely many more. Just think that if all the native American Indian tribes had survived until now there would be over 300 languages on the east coast of the US alone. Over just the last century, languages have been dying out at an alarming rate. If you consider a definition of language to be: "a systematic means of communicating by the use of sounds or conventional symbols," this means that whole modes of communication, whole means of transference of knowledge and meaning from one person to another have been and are being lost forever. The diversity of the world is decreasing, homogenization is winning. This is also a concern for musical expression.

Using the definition of language in the previous paragraph, we can draw some parallels with music. Music is definitely systematic, even mathematical on a physical level, and as notated (such as with classical methods) can be summarized as a collection of symbols. But anyone who plays and performs music can tell you that this is not all that music is. There is expression and interpretation. A good performer will use their body as much as their instrument, stretching and shortening time, manipulating mood and intensity, to convey the emotion of the music and express a particular meaning, a truth, to the recipient, than cannot be fully expressed otherwise. It's just like language, only without the necessity of words. To some degree, this meaning can be conveyed across cultures, across languages, but not always.

It is important to note that culture and language are part of an interconnected puzzle of many pieces. The way that we understand and describe the world around us gives us language, which in turn affects the way we interact with our environment and the people in it. Music is simply part of the puzzle, albeit an important one. Music often gives emotional expression to our thoughts and feelings in a way that words alone cannot. But the musical system used by every culture is slightly different, so that while music functions as a communicator of meaning, the way it communicates will be different for every culture, as it is (arguably) for each individual.

If we look at language in greater detail, it may help us understand music better. As an example, have you noticed that native German speakers learning English can't pronounce "w" easily at the beginning of an English word, producing a "v" instead? It's because "w" does not exist in their language at the beginning of words, while "v" does, so they didn't grow up practicing "w." English children have many words like "wine" and "vine" to show them that these are two separate sounds at the beginning of a word. Produce the wrong sound and you may not be understood by your fellow English speakers. As for the German speakers, they are producing the closest equivalent of "w" (to their ears) from their native language.

The study of sounds in a language is called phonetics. A "phone" is taken to be the smallest unit of sound in language. "Etic" is a term that means "from an outsider perspective," as opposed to "emic" which means "from an insider perspective." (The terms "etic" and "emic" were first coined by phonetician Kenneth Pike in the 1950s, and have since been applied to many different spheres of thought.) In the phonetic alphabet there are over 300 phones (including qualities) that languages have been found to differentiate between, but none of the languages differentiate between all of the sounds. Instead, each language has its own "phonemic" inventory—a group of sounds that speakers of the language differentiate between, like "w" and "v" for English.

The fact that language is based on smaller units of sound that make a difference in particular contexts can be applied in attempting to understand other systems. It can even be applied to music. Music as a system is based on sound, similarly to language, but in contrast to a "phone" (the smallest unit of language), music's smallest unit is commonly called a "note" or a "tone." Unlike language, however, music is not made universally with a common instrument, at least not in the same way that all humans use their vocal apparatus to produce the sounds of language. This makes a descriptive etic perspective rather difficult. But is there something common to all music that we can use as a framework to notate/compare music? I would suggest that there is a common thread, something other than a note or tone: rhythm.

Rhythm is common to music in all cultures, where tones occur over a pulse (however regular or irregular) that prescribes a beginning and an ending. This pulse provides a universal framework for music in the same way that phonetics provide a universal descriptive framework for language. However, this is the outsider's "etic" perspective. From the insider's "emic" perspective, the way that rhythm is laid out depends on the stylistic framework of a song within a particular culture, suggesting that a beat or rhythmic pattern is less like an etic marker and more like what phonemes are to language—dependent on context.

PUTTING IT ALL TOGETHER

Okay, so if all music has rhythm, is rhythm then universal, therefore music is a universal language? Not quite. Every culture has its own kind of rhythms, and most have multiple kinds of music distinguished by rhythmic differences. Suffice it to say that rhythm gives us a purely descriptive framework to help us understand and notate these different kinds of music, but in many cases this is where the "universality" of the music ends. Music is tightly tied to culture—it is the means of expressing deep personal and societal realities within a culture that cannot be easily expressed with spoken or written language.

To make it more complex, expression is interpreted in a variety of ways depending on the cultural context. In western culture, music is based around twelve distinct tones/notes that combine to form chords and modes. Certain combinations of notes create different emotional moods—notice the difference between a major and minor scale, for example. The former sounds "happy" and the latter sounds "sad" to the western ear. Bring those scales elsewhere in the world, however, and you may find this is not the case.

Take the Canela people of Brazil, for example. Ethnomusicologist Tom Avery learned that the Canela's traditional (and favorite) kind of music involves harmonies sung in parallel tone clusters. These songs sound dissonant to a western ear, with several close chords (or semi-chords) layered on top of each other. For the Canela, however, this is a joyous expression of emotion and meaning, and it wasn't until Tom helped the Canela to compose scripture songs in this indigenous style that they really started to understand and respond to the love God had for them.

Another example is a friend who is a Bible translator in Mali and loves Celtic music. He used to take his mandolin to his front porch in the evenings, playing through reels and jigs. Finally one day his Malian neighbor came over and asked him to stop because the music was so annoying. "I just can't hear [understand] that music!" he said. What one culture views as communicating in a certain way is not necessarily viewed in the same way by another culture.

Scales or "steps" between notes or tones are often quite different from culture to culture, dependent to some extent on functional realities such as what materials are available for instruments. Western music has twelve notes in its scale, with ten semitone intervals, but middle-eastern music in the Hejaz tradition has intervals of three semitones between major notes. Indian classical music has a moveable scale of seven notes, and their ragas even use intervals smaller than a semitone.

WHERE THAT LEAVES US

I think the above examples will give the detractors more to think about, but what about the fear that world music is becoming homogenous? Is universalism something to strive for, or something to be feared? It should be understood that each culture generally also has many different kinds of music internally with which to express themselves. Borrowing western music is simply another language to add to the basket. It may be that the prevalence of media in the developing world, or the simplistic nature of pop music (read: easily accessible) is the reason for the growth of popularity of western styles, but in many places (as my friends at Heart Sounds International will tell you) indigenous styles are alive and well, particularly in worship. When indigenous music styles are used along with scripture in the people's language, these songs become foundational to worship in the local church, as they are able to communicate more effectively than any translation or adaptation of a western song could.

It should also be clear that the impact of "worship imperialism" is still being felt among earlier-reached groups. Many times in the early part of the twentieth century missions movement, when missionaries entered an area for evangelism, they easily confused their own Western culture with Christianity. As a result, they brought ways of dressing, ways of praying, ways of preaching, and ways of singing into the local church. At the same time, many believers around the world see the Western world as the source, the homeland, of Christianity, and try to model western church culture (and what we sing) as much as possible, in part because it makes them feel closer to the Church universal. Changes are always introduced after a cross-cultural encounter, but they don't necessarily impact the culture negatively in the long run. Where I was born and raised in Ghana, the church was full of local worship songs with complex rhythms accompanied by joyous shouts and dancing, a far cry from the staid, still hymn-singing that came with the first missionaries.

To bring the diversity of music closer to home for most of us, notice the variety in western culture alone. Scanning through the radio stations on your dial will bring you classical, jazz, blues, rock, folk, metal, and everything in-between. Each type of music has a different "feel." These genres are set apart by instrument and content differences, but also by rhythmic differences. Even within classical music there is a difference in rhythmic pattern between a march, jig, waltz, or swing tune.

In Ghana, beats are understood to be cyclical patterns of emphasis and are layered on top of each other in a prescribed manner. What is essential to the community is that they can comprehend the nature of the rhythm and fit themselves into it. Ghanaian drummers are masters of changing emphasis to fit the situation, using drum patterns as a language that can actually speak proverbs, genealogies, and stories to their audience. But the prescribed patterns are also dependent on the kind of song they are playing—is it a war song, a farming song, a hunting song, a mourning song, a love song? Each kind of song requires a different rhythmic emphasis played on the instruments at their disposal.

How Then Shall We Live?

The diversity of expression in different cultures means that the world is full of brilliant colors, reflecting our different understandings of life and what is important. Yet is there something universal, something all-encompassing that we should strive for, beyond diversity? I believe our differences are important and essential, that our differences allow us to learn from one another. Living in Ghana has taught me the importance of context, that just as we create from community, we must understand the gospel as a context for our creativity in all aspects of our lives. Perhaps this is what is universal to our musical expression. We are a particular people. We live within a particular context, in a particular environment, and we see the world through our particular colored glasses.

As Christians, the culture and environment in which we live is not our ultimate contextual reality. The kingdom of God is. We are wanderers in a foreign land. We are Israelites in the land of Babylon. This is the context in which we must create music. What exactly does this mean for musicians? Our reality is that we have a purpose in the kingdom of God. We have been created to worship God. We are a stone in the building of His church. We exist to encourage others along the path. Our lives are intended to give expression to the grace we have received. And ultimately we are called to reflect our Lord and Savior as a particular facet of the priceless jewel that is his church, his bride, worldwide.

Music is an aspect of community and culture, a social instrument. We share music with each other the way we share books, ideas, food, thought, events, faith. And music as a creative endeavor can only happen within community. Though created perhaps by individuals, it is grown from the soil in which those individuals are planted. This creative process ought to be grounded in the reality of our existence in Christ. Our music, like our lives, are a testament to the redemptive power of the Gospel. We create with an understanding of the Kingdom of God as extending around the world beyond cultural boundaries to include members of "every nation, tribe, and tongue."

Sadly, most World Music in today's mass-media driven world is only successfull if it appeals to a western palate, which prefers tonic scales and harmonies. Rarely will you find groups like Gipsy Kings, Ladysmith Black Mambazo, Angelique Kidjo, Yothu Yindi, and Aradhna who are true to their own cultural music style and still appeal to a western sensibility of music, bridging the gap between different cultures. But locally, wherever you go around the world, you will find that indigenous music is more popular than any western song. Whether it's played on a tape deck, a CD player, a cellphone, a USB drive, or live in the community, the music is here to stay. Most of it I "can't hear" very well, just like our Malian friend, but with a little time and effort, and in the light of eternity, maybe I can.

In Ghana, among the Buem people, ethnomusicologists were invited to come and lead a workshop. My parents, as Bible translators, had been working for many years with the local people helping them develop an alphabet, start literacy classes to read and write their own Lelemi language, and had translating the New Testament into Lelemi. At this workshop, people were being taught how to use their own song styles as the basis for creating new songs in the Lelemi language with the translated scripture as text. Within a week, they composed more than twenty new songs in the styles of war songs, hunting songs, farming songs, and many others. The one style they decided could not be used was the style of song dedicated to the fetish priest—the worship of spirits.

As we look at the styles of music in our western culture, are there any rhythms that are dedicated to worshiping things other than God? Perhaps not in the strictest sense. But there are deeper rhythms that surround us at all times and places. In the music of the natural world, of plants and animals, wind and weather, even the chatter of mechanical things that humans use, cars, trucks, traffic, electrical appliances, tools, and implements. Humans are beings that seek consistency, pattern, and dislike changes that interfere with that pattern. There are natural cycles that we engage in and respond to and that we observe in the world around us. It almost seems that if we could pull far enough back from our understanding of time, we would be able to hear all of these sounds together and discern a larger movement of harmony or dissonance in the whole.

It is in this sense that our rhythm as Christians needs to be continually reassessed. So many of the rhythms that surround us are counter to the context of the kingdom in which we have our ultimate being. In places like Africa, it may explicitly be the worship of spirits. In the US, it is implicit worship of spirits in the form of success, materialism, selfishness, consumption . . . the list goes on.

Rhythm can be a beautiful pattern that allows musical tones to form in a timely manner to each other, so that the structure of sound creates something bigger than each individual note. In this it mirrors life—the order that we observe around us in the world, the symmetry of form, and the relationship of living organisms to each other. In many ways it is as if rhythm condenses the physical, visible world into an audible shape, a microcosm of sound, a story of the universe. Rhythm is the framework that gives measure to time.

This framework for music has spiritual parallels. Just as an orchestra ought to be aligned with the conductor, we are called to align ourselves with God's "timing," with His pacing for life. He says, "Come and taste and see that I am good." When we align ourselves with His pace, we are filled with His spirit, begin to see the world through His lens, and begin to walk and act in accordance with

Him and each other. We are His orchestra, and He is most glorified when we move together in His rhythm.

Our alignment with God's Holy Spirit is dependent on how well we know Him. Just like how well we know other musicians (our ability to "sync" with them) depends on how much we practice with each other and how aligned we are to the same groove. How are you able to "feel" the rhythm of the Holy Spirit? Spend time with Him. Read the Bible both alone and with others who are trying to align themselves with it. Pray.

Most musicians will tell you they don't practice their instrument enough. This is true for my own life, but more importantly there is always more to do in practicing the presence of God. As I grow in my musical ability and faith, I am continually re-examining my life to discover whether I am using my gifts to the fullest, and in the service of the Kingdom of God.

Looking back over my short life, the path has not been straight, more winding and circuitous, across many borders, languages, and cultures. But throughout the journey I've tried to be faithful, staying where I am planted and going where I'm called. This choice stems from my understanding of God as a sovereign creator who guides and directs His people, in part through circumstances. If His will is that we should all grow into the likeness of His son, Jesus, why do I so often try to do things in my own strength, to make things happen without the leading of His hand?

My experiences have shown me that for a Christian musician, music is not the be-all, end-all. It is a calling, something you do, a way to mirror Christ to the world as you grow in Him. I think particularly of the world's empty promise: "follow your heart and you will find what you desire." Jesus tells us, "Follow me, and I will give you the desires of your heart."

It's in hindsight that I can see how remaining where I am planted has enabled the soil of my life to be enriched by God's word and the community around me. My life has been cultivated and I have become more rooted in the truth of who God is and who I am in relation to Him. It is only as I grow to know Christ more as the foundation of my life that I can follow where He leads. This is true worship. God leads us in many directions, but ultimately He is the center of a Christian's life, and if He is leading us, our path can only end at His feet. The Westminster Confession tells us that the chief end of man is "to glorify God and enjoy Him forever."

True Universals

I am reminded of the quote from Jim Elliot before he was killed by the Auca tribe in Ecuador: "Missions is not the goal of the church, worship is. Missions exists because worship does not." I used to think that this meant the church wasn't worshiping God properly, that if we just worshiped God better, we wouldn't need to tell people about Christ, or to bring them the Bible so that they can know God as we do. In a sense this is true, but I'm learning that what the quote really means is that God is not being worshiped in the way that He desires—by people from every tribe, tongue, and nation.

There are still more than 2,000 languages (tongues/nations) in the world representing over 350 million people that have no access to scripture in a language they can understand. In many cases, these languages are not even written down. How can we worship God properly when people around the world do not know about Him? His orchestra is not yet complete.

So, is music a "universal" language? Perhaps not. But the Gospel of our Lord and Savior Jesus Christ is. It is the good news of salvation, of redemption for the whole world, of freedom that allows for diversity of expression, of worship, in the music that is nearest and dearest to each person's heart and soul. When the musics of the world join together in celebrating this universal theme, that will be a glorious day indeed.

TRUTH
containers

Shai Linne is a Hip-hop artist, theologian, poet, and pastor-in-training. He has appeared on numerous independent and national Christian hip-hop releases as well as having released 5 solo projects of his own. He is known for having coined the phrase "lyrical theology", which has become a prominent sub-genre of Christian Hip-hop. He has been featured in publications such as *Christianity Today* and *World Magazine*. Shai lives in the D.C. area with his wife Blair and their son, Sage.

How does hip hop get at Truth better than other genres of music?
I *don't* think that Hip-hop necessarily gets at Truth better than other genres of music. Every genre has its own benefits, as far as form is concerned. Hip-hop has the potential to serve Truth well because it has an immediacy of form that tends to be very direct. It's also very clear and propositional. That is a distinct characteristic of Hip-hop's style. The MC (that is, the rapper) is making assertions about life, about their worldview. Because of this, there are some inherent expectations within Hip-hop culture that both listener and artist bring to the table. There are cultural ground rules that have been in place from the very beginning, such as the notion of authenticity, or "keepin' it real." There is an expectation that the MC (unless he states otherwise) is being truthful about his life. Other genres like R&B and Country don't necessarily have that expectation. For instance, an R&B singer can write about an adulterous affair in the first person, but the audience doesn't expect that the song is true of the singer. Whereas with Hip-hop, there is that expectation. So what that produces within the confines of the genre is a heavy

emphasis on propositional truth. Therefore, due to that cultural expectation, it can be a great vehicle for Truth.

How can the genre get in the way of Truth?

Well, another cultural expectation is that Hip-hop is not just about lyrics, but also the music that goes along with it. The music has evolved and taken different shapes and forms over the years. There are different subdivisions within the culture itself and they tend to be based on region. Most of the popular forms of Hip-hop that you hear today emphasize the beat, the rhythm, the drums, and the bass. Much of it is designed for a dance club atmosphere. Obviously, the purpose of the music in a club is to facilitate dancing. In those cases, Hip-hop is not so much about what is being said, as the way it is being said and the music that is accompanying it. Whenever the music overshadows or dominates the lyrical aspect, at that point you're in danger of the truth being obscured.

Ironically, the form and style of the *lyrics themselves* can obscure the truth in the lyrics. There are many things that make a good MC. One of those things is known as *delivery*. That is, the MC's approach to speaking the words. Delivery deals with questions like, How well does the MC "flow"? (Is the MC rhythmically complimenting the beat well?) How many syllables can the MC pack into the bars of the music?, etc. Some MCs pack so many syllables into their rhymes that it can be difficult for even the well-trained ear to understand what they are saying. When that happens, as amazing as it might sound, if the listener is not able to make out the lyrics because of the delivery of the MC, it will contribute to obscuring the truth.

I understand that John Calvin once wrote, "If we regard the Spirit of God as the sole fountain of truth, we shall neither reject the truth itself, nor despise it wherever it shall appear . . .." But it is easy to imagine that you have received a great deal of negative feedback over the years that said the truth is obliterated in your music because it is hip hop music. How do you respond to such criticism?

I use the analogy of container and contents. I focus on the difference between the container that something is in, and the actual contents of the container. In this analogy, the form of the music is the container and the truth is the contents. We often confuse the two and assume that certain contents can only come in certain containers.

From a Christian standpoint, what we are first and foremost called to do is discern the contents. Do the contents line up with Scripture? Is the song in line with a biblical worldview? Does it tell the truth? The secondary consideration from a Christian standpoint concerns the container. In what sort of packaging is the truth coming? If we've discerned that it is truthful, then we need to determine whether we are a cultural insider or outsider when it comes to the particular container. If we are cultural outsiders, a spirit of humility needs to be exhibited. We are going to need to educate ourselves on the particulars of the container. It could very well be the case that a particular container isn't as helpful as another may be in holding certain contents. A strainer, for example, is great for noodles, but horrible for liquids. But as cultural outsiders, before educating myself about the nuances and rules of that particular genre, I'm not in a position to properly critique it. I am always in a position to critique whether or not it is communicating truth as a Christian. But as it relates to a particular genre, I must learn about it first.

Now I won't say that every container is equally valid, useful, or helpful in presenting the truth. However, we have to recognize that containers are culturally conditioned and the way that we receive the containers is based on how we were socialized. So we must be careful when critiquing Hip-hop (or any form of music for that matter) to not exalt the container over the contents and not to conflate the two.

A plate and a bowl are going to present the diner with different experiences of soup. Punk rock as a container is going to give the listener a different experience of contents than a classical music experience. Therefore, if we conflate the contents with the container we may miss out on the truth of the contents because it is coming to us in a form that either we are unconditioned for culturally, or it is simply a form that is not useful for transporting those contents. Some ideas are simply more suited to one genre over another, in the same way that soup is better suited for a bowl than for a plate. Punk rock may be a great way to communicate your angst at the world but might not be the best way to share how much you love your newborn child.

Absolutely. That's excellent. I think this is the beauty of God's design of diversity in culture. If we see God's glory as a bright shining light, then the culture would be the prism or the facets of the jewel in which the light is reflected. Every facet is going to capture an aspect of His Glory, but no one facet can capture every aspect. This is why I would make the argument that every culture since the fall has pros and cons in terms of their ability and capacity to reflect the light of God's glory. Each has inherent limitations. We should be musical and cultural pluralists in the best sense of the term. This is what makes bringing together many different cultures under the banner of Christ so important. It's also why we need churches that are diverse ethnically and culturally- because each culture has its own blind spots. We can't see our own blind spots. It takes someone outside our cultural context to say, "What you're doing is not neutral. You are one facet and I am another facet. What you are doing in this one area is great, but have you considered this in that other area?"

For example, a church might have great teaching and excellent classical music but begin to believe that their form of music is the only way to bring glory to God. And if they are the majority culture, there might not be anyone there to point out to them that they have confused their preference with God's proclamation. I've seen this in blogs when this conversation comes up. If we are not careful we can take our pet forms and become elitist concerning them. Elitism is definitely a sin and a result of the Fall. It's a complete dismissal of other containers without taking time to understand them. That is a result of pride.

And this kind of pride isn't just the sin of high art practitioners. You can have low art elitism too. It is hard to imagine listening to high art folks bashing you your whole life and then turn around and do the exact same thing. This leads me to want to ask if you think there is any place for hip hop in the worship of the Church.

Yes, both the music of Hip-hop and the poetic style of Hip-hop (that is, rap) have a place in corporate worship. I've seen them both used well and both used poorly. But I would say that about other musical and poetic forms as well. As I've travelled around the country and experienced many different settings of people engaging in corporate worship, my general observation is that in American Evangelicalism there seems to be very little theological reflection concerning what happens at corporate gatherings of God's people.

I'm committed to the idea that the congregation is the chief musician in worship and everything that is done musically should be directed at helping them praise God the best way they can. I've been in churches where the attitude is "We're using an organ, so it must be good." But how many churches are using an organ—or a praise band—and it is, in fact, getting in the way of worship?

That is so true. In most churches I visit, that is a common problem. Jonathan Leeman of Nine Marks says, "In the corporate worship gathering the most important sound is the voices of the congregation." I think that is right on. For Hip-hop or any other form of music to be used well in corporate worship there needs to be good theological reflection on the part of those who are attempting to incorporate it.

Many forms of Hip-hop are great at communicating celebration. The music of Hip-hop is a mosaic that draws on the strengths of so many diverse and exciting styles of music. Music that is upbeat is often meant to communicate joy, triumph—ideas obviously imbedded in the Gospel. Also, from the standpoint of engaging the affections properly with particular truths related to the Gospel, there are forms of hip hop that are IDEAL musically for encouraging appropriate physical expression.

Beyond the music of Hip-hop, you have the call and response aspect that is imbedded into it. It mirrors the angels in Isaiah 6, who day and night are crying out antiphonally, "Holy, Holy, Holy is the Lord God Almighty." Another example is Psalm 136. The line "His steadfast loves endures forever" is meant to be back and forth between the one leading and the congregation responding.

You could almost say that it is the first hip hop psalm.

Exactly. We find responsive readings (where the leader will read one section and the congregation will read the next section) in many Christian traditions—there just isn't a funky beat behind it.

As far as the rap element of Hip-hop, that would be a little more difficult to do congregationally. I don't think it is impossible, but it would take a congregation that is really steeped in the Hip-hop culture to be able to do it well. And it would take serious theological reflection on the part of the one leading. But I do believe that it can be done. Now as far as special music, Hip-hop absolutely has a place in the corporate gathering of the saints—provided the content of the rap is edifying, God-glorifying, and Gospel-saturated.

In the '80s and early '90s hip hop was growing and developing. It had diversity, quality, innovation, and influence. Then gangsta rap came on the scene. Was this the end of good hip hop?

No, it wasn't the end of good Hip-hop, but what happened it that a lot of good Hip-hop went "underground". From the late '70s to the early '90s there was a great deal of creativity in Hip-hop—even towards the end with groups like A Tribe Called Quest and De La Soul. Even Public Enemy was making powerful music- so much so that they actually were under FBI surveillance for a while. The government found their music and influence important enough to keep them under watch—which goes to show you the power of the medium and its ability to rally people. This is what I love about Lecrae. His early music sought to rally Christians around the Truth. He has a song called "Send Me." It is quite blatantly a rally call for missions. It's an amazing thing to be at a concert and see 10,000 young people excited, chanting the words: "Send me, I'll go/ Send me, I'll go/ Send me, I'll go/ Let me go! Let me go!"

But back to the question of the end of good Hip-hop.

What happened when gangsta rap came on the scene was that there was an immediate split. To be clear, gangsta rap is something that corporations saw economic value in and completely exploited. When some of the West Coast guys came on the scene (Dr. Dre, Easy E, NWA) and went gold with *zero radio play*, it was unprecedented. The corporations saw value in that. So over the next four to five years A&Rs stopped signing groups like De La Soul and A Tribe Called Quest—positive Hip-hop music. At that time, to get signed by a major label you had to be gangsta. You had to talk about Bloods and Crips. What wound up happening was that there were people who embraced that and said, "Yes, this speaks for me and for the realities of life in the hood." But then you had others who were saying, "No, that is not representative of everybody in the hood. In fact, it is destructive, and we find it to be ignorant, offensive, and a horrible portrayal of young African-American men." So that produced this split between the East and

West coast. With that split, some retreated into the underground, which explored different themes. The underground was more nuanced and intellectual—even heady at times. Artists like Mos Def and Talib Kweli made Hip-hop music that was more geared towards a listener rather than a dancer. It was what some would call real Hip-hop. So, to answer your question, gangsta rap was not the end of good Hip-hop.

In many ways, what Christian Hip-hop has done since the late '90s is take that underground aesthetic and inject God's truth into it. It has branched out musically since then, but what was distinct about the underground was that it was lyrically driven. So the music was intentionally a backdrop rather than domi-nant. There is a new wave of theological hip hop—Lamp Mode Records, Reach Records and others. Our roots are grounded in what a Philly group called Cross Movement was doing between 1996 and 2007. They are really the pioneers of this new theologically driven Christian Hip-hop.

For our readers, we don't want to imply that there wasn't any Christian hip hop before 1996. In the late '80s and early '90s there were artists like P.I.D. (Preachers in Disguise), S.F.C. (Soldiers for Christ—featuring Super C and DJ Dove), Dynamic Twins, Freedom of Soul, 12th Tribe and others, even including the more mainstream group dc Talk.

Everything I'm telling you is what I've been told because I didn't enter the scene until 2001. But, yeah, Dynamic Twins, S.F.C., Gospel Gangstas—a lot of those guys were on the West Coast. It is interesting because even with those groups, what they were attempting to do was to be a Christian presence in the West Coast underground Hip-hop scene. What Cross Movement began to do was be more overt and explicit in their theological emphasis and approach. Actually, that created a split within Christian Hip-hop. It was the difference between art *for* the Church (music meant to point to the ministry of prayer and the Word) and art *from* the Church (music meant as salt and light in the culture that was not neces-sarily explicit in its theological emphases).

Instead of seeing the need for both? In pop music you would have Caedmon's Call or Indelible Grace as for *the Church music and Switchfoot, The Fray, and NeedtoBreathe as* from *the Church music.*

Exactly. In Christian Hip-hop, Lamp Mode would be considered primarily art for the Church. In his last two albums Lecrae made a shift and is reaching out into the mainstream. His most recent album, *Gravity,* hit #3 on Billboard. If you listen to his album, he hasn't taken Jesus out of his music, but he's moved from the anthems that rally Christians to attempting to find common ground with the unbeliever and speaking to them from that place.

So there was, and still is, a split within Christian Hip-hop, a kind of "warring" between the two sides. One side saying "you guys are afraid to talk about the Lord, you're ashamed of Christ" and the other side saying "You're stuck in the four walls of the Church, you're not reaching out to the world."

In the early 2000's, Cross Movement kind of drew the line in the sand on the explicit side of things. Then there was a group called the Tunnel Rats who were symbolically on the other side. In the minds of the fans, there was this "war" between Cross Movement and Tunnel Rats. Lamp Mode is kind of under the Cross Movement umbrella. We are different from Cross Movement in that we're more explicitly Reformed. Cross Movement was more broadly evangelical. If you were Reformed theologically you would hear some of those themes in their music, but they weren't explicit about that. We just took that and said, "We're going to be clear about the Doctrines of Grace in our music." But what has happened is, with the success of Lecrae and Reach Records, there are more opportunities for entrance into mainstream venues. So it has come full circle again. In some ways we are back to where we were in the mid '90s where there is a move back towards "Let's not be as explicit. Lets do what we can to reach the surrounding culture." There has been a lot of debate about that.

Let's return to the container *and* contents *discussion. Please expand more on the concept of packaging the truth in different ways for different groups of people.*

I like to sum it up in the following categories: "theology-doxology-sociology." *Theology* is the study of God, *doxology* is an expression of praise to God, and *sociology* is the study of human behavior.

Theology was never meant to be done in isolation as a goal in itself. It should always go somewhere. Good theology should lead to doxology. Theology that doesn't lead to doxology is dead orthodoxy. And all doxology should be grounded in good theology. Doxology that is not grounded in good theology is idolatry.

But then the question becomes: "Okay we have the truth about God, we are called to respond to God with praise . . . but what is that praise going to sound like? The song that we sing as an expression of good theology—what kinds of harmonies will it have? What instruments will we use? Those are questions of sociology. Again, as we travel around the world we should expect the contents in the universal church to be the same. The truth is the truth no matter where you go, no matter who is saying it. From the streets of Chicago to the secret house church in Afghanistan, it should be the same, because it is the *truth*. Christians from Chicago and Afghanistan should be responding to the truth with doxology, but the form of that doxology SHOULD be different. One of my biggest gripes is when missionaries go to other places and teach not just the *content*—the truth of the Gospel of Christ—but impose their *container* as well.

Keith Getty addresses this same concern elsewhere in this book where he laments seeing African kids who are excellent in their own kind of music adopting Hillsong praise songs.

Right. They don't have the theological discernment to separate the contents from the container. I was talking to a guy who is involved with a church plant in the Middle East. In this church plant there are ex-pats from many different countries. You have this melting pot of people from all around the world. I was excited about his new work and I asked him, "What does the worship sound like?" And he said, "It is basically what you would hear at a church in Maryland"

That's problematic. But I think what happens is that people who go to be involved in works like that don't know anything but what they have experienced and what they like. I'd like to see them stop and instead as themselves, "What is the dialect of this region?" And then go and help the facilitation of create fresh new works from that particular place and cultural context. But when you've been the majority culture your whole life, it is hard to go somewhere else and not assume the position of the majority culture.

Or be self-reflective enough to realize you have preferences that aren't necessarily biblical.

Absolutely. And it makes sense. If you don't have to reflect, you just swim along merrily. Does the fish know that the water is wet? It's that kind of thing.

There is a conflation of contents and container. A lot of times we think the way we do it is the biblical way to do it. Not just that what we are saying is biblical but that the actual *form* is biblical.

Yes, everyone knows Jesus sang a Fannie Crosby hymn with the disciples before going out to the garden of Gethsemane.

Exactly. And you have to understand that if you heard the style of music David used in the Old Testament, it might rub you the wrong way. In fact, you might hate it. But at that point the question that you need to ask yourself is: *Is it the Truth?*

INSTRUMENTS
are good

In the story of my life, music is important. One of my first memories was playing with records, RCA Victor 45 rpm vinyl recordings. My mother tells me that I played Elvis records over and over when I was three or four years old. As much as the sound, I think I was fascinated by the dog barking into the "Victrola."

I have always been fascinated by musical instruments. I fiddled around with an old piano at my grandmother's house as early as I can remember. I liked messing with a ukulele that my uncle brought back from Hawaii while he was in the Navy. I could play "Cat Scratch Fever" on it. When I was in middle school I started studying the trumpet in band. Through high school I played several other brass instruments like tuba and baritone. In the eighth grade I marched with a sousaphone—one of those big, partly-brass-with-white-plastic contraptions. It was in my high school years that I discovered guitar at the time when Eddie Van Halen was all the rage. I learned to play guitar with an Eagles Greatest hits book and an "Eight Track" tape of the recording. In college after a couple of years studying trumpet I switched to classical guitar.

In college, Christ revealed Himself to me. I began to follow Him as a disciple in the context of the Navigator ministry. During my first few months as a committed disciple, someone I met at a church concert shared the gospel of anti-contemporary Christian music with me. He explained that all music with a backbeat was sinful and appealed only to our flesh. The melody appeals to our spirit, the harmony appeals to our soul or mind, but the beat of music appeals to our sinful flesh. So essentially all pop styles of music which have a beat fail to be good music. This was my first introduction in the mid 1980s to the "worship wars."

During those years in college I was always writing songs, leading praise groups, playing guitar/voice pieces for church, doing recording sessions, and rewriting hymn tunes.[1] In my last term before graduation, I organized a rock group with my friend Don Inkster, ITR ("In the Rock"). We played at camps and churches, doing some pop Christian music, my own songs, and hymn arrangements, as well as a few tunes like "Help" by the Beatles.

From there I went to seminary and was hired as an adjunct professor in the music department at Columbia Bible College and Seminary (1987). There were strong opinions on both sides about breaking with traditional forms of music in church. Through my three years in seminary, I enjoyed serving in music at a couple of very different churches and leading several different music groups for youth events and missions conferences. One year I led worship at a Baptist church that prescribed that I select from exactly twenty-five hymns they knew from the Broadman hymnal. Then I led the worship team at a church that was very charismatic, along the lines of the Vineyard church movement. It was quite a contrast.

I was asked to lead one of the touring musical groups for the College and Seminary during the summer prior to my last year. We traveled and performed in a number of different kinds of churches and church camps. Our music was sacred with some traditional hymns and a few contemporary pieces (circa 1989). In our chapel concert before touring we played, "Turn, Turn Turn." "To everything (turn, turn, turn) / There is a season (turn, turn, turn)," a song by the Byrds, with lyrics from Ecclesiastes chapter 3. This seems pretty tame to me now, but at the time it was seen as rebellious and some of the professors thought I was desecrating the memory of Vietnam Vets. Actually it was just a song with a cool guitar part suggested by one of the female vocalists, Holly.

Looking back on our few weeks of touring, it's like the Johnny Cash song, "I've been everywhere, man." We performed in churches and camps in North Carolina, Virginia, Illinois, and Iowa. I remember a Pentecostal camp in Kentucky where the leader told us that most of the kids go to snake-handling churches. In Ohio we were in a Mennonite church An older gentleman from the church met us and said, "I saw that you had electric instruments in your picture" (e.g., a bass and a keyboard), "those won't be acceptable in our church" He said only recently had their congregation permitted instruments at all. We were fine to sing and play only acoustic instruments. Of course we did sing into microphones. But what I most remember was this man took us out to an actual Five Star restaurant! This is not something that happens in these kinds of church concert tours. Then that evening my wife and I stayed with a family from the congregation. The husband had just returned from an African Safari. He had a seven or eight foot tall mounted giraffe head and neck and a dozen other mounted trophies. This was my introduction to Mennonites, which is funny since I now live in

Mennonite-central, Lancaster, Pennsylvania. I don't see too many of the Five Star Safari Mennonites these days, but many of the more conservative groups still do not use instruments in worship. They sing beautifully.

My last year in seminary I did two musical outreaches which helped me see how much music creates opportunities for relationships. In our church, one of our small group members, Beth, had the idea that we could regularly listen to local live jazz groups. By supporting them in attending their pub performances we could get to know the musicians and share Christ with them as our relationships developed. Over that time we got to know several of the musicians and I learned a lot about playing jazz guitar, too. Then with some friends from the Navigator ministry (University of South Carolina) we formed a blues band and regularly played at a bar on open mic night. We played some classic rock and blues and looked for opportunities to befriend other musicians to share Christ with them.

After seminary I served a wonderful congregation on the pastoral staff, Audubon Drive Bible Church At that time the church had many families influenced by Bill Gothard's ministry, i.e., "Basic Life Principles." He spoke very strongly against pop music and any Christian music with a beat. He taught this music affects you both physically and spiritually in a negative way. By listening you were enslaving yourself to dark spiritual forces. There was a great deal of tension about the "right" kind of music at church during those days.

It was in this context that I began to research the idea of contemporary music and contemporary music styles, and music in the Bible. A few years later I presented these ideas at the Evangelical Theological Society meeting in 1998 in Orlando, in a paper called "Music in the Bible and Music on the Radio."[2] Many people are still interested in this topic and I have presented this to some very different audiences from high school students to seminarians in Russia and even at a Seventh Day Adventists worship conference.

In the early days of the worship wars it seemed like some were saying about nineteenth century "gospel hymns" what others had said about the King James Version of the Bible: "If it was good enough for Paul, it's good enough for me." However music has always been a cultural expression and has radically changed over civilizations and culture. Music even in the most traditional services is unlike any music that was heard in biblical times.

The next music controversy was because our evangelical Bible Church was moving in a decidedly Reformed direction. Our elders and pastor were reading the Reformers and the Puritans. This is like worship wars "2.0." Now the challenge was the Reformed and Puritan "Regulative Principle" of worship: only what is warranted in the Bible may be done in worship. "But the acceptable way of worshiping the true God is instituted by himself, and so limited by his own revealed will . . ."[3]

This warrant doesn't have to be so specific as to find a verse that endorses playing Fender Stratocasters. But as it turns out, one does have to prove the use of instruments in worship. Following this principle, many have concluded that musical instruments should not be used in worship. In this tradition, Presbyterian writer G.I. Williamson says, "The conclusion to which we are driven is this: God has not commanded us to use musical instruments in New Testament worship."[4] Here the most rigorous Reformed Protestants and the most conservative Anabaptists (Mennonites and Amish) share a common liturgical practice.

Though we seriously studied the Regulative Principle in our reforming Bible Church, at the time we never ceased using musical instruments. But I think if we had been more rigorous, we may very well have limited our music and musical instruments. Through almost a decade of experience with that church, a lot of young musicians played in the service. We raised a small orchestra of young folks on keyboards, as well as percussion, strings, and wind instruments. Some of those musicians became quite good and even professional music teachers. Quite a number of young musicians could have been adversely affected had I led in the direction of a more restrictive use of musical instruments.

Since 2002, I have been serving a church which embraces historical liturgical practice and weekly Eucharist. The purpose of our music in the liturgy is to serve the basic events of the service: The Call, Confession, Consecration in the Word, Communion, and the Commission to depart and serve. We still use a variety of musical instruments in the service and include many ancient and Reformation era ("renaissance") psalms along with traditional hymns and contemporary compositions. We have a small orchestra playing in worship. In our church and school community I've worked with a lot of young musicians to help them learn to play pop music too, from "old timey," "O Brother, Where Art Thou" music to the blues and classic rock. I enjoy the contrast of paleo-hymnody in the liturgy and blues at a Pentecost feast.

On a missions trip to Ukraine in March 2012, I enjoyed participating in a birthday dinner for a pastor with a group of Reformed Pastors and several Catholic priests. This was a true cross-cultural celebration experience. I think it was after serving the grilled Carp (fish), that the four Roman Catholic priests announced that they would sing something from their liturgy. It was the Lord's Prayer. As they began to sing one of their ancient songs, I realized that we sing that same tune in our own service in Lancaster, Pennsylvania. While there is diversity to be celebrated across time and culture, there is also a precious unity that I wish we all experienced more. There is no good reason that everything in Christian liturgies should be the same, but there is even less reason that all things should be different.

MUSIC IN THE BIBLE

Now I've laid out some of my autobiography on music and you can see that I am not neutral about the value of musical instruments. But I would like to offer what I consider an objective Biblical study of instrumental music for God's kingdom.

Many biblical passages support the use of music generally as a fundamental category in the worship of the new covenant church (Matthew 26:30; 1 Corinthians 14:19, 14:26; Ephesians 5:18–20; Colossians 3:16; Hebrews 2:12). Music is a means for praise, expressing joy, thanksgiving, even sorrow for sin (Isaiah 16:10), prayer (1 Corinthians 14:15; Psalm 72:20), and a means of teaching and spiritual communication (Colossians 3:16; Ephesians 5:19). In these later texts we "teach" or "counsel" (*noutheteo*) with music.

In Scripture the music makers are both professional as well as nonprofessional (1 Chronicles 15:22; 25:7; Isaiah 5:11–12; Ezekiel 33:32). There are those who direct music and teach music (Psalms 4:1, 5:1, 6:1, etc.; Nehemiah 12:8, 1 Chronicles 15:22). The people of the Bible overflow with music in every circumstance including cultural uses which are both godly and ungodly. Music sounded in every aspect of life—work, play, celebration, and war (Isaiah 16:10; Jeremiah 48:33; Matthew 11:17; Luke 15:25; Genesis 31:27; Exodus 32:17–18; Ecclesiastes 2:8; John 11:34–35; 2 Samuel 19:35). Jewish musicologist Abraham Idelsohn says, "As many references in the Bible to the music performed in secular life testify, Israel enjoyed life through music both vocal and instrumental, and associated music with dance and wine in which men and women participated."[5]

INSTRUMENTS IN THE BIBLE

The use of musical instruments is evident in the many commands and examples in Scripture from the timbrels of Miriam to the harps of Revelation (Exodus 15:20; Revelation 5:18, 14:2, 15:2). In the Psalms we read such commands as, "Give thanks to the Lord with the lyre; Sing praises to Him with a harp of ten strings" (Psalm 33:2). "I will also praise Thee with a harp, Even Thy truth, O my God; To Thee I will sing praises with the lyre, O Thou Holy One of Israel" (Psalm 71:22). Many references to instruments may be found in the prefaces to the Psalms (4:0; 6:0; 11:2; 21:12; 33:2; 54:0; 55:0; 61:0; 67:0; 76:0).

The most well known instrumentalist in the Bible is King David. David's "heart after God" (Acts 13:22) is seen in the many expressions of praise in the Psalms, including his praise with instruments. David was a skillful instrumentalist. After he was anointed privately by Samuel, his first action as the anointed king (or king-elect) was playing the harp. "And so it was, whenever the spirit from God was upon Saul, that David would take a harp and play it with his hand. Then Saul would become refreshed and well, and the distressing spirit would depart from him" (1 Samuel 16:23). The very term "psalm" originally meant plucking a stringed instrument or "music of the lyre" which seems to have originated with David's instrumental worship.[6]

United with David's Psalms of praise is his creative introduction of various instruments. For example, Psalm 8 is a well known, "O LORD, our Lord, How excellent is Your name in all the earth." It goes on to address the restoration of man's true dominion. "You have put all things under his feet" (Psalm 8:6). Because of this, it is cited repeatedly in the New Testament of Jesus Christ (Matthew 21:16, 1 Corinthians 15:27, Ephesians 1:22, Hebrews 2:8). The preface to Psalm 8 says, "To the Chief Musician. On the instrument of Gath. A Psalm of David" (NKJV).[7] David praises God and prophesies of Christ with a Philistine musical instrument. David has plundered the Egyptians, musically.

David was an instrumental entrepreneur who created and apparently imported a variety of instruments. One passage speaks of the "musical instruments, 'which I made,' said David, 'for giving praise'" (1 Chronicles 23:5). These instruments were emphatically approved of God for later temple service (2 Chronicles 29:25). They are referred to as "the musical instruments of God" (1 Chronicles 16:42 NKJV). Only after David do we find instrumental music incorporated into the cultic service at the temple, both Solomon's temple and the rebuilt temple of Zerubbabel (Nehemiah 12:36).[8] David's "instruments *of God*" may be reflected in the redeemed and faithful who play "harps *of God*" (Revelation 15:2-4, emphasis mine).

About half of the 150 Psalms are attributed to David. Given David's foundational role in the Psalter and his instrumental exuberance, it is not surprising to see the symphonic climax of the Psalter filled with instruments for praise. Psalm 150 is a summative statement:

> Hallelujah. Praise God in His sanctuary; praise Him in the sky, His stronghold. Praise Him for His mighty acts; praise Him for His exceeding greatness. Praise Him with blasts of the horn; praise Him with harp and lyre. Praise Him with timbrel and dance; praise Him with lute and pipe. Praise Him with resounding cymbals; praise Him with loud-clashing cymbals. Let all that breathes praise the LORD. Hallelujah.[9]

This list of instruments culminating the Psalter covers every fundamental kind:

> from chordophones (lyres, harps, kinnors), to membranophones (timbrels), to aerophones (flutes, trumpets, shofars, pipes), to metalophones (cymbals).[10]

INSTRUMENTS IN THE HISTORIC CHURCH

Despite all of this, if we could travel together through time and space, we could visit churches for centuries all over the world where no musical instruments were used and were, in fact, forbidden. In some ancient and modern traditions it is still the case that musical instruments have little or no role in worship. Very few (Eastern) Orthodox churches permit instruments. Those that do, permit an organ in a few parishes. This only developed in twentieth century in America.[11] The

(Western) Catholic church did not admit instruments until very late, around the seventh century and then many Protestants and Anabaptists objected to their use in the sixteenth century and beyond.

There are two main arguments against musical instruments in worship. First, early on in the history of the church there was concern about looking and sounding like pagans.[12] Instruments were connected to the often immoral Greco-Roman theater. "There is hardly a major church father from the fourth century that does not inveigh against pagan musical practice in the strongest possible language."[13]

The second reason is that there is a relative silence in the New Testament on instruments. Without an explicit endorsement in the New Testament, many theologians argued against musical instruments, seeing them as wedded to the sacrificial system.[14] Like Augustine and Chrysostom before, Calvin saw the musical instruments of the Old Testament as typological of the people of God in the New Testament.

> With respect to the tabret, harp, and psaltery, we have formerly observed, and shall find it necessary afterwards to repeat the same remark, that the Levites, under the law, were justified in making use of instrumental music in the worship of God; it having been His will to train His people, while they were as yet tender and like children, by such rudiments, until the coming of Christ. But now, when the clear light of the Gospel has dissipated the shadows of the law, and taught us that God is to be served in a simpler form, it would be to act a foolish and mistaken part to imitate that which the Prophet enjoined only upon those of his own time.[15]

Southern Presbyterian R.L. Dabney (1820–1898) argued against the popular movement of adding organs in Presbyterian churches. He wrote, "For as the temple-priests and animal sacrifices typified Christ and his sacrifice on Calvary, so the musical instruments of David in the temple-service only typified the joy of the Holy Ghost in his pentecostal effusions."[16] Adam Clarke (1762–1832), the noted Methodist commentator, said, "Music, as a science, I esteem and admire: but instruments of music in the house of God I abominate and abhor. This is the abuse of music; and here I register my protest against all such corruptions in the worship of the Author of Christianity."[17] The Baptist, Charles Haddon Spurgeon (1834–1892), did not permit instruments or choirs in his Metropolitan Tabernacle. He said, "No musical or aesthetic accompaniment will ever be used."[18]

Often the arguments against instruments tend toward the claim of Old Testament vs New Testament spirituality. Non-instrumental music is more "spiritual" and fitting for "the more spiritual dispensation" of the new covenant. I challenge this trajectory. Scripture drives us toward a creational embrace awaiting a consummation which is even more robustly creational.[19] On what grounds may we call human voices *spiritual* while we charge David with *carnality* because he made sounds from the materials of a good creation? The sounds of voices register the vibrations of created matter just as do the sounds of non-vocal instruments. A larynx is not more creational than a string. Air flow through nasal cavities in singing is not more creational than that in the mouthpiece of a trumpet. Instruments are creational extensions of persons.

Beyond debunking bad philosophical arguments mustered against instruments, is there a positive case, Scripturally? Can it be shown that the Bible expects instrumental music in new covenant worship? I believe so.

INSTRUMENTS IN THE TABERNACLE OF DAVID

A strong line of defense for musical instruments is found in the example of the "Tabernacle of David."[20] The Tabernacle of David was the tent for the Ark of the Covenant during David's reign, prior to the construction of Solomon's temple. David brought the Ark into Jerusalem in the famous episode where he danced before the Lord (2 Samuel 6:14).[21]

David established this house of worship in Jerusalem on Mount Zion, even while the Tabernacle of Moses was in Gibeon. Mosaic sacrifices continued to be offered in Gibeon (2 Chronicles 1:3). Janice E. Leonard writes about the Tabernacle of David, "Priests and Levites were sanctified to carry on worship before it, but except for the initial dedication ceremonies, this worship did not involve burnt offerings."[22]

> So they brought the ark of God, and set it in the midst of the tabernacle that David had erected for it. Then they offered burnt offerings and peace offerings before God... And he appointed some of the Levites to minister before the ark of the LORD, to commemorate, to thank, and to praise the LORD God of Israel: Asaph the chief, and next to him Zechariah, then Jeiel, Shemiramoth, Jehiel, Mattithiah, Eliab, Benaiah, and Obed-edom: Jeiel with stringed instruments and harps, but Asaph made music with cymbals; Benaiah and Jahaziel the priests regularly blew the trumpets before the ark of the covenant of God. (1 Chronicles 16:1–6 NKJV)

Three important matters stand out about the Tabernacle of David in contrast to the previous Mosaic Tabernacle.

Unlike the Mosaic Tabernacle, the Ark was not hidden behind a veil or curtain. Worshipers were "before" the Ark which was in the "middle of the tent" (2 Samuel 6:17 NET, 1 Chronicles 16:4).

Unlike the Mosaic Tabernacle, the worshipers included Gentiles along with Jews, namely Obed-Edom the Gittite (1 Chronicles 16:5, 2 Kings 6:10–11).

Unlike the Mosaic Tabernacle in which there were no songs of praise, worship at the Davidic Tabernacle emphasized praise with musical instruments.[23]

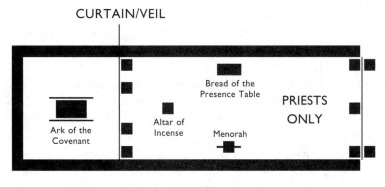

CURTAIN/VEIL

Bread of the
Presence Table

PRIESTS
ONLY

Ark of the
Covenant

Altar of
Incense

Menorah

MOSES' TABERNACLE

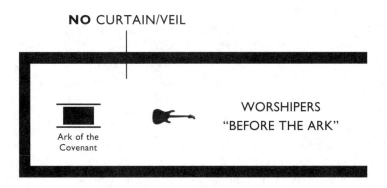

NO CURTAIN/VEIL

WORSHIPERS
"BEFORE THE ARK"

Ark of the
Covenant

DAVID'S TABERNACLE

Therefore, the Tabernacle of David provides the first example of direct access before the Lord in worship by multi-ethnic worshipers with instrumental, praise-centered worship. It provides a foretaste of new covenant worship in which the temple veil has been torn apart so that all nations may have equal access to give praise to the Lord with their music (Matthew 27:51, Mark 15:38, Luke 23:45). This Tabernacle is prophetic of the new covenant in which the promise of God is for Jews and Gentiles to come into Christ as a New Man, a new Adam, or "new humanity" (Ephesians 2:15 NRSV).

It is surprising to discover Gentiles and Jews worshiping together before the Lord in the Old Covenant. But like Rahab and Ruth, many Gentiles have populated the genealogies of Israel. Likewise, the musician Obed-Edom, was a

"Philistine from Gath who apparently was loyal to David and Israel. At Obed-edom's house David left the ark of the covenant following the death of Uzzah at the hand of God (2 Samuel 6:6–11)."[24] Peter Leithart says, "Moreover, the blessings upon Obed-edom reveal that the Davidic covenant will be a covenant of blessing to Gentile nations, a promise fulfilled especially in Solomon's reign, when the nations came to learn wisdom from Israel's king (1 Kings 10:24), but also seen earlier as many foreigners come to join David and become mighty men (like Uriah the Hittite)."[25]

This example of worship might still lie undisturbed in the annals of Chronicles except that it was cited in the New Testament. The inclusion of Gentiles in the Church was the subject of the first Church council in Acts 15. In summary James cites Amos 9:11 which refers to the Tabernacle of David. It is precisely because of Gentile inclusion in the Church that he references this Tabernacle. By rebuilding this Tabernacle there will be salvation to the Gentiles. Jews and (uncircumcised) Gentiles will now assemble together in the name of Jesus to worship the true God.

> Men and brethren, listen to me: Simon has declared how God at the first visited the Gentiles to take out of them a people for His name. And with this the words of the prophets agree, just as it is written: 'After this I will return And will rebuild the tabernacle of David, which has fallen down; I will rebuild its ruins, And I will set it up; So that the rest of mankind may seek the LORD, Even all the Gentiles who are called by My name, Says the LORD who does all these things.' (Acts 15:13–17 NKJV)

Some commentators think the Tabernacle here is just the Davidic "house" or "dynasty." But the Gentile connection is strong evidence that James and Amos understood their inclusion in the distinctly Davidic worship on Mount Zion. Even more, David's psalm of dedication for the Tabernacle emphasizes Gentile worship, "Sing to the LORD, all the earth ... Declare His glory among the nations, His wonders among all peoples ... And let them say among the nations, 'The LORD reigns.'" (1 Chronicles 16:23–24, 31, also Psalm 105). David's Psalms emphasize Gentiles worshiping Yahweh. "Therefore I will give thanks to You, O LORD, among the Gentiles, And sing praises to Your name" (Psalm 18:49). "All the ends of the world shall remember and turn to the LORD, and all the families of the nations shall worship before You" (Psalm 22:27). The bold Messianic Psalm 2 says, "Yet I have set My King On My holy hill of Zion ... Ask of Me, and I will give You the nations for Your inheritance" (Psalm 2:6–8).

David's worship at Zion's hill becomes connected with not only the renewal of Israel, but also the inclusion of the nations. In an ode to Zion the sons of Korah wrote, we read, "The LORD loves the gates of Zion more than all the dwellings of Jacob. Glorious things are spoken of you, O city of God!" (Psalm 87:2–3). From

Zion flows living water, "Both the singers and the players on instruments say, 'All my springs are in you.'" (v7). This Psalm about Zion explicitly refers to the inclusion of other nations in the register of Zion. "I will make mention of Rahab and Babylon to those who know Me; Behold, O Philistia and Tyre, with Ethiopia: 'This one was born there.' And of Zion it will be said, 'This one and that one were born in her; And the Most High Himself shall establish her'" (vv4–5). Commentator, Derek Kidner explains, "A representative sample of the Gentile world is being enrolled in God's city ... Towards the people of God they are not mere proselytes: they can avow, as Paul said of his Roman status, 'But I was born a citizen' (cf. Acts 22:28). This is the gospel age, no less."[26]

Isaiah 16:5 uses Zion's Tabernacle as the very place of Christ's reign over all the world, "In mercy the throne will be established; And One will sit on it in truth, in the tabernacle of David." Throughout the Old Testament Zion becomes the location of God's special presence with His people: "God is in the midst of her, she will not be moved" (Psalm 46:5). "His tabernacle is in Salem; His dwelling place also is in Zion" (Psalm 76:2). "Out of Zion, the perfection of beauty, God has shone forth" (Psalm 50:2).

Even more striking is the fact that while we popularly associate Mount Zion with going up to worship at the temple in Jerusalem, *neither* Solomon's temple *nor* the later temple of Zerubbabel and its expansion by Herod were built *on Mount Zion*. The temple was built on Mount Moriah. "Now Solomon began to build the house of the LORD at Jerusalem on Mount Moriah ..." (2 Chronicles 3:1). In fact, after the temple was constructed they removed the Ark from Mount Zion and brought it to the temple on Mount Moriah (2 Chronicles 5:2). The only worship that happened on Mount Zion was at the Tabernacle of David.

A striking truth for those who love the Psalms is that David's place of worship was this place, not the later temple built by Solomon and not the Mosaic Tabernacle located in Gibeon.[27] So in the Psalms when we read that David longed to be at the House of the Lord or meditated on the beauty of God in His temple, he was referring to this Tabernacle (of David) (Psalm 5:7, 11:4, 18:6, etc). Psalm 27 says "One thing I have desired of the LORD, That will I seek: That I may dwell in the house of the LORD all the days of my life, To behold the beauty of the LORD, And to inquire in His temple" (Psalm 27:4). When David was beholding the beauty of the Lord, he was doing so in praise, seeing the Ark at the place known to us as the Tabernacle of David.

The biblical theology of the concept of Zion is a golden stair-case winding to heaven. While this Tabernacle is the place of the first and only worship on this mount, Zion truly becomes an icon of heaven's worship. The Tabernacle of David is the origin.[28]

The concept of Zion is also significant in the New Testament. Hebrews 12 contrasts two mountains. "But you have come to Mount Zion and to the city of the living God, the heavenly Jerusalem, to an innumerable company of angels, to the general assembly and church of the firstborn who are registered in heaven..." (Hebrews 12:22). The other mountain is *unnamed*, but described as "the mountain that may be touched and that burned with fire, and to blackness and darkness and tempest, and the sound of a trumpet" (Hebrews 12:18–19). Mount Sinai was the place of the giving of the law and certainly fits the description. But perhaps the reason Mount Sinai is not named is because there is a more subtle contrast with the standing temple in Jerusalem on Mount Moriah. Throughout Hebrews the appeal is made toward those tempted to return to old covenant forms (without Christ) rather than persevering with the new covenant assemblies of Christ. It is not that they would literally return to Mount Sinai, rather they may actually return to Mount Moriah, the temple in Jerusalem, forsaking the new covenant Church (Hebrews 10:28).

In the triumph of the Lamb in Revelation 14 and 15 John brings together Zion, instruments, and all nations. He sees "a Lamb standing *on Mount Zion*, and with Him one hundred and forty-four thousand" who "were redeemed from the earth" with "the sound of harpists playing their harps" and "they sang as it were a new song before the throne" (Revelation 14:1–3 emphasis mine). In chapter 15 with "harps of God," they sing, "Great and marvelous are Your works, Lord God Almighty! . . . *For all nations shall come and worship before You . . .*" (Revelation 15:2–4, emphasis mine).

INSTRUMENTS IN CHRISTIAN CULTURE

I have argued that the deepest biblical proof for the value of musical instruments arises from the typological example of Davidic worship on Mount Zion which is the basis for much of the instrumental references even in the Psalms.[29] This *type* of the new covenant includes direct access to the presence of the Lord, a world of multi-ethnic worshipers, *and praise with instruments*, as a model of new covenant worship. In the name of great David's greater Son, we, from all nations, have access through one Spirit to praise the Father (Ephesians 2:18).

It is fitting then that our worship should include praise with instruments in a multi-ethnic Church Instruments arise from culture. Musicians make sounds with the particular cultural artifacts of their times and places, whether Gath or Germany. Further refinements culturally and technologically necessitate different musical sounds. Before the technology to make valves for brass instruments or hinged keys for woodwind instruments, wind instruments had different sounds with limitations in range and technique. Therefore, musical sounds develop over time even by virtue of the technological and material changes.

By the development of instruments we "have dominion" over the raw elements of creation, like wood and metal, ebony and ivory, in order to transform them into tools for sound. With musical instruments we explore creation finding and expressing more of the reality God made in the soundscape. By the work of luthiers and instrumental artisans, combined with the creative skills of musicians, auditory art embellishes the native creation which enriches creation.

We show the *imago dei* as we make sounds which aim to musically re-create. Through such musical *work,* we *glorify* (add weightiness to) creation and the Creator. Our rightful dominion is a cultivation which produces new fruits. These fruits require the work of human hands. This is beautifully illustrated in the Eucharist service. We pray, "Blessed are you, Lord God, King of the Universe who gives seed to the sower and bread to the eater (Isaiah 55:11). Through your goodness we have received this bread, *which the earth has given and human hands have made,* and through Your surpassing mercy You have given us the bread of life. Blessed be God for ever. Amen."

The Eucharist follows the Offertory because we are really and symbolically bringing the work of our cleansed human hands into God's presence. On the Table is bread, not unprocessed wheat kernels. Bread is required and bread requires the fruit of the earth and the time of the fruitful labor of human hands. Wine is not raw grapes (nor mere grape juice). It requires the fruit of the earth and the fruitful labor of human hands in time. This is a model for all of our labor, musical or otherwise. We add to the beauty of creation.

What should we expect then in the developing global Christian cultures? Scripture demands the praise of the nations (*ethne*). For example, Isaiah commands, "Sing to the Lord a new song, sing His praise from the end of the earth! (Isaiah 40:10). "Sing to the Lord a new song; sing to the Lord, all the earth" (Psalm 96:1). "New songs" are being commanded from other nations. Worship from other nations is a climactic hope in the drama of redemption. God desires for "the Gentiles to glorify God for His mercy" (Romans 15:9-11).

We should expect that a "new song" will arise from all nations. This is envisioned in Revelation. The elders with harps (*kithara*) give praise. "And they sang a new song...Thou wast slain, and didst purchase for God with Thy blood men from every tribe and tongue and people and nation'" (Revelation 5:8-10). A "new song" "refers to the introduction of a new composition for the purpose of celebrating..." The call for a new song rings out seven times in Scripture (Psalms 33:3; 40:3; 96:1; 98:1; 144:9; 149:1; Isaiah 42:10).[30] The salvation of a world of peoples is much to celebrate.

Christ is saving a whole world of different cultures, thus the music of the redeemed will flow from all redeemed peoples and cultures. This is God's plan of world redemption. This strongly implies that the nations will use their music in their language to glorify God. Since more peoples are saved and sanctified, there will be a greater expansion of the praises to our Triune God reflected in different kinds of music and musical instruments that arise from different cultures. We must rejoice in this rather than restrict it. Our Triune God's praises cannot be exhausted. His fullest praise requires worlds of music and musical instruments for Mount Zion's Lamb of God. Hallelujah!

Endnotes

1   Some of those are now available in iTunes, search "Strawbridge House."

2   An expanded version of this is still available here: http://www.wordmp3.com/details.aspx?id=222

3   Westminster Confession of Faith 21:1.

4   http://www.westminsterconfession.org/worship/instrumental-music-in-worship-commanded-or-not-commanded.php

5   Jewish Music: Its Historical Development (New York: Dover, 1992 [1929]), 21.

6   One source says, "psalmos, psalmou, ho (psallo), a striking, twanging (Euripides, others); specifically, a striking the chords of a musical instrument (Pindar, Aeschylus, others)" THAYER'S Greek-English Lexicon of the New Testament, n.p. Also http://en.wikipedia.org/wiki/Psalms.

7   The Jewish Publication Society translation and others have this as "on the gittith," also in the preface to Psalm 81 and 84. While this term possibly refers to the name of a tune or "winepress," evidence points to an actual instrument just as the NKJV translates it. The ancient Targums (Aramaic version) has it as, "For praise, on the lyre that he brought from Gath. A hymn of David." http://targum.info/pss/ps1.htm

8   "David introduced music into the Tabernacle and Temple services (1 Chronicles 16:4-7)." On Psalm 150, Life Application Study Bible (Accordance electronic ed. Carol Stream: Tyndale House Publishers, 2004).

9   The JPS translation (1985) Tanakh: Jewish Publication Society.

10 See "Music: Musical instruments" by H. M. Best & D. Huttar in M. C. Tenny, ed., Zondervan Pictorial Encyclopedia of the Bible (Grand Rapids: Zondervan, 1976), 311-324. Also Andrew Wilson-Dickson, The Story of Christian Music: From Gregorian Chant to Black Gospel (Fortress, 1992), 17.

11 The irony of the organ as a sacred instrument is that it mimics instruments of an orchestra, including percussion.

12 Andrew Wilson-Dickson, The Story of Christian Music: From Gregorian Chant to Black Gospel (Minneapolis: Fortress, 1992), 28.

13 Music in Early Christian Literature, ed. James W. McKinnon (Cambridge: Cambridge University, 1987), 2.

14 John L. Girardeau, *Instrumental Music in the Public Worship of the Church* (Edmonton, Alberta: Still Waters Revival Books, [1888] 2000).

15 On Psalm 81:2 in John Calvin, Calvin's Commentaries (Complete) (trans. John King; Accordance electronic ed. Edinburgh: Calvin Translation Society, 1847), n.p.

16 Dabney wrote this in a review of the classic treatment of the Puritan Regulative Principle view espoused by Columbia Theological Seminary professor, John L. Girardeau, Instrumental Music in the Public Worship of the Church http://www.naphtali.com/articles/worship/dabney-review-of-girardeau-instrumental-music/

17 Adam Clarke, Adam Clarke's Commentary on the Whole Bible (Accordance electronic ed. 6 vols.; Altamonte Springs: OakTree Software, 2004), Vol. 4, page 684.

18 Lewis A. Drummond, Spurgeon: Prince of Preachers (Grand Rapids: Kregel, 1992), 351.

19 See the literary defense of this point in C.S. Lewis's classic, The Great Divorce, in which the inhabitants of hell are vaporous, isolated ghosts and heaven is hard and heavy creational wonderland.

20 I am indebted to Peter J. Leithart in his recorded lectures in the Christ Church Ministerial Conference, "The Other Day the Music Died" (Moscow, ID: Canon Press, 2000). These ideas are more fully exposited in his, From Silence to Song: The Davidic Liturgical Revolution (Moscow ID: Canon, 2003). This book is not only a needed exposition of this Tabernacle, but provides a biblical theology of Chronicles, p. 19ff.

21 The Augustinian-Calvinian and Puritan arguments take no account of this distinctive advance in biblical worship, but seem to lump it into the Levitical temple service.

22 The Complete Library of Christian Worship: The Biblical Foundations of Christian Worship, Vol. 1, Robert Webber ed. (Peabody MA: Hendrickson, 1993), 121. The idea that animal sacrifices ceased after the dedication seems to be drawn from 1Chronicles 16:37–43, distinguishing the ministry at the ark (music) with animal sacrifices at Gibeon. One exception is that after receiving divine wisdom (in a dream at Gibeon), Solomon came to Jerusalem, "stood before the ark of the covenant of the Lord, and offered burnt offerings and made peace offerings, and made a feast for all his servants" (1Kgs. 3:15). See Leithart, From Silence to Song (55–56).

23 Prior to this the only use of instruments at the Mosaic Tabernacle was the two silver trumpets "for calling the congregation and for directing the movement of the camps" (Num. 10:1–10).

24 "OBED-EDOM," Holman Illustrated Bible Dictionary, Eds Chad Brand, Charles Draper, Archie England (Nashville: Holman, 2003. Electronic text hypertexted and prepared by OakTree Software, Inc.

25 "Death and Resurrection of the Tabernacle" (Biblical 53 Horizons, February, 1999), www.BiblicalHorizons.com.

26 Derek Kidner, Psalms 73–150: An Introduction and Commentary (TOTC 16; IVP/Accordance electronic ed. Downers Grove: InterVarsity Press, 1975), 346.

27 "David had actually been barred from Gibeon because he was afraid (cf. 13:12) and unable to enquire of God." Martin J. Selman, 1 Chronicles: An Introduction and Commentary (TOTC 10; IVP/Accordance electronic ed. Downers Grove: InterVarsity Press, 1994), 219. Leithart teaches that the divided worship of Gibeon (Mosiac) and Zion (Davidic) was united by Solomon in the temple. 1&2 Kings; Brazos Theological Commentary on the Bible (Grand Rapids: Brazos Press, 2006), 67.

28 Some might argue that Zion simply becomes another name for Jerusalem. This may be so for some texts, but there is a clear origin of this iconic location.

29 It was precisely because of David's use of instruments that they were taken up into temple service later. This fact seems to be overlooked by critics of instrumental music in worship.

30 David E. Aune, Revelation 1–5 (Word Biblical Commentary 52A; Accordance/Thomas Nelson electronic ed. Dallas: Word Books, 1997), 359.

TEACH US
to sing

Whenever the Psalter is abandoned, an incomparable treasure vanishes from the Christian church. With its recovery will come unsuspected power.
    —Dietrich Bonhoeffer[1]

There was a time in the Reformed tradition when the only permissible singing in church was the singing of psalms; nowadays, however, Protestants have learned to sing everything else—from sacred country music to sacred rock—except the psalms!
    —Simon Chan[2]

Put yourself in my shoes. You're the new director of worship and music at an evangelical church. You're not the kind who tethers every song in a service to the sermon, but you do come to the task with this conviction: the ministry of music is a ministry of the Word of God; music, like preaching, should reflect the whole counsel of God and not just a few of our favorite things.

Now: Once the pastor begins to unpack a biblical book with more gravitas than many of evangelicalism's greatest hits can bear, what will you have the congregation sing?

Four and a half years ago, I found myself asking that question. I had arrived at the church just before Christmas. Christmas behind us, we made a beeline from the manger to the Apocalypse. Little Lord Jesus (no crying he makes) was suddenly the exalted Son of Man, his voice like many waters, his word to the churches a healing sword. Alpha and Omega, First and Last, he stood among stars and burning lampstands, a white shining figure before whom John the seer fell as one dead. The Revelation, like the Lion of Judah it reveals, sometimes shakes its mane and roars. Where was the music to match?

From the Apocalypse, we turned to the psalms. The pastor preached about a third of them. Not long into that series, despair set in again. Week after week, I wondered, What do we know that measures up to the psalms? There is something incongruous about singing, say, "Now I am happy all the day" while the Word of God is singing things such as

My tears water my bed day and night.
How long, O LORD?
Now therefore, O kings, be wise;
    be warned, O rulers of the earth.
Serve the LORD with fear,
    and rejoice with trembling.
The LORD abhors the bloodthirsty and deceitful man.
My God, my God, why have you forsaken me?
They kill the widow and the sojourner, and murder the fatherless.
Darkness is my only companion.

Where were the popular hymns and songs that spoke in those ways? The logical solution was to sing the psalms themselves, of course; psalms, however, are not part of the typical evangelical repertoire.

Between the Bible and our praise is a disconnect, but we scarcely notice it. When it comes to worship, most of us like what we like without further thought. We seldom pause long enough to see that what we sing, taken as whole, falls short of the depth and breadth of the Word of God. Our worship music isn't well, and full healing won't come without a reopened Psalter. Apart from the psalms, our worship will never be fully biblical. So long as the psalms lie dormant, our worship will never be fully biblical.

I want to offer here a winsome case for returning the psalms to their most natural habitat—our hearts and lips in the worshiping assembly. But critical words about today's evangelical worship will be needed. I hope not to offend or embitter. I hope, too, to allay any fear that my pleas are the machinations of a crypto-Papist. I am, rather, a child asking for bread. It would be good if we could simply be reminded of what we no doubt already know—that Paul commended psalm singing, that the psalms belong to Jesus, and that if they are worthy of his voice, they are worthy of ours—and leave it at that. Alas, even if we know such things, we have not proved consistently faithful in acting on them. I aim to say a helpful word, not the last word. Can we reason together?[3]

SINGING THE BIBLE

Christians need to think more deeply about what they sing, and why. Not all that's old is good. Not all that's new is bad. But the psalms and biblical canticles are the measure of both. Any congregation that rallied around that point would eventually see musical tastes transformed. The best would drive out the pretty good, regardless of age. Almost miraculously, water would be displaced by wine.

Our songs shape us. We own them, or they own us, in ways that we never own sermons. More than most preaching, music is what sticks with us after we exit the pew and pass through the back door. If we wallow in schlock and schmaltz, our devotion grows schlocky and schmaltzy. Our faith becomes long on sentiment, short on substance. It is one thing to sing a row of pretty *alleluias* with no other content; it is another to sing, with the author of Psalm 119, "It is good for me that I have been afflicted, that I might learn your statutes." We can (and should) outgrow ditties and bad hymns. We cannot outgrow the psalms. Psalms both sensitize us and toughen us up. They mature us.

Biblical music is a gift of God. Scripture is full of songs—those of Miriam, Moses, and Hannah, of Zechariah, the Virgin Mary, and Simeon. The letters of Paul contain hymns, or hymn-like material, and so does the Revelation. The Bible doesn't come to us first as theology textbook but as storybook and songbook. We're invited to put ourselves into the story (by faith and baptism) and then to join the songs—the songs of God for the people of God.[4]

Behold, I tell you a mystery: The churches that claim to make the most of the Bible in their theology make the least of the Bible in their worship. For all their emphasis on the authority and God-givenness of Scripture, evangelicals often have the least biblical worship in Christendom. We have fostered churches— some even bear the name "Bible"—where the Scriptures lie shut, liturgically speaking. They are not sung. They are not prayed. They may be read only mini- mally, and in a rush, as an appetizer before the sermonic main dish.

By contrast, Roman Catholic, Anglican, and Orthodox services, when they are at their biblical best, abound in biblical song. People in those communions often sing psalms and other biblical canticles. They sing the Beatitudes and the Lord's Prayer. They sing songs full of biblical language and imagery—the *Gloria*, for example, and the *Te Deum*.

To make those observations is not to vilify one tradition and idealize others. Admittedly, some churches that do sing the psalms actually assign the privilege to choirs or cantors alone. Or they settle for abbreviated psalms and intone them without the vigor that the children of the resurrection elsewhere, at *their* biblical best, long for in their music-making ("shout," "make a joyful noise," and the like are not synonyms for "coo" or "purr"). Every tradition has its liabilities. But believers in congregations that wrangle over worship would do well to learn from others who have not forgotten that the psalms remain the church's first and finest hymnbook.

PRICELESS

Two disparate Protestants who call us to remember are Charles Haddon Spurgeon, the great nineteenth-century English preacher, and Dietrich Bonhoeffer, the young German pastor-theologian executed by the Nazis in 1945. Spurgeon first, deploring more than a century ago what he could have deplored today: "It is to be feared that the Psalms are by no means so prized as in earlier ages of the Church. Time was when the Psalms were not only rehearsed in all the churches from day to day, but they were so universally sung that the common people knew them, even if they did not know the letters in which they were written." Spurgeon ministered at the Metropolitan Tabernacle in London, and in the hymnbook that he himself compiled, all the psalms (in metrical versions) are represented. "Time was when bishops would ordain no man to the ministry unless he knew 'David' from end to end, and could repeat each Psalm correctly; even Councils of the Church have decreed that none should hold ecclesiastical office unless they knew the whole Psalter by heart."

Spurgeon was not romanticizing the past. He knew that bad habits have marred the church in every era. He also knew not to toss out the baby with the ancient and medieval bathwater: "Other practices of those ages had better be forgotten, but to this"—to the early Christian premium on the Psalter—"memory accords an honourable record."[5] It is no Roman Catholic or High Church Anglican or Eastern monk saying all that, but a Baptist. A Bible-believing, Bible-preaching, Bible-loving Baptist.

Bonhoeffer, in a pithy little book on the psalms, notes some of the same things as Spurgeon. "In many churches," Bonhoeffer writes, "the Psalms are read or sung every Sunday, or even daily, in succession. These churches have preserved a priceless treasure, for only with daily use does one appropriate this divine prayerbook."[6]

Priceless treasure? Few who experience evangelical worship today would know it.

PETER, PAUL, & MOSES

Why sing the psalms? At a surface level, we want to master the whole collection—or, better, to be mastered by it—for the same reason that George Mallory reportedly wanted to climb Mount Everest: *Because it's there*. The psalms are God's "praise songs," which is one way to translate *Tehillim*, their Hebrew title, and he wants us to sing them. But we can say more. If we leave the matter at "God said do it, so do it," we risk giving the impression that he has burdened us with some arbitrary rule. The truth is richer.

What is the Book of Psalms about? Many things, of course. Praise and lament, wisdom and wickedness, warriors and kings, secret sins and tender mercies. But the deepest Christian conviction about the psalms is that ultimately they speak of Jesus in his suffering and glory. It is a conviction that springs from words of the risen Lord himself, who opened his disciples' minds to the things concerning him "written in the law of Moses, and in the prophets, and in the psalms" (Luke 24:44). The psalms are the soundtrack of the gospel, the Old Testament book most quoted in the New. That is more than a random bit of Bible trivia, and it can be put more poetically: Matthew, Mark, Luke, and John, Peter, Paul, and the writer to the Hebrews—they all love to tell the old, old story of Jesus and his love, and none tells it without recourse to the Psalter. Like their Lord, they hear within its ancient lines fresh, Jesus-shaped significance. If we, in our worship, comfortably tell the story without psalms, how biblical is the story we tell? How biblically are we telling it?

The psalms speak of Jesus; they also speak *for* him. Their voice is his. "I will tell of your name to my brothers; in the midst of the congregation I will sing your praise." The words are from Psalm 22, attributed to King David, but the writer to the Hebrews hears Jesus (2:12). The psalms are Jesus' singing voice, in words with power, within the worshiping church. Some psalms make this hard to believe, of course. How can it be the voice of Jesus we hear when, for example, the guilty psalmist confesses wrongdoing and cries for forgiveness, as in Psalm 51?[7] What need has Jesus of forgiveness? None. But even here, we may believe, he speaks. He who, in one sense, knew no sin, in another sense knew it most profoundly. And he has made the weight of sin that the psalm describes—its shame, its brokenness, its filth and guilt—his own. In the sinless Jesus, the king's confession is a word made flesh in a new way. What belonged to David in his darkest hour belongs also to David's greater son in his solidarity with sinners.

TOLLE CANTARE

There is another voice to hear in the psalms, if only they are sung: our own. Is singing really necessary? If a church is content to read them, isn't that enough? The answer depends on what we mean by *necessary*. I suppose that *singing* the psalms is no more "necessary" than *singing* "In Christ Alone" or "How Great Thou Art." Yes, any text can be read instead of sung. But why? Why say it when you can sing it?[8]

God gives us songs. Singing them needs no further justification, no more than rendering a Mozart symphony as an orchestral piece needs justification. Symphonies are for orchestral playing. Songs are for singing. No congregation would tolerate merely reading "Holy, Holy, Holy" or "Shout to the Lord." It makes no more sense to do it with the psalms. The call into the Psalter is not just *Tolle lege* but *Tolle cantare*—not take and read but take and *sing*.

Song is speech with glory. It is more glorious to say "I love you" clearly and with conviction than to grunt it. But more glorious still is to sing it, as my mother used to do from the hallway at bedtime. Love sings. Glory sings. "As long as Christians will *love* the Kingdom of God, and not only discuss it," writes the

Orthodox theologian Alexander Schmemann, "they will 'represent' it and signify it, in art and beauty."[9] The song of those who love the kingdom creates in their assembly a sort of audible glory cloud, a prayer that rises like incense. Mere speech is not enough.

How then shall we sing?

Here we face a problem. The psalms, even the Hebrew originals, do not do what many modern Westerners expect a poem or hymn to do. Consider the first four lines of Psalm 23 in the Authorized Version:

> The LORD is my shepherd;
>> I shall not want.
> He maketh me to lie down in green pastures:
>> he leadeth me beside the still waters.

The words do not rhyme. Lines are uneven. What comes through clearly, even in translation, is the psalm's "parallelism," a hallmark of Hebrew poetry: In a pair of lines, the second "parallels"—elaborates on or contrasts with—the first. It is impossible, given the psalm's structure, to write a melody that fits verse after verse the way the tune for "Amazing Grace" fits each of its verses. And so we must choose: either find a way to sing the text as is, or rewrite it to rhyme and fit a particular meter. "Metrical psalms" represent the second choice. A famous example from the *Scottish Psalter*:

> The Lord's my Shepherd; I'll not want.
>> He makes me down to lie
> In pastures green; He leadeth me
>> The quiet waters by.

The vocabulary is almost identical to that of the Authorized Version. But this version obscures the parallel structure of the original. Musically and metrically, "He makes me down to lie" sounds as if it stands on its own. "In pastures green" sounds as if it goes with "He leadeth me" (rather than the previous line), leaving "The quiet waters by" to dangle. "Down to lie" and "waters by," meanwhile, represent the quirky turns of phrase that prompt some people to call older metrical psalmody "The Psalms According to Yoda."

There are in fact ways to sing a psalm without torturing its syntax, and most of them go by the name of *chant*. Chant is simply reading on pitch. Unlike most of the music we are used to singing and listening to, chant has no regular rhythm, but it would be wrong to say it has no rhythm at all. Its rhythm is the rhythm of human speech.

The word itself—*chant*—spooks many evangelicals. Chant is what *Catholics* do; *we sing*. But chant is not something other than singing, much less its opposite. Indeed, *chant* is a French word for *song*.[10] In English, it has proved useful for distinguishing a particular *type* of song. But because some people dislike the word, I have often dropped it and spoken instead of "spandex music." *Spandex* is an anagram of *expands*, and that is what chant does. It expands (and contracts) to accommodate written lines of unequal length. This is its strength, its unique virtue. Anything—phone numbers, lists of pizza toppings, Dr. Seuss, conjugations of Old Norse verbs—can be chanted.

Is chant "Catholic"? That would be news to millions of psalm-singing Orthodox, Anglicans, Lutherans, and other non-Catholics, including (so I hear) some Australian Baptists. It would be news to the editors of the Reformed Presbyterian *Book of Psalms for Singing*, which majors in metrical psalms but nonetheless applauds the general superiority of chant—"the music completely serves the text"—and offers a succinct tutorial.[11] Not to mention Jews, among whom the whole psalm business got started.

No, chant isn't the only way to sing psalms, but it is the easiest, most suitable means at hand. Its flexibility makes it a perfect fit for the psalms, line after uneven line. It keeps their shape as well as their language intact. They get to say what they say *the way they want to say it.* Agreed: A little Lutheran psalm tone or a simplified Anglican chant is not as ear-grabbing as "For All the Saints" or "The Maple Leaf Rag." At least not in the same way. But chant is on a different mission with glories of its own. In all its various forms—Eastern, Western, Catholic, Protestant—chant adopts a posture of humility before the text of Scripture. It seeks only to give the inspired word pre-eminence, to be conformed to it, to glorify it. Ideally, it bends the worshiping assembly to do the same.

We need this, no? It may not be what we like or are used to. But having learned too well to approach worship as consumers looking for what we like just because we like it, we need this. Jesus makes us priests and kings to God, not worship consumers.

WHAT IF?

So suppose we do it. Suppose we bend and do the hard work of reformation, restoring the psalms to our worship. What can we expect?

First, a shock to the system. After decades of neglect, we step into the Psalter as strangers in a strange land. Its terrain, apart from well-worn paths through a few favorite verses, is alien. To some people, it will seem downright uninhabitable. This is why Bonhoeffer advised getting into the psalms daily. "When read only occasionally, these prayers are too overwhelming in design and power and tend to turn us back to more palatable fare."[12]

The psalms will teach us that worship is part spiritual warfare against powers and principalities and strongholds. God has not given most of us the wherewithal to go do something for suffering Christians in North Korea, parts of Africa, and other troubled areas. But he has armed us with Psalms 2 and 3 and 5, and 82 and 94 and 146. The psalms speak for the persecuted and afflicted. They give us a way to identify with people who share the sufferings of Christ in ways that many of us are spared, and to remember them before God. They express the longing—even if we perhaps do not feel it as acutely as the psalmists—for a world in which God puts wrong things right. A church that resists singing psalms is like a football team that spurns the best of its playbook as somehow at odds with the sport. It is an army that wars against its own weapons.

The psalms will give our worship breadth. Evangelicals fret too much about a "blend" of musical styles and too little about breadth of content. If we want music ministries marked by wholeness, it is too little to ask of each individual song, "Is it biblical?" We can have a hundred hymns about justification by faith (or conversion, or something else) that, taken individually, are all biblical. But if we sing little else, our vision and expectations are distorted. So is truth. The psalms restore balance. Singing whole psalms—not just favorite slivers tweezered out of context—brings before the Christian assembly a range of concerns that much of our current music ignores: the dark night of the soul, the plight of the poor and vulnerable, strangers and widows and kids without fathers, bracing words against abusers of power, and so on.

The psalms will give our worship greater depth. American Christians are not better placed than the Holy Spirit to pronounce what makes a great "praise song." Next to what the Spirit has given, even some of our most popular "praise and worship" fare is shown up for what it is: Psalms Lite. The difference, as Mark Twain said when comparing the right word and the almost right word, is the difference between lightning and the lightning bug.

In too many quarters of evangelicalism, blessed are those who hunger and thirst for the ephemeral, the faddish, and perpetual adolescence, for they shall be filled. But others—including adolescents—starve. Tired of songs whose watery lyrics seem (as one teen put it to me) bent on stagnation, they want something more, something rooted, something with oomph, something big enough to take on the world.

Is that not what we all, in our best moments, want? Something deeper, richer, more God-focused than our tastes or feelings? Encouragingly, even young people are saying yes.

I have done two psalm workshops at Dallas Baptist University, where the response both times was enthusiastic. Students sang without hesitation and confirmed that, yes, evangelicals can do this. They voiced their dissatisfaction with a lot of contemporary Christian music. And on both occasions, some students responded along these lines: "I like this music because it doesn't call attention to itself. It makes the Word central."

At my church, we have sung Psalm 46 several times in the past year. A college student in her early 20s recently sent this e-mail: "My Bible reading for today included Psalm 46, and I just want to let you know I found myself singing the whole thing in my head. Guess the whole 'singing the Psalms' thing really does help ingrain them into the mind!"

"Love it," another young person has said, calling the psalm "one of the most inspirational pieces of music I've ever heard in my life." Remarkable praise, given that the music could hardly be simpler—a string of eight notes sung six times. But this young person knows where the power lies: "When we sing it, it gives me hope. I feel like, whatever happens in my life, with God I'll be victorious. And it's not just something written by some guy who thought it was what the Holy Spirit wanted him to say. It actually *is* the *Word of God*."

Not all Christians think like that, of course. Even if they did, that alone would not be the church's cue to sing the psalms. A church that sings psalms *only because people want them* is likely to abandon them when people lobby for something they like better. In the worship of the living and true God, fickle taste cannot be trusted. Worship is called not just to reflect tastes but to transform them.

"Be filled with the Spirit," writes Paul, "speaking to one another in psalms, hymns, and spiritual songs, singing and making melody in your heart to the Lord" (Eph 5:18–19). I have waited until now to quote him, hoping to show first that the incentive to sing psalms does not hang on a single proof-text or two. But if a proof-text is wanted, here it is. The apostle has already called the church a new temple (Eph 2:18–22)—an image more provocative than picturesque. It means that ordinary believers in Ephesus and elsewhere—some Jewish, some non-Jewish—have taken up the vocation of the old temple in Jerusalem. They have become the dwelling-place for God through the Spirit, a house of prayer for all nations. No surprise, then, to find Paul bringing fullness of the Spirit and the new temple together with the psalms, the temple music *par excellence*. Near the end of his letter, Paul encourages the Ephesians to take up "the sword of the Spirit, which is the word of God, praying at all times in the Spirit . . . making supplication for all the saints" (6:17–18). The psalms empower us to do both at once.

"What do we accomplish by singing Psalm 51 this evening?" I asked one informal Sunday-night gathering. We rehearse Scripture together, someone said. We acknowledge the waywardness of our own hearts, said someone else. Good answers. But, I suggested, there is more. "How many of us know someone who needs the forgiveness and healing that this psalm speaks of?" Up went nearly every hand. Remember, I said, Jesus sings the psalms. What if we use this one to bring before God the people we just named in our hearts? They may not pray for themselves, much less sing a psalm. But *we* can kneel in solidarity with the One in solidarity with us, and together raise a psalm-filled voice for their sake.

Such an approach, I have found, can help us begin to hear the psalms (and rethink the purposes of worship) in new ways. We suspend our worship consumerism and start acting as priests. Receive a psalm as a gift for sharing, and you are less likely to think of singing it as merely something you *have* to do—raw duty—and more as what you *get* to do, with Jesus.

A Korean congregation meets at my church. I was recently at the pastor's house. Pastor Kim and his wife, Mijeong, speak more English than I do Korean, but communication can still be a little hard at times. Late in the evening, I wondered aloud whether they knew a Korean song that I had heard somewhere and liked. I sang the first word (the only one I knew) and hummed the rest. Within seconds, Mijeong went to the piano and produced the sheet music. I played, they sang. I sang a little, too, but not like they did. They sang out, and beautifully. This was their music, after all: the music of home. After that song, Mijeong pulled out another for us. We sang through both several times. Making music together seemed to be making new connections between us, or strengthening old ones. Music became a means of communion.

Does something like that happen when we sing Jesus' songs with him? I think so. Imagine being invited to a dinner party where Jesus plays host. Having served bread that strengthens the heart and wine to make it glad, he invites us to talk. "Lord," one of us says, "teach us to pray." Jesus begins to sing. "Oh give thanks to the LORD, for he is good; for his steadfast love endures forever!" The music sounds foreign, unlike anything we are used to. "Out of my distress I called on the LORD; the LORD answered me and set me free. . . . I shall not die, but I shall live, and recount the deeds of the LORD." Jesus pauses, asks us to join him. Who will balk, even if the music seems too exotic, or too simple, or "too Jewish"? Surely even our first efforts to sing with him, perhaps as fumbling as my attempt to sing Korean, will rejoice his heart. These are his songs, the music of home. Imagine what it would be to commune with Jesus, crucified and risen, in such a way.

Imagine. And sing.

Endnotes

1   Dietrich Bonhoeffer, *Psalms: The Prayer Book of the Bible* (Minneapolis: Augsburg Fortress, 1970), 26.

2   Simon Chan, *Liturgical Theology: The Church as Worshiping Community* (Downers Grove: InterVarsity Press, 2006), 158.

3   I acknowledge with thanksgiving three people who have helped me think about the psalms: the Reformed theologian James B. Jordan, whose writings on worship never fail to provoke thought; Peter Enns, who taught me at Westminster Theological Seminary; and Archbishop Dmitri Royster, of the Diocese of Dallas and the South of the Orthodox Church in America. As the dear archbishop lay dying in late August 2011, I was honored to be among those reading the Scriptures to him, in my case mostly from the Gospel of John and a few psalms. Especially with respect to Jordan, I am largely thinking his thoughts after him. From him I learned that it is enough to say a helpful word without saying the last word. I am grateful to all three. Of course none would necessarily endorse every word written here.

4   I will not go at length here into the question of "exclusive psalmody," the belief of some Reformed Christians that nothing but psalms may be sung in formal worship. For the record, I am not a proponent of exclusive psalmody. But I am also (obviously) not a proponent of many churches' apparent default position, which is *excluded* psalmody. One further thought: Those who believe

that only the psalms may be sung tend actually to sing songs *based on* the psalms rather than the real thing. Of course, churches could do far worse than to sing good psalm-based songs.

5   Charles Haddon Spurgeon, "Preface," *The Treasury of David: Volume Three*, (McLean, Virginia: MacDonald Publishing Co., n.d.).

6   Bonhoeffer, 25.

7   Even more troubling for many people are the psalms that urge God to intervene on behalf of the exploited and the abused. This issue deserves a fuller treatment than can be offered here. For a helpful word, see "Appeals for Divine Intervention" in Gordon J. Wenham, *Psalms as Torah: Reading Biblical Song Ethically* (Grand Rapids: Baker Academic, 2012), 167–179.

8   A motto inherited from James B. Jordan.

9   Alexander Schmemann, *For the Life of the World* (Crestwood, NY: St. Vladimir's Seminary Press, 1963), 30 (italics his).

10   Note the title of a liturgical work by John Calvin: *La forme des prieres et chantz ecclesiastiques—* "The Form of Prayers and Ecclesiastical Songs."

11   *The Book of Psalms for Singing* (Pittsburgh: The Board of Education and Publication, Reformed Presbyterian Church of North America, 1973, 1998), 440. "Chanting has several advantages over metrical Psalmody, stemming from the fact that in chanting, the music completely serves the text. The music is not difficult or interesting in itself, but has character and meaning only in conjunction with words. The meaning of the text is thus more immediate, and the parallel structure of the Hebrew poetry is more apparent. The difficulties of translating ancient non-metrical poems into sensible English rhyme are rendered unnecessary. Chanting encourages the use of entire Psalms rather than selections."

12   Bonhoeffer, 25.

further READING

Some readers, naturally, will want to hear what psalm chant sounds like. I wish there were a slew of recordings to recommend. There is no shortage of recorded Gregorian chant, of course, but not much is in English or involves the psalms. There are also plenty of recordings of Anglican chant, sung by English choirs. The whole Psalter, as recorded by the choir of St. Paul's Cathedral in London, is available on the Hyperion label. But much recorded Anglican chant sounds—to these ears—rather bloodless. I go to a little conference every year where we use Anglican chant for the *Te Deum*, the Beatitudes, and the *Magnificat*. But we sing them more vigorously and enthusiastically than the choirs on most recordings. For a couple of lively contemporary renditions (Psalms 15 and 149) based on Gregorian tones, check the links below.[1]

A further frustration: I don't know of a single Psalter to recommend without reservation. Please take this as a sign that we have work to do and not as a sign that psalm-singing is not worthwhile. Use your imagination. Examine the resources. Be open to the thought that something like this could be done and done well.

Some readers will wonder whether we really have to chant. Can we not write other music? By all means. A half-way house between chant and metrical song is "through-composed" music. A through-composed song has more melodic shape than a simple psalm tone, but unlike most hymns and songs, its music does not repeat (at least not exactly) from verse to verse. Two pleas to musicians: Write for whole psalms, not just favorite verses. We need whole psalms. And live awhile with forms that already enjoy currency in the church. Get to know the Gregorian psalm tones.[2] (At least one is known by just about everyone; it is the basis of the Lowell Mason tune most commonly associated with "When I Survey the Wondrous Cross." Yes, one of the most beloved evangelical hymns is sung to Gregorian chant.) Study the tones from Saint Meinrad Archabbey.[3] Become familiar with Anglican chant[4] and Orthodox music.[5] Explore, listen, sing. Then write.

Reading the Psalms With Luther (Saint Louis: Concordia Publishing House, 2007). This little book includes all the psalms, from the English Standard Version, "pointed" for singing. ("Pointing" refers to how the psalm and the music are made to fit together.) Each psalm is accompanied by a short introduction and prayer by Luther. Eight psalm tones are provided, but similar tones from other sources could be used as well. The user is left to decide which tone to use with which psalms. I would point some lines differently, seeking more consistently to place the last accented syllable of each line on the last note. To my ears, that sounds more natural than what the book often suggests. Because of that, I find this Psalter better suited for private use—I can change the pointing on the fly—than for congregational.

Psalms for All Season: A Complete Psalter for Worship (Grand Rapids: Faith Alive Christian Resources, 2012). All the psalms are here. Each is presented in a version for responsive reading and versions for chanting; there are also multiple metrical psalms, paraphrases, and so forth. The big liability (as I see it) is the New Revised Standard Version because of its "inclusive language." Consider Psalm 1. The first verse, in its ancient Greek translation as well as in the Hebrew original, definitely speaks of a "man." Blessed is the man who walks not in the counsel of the ungodly. NRSV: "Happy are they . . . " There is no denying that women, too, are blessed. The problem is this: The Psalter has been assembled with care. It is no accident that the first two psalms are the first two psalms. They are like the two doors of a great gate into the Psalter. Psalm 1 introduces a "blessed man." Psalm 2 introduces a king. A long tradition in the church sees Jesus as the fulfillment of the blessed man of Psalm 1. Is it possible that the king, Son of Yahweh, enthroned in Psalm 2 can be identified with the blessed man of Psalm 1? Perhaps. But any translation that renders Psalm 1:1 as "Happy are they" obscures the possible connection.

The Psalter: Psalms and Canticles for Singing (Louisville: Westminster/John Knox Press, 1993). This is not a complete Psalter, and again I prefer stricter translations, but musicians may find it a good place to begin getting a taste of various styles of chant. *Psalms for All Seasons* includes every psalm, but as an entrée to chant, this one is better. One beauty of this music is that you can sing any translation you want with it. Make it a faithful one.

Reginald Box, *Make Music to Our God: How We Sing the Psalms* (London: SPCK, 1996). This book surveys the ways in which the psalms have been sung in English and proposes solutions to various difficulties. It includes many musical examples.

Michael Wilcock, *The Message of Psalms 1–72: Songs for the People of God* and *The Message of Psalms 73–150: Songs for the People of God*, The Bible Speaks Today (Downers Grove: InterVarsity Press, 2001). A popular-level commentary.

Endnotes

1   See http://vimeo.com/9294522 and http://vimeo.com/7718951. For printed music, see David Erb, *Cantica Sanctorum: A Collection of Psalms, Hymns and Spiritual Songs* (Moscow, Idaho: Canon Press, 2012).

2   The Gregorian tones, written for Latin, present challenges for English adaptation. For a discussion of possible solutions, see Anthony Ruff, "Gregorian Psalm Tones with English Texts?" in *Custos* (Issue 2, 2009), 1–10: http://www.npm.org/Sections/Chant/images/Custos%202.pdf.

3   These flexible tones can accommodate four-, five-, and six-line psalm "stanzas." A set of tones can be viewed online: http://www.saintmeinrad.org/media/28541/ModalPsalmTones(Organ).pdf. The simple accompaniments are written for organ, but other instruments (guitar, piano, strings) could be used. For audio demonstrations, go to http://www.saintmeinrad.org/the-monastery/liturgical-music/downloads/. Under "Downloads," click "Other," and see No. 16 at the bottom of the page. Keep in mind that the solo voice there can scarcely hint at how beautiful the psalm might sound if sung by multiple voices in a resonant space.

4   See, for example, Alec Wyton, ed., *The Anglican Chant Psalter* (New York: Church Publishing, 1987). Wikipedia has a color-coded example that some readers may find helpful: http://en.wikipedia.org/wiki/Anglican_Chant

5   For a sampling of Russian tones, see http://commons.orthodoxwiki.org/The_Modern_Russian_Eight_Tones.

Hymns
and innovation

When truth gets into a creed or a hymn-book, it becomes the confident possession of the whole church.
—Alec Motyer

As a church sings, so a church will live.
—Alistair Begg

In this conversation Robert Bigley and Ned Bustard talk with modern hymn writer Keith Getty. As they spoke together on a rainy Wednesday afternoon, they meandered through aesthetics, architecture, thankfulness, criticism, acoustics, and even U2. But of course, they couldn't begin without mentioning "In Christ Alone," Getty's most famous tune.

Owl City's Adam Young recorded a version of the hymn and said: "I'm twenty-four years old, yet something about this song makes me bawl like a baby. The way the melodies and lyrics swirl together is so poignant and beautiful. If I were to count on one hand, the number of songs that have ever deeply moved me, this one would take the cake." Getty's wider catalog of hymns has also been recorded by artists throughout the world of music—country artists Alison Krauss and Ricky Skaggs, Irish musicians Moya Brennan and Anuna, and contemporary Christian musicians Natalie Grant and the Newsboys. They are sung in small churches, large cathedrals, and concert halls around the world.

Keith Getty: "In Christ Alone" was my first and remains to this day our best-known hymn. I co-wrote it with Stuart Townend when I was 25 and still play it more often than anything I've written since. But, I take comfort in the fact that Elton John wrote "Your Song" in 1973, and he has had to perform it every night since then. He said he can't deal with the backlash if he didn't perform it. He has written so many good songs since then, but that still stands above the rest of his work. I realize that I face the distinct possibility of working for forty more years and writing things that aren't as well-loved as that first one.

In light of such a potentially bleak future, what do you do with that as a musician who is a Christian?

Well, I think there are several things. In all things in life, you need to begin with thankfulness. If not, it leads to cynicism, or exhaustion, or to being critical of others, or pure pride. I am thankful for it because it gave me a flagship hymn— that I don't have to explain to people what a modern hymn is. You just say "In Christ Alone" and many people say, "Okay, I get it." It gives a great platform from which to work and to expand ideas on church music.

So, "In Christ Alone" gave us a starting place, a leaping off point. Since then, I have constantly tried to improve as a songwriter—taking on new challenges, listening to new music, co-writing with new people, going to new places, creating new deadlines for songs and projects, trying songs out in new ways with congregations, steeping myself more in the rich traditions of church music throughout history. Even more so, the challenge, which does not exclude artists, is to be growing as a Christian—growing in wisdom and knowledge but also growing in a sense of empathy and love and urgency toward the world around us.

If the current song, the current project, is not the thing we're most excited about right now, we need to ask serious questions about the development of our own gifts or the state of our own spiritual walk.

Jeremy Begbie has written that when "Christians start talking about music, they love to change the subject: they speak about lyrics, texts, titles, and the musical sounds are often forgotten."

At the end of the day, it is so much about the music. If you have good music and good words, you have a good song; if you have bad music and bad words, you have a bad song; if you have good words and bad music it is still a bad song. But, the problem is, if you have bad words and good music, it is a popular song. At the end of the day, the music is of critical importance. Jeremy is right—church leaders have a responsibility to have a critical awareness musically as well as theologically. It's just too important to simply wash their hands of it.

Sting said, "Sometimes mediocre poetry becomes incredible song material."

Yes—it's all about the music! Songs are an art form all their own. Trying to force people to sing good words to bad music is just the artistic extension of trying to get someone to become a Christian only by beating all their arguments up. It ignores the reality that our lives and emotions are richly connected to the songs we sing.

The first volume of It Was Good *starts with the assumption that the reader understands the legitimate calling of the believer to work in the arts. From there it asks how being followers of Christ impacts their craft. So if you were sitting in front of a huge assembly of the next generation of music makers in the Kingdom of God, what is the most important thing you would tell them that they need to do?*

I want to say something really significant here.

Hmmm.

When I was trying to decide basically whether to be a musician or a pastor, Kristyn's Uncle John (John Lennox, the noted mathematician and philosopher) challenged me to be a musician but to be the best musician I could be and to be sure that my faith grew faster than my music. Whether a hymn writer, a film-maker, graphic designer—whatever it is - the same thing applies: to take each of our God-given talents and turn them back into service requires a life-long dedication to both our craft and our spiritual lives. We are, after all His workmanship. The most lasting impact we have is His development of our spiritual lives. C.S. Lewis reminds us that the eternal things in this world are neither symphonies, sculptures, nor architecture, but the people beside us on the bus.

With regard to church music, I simply couldn't recommend it highly enough—to be able to write beautiful music with Christian themes that God's people sing is just a huge privilege.

If "every culture has its own language and its own music," have you found that your hymns work in other cultures?

Well, yes and no. I think every culture has its own indigenous musical language and is poorer for not making more use of it. But that said, the fact of the matter is that Western music is wanted all over the world. So, Western music does translate in terms of popular culture, but I think it's a sad thing when it completely replaces the indigenous music.

I was delighted when I got to work with a group of kids from Uganda who have studied percussion their entire lives and are geniuses. Then I found out that all they want to do is sing Western music. I thought, "What on earth? You are geniuses—do *your* thing!" The trend toward homogenization in all areas of art is frightening. And it isn't limited to Africa. It would seem everyone around the world—from Brazil to India to Africa—everyone wants Western songs. From my experience, given the richness of traditional Irish music, I'm perplexed that more of my countrymen don't use it as a primary inspiration for composition of church music.

But I'd say that I do believe if music has a universal language, it is found in the pentatonic scale. Bernstein, in his Harvard lectures, talks a lot about the parallels in Chinese, Eastern European, and Celtic folk music, because they are built around those scales.

For our readers with less music theory under their belts, the pentatonic scale is the most commonly used scale world-wide. It can be found in folk melodies from the Far East to Europe, Africa, and the Americas. It consists of only five notes (hence the root "penta"). If you imagine the major scale ("do, re, mi, fa, sol, la, ti") and remove the "fa" and "ti" you have the traditional pentatonic scale. Likewise, if you play only the black keys on the piano you will be playing a pentatonic scale. Because there are no semitones (half-steps), the notes of the scale can be played in any order without severe dissonance and without a pre-established sense of tonic. The nineteenth century Appalachian folk tune "New Britain" became the best known pentatonic-based song in the world when it was published in Southern Harmony as the tune for "Amazing Grace."

Right. Therefore all folk musics are more closely related than classical and popular. That is why *The Chieftains in China* is such an intriguing album. It's why Riverdance is such an intriguing project. It took the Irish diaspora around the world and linked its music with the cultures that subsequently absorbed them. The Irish stuff—folk music—is easier to translate into other cultures. And I think we have found that in the sense that many of our melodies sound well in other languages—they've resonated with Chinese churches and with Eastern European churches who have adopted our songs in ways that you would almost not recognize. I didn't set out to write music that would work in different cultures, but apparently the melodies are useful, maybe partly because they don't always require band accompaniment. As melodies, they are not as individualistic but more inherently suited to group singing.

Most of today's Top 40 songs are rhythmically-driven, often with very little attention to melody. While they serve their own purpose, they lack that single element that could enable them to have staying power.

Sure - we often cite "Be Thou My Vision" as an example. The lyrics date to around the sixth century, but it is still being sung today. You have heard it with a rock band (so it works rhythmically) and you have heard it with just voices. It is incredible what you can do with that folk melody. It is a great example of how a well-written song continues to be relevant. Just like "Amazing Grace," or "Come Thou Fount of Ev'ry Blessing." "Be Thou My Vision" is not bound by any generation or style.

Let's delve a bit into the influence of Top 40 over contemporary worship music. Besides the inherent constraints of pop-influenced music, what is lost when the Church allows the radio to drive worship.

When you consider all the forms of music that people might listen to during the week—pop, baroque, hip-hop, early music, bluegrass, opera, jazz, indie, reggae, techno, americana, orchestral, r&b, new wave, blues, swing, electronica—what we sing in church is remarkably predictable compared to that. I also fear there's a shortened list of things we sing about in churches today. In the Psalms, we have the whole gamut of God's character beautifully sung, and the Psalmist seems to live in almost every human emotion imaginable. By contrast, much of what is written today is singularly focused on how God makes me "feel." It gives little time to mournful reflection, it gives little time to plying deeply into truth, it gives little time to darkness, and it would seem that it avoids anything that does not lead to a feeling of ecstasy.

The next thing I would say is that we seem to have lost a sense of Story and telling the Story the way God's songs of faithfulness are told throughout Scripture. For example, the Song of Moses talks about His faithfulness, the Psalms talk about His faithfulness, right through to the Magnificat—which ultimately isn't about Mary telling everyone how good it is to be pregnant, or how she "just wants to praise Him," but it is, again, about His faithfulness from generation to generation.

How do you think the architectural design of modern churches affects congregational worship? It seems most churches care more about the sound coming through the speakers rather than the sound coming from the congregation. So we see them building puffy padded worship centers with no natural acoustics, in order that they not compete with the praise band blaring through the speakers.

Anything that makes something sound better is helpful. The better the acoustics for congregational singing then the better the acoustics for congregational singing. I see it as important, but not crucial. If you are building a new building, and have the money for it, then acoustics is an issue. But for my friend who is going to Nigeria to teach future pastors, acoustics is not an issue. For the people another friend told me about recently that met together in North Vietnam every week for a worship time and whispered hymns in rhythm so they wouldn't get caught by the authorities, acoustics is not an issue.

We have had the privilege to collaborate on some hymns and spiritual songs for our church. When we have done that we have received immediate feedback: they either sing it well, or they don't. With your lifestyle of being on the road so often, do you see the need to have a local church body as part of the creative process?

Trying the songs out is the key. When I was at Allistair Begg's church I was a writer-in-residence of sorts and they'd try out my songs. It was great for us. As we reviewed a song the final analysis of its success wasn't based on musical arrangement or vocal performance. It boiled down to: "Were these words feeding our congregation and was the congregation engaged in passionate singing?" Inevitably we would make some alterations to it. In fact, we have never had a song that after one, two, or three performances did not get changed in some way or another.

Many of the greatest songs ever written are not singable by congregations and thus are not good for congregational worship. Those of us who are musicians tend towards songs that are most musically interesting, or sound best on a recording or even at a major event with a professional band. However, this really does not feed the congregations we lead. If the people are unengaged and are just spectators we have missed the point. Truly effective church worship is where people of every generation, cultural background, social status, and stage in life can sing melodies together as a family to their Creator and Redeemer. It is a microcosm on earth of what we look forward to in Heaven.

Therefore, when we write modern hymns, we are aiming to write melodies that people of different ages and backgrounds can (and will) sing. So I am always chasing that melody that might transcend all those boundaries and, frankly, just be easy to sing. I have never had a very high success rate as a melody writer in comparison to the number of melodies I've written. The importance of working at it, as any other craft, cannot be overstated. A melody only eventually makes it after many drafts. In the past few months I've probably written 300 melodies, and I'll only use two or three of those.

Typically when Stuart and I write songs we run them by our pastors. And we use theologians at both ends of the process. We use them at the start of the creative process. I call three or four theologian friends and ask them to talk with me about the project I am working on. And then at the back end we let them see where we've gone.

In conclusion, as you look at the future of music in the Church, how do you propose that we extricate ourselves from the mire of contemporary worship?

We've seen the model in every period of church music history where lasting art has been created: it has been the fusion of pastoral and theological leadership with the highest musical expression of the time. Throughout the Old Testament and New Testament and church history since, great church music has poetically combined rich theology with melodies written for an artist called the congregation. When these songs are artistically inspiring, we can't help but pass them on from generation to generation.

LOVE THE ONE
you're with

Working as a minister of music in a small inner city church is a wonderful and unique challenge. I have been the minister of music at Abbott Memorial Presbyterian Church in Baltimore city for fourteen years. Abbott has about 180 members on the books, and about 130 people attend our Sunday worship service. The joy and the challenge of ministry in a small church is to create a music program that recognizes my giftedness, and fully utilizes the talents of our congregation, and the resources of our community. I don't want to get stuck in the mire of thinking *"If I could only . . ."* or *"If I only had . . ."* By the grace of God, our church has a vibrant music ministry to church attenders and outreach to its community. My hope for this essay is to encourage ministers of music in similar circumstances, who hope to share the gospel through music in a small church setting.

RELATIONSHIPS ARE KEY

While I was pursuing my Bachelor's degree, I was an organist at a small Baptist church. The minister of music, Keith Vincent, was a great mentor to me. One of the most important things that I learned from him was that relationships are just as important as the music. I observed that the success and failure of many music programs was more a result of relationship building than any particular musical abilities. I have seen successful ministries with musicians of all skill levels. Those who weren't skilled performers themselves were able to surround themselves with the talent necessary to implement the musical vision of the church. Those who didn't spend time developing relationships with people in their church and outside their church often could not get their programs off the ground, or would watch them fizzle out. The music minister may have been fully committed to his vision, but others in the church were not. Music is a social artform often requiring collaboration and a team mentality. Without others behind you, your dreams will never become reality.

Music ministers come with wide variations in their skill sets. Their primary giftedness can vary from administration, performance, or teaching, to pastoring, conducting, composition, or arranging. Music ministers who are not performers can be just as effective as those who are. Often musicianship and administration are on opposite ends of the gift spectrum. The key to a music minister's success or failure is his ability to identify his own weaknesses and compensate for them by building relationships with people, learning their strengths, and finding a place for them in the musical framework of the church. Someone with strong administrative and people skills can use those gifts to build a team of talented musicians who can work together to meet the needs of the church in worship and develops additional musical resources for the future. Coffee breaks and jam sessions can be just as important to a healthy church music program as hours spent locked in an office "getting things done."

100% Organic

A local pastor visited me with the hopes of learning how he could start a music program similar to the one we offer at Abbott. He hoped for a how-to guide. The problem was that I couldn't give it to him. The needs of every community are different, and the way a church can best meet those needs is also different. Instead of a how-to-guide, I described the process I went through to develop the music programs offered at Abbott.

The music ministry at Abbott has many different facets. In addition to what we do on Sunday morning, we also house Abbott Center for the Arts. Abbott Center for the Arts' goal is to train musicians in our congregation and in our local community. My ministry through the Center is a combination of the specific needs of our community and our talent pool. First we identified a need in our church and community. For example, when I started at Abbott, the schools did not have instrumental music programs, and there was no organization meeting that need. Also, the families in our neighborhood are primarily low income. Even if someone was offering music lessons, most of the families wouldn't be able to afford it.

Then came the realization that we had a number of people who could meet these needs. Before I came to the church, I taught private lessons at a community college. I decided I would continue to use my teaching gifts by offering private lessons at the church. One of my former students in the congregation was skilled and interested in teaching, so he taught guitar and drums. I had two friends from the Peabody Institute of the Johns Hopkins University who were looking for opportunities to teach. They joined us as well.

As I was developing the private lessons offered at the church, I became familiar with Music Together®, an early childhood music program that invites families to make music together in small classes. Its primary focus is on children ages birth to four and their parents and caregivers. I had tried offering small group music classes for older students, but without a budget to market the classes, those early attempts were not long-lasting. Baltimore is famous for our formstone row houses. Growing families quickly feel the pinch living in a narrow row house without a backyard. Our community is filled with young families with small children, but once their children get older, a lot of families move away from the area for better schools, or just more space. Music Together® seemed to meet the needs of our neighborhood perfectly.

Once again, I looked at the human resources God provided in the congregation. There was a woman who had a passion for teaching young children. We sent her to be trained, and she ran the Music Together® center as part of Abbott Center for the Arts. These classes are now the largest outreach offered through the center. We have about fifty families, mostly from the community, enrolled in these classes.

While it is possible to re-create the opportunities offered at Abbott, it is probably not the best option in another situation. If the local schools offered a good music program, or another organization met that need in the school, the community might not need a church program like the one we offer. If your community isn't saturated with young families, offering early childhood music classes may not meet the larger needs of the community. It would be better to ask yourself a series of questions: What do I feel is the greatest need in my congregation and in my community? Has God gifted me in a way that could meet that need? Is there anyone else in my church or in the local music community who would join forces with me?

TELLING THE TRUTH

So far, I have focused on the music outreach programs offered at our church, but what about the music in the worship service itself? How can a music minister enhance the music he plans for his congregation? How can he make it great music? How can he be original and inspired and so inspire the worshipers he leads? C.S. Lewis writes,

> Even in literature and art, no man who bothers about originality will ever be original: whereas if you simply try to tell the truth (without caring twopence how often it has been told before) you will, nine times out of ten, become original without ever having noticed it.

How can we tell the truth musically? So often, we are looking at what we have to work with and thinking, "If only I had this drummer, or singer, this instrument or this piece of equipment, then we could pull off this piece." My answer to that is to be honest about your resources. Embracing what you do have and highlighting the gifts of the people who worship alongside you, you are more likely to come up with music that is great, original, and will offer a conduit to true and authentic worship.

Two years ago, a friend gave me an accordion and told me I should learn to play it. I did, and it turns out that I love it. When Christmas came around I wanted to do the Sarah McLachlan/Barenaked Ladies version of *God Rest Ye Merry Gentlemen*, but we didn't have the singers to pull it off. So, I strapped on the accordion and asked my guitar player to bring in his mandolin, and we did the song with a pop-meets-bluegrass flair. The arrangement was great because it highlighted our strengths, unique because we used whatever we had, and honest because it was what we liked to play. The congregation *loved* it and this has become a signature sound for us.

My pastor likes to see our church members involved up front with the music on Sunday morning. One of our members, Michael, is often available to play for the service. Michael is one of our music school students. Sometimes I look at the arrangements I would like to do and I start thinking, "How is Michael going to pull this off?" Rather than seeing who I can bring in to cover the part, I'm forced to be honest and creative. I know his playing, so my task is to think about what the song needs and come up with a part he can play successfully that enhances the performance of the song.

Save the Casserole for the Pot Luck

Today's church musician has an incredible variety of music from which to choose. Even the most traditional hymnal contains music from a multitude of traditions and various styles. We still use the 1961 version of the Trinity Hymnal. It contains everything from *A Mighty Fortress is Our God* to *His Eye is on the Sparrow*. In it are majestic chorals, gospel songs, Irish, Welsh, Jewish, and German hymn tunes, camp meeting songs, and hymns from the Renaissance. If you're in a church like mine that also sings contemporary hymns and worship songs, you have a musical smorgasbord. It's a musician's dream.

In all the variety and diversity available to church musicians, there is still the tendency to play all the songs in similar styles, and with the same instruments. Another mentor of mine, Dee Solomon, said to me, "If you're going to do a variety of music, let each piece retain its unique flavor." Don't get stuck in musical ruts so that everything sounds the same. We miss out on just as much by playing everything on the organ as we would if we played everything on the guitar, turning a smorgasbord to a casserole in which the peas, carrots, and chicken no longer have distinct flavors.

The contemporary church can fall into this just as easily as the traditional church. Don't get stuck thinking there always has to be a drum set and guitar. Leave the piano out one week. Start asking around about hidden talents, people in your church who might play harmonica or clarinet. It might be a challenge to include instruments that don't usually appear in your worship set, but including church members in leading worship and changing up the sound week to week and song to song will help everyone get excited to participate.

WHAT I'VE LEARNED FROM THE BEATLES

I'm a big Beatles fan. (I'm sure that my friends reading this are wondering how I managed to go this long without mentioning it.) Their music might be described as simple, but that simplicity is only on the surface. What can be said about the Beatles' music can also be said about good worship music.

The thing that makes The Beatles music great is that the melody and arranging are strong. A strong melody is what carries the song and creates interest. Many of these songs sound just as good played solo on guitar as they would if played by a full band.

The music is designed to be accessible to a large audience, so the melody tends not to have a huge range, and the chords tend to be straight forward, but as I said before, this is only on the surface. I think there is a lot we can learn from the Beatles that will enhance our worship songs.

Listen to just about any Beatles music and you will find that no two verses of a song are arranged in exactly the same way. It might be something as simple as the addition of a shaker or tambourine, but there is always something that is changed. If you have never noticed this before, listen and you'll be amazed. It's also important to realize the structure of the song, i.e. verse, chorus, and bridge. What are you doing dynamically and instrumentally to distinguish these sections? Playing music without these distinctions is like walking through a house without being able to identify whether you are in the living room, kitchen, or bedroom.

How might this apply to your worship band? You might try having the drums or bass lay out for the first verse. When they come in on the chorus you really notice it. It gives the song a shot of energy. If the structure of the song is two verses and three choruses, and you have drums, bass, piano, guitar, keyboard, and mandolin, you have a lot of different combinations that can make the song interesting. Find music that you like, and listen to it with the ear of a producer. Identify each instrument in the texture. Notice how it is being used to create the feel of the song. And as I said earlier, listen to how the instrumentation is used to define the structure of the song. Every discovery can be a creative tool you can use to shape and enhance your worship music. Don't be afraid to experiment. By trying different things, you start to be aware of the effects you can create and the possibilities of each instrument. What you want to avoid is the pick-up band syndrome where everybody plays everything all the time.

Since the songs are largely based around triads, the occasional addition of 6ths, 7ths, or 9ths add a nice touch of seasoning to the song. In the chorus of *Let it Be,* the chords are written as Am, G, and F. McCartney holds the E through all three chords and the result is actually Am, G6, and Fmaj7. It's a subtle difference, but once you play it that way, you never go back. The bass player can also add interest by not always staying on the root of the chords.

STAY CONNECTED

It cannot be overemphasized that you should make sure you are carving out time for your devotional and prayer life. It's important to have quiet time, and it's just as important to be in relationship with others with whom you can grow, share your struggles, and be accountable. Jesus admonishes us in John 15:5 "I am the vine; you are the branches. If a man remains in me and I in him, he will bear much fruit; apart from me you can do nothing." I have always taken this to refer solely to our time in prayer and meditating on scripture. As I have faced various trials, I have learned that this also refers to the body of Christ, the Church.

As a musician and artist, it is very easy to be isolated. Our practice and work often have to be done in solitude. To make matters more difficult, we spend the days alone because our volunteers are all working, and in the evenings we spend time working on music to the neglect of our families. It can be difficult to create a balance between time spent alone, time spent with the church family, and time spent with our families. Additionally, it is crucial that you take care of your physical and emotional health. When I started working on this essay, I was swamped in busyness. I had to see my doctor because of stress and anxiety, my blood pressure was through the roof, and I was suffering from acid reflux. Six weeks later after clearing my schedule, going to the gym every morning, and taking a wonderful vacation with my family, my blood pressure is ideal, and I'm not dealing with heart burn. Now I'm not feeling torn between family and ministry as if it was an either/or choice, and I feel joy entering my life again. I found that it is important to establish a schedule that, while flexible, allows us to capture the proper balance in all facets of life.

I would conclude by saying that spending time with God in prayer is incredibly important especially when things are going well. When there is success in ministry, the temptation is for that ministry to become our identity. When ministry is our identity it becomes an idol and we live and die by our own success and failure rather than living in the freedom and security that Christ has earned for us.

There is a large oak tree outside my home office which acts as a reminder to me of the man in Psalm 1:3 who is described as "a tree firmly planted by streams of water." Like the tree in Psalm 3, we have to sink our roots deep in the soil in order to tap into that life-giving stream. In the 2nd verse of *A Mighty Fortress*, Martin Luther sums up well what I'm trying to say.

> Did we in our own strength confide, Our striving would be losing.
> Were not the right man on our side, the Man of God's own choosing.
> You ask who that may be? Christ Jesus it is he,
> Lord Sabaoth his Name, From age to age the same,
> And he must win the battle.

WORK
as worship

Nobody tells this to people who are beginners, I wish someone had told me. All of us who do creative work, we get into it because we have good taste. But there is this gap. For the first couple years you make stuff, it's just not that good. It's trying to be good, it has potential, but it's not. But your taste, the thing that got you into the game, is still killer. And your taste is why your work disappoints you. A lot of people never get past this phase, they quit. Most people I know who do interesting, creative work went through years of this. We know our work doesn't have this special thing that we want it to have. We all go through this. And if you are just starting out or you are still in this phase, you gotta know it's normal and the most important thing you can do is do a lot of work. Put yourself on a deadline so that every week you will finish one story. It is only by going through a volume of work that you will close that gap, and your work will be as good as your ambitions . . . It's normal to take awhile. You've just gotta fight your way through.
  —Ira Glass, *This American Life*

I first fell in love with the word "vocation" some three years ago—nine months after leaving my publicist job to pursue a career in music. For me, music had become more than just a hobby and even less a job. It was a calling. Most people thought I was crazy. They believed I had potential but that I was foolish and maybe too hopeful. No one blatantly voiced their concern, but I could see it in their eyes and their roundabout questions:

"You quit your day job?"

"Yes."

"This is *all* you're doing?"

"Yes."

"So do you still live with your parents?"

"No."

Not that there's anything wrong with that. Parents are great. And when I launched out on this new career I expected things to be hard, but I also expected to be happier. I took a major pay cut, making less than thirty percent of my salary from my previous job while working twice as hard with twice as many hours.

Work, I've learned, is an act of worship. As a child raised in a devout Christian home, I regarded worship as an act of submission and praise; but my understanding had always been limited to music, the lifting of hands, and, coming from a Nigerian background, dancing. As I ventured into the unknown territory of self-employment, I began to notice how the Word of God beautifully illustrates the posture we are to take towards our work. Genesis, after all, begins with an introduction to work . . . and yes, creativity. Not a coincidence.

THE SEED

Do your planning and prepare your fields before building your house.
—Proverbs 24:27 (NLT)

In the New Testament, Jesus shares a parable about a farmer and his sown seeds—some sown on shallow, rocky soil, some on a treaded path, falling victim to the birds, some sown among thorns, and others sown on fertile soil. As the story goes, each seed eventually dies except the ones sown on good ground.

As music makers, we often spend so much time thinking about the product that we forget the process. During my years as a publicist, I learned that most authors think their work is finished when the book is finished. And unfortunately, most musicians think the same way. But the work has barely begun! Let's say you've just spent one month in the studio, one month mixing/mastering your project, and one month putting together your album artwork. Two weeks ago you sent everything to the printer, and now you have 1,000 units of your album sitting in your living room and several thousand dollars "missing" from your bank account! Does this sound familiar?

Here's the thing: you can't just write a song and put it out there, because no one will hear it. And by "no one" I mean no people outside of your immediate family and friends. You need a game plan, a marketing plan that adds fuel to the fire. There's nothing like putting your heart and soul into a project, completing the project, and discovering that it's just sitting there, waiting for someone to care. Nobody wants that. So what is your fertile soil? Is it a network of support that you have spent months creating? Is it the research you have done to guide you in your new venture? Have you connected with others who are on a similar journey and who can mentor you? And most importantly, do you believe in your vision enough to make others believe in it? You can build a house, but if you build it on sand, it will eventually fall over. It might be great for a day, a month, or even year, but it will eventually fall. The foundation, the preparation, the seed is more important than you or I will ever know.

THE WATER

Work willingly at whatever you do, as though you were working for the
Lord rather than for people."
  —Colossians 3:23 (NLT)

I am convinced that true, lasting work rarely ever sees immediate return—that true work involves preparing the ground, planting the seed, and watering. . . then watering some more. . . and then pruning. . . and then continued watering. The problem with this is that, in a culture where we've become accustomed to getting what we want, when we want it, and how we want it, working for anything just doesn't seem fair, especially if we're not getting paid immediately. How tragic to think that we are cheating ourselves from true success because of our selfishness and impatience.

Nestled in between a verse on pride and a verse on hope is the following: "Wealth from get-rich-quick schemes quickly disappears; wealth from hard work grows over time." —Proverbs 13:11 (NLT). I don't see this placement as sheer coincidence. In fact, these words carry even more weight in context. For many of us working musicians, trust for provision is a constant struggle that requires humbling and hoping (or confidently believing) that we will see the fruit of our labor. So in a perfect world, we are to be diligent knowing that we labor not in vain, but instead with an expectant heart that trusts in God for a full return of our investment—one that will grow over time.

"So, why aren't my albums selling? Why can't I get a good gig? Why don't I get any traffic on my website?" Well, how much time do you actually *invest* in your art? Just like any career, your art requires time, money, and patience. "Big breaks" are a thing of the past, and really a negative by-product of the fast-food world we live in. As we work to perfect, produce, and present our work, we are called by the Scriptures to work as if we are working for the Lord—the boss of all bosses, and the ultimate investor. Invest in your work as if you have been commissioned by the Lord himself. With that in mind, remember these three things:

Money
Reward will always require risk. You will have to spend money to make money and you will have to spend even more to make even more. I think of art-

ists like Derek Webb, independent singer/songwriter and founding member of Caedmon's Call. In 2006 he began Noisetrade, a platform created for artists to gain exposure by giving their music away. He first tested the idea with his self-released project, *Mockingbird*, asking fans for their contact information and also to share the music with their friends. For most people, the idea was ludicrous. How does someone spend thousands of dollars out of his/her own pocket just to make $0 in return? And more importantly, *why* would anyone want to do this? Well, it actually made a lot of sense! By the end of *Mockingbird*'s shelf-life, Webb had given away over 80,000 downloads and garnered over 80,000 emails (and other data) from old and new fans alike. That, my friend, is a harvest that will become sweeter over time. As Webb's fans carry over from one release to the next, fan support will translate into ticket sales, merchandise sales, and even more fans through word-of-mouth.

Time

Time cannot be found, but it can be lost. You either do your passion or you sit back and watch others do theirs. So many of us waste time by talking about our ideas, but never actually act on them. American poet, musician, and author Gil Scott Heron says, "If you not gon' work... If you not gon' help, do not complain about what ain't happenin'. Because you could be doin' that." Everyone's got a good idea. But unfortunately, unless you're Steve Jobs or Bill Gates, you don't get paid for your ideas. You get paid for doing something with them. Take action and work for what you want. Don't expect it to spring up overnight; but *do* expect it to bear fruit over time. "A little extra sleep, a little more slumber, a little folding of the hands to rest—then poverty will pounce on you like a bandit; scarcity will attack you like an armed robber" (Proverbs 6: 10–11 NLT).

Patience

It will not be easy but it will be worth it. This one is hard.

The Waiting

We can make our plans, but the Lord determines our steps.
—Proverbs 16:9 (NLT)

As I write this, I am sitting in the middle of a year-long waiting room. Not knowing what comes next is very much a foreign concept to me and the feeling of uncertainty is pretty miserable. But as a recovering control freak, the biggest lesson I have learned over these last twelve months is that I am not in control. God is not Santa Claus and I cannot have what I want, when I want it. This sucks. For a few months I became a casualty of complacency—trapped by lack of direction and an abundance of doubt. I doubted God's sovereignty and began to brainstorm ways to "make things happen" in my life and career. God responded with more silence and essentially said (or didn't say), "Hey, you're not in the driver's seat!"

I now believe that the process of waiting is what distinguishes "vocation" from "job." Vocation, or "calling," implies that one must be called before they can go. Sometimes that call will come quickly, but other times you will need to wait. If I can assert this, the waiting season has less to do with what you're waiting for and more to do with *you*. You can be overqualified for the task and equipped to carry it out, but if your integrity is lacking, or your work ethic is lacking, or if you're flat-out unprepared for what God has in store (only God knows), then allow this season to wash over you. Welcome it with open arms and expect God to develop your character and your capacity to handle what he has on the way.

Here's something else: Waiting, defined as active readiness, is not to be confused with inaction. In fact, waiting forces us into a season of preparation. I think of the parable in Matthew 25 where ten bridesmaids go out to meet their bridegroom. Five bring oil for their lamps while the other five foolishly leave unprepared. But the bridegroom tarries and the women fall asleep. And then, lo and behold, in the middle of the night someone shouts, "The bridegroom is coming," and suddenly the five without oil begin to scramble and beg the others for some of theirs. But they don't share because, "We don't have enough for all ten of us! Go get some of your own!" And as they leave in one direction to go find oil, the five prepared bridesmaids leave in the other direction with the groom. When they return with their newfound oil and beg to be received, the Lord says, "It's too late! I don't know you! You wasted your time! Why did you sleep your life away? Why were you not prepared?"

As you wait, seek the face of God. Make sure you are ready for the season that is to come and prepare yourself for the call.

THE REAPING

If you write a song and nobody hears it, does it really exist? No. This is more a personal opinion than an absolute truth; but your answer to this question will be the lens through which you view your music-making career. I think of a talented carpenter who builds a warehouse full of furniture that has never been used; or an artist with a studio full of paintings that have never been outside its four walls. Yes, we bring joy to the heart of the Lord when we create; but we also give him Glory when we share what he has done in us with others. We are vessels after all—poured into so we can pour out.

In the parable of the talents (Matthew 25:14–29), Jesus likens the Kingdom of God to a businessman and his three servants. Before leaving town, he gives five mina to one servant, three to another, and one mina to the third. Mina, by the way, was a unit of currency. Upon his return, the businessman asks his servants to give an account of how they used what they had been given. The first two servants multiplied their allowances, turning five into ten and two in four. The servant who had been given one mina did nothing; and the businessman responded: "To those who use well what they are given, even more will be given, and they will have an abundance. But from those who do nothing, even what little they have will be taken away." —Matthew 25:29 (NLT)

So what does this mean about how we are to use our gifts? In my opinion, it is a reality check. We can't do nothing! We can't just sit on our talents knowing full-well that God actually *wants* to bless and multiply the work of our hands. That's like asking for a stone in place of bread.

The dictionary defines harvest as "a supply of anything gathered at maturity." It's the point at which everything you've planted is finally ripe for the picking. In essence, it's the payoff!

How sweet it is to witness one seed bear multiple fruits that contain even more seeds that will one day bear even more fruit!

A TREE

What if you could think of your career as a plant? Its success would depend heavily on the condition of your soil and how well it was taken care of. I think Jesus shared parables to help us live out our earthly callings with divine discipline. I love the Ira Glass quote at the beginning of this chapter because when I think about my career, I wrestle with never being fully satisfied with the quality of my music. I know it can be better and I want it to be; and even after seven years of performing (half of those professionally), I still have a long way to go before I can look back and say will full confidence "It is good." As an artist I urge you to live and work like a tree planted by a river a water so that you may bring forth fruit in due season (Psalms 1:3). May all that you do prosper, and when it is all is said and done...

"May the beauty we love be what we do."

AMPLIFIED
experience

To be fair, not all Christians have insane ideas about music.
—Headline from Idolater.com[1]

The first thing visitors to the Student Activities Offices at Calvin College notice is the contrast. Buried within the institutional labyrinth of white cinder block walls and fluorescent lights framed in drop ceilings is an incandescent grotto adorned with the icons of pop music. Dave Mathews is here, and Lupe Fiasco. Emmylou Harris, Neko Case, and Patty Griffin converse quietly in the corner, while Ben Harper and Iron & Wine peek out from behind the door. Joanna Newsom and Andrew Bird cast their characteristically eccentric gazes at one another across the room. Mavis Staples and the Blind Boys of Alabama inject both levity and gravity into the space, surrounded by multi-color multi-generations of artists whose trails they helped blaze.

The décor is practical: in two decades of booking concerts, you simply collect a lot of band posters, and all of the above artists and more have performed at Calvin College. But the décor is also theological. It's a messy witness, tacked to the walls with duct tape and poster putty, on display for all to see and to discuss and to question. The motto of the Student Activities Office (SAO) is "changing the conversation about popular culture" and even the posters serve this purpose. But anyone can stick pieces of paper on the wall. Beyond the physical space is where the conversation really heats up, as live concerts draw people into the circle with all five senses. Lights and speakers, instruments and microphones, musicians and fans converge in a big room for just a moment in time and each moment is precious enough to frame.

But it all begs bigger questions. Why should Christians spend time and money on such activities—and not just as observers, but as promoters? What, if anything, would make a concert venue run by Christians different from other venues? This chapter will use the Calvin College concert series as a case study for reflecting more deeply on the potential for concert venues informed and shaped by holistic Christian values.

EXHIBIT A

Backed by a stand-up bass and acoustic guitar, the vocalist croons into the microphone. The audience is rapt, transported to an earlier decade when the historic Ladies Literary Club heard music such as this the first time around. Footlights and fedoras complete the look, but it's not 1930—it's October 23, 2009.

Applause rings around Katy Bowser's glowing face as she finishes singing another artfully homegrown tune. An opening artist this evening, Bowser has performed for Calvin audiences before and she's keenly aware that it's a unique opportunity. "You should know what you have," she advises the students in the crowd. "I've been to many other Christian colleges and you should know how special it is that you have access to so many wonderful concerts."

Bowser is just one of a throng of artists, students, and concert goers who, over the past two decades, have recognized how special the concert series at Calvin College is. So what exactly is it that Calvin students have? Why should they be so grateful?

The legacy of the series began in 1993 with a modest proposal: Ken Heffner applied for the new position of director of Student Activities with more than just amusement in mind. With ten years of concert promotion experience, Heffner proposed a model of student activities that would foster conversation around quality, contemporary, popular art.

Prior to coming to Calvin, Heffner had been involved with the National Association for Campus Activities for several years, attempting to articulate through speaking and practice how the traditional model of student activities as entertainment was counterproductive for higher education in general and Christian higher education in particular. During this time, he began booking shows as part of his college student activities work. "I was doing Billy Joel, Vienna Boys' Choir, and all kinds of concerts there and I loved it and began crafting a Christian philosophy of concert booking back then, which would have been in the late '70s," Heffner recounted. "And I've always been fascinated with contemporary music going back to being a little kid listening to the Beatles."[2]

Equipped with an "all things" theology inherited from the late neo-Calvinist visionary Peter Steen, Heffner didn't arrive at Calvin hoping merely to recreate what already existed at other colleges, which tended to follow an entertainment model rather than an arts education model. Instead, he hoped to combine his passion for live music with the robust theological and educational mission of the college. Such a programming agenda held the potential to challenge and support students to approach popular culture as art and look for God's redemptive work in the unexpected corners of rock concerts, television shows, films, and more.

The result has been a concert series that functions more like a club than a college. Heffner and his small staff have built up a season with national renown among students and local concert goers, as well as artists of diverse faiths and genres. Then, as now, the selection of artists who visit Calvin's stages is a living mystery that testifies to a strong belief in God's ongoing redemption of all things. Notably Christian artists line up alongside those who don't publicly profess any faith, but bear the image of the Creator in their technological innovation or stunning harmonies or brilliant poetry. As Heffner explains the motivation behind the series:

> It's not a secret desire for fame, it's this desire for the Kingdom of God to go public, to break out of this privatization of the gospel and of Christian experience. [It's about] constantly looking for new ways that we can show up in the public square and witness to something there with mixed results and mixed faithfulness, but still just go and do it, show up, take this vision and run with it and take the talents you have combined with the vision and support community and go and do something.

IN MY FATHER'S HOUSE, THERE ARE MANY ROOMS

If the Calvin concert series functions more like a club than a college, then the application of its principles extends far beyond Christian higher education. The foundational idea that Christians should be participants in God's transformation of all aspects of human culture runs deep, and a profound articulation is found in the neo-Calvinist tradition that originated in the Netherlands.

In the canon of influential figures in Reformed Christianity, Abraham Kuyper is a prominent member. Though it's important to acknowledge that his political authority in the Netherlands coincided with grave abuses by Dutch colonials around the world, elements of Kuyper's philosophy are fundamental for understanding the why's and how's of something as seemingly oxymoronic as a Kingdom-oriented rock concert series. Kuyper's vision for Christian purpose in the world extended to all aspects of human culture. Rather than drawing lines based on simplistic moral assessments, Kuyper characterized human culture, systems, and institutions as a house in need of renovation.[3] According to Kuyper, demolition of the entire house would not solve the problem of evil; rather, humans are called to work constantly and faithfully at re-forming all rooms of the house toward God's design.

This idea isn't just the copyright of a nineteenth century statesman, but has roots in the biblical narrative. In the slim and powerful volume *When the Kings Come Marching In*, Richard Mouw reiterates Kuyper's sentiment in light of Isaiah's prophecies about the new earth. Mouw explains that "when Isaiah looks to the fulfillment of God's promises, he envisions a community into which technological artifacts, political rulers, and people from many nations are gathered. God intended from the beginning that human beings would 'fill the earth' with the processes, patterns, and products of cultural formation." Later in the story, in a letter to the Colossians, Paul summarizes Christ's shaping of such a vision through the whole story, from creation to consummation:

> He is the image of the invisible God, the firstborn of all creation; for in him all things in heaven and on earth were created, things visible and invisible, whether thrones or dominions or rulers or powers—all things have been created through him and for him. He himself is before all things, and in him all things hold together. He is the head of the body, the church; he is the beginning, the firstborn from the dead, so that he might come to have first place in everything. For in him all the fullness of God was pleased to dwell, and through him God was pleased to reconcile to himself all things, whether on earth or in heaven, by making peace through the blood of his cross. (v. 15-20)

While those of us who prefer the Bible's personal moral and spiritual advice might squirm, what Paul is putting out here is a powerful political and cultural statement about how Christ relates to the entirety of creation. In seeking faithfulness to the resurrected Christ, Christians have to reconcile themselves to their Savior's creative, all-encompassing character and intentions. How then can we humans think and act to destroy a house that God has built and is reconciling in its entirety?

If destruction of the entire house is one temptation, another is to prioritize some rooms, while locking the door and throwing away the key to others. For Christians inclined to declare certain rooms off limits, popular art is an easy target for neglect, while rooms like worship and the family are safe havens. For others, however, the normative, faithful path is to show up everywhere as listening, learning, compassionate, prophetic witnesses who are agents of the radical Christ. In this sense, the messiest, loudest, most provocative room might be just the place to start. If we don't walk through that door, we stand to lose more than just our ability to converse casually about Lady Gaga around the water cooler; we stand to lose our humanity. In her classic treatise on faith and art, Madeleine L'Engle writes,

We are afraid of that which we cannot control; so we continue to draw in the boundaries around us, to limit ourselves to what we can know and understand. Thus we lose our human calling, because we do not dare to be creators, co-creators with God. Artists have always been drawn to the wild, wide elements they cannot control or understand—the sea, mountains, fire. To be an artist means to approach the light, and that means to let go of our control, to allow our whole selves to be placed with absolute faith in that which is greater than we are.[5]

The room of popular art can be raucous and racy, but, precisely *because* of its risk-taking nature, it's a place where significant conversations can happen. The conversations generated by such risk-taking are strengthened when they take place not just among Christians and for Christians, but in the public square as well.

ART IN THE PUBLIC SQUARE

The biblical narrative, along with historic figures like Abraham Kuyper, can help us understand why Christians should be making and promoting art in the public square, but they don't say much about how something as specific as a rock concert venue ought to be run. At this point, we'll return to the question of what practices might distinguish a venue run by Christians in some particular aspects of that vocation. I'll try to speak broadly to a wide range of venue types—from DIY to arenas—while continuing to extrapolate principles from the example of the Calvin College concert series.

Forming a Community of Leadership

A community of leadership with a shared vision for the venue is essential—whether these leaders are paid staff, volunteers, a board of directors, or even just a group of friends—and such a collaboration can help avoid pitfalls like profit-mongering and pietism. A huge temptation both for Christian concert promoters and others is to follow the profit stream. The Christian music industry in particular comes with a devoted target market whose pursuit of cool is often couched in terms of moral obligations and boundaries—a powerful combination that unlocks the wallets of teenagers, parents, and adults everywhere. "Christian, Inc." can become a new form of baptized consumerism in which anything stamped with a Jesus quotient is fit for consumption in large quantities. As they resist temptations from both pietism and profit-ism, a strong leadership community stewarding a concert venue will seek to be discerners of the prophetic, wherever it is found among the powerful tides of the status quo. As people of faith or even as a collective of diverse people committed to an agreed-upon set of founding principles, a group can share in accountability and creativity through a wide range of joys and challenges. It will be helpful if all members of the group love live music, but also have diverse gifts from aesthetic sensibility to crunching numbers.

Toward these ends, the SAO concert series has been stewarded by several groups serving various purposes. Paid staff people handle the logistics of booking, marketing, and finances, as well as education around the vision of the venue. A group of student volunteers contribute fresh ideas and firsthand market analysis, while helping with show day tasks like load-in, load-out, and hospitality. An advisory group of college staff and faculty members assists with discernment and risk assessment. Altogether, these individuals surround the series with prayerful intention.

Crafting a Venue

One very practical necessity for a concert venue is a space. This observation may seem painfully obvious, but it's incredible how often the crafting of a space is an afterthought and how often the expense of maintaining a space is the demise of the venue. The location and aesthetic of a space will dramatically influence the audience, and the building or renovation of a space offers creative potential for expressing core values. Beyond the usual questions of logistical viability, some questions to consider include:

- What existing spaces capture the desired "spirit" of the venue in some way?
- Will my target audience feel comfortable entering this space? This question is especially important to consider when dealing with religious spaces.
- How accessible is this space to people with limited mobility? To people with limited income? To people who don't drive?
- How will this space be a blessing to its surrounding neighborhood? What neighborhood leaders and partners should be engaged?
- How could the space be crafted to use fewer resources, both to keep overhead low and demonstrate stewardship of creation?
- As a space for art, how will core values be communicated artfully, rather than didactically?

A community of leadership working toward a vision together will be helpful in discerning the answers to these kinds of questions and coming up with creative solutions. The spirit of a space is a multisensory communicator that should not be underestimated.

Selecting Artists

Booking concerts as a faithful Christian practice deeply shapes the selection of artists. Several criteria come into play, including price, routing and venue availability as well as the quality of content, stage presence, and audience appeal. Because diversity and creativity are inherent to art, each artist will fulfill criteria to varying degrees.

Christians working in the arena of concert venues need to make choices about the kind of venue and the audience, but they don't need to feel bound to some sort of superficial definition of "Christian music." As the Christian scholar Hans Rookmaaker explained in his classic 1970 text on faith and art, "What is Christian in art does not lie in the theme, but in the spirit of it, in its wisdom and the understanding of reality it reflects. Just as being a Christian does not mean going round singing hallelujah all day, but showing the renewal of one's life by Christ through true creativity, so a Christian painting is not one in which all the figures have haloes and (if we put our ears to the canvas) can be heard singing hallelujahs."[6]

As Heffner explains regarding the SAO's criteria, groups are considered within three categories: Christians doing prophetic work within the Christian music industry, Christians doing prophetic work in the public square, and artists with other or no faith claims who are creating truthful work. For many outside observers of Calvin's concert series, these first two categories just make sense. Of course, a Christian institution would be on the lookout for good work happening within the body of Christ, but the third category alternately disappoints, mystifies, and thrills observers. As Heffner explains,

> Discernment is having ears to hear and eyes to see and being attentive to where God is at work . . . and sometimes the way God is at work is rather subtle and nanceful. It's not going to be [as obvious as] Steve Earle who probably wouldn't call himself a Christian, but whose music just drips with biblical imagery . . . or like Iron and Wine who just serves it to you in big slabs of biblical ideas, even though he himself isn't sure he believes in any of it. But it's also going to happen in an Andrew Bird who is doing something redemptive, but it's suggestive, it's imaginative, it's not didactic. . . . It'll be in the Hold Steady—in a band that it comes through as much in the music as in the text. It'll be in Lupe Fiasco, who clearly makes no claim of being a Christ-follower, but whose music is moving us closer to what rap could be . . . . There's a truthfulness in part in the work of Lupe and we want to honor that and affirm it and say, "Yes, thank you for that."

Now, not every venue needs to book artists in all three of these categories, or even in the range of genres Heffner references. However, I would suggest that a venue shaped by Christian commitments won't just seek artists who fulfill a Jesus quotient when you proof text their lyrics. Rather, selecting and booking artists provides an opportunity to witness to the incorrigible wildness of a common grace Kingdom that breaks through in the work of all kinds of fallen human beings.

Marketing Shows

Ticketed concerts have a way of bringing the conversation about art and faith to a new level in the public square and the desire to foster a public conversation has very practical implications for marketing a concert series. As Heffner points out, promoting an internal conversation among Christians is much different than promoting an artistic experience as an open conversation. "Your rhetoric changes the way you present it: where you go to advertise it changes how you make it look visually, the design, the way you introduce it, etc.," he explains. "It's all a challenge to figure out how you do that, how you do these things in a public way so as not to be constantly going on about the confessions behind what you're doing." Announcements about upcoming shows can make their way not just into student news digests, Christian radio stations, and local church bulletins, but into local newspapers and music magazines, as well as in local music stores and on Facebook, Twitter, LastFM, and other media outlets. Even advertising becomes part of the witness, as those who are paying any sort of attention wonder at the strangeness of Switchfoot sharing ad space with OK GO or Lupe Fiasco with Over the Rhine.

Cultivating Hospitality and Ritual

When the leadership behind a concert venue lacks vision, consumerism tends to fill the vacuum. As long as tickets sell, who cares if the bathrooms are disgusting and the green room is trashed? As long as alcohol sales keep the budget afloat, who cares if the audience wants to buy enough beer to annihilate any memory of the show? When attendees are mere consumers and artists are just a product being sold, the end result is an experience that's greatly inferior to what it could be for both the audience and the artist.

As a steward of the rare intersection of Christian college students, the general public, and artists, Heffner seeks to create an atmosphere of hospitable engagement, rather than diversion. In doing so, he swims against a tide of consumerism that has been shaping the concert industry at large in significant ways over the past several decades. "I understand that there's an economic side to doing art, there's an economic side to almost everything. It just shouldn't be allowed to be the dominant side," says Heffner.

Concert promoters have a wonderful opportunity to set an alternate tone and the desire to make a concert series about art first and commerce second can be reflected in many of the routine practices surrounding every show. Some of these practices that demonstrate hospitality to both artists and the audience might include:

- Providing a quality venue with good equipment.
- Introducing artists from the stage in a way that communicates knowledge and appreciation of their music.

- Creating opportunities before and after shows to connect with repeat attendees to your venue, recognizing their role as invested participants and listening to their suggestions.
- Creating space before or after shows for artists and audience members to be in meaningful conversation with each other.

This last practice of holding artist conversations has become a hallmark of the SAO's shows, and something that is sought out by artists and listeners alike. In the routine conversations that precede or follow shows, fans receive the opportunity to ask good questions of their favorite musicians and learn something more about the music they love. A moderator frames the time by explaining that it's not a meet-and-greet or an opportunity to gush about the artist's celebrity, but a time for genuine inquiry and respect. Beyond just being passive reactors, the audience becomes a conscious participant in the artist's story just by showing up. "Artists write music, record it, and go on the road because they want to connect, they want to tell their story," says Heffner. "And when you remember that as a concert venue or promoter, when you remember that that's what it's about, that's why we do this, and you provide some ways in which you're honoring that, you're doing hospitality." Audience members serve artists well when they're attentive and responsive, whether the appropriate response is to dance and sing along at the top of our lungs or to listen so quietly even breathing seems to cease. Hospitality means crafting rituals that, at their best, allow both artists and audience members to leave a venue feeling loved and valued.

HOLY EXTRAVAGANCE, LIVE AND IN PERSON

At Calvin College and elsewhere, the anecdotal evidence is striking that concerts conducted in the public square can illuminate the depth of a Christian vision for all things. However, in a world full of brokenness and suffering, doubt lingers for concert promoters like Heffner, especially when a single show can cost as much as double a year's tuition at a private college. "I do think, shouldn't I just go to Honduras and learn Spanish and go work with people there? Isn't this an example of privilege, of affluence—being able to do this thing? Does this make any sense?" But Heffner is quick to point out his own logical fallacy: "It's not art *or* caring for the poor, it's art *and* caring for the poor. And it's also that art matters to the poor; it's not a rich man's game."

Heffner and many culture makers and artists all over the world are fortunate to have a cloud of witnesses to remind them why they do what they do. The biennial Festival of Faith & Music at Calvin offers an opportunity to gather some of these witnesses into one place for two and a half days of remembering and experiencing. In March 2007, author Lauren Winner took the stage as one of the keynote speakers to remind listeners that "we are invited to be beautiful and lavish in our artistic production and to do that at the invitation of a God who is himself whimsical and lavish and abundant."[7] Winner's conviction was based not on a selfish justification of her own craft, but on a deeply studied understanding of who God is and what kind of economics God calls us to. Calling out the church's general inattentiveness to art, Winner said,

> It seems to me to not be a very faithful question to ask, "Oh, how come you as a Christian aren't devoting all of your energy to ameliorating poverty?" At least it is not a question that is forged in the idiom of a God of abundance. We live in a secular world governed by a capitalist model of scarcity. There's never enough money in our world. There's never enough time. All of our resources are scarce. But by contrast, our God gives us a very different economy. Our God is a God of overflowing creative fecundity; a God of inexhaustible Eucharistic offering; a God, after all, who multiplies loaves and fishes. So, to borrow Marva Dawn's phrase, one of the things that marks us as followers of that God is the consistent practice of being royally wasteful, of wasting time by praying and worshipping, an activity that by the world's standards is at least unproductive, and maybe psychotic. We might all be standing in a room, you know, *talking to ourselves.* Christians need not, because of our God of abundance, always be concerned about the evident utility of everything that we do. We are instead called to worship and reverence a God who is a God interested in whimsy and not just utility. Cultivating art, I think, is one of the ways that we do that, because art is not done in the service of utility . . . . The logic of scarcity in our surrounding world is different from the Christian logic, which is a logic of abundance. And one of the ways that we can testify to that abundance is through our devotion to art.

Two years later at the 2009 Festival of Faith & Music, visual artist Makoto Fujimura echoed similar sentiments. Fujimura emphasized that art should be transgressive, pointing out our personal and cultural flaws, often in ways that make audiences uncomfortable.[8] Such provocation isn't in the interest of fame or narcissism, but in the interest of standing in the best of the prophetic, apocalyptic Judeo Christian tradition. In *The Irresistible Revolution*, Shane Claiborne writes, "There is a pervasive sense that things are not right in the world, and the gentle suggestion that maybe they don't have to stay this way. . . . But most Christian artists and preachers have remained strangely distant from human suffering, offering the world eternal assurance over prophetic imagination. Perhaps it should not surprise us that Jesus says that if the Christians remain silent, then the rocks will cry out. . . or the rock stars, I guess."[9] Putting on concerts can create one more outlet for the prophetic voice. And yes, putting resources into art means that we won't be investing in other things, but, according to Heffner, "The doing of art is extravagant and being extravagant is part of the point. It's not [just an] unfortunate side effect. It's supposed to be extravagant to some degree." In this context, creating space for live music isn't just a clever and expensive attempt to entertain or offer surface-level evangelism to impressionable college students, but an opportunity to invite prophetic truth-telling, under the lights and in full stereo sound.

If cheap diversion is not the objective, neither is perfection. Heffner notes, "The problem we get hung up with within the Christian community, particularly the evangelical Christian community, is that we have this notion that it has to be altogether good . . . . [But] we're not looking for perfection, we're looking for faithfulness. We're looking for attempts to witness to a good thing, which will always be flawed until the New City." The objective is to wait for that future promise with our lamps lit, be they clip lights on a makeshift platform or a flown rig of remote controlled lasers in an arena.

And so we come back to the funky little office that, this side of the New City, serves as mission central for one concert series that's seeking to approximate a Kingdom vision for a particular area of life. Some of the memories taped to the wall are reminders of risks that, in retrospect, weren't worth taking; of failures to show adequate hospitality; of concessions to a dualist worldview that would limit the series to praise bands. But there are also moments of grace whose harmony wakes us up to the world that is to come. There's the transgendered musician whose presence taught a student about the depth of God's unconditional love. There's the singer whose rigorously trained voice gripped an entire sold-out crowd in utterly silent awe. There's the band that lured dancers from age seven to seventy onto the stage in a collective salsa frenzy. These are the kinds of encounters that simply can't happen in the small space of a brain between headphones. In the setting of a live concert that's done well, says Heffner,

> It's the artist there who crafted this piece presenting it for you in person with great sound . . . and great light, so that the whole experience is amplified, literally amplified, and I guess we could say figuratively amplified . . . That's why I'd make the case for going to live concerts. It is okay to listen to music in your room with your friends on a decent stereo; it's better yet to go to a 2,000-seat room with your friends and make a night of it and experience the artist right there.

To create space to hear echoes of the incarnation in the reverberation of sound—that's a high calling, indeed.

Endnotes

1   Gibson, Dan. "To Be Fair, Not All Christians Have Insane Ideas About Music." *Idolator* N.p., 27 Feb. 2009. Web. 23 Dec. 2009. <To be fair, not all Christians have insane ideas about music.>.

2   Heffner, Kenneth. Personal interview. Apr. 2009. Quotes throughout from Heffner originate with this interview.

3   Kuyper, Abraham. *The Problem of Poverty*. Grand Rapids, MI: Baker Book House, 1991.

4   Scripture quotations throughout are from the *New Revised Standard Version*.

5   *Walking on Water: Reflection on Art and Faith*. Wheaton, IL: Harold Shaw Publishers, 1980.

6   *Modern Art and the Death of a Culture*. Wheaton, IL: Crossway Books, 1994.

7   Winner, Lauren. "Embodying the Incarnation: Christianity and the Arts." Calvin College. Grand Rapids, MI. 30 Mar. 2007. Web. 13 May 2009. <http://www.calvin.edu/admin/sao/festival/2007/audio/podcast/lauren-winner_keynote.m4a>.

8   Fujimura, Makoto. "Creating and Transgressing in Love." Calvin College Festival of Faith & Music. Grand Rapids, MI. 2 Apr. 2009.

9   Grand Rapids, MI: Zondervan, 2006.

NOT STRANGERS
in this crowd

My family took vacations twice every year and by the time I graduated from high school I had been to forty-two states. So the idea of packing up a car and traveling around the country was not very foreign to me. After college I bought a Volvo station wagon and began to book shows across the Southeast. Then I got picked up by a college booking agency, and they soon had me playing all over—community colleges, lunchrooms, trade schools, big state schools, small liberal arts colleges. Just me, my guitar, my Volvo, and a string of Super-8 motels. It was adventurous and lonely. It was just to pay the bills. I'd be lucky to sell five CDs per event. But I slowly developed a band and a fan base (one big factor that contributed to growing my fan base was playing at YoungLife events). I was working hard to follow my dream, and now my dream had become my business. And that change threw in all kinds of wrenches. Was music my calling or was it my job? It was a strange transition. I get an incredible amount of joy out of making music for people, but it is my job, too. And ninety percent of my job is very un-glamorous! Yet there is something in the remaining ten percent that is pretty incredible. What happens at a concert can be life changing. I have a song I wrote about the concert experience that might help capture what I mean. The song is from our record *Passenger Seat* and it is called "Hallelujah." The song begins:

> *Blue jeans on in the living room*
> *Mother's busy with a kitchen broom*
> *Nine o'clock, headlights cross the wall*

What is interesting about that song is that I am putting myself in the shoes of a kid going to a concert—well, really, the song is about me in many ways. I used to go see live music all the time. There is something alive, fresh, and a little bit out of control about a live show. I saw Bob Dylan twice, the Dave Matthews Band a bunch, and in college the amount of concerts I attended were beyond number. A lot of the college events were road trips from Knoxville down the interstate into Asheville. I can remember being fifteen, like the boy in my song, waiting for my older friends to come pick me up. I lived in the suburbs, a good twenty minutes to any decent concert venue. I remember the anticipation, the waiting, and then the person comes and picks you up, heading downtown to the show. We were going to experience this bizarre, communal experiment with a bunch of strangers.

> *The white lines dance on the interstate*
> *Going downtown, gonna stay out late*
> *The band plays and they're singing "Hallelujah"*

What would the band play that night? How many set lists did we make up as we drove to those concerts in Asheville? Creating a set list is almost like writing a play. You want to have a strong opening where you immediately capture the attention of the audience. You are trying to get them to buy into what you are doing right out of the gates. From then it is a little bit of a roller coaster. You don't want to play all your fast songs at first because then the second half of the show is very boring. Banter, too, is an important thing to think about when you are making a set list. Where do my good stories fit in? I don't want to have my good story songs all together then the rest of the show have nothing to say. You are kind of taking people on a journey through the set list. But you also have to keep in mind things like, "Oh, I have five songs in the key of D—I don't want to do five songs in a row in the key of D."

After that it is about making "moments." NeedtoBreathe has taught me this well. They have a variety of "moments." For example, they might break away from the mic and play the acoustic guitar for a bit before jumping into a massive, bring-the-house-down tune. Which leads to the next concern with set lists—finding the right song to end the show, a big thing that fills the room with energy. I will usually spend twenty minutes each night working on the set list before I give it to the band. And then every once in a while in the middle of a concert you call an audible when something doesn't feel right and you know that the next song you were planning to do would continue the negative reaction you are getting from the crowd. You're losing the audience . . .

> *Some are sinners, some are saints*
> *Singing the songs out loud*

They all come for different reasons
They're not strangers in this crowd

I used to feel like I had something to prove to the audience. And that the concert was about me trying to prove my value to them. Now I think of my audience
as people with whom I share something in common. I want to communicate to
them in a way that encourages and challenges them. In that way, it is not a far cry
from preaching to playing music on a stage. You can see that played out in soul
music with musicians like James Brown, Otis Redding, and Muddy Waters. Those
guys basically worked the crowd into a frenzy. Bruce Springsteen does the same
thing nowadays. Yet not all artists have that mentality. There are some artists who
just play their songs and leave it at that. But the bands that I tend to look up to
treat it more as if the audience is an extra member of the band. And how well the
audience participates determines how well that night's concert goes.

The most obvious way to get the crowd participating is to teach them a bit of a
song and ask them straight out to sing along. Often I just rely on the hooks in my
songs to get them swept up into singing. Another approach I will take from time
to time is taking requests. I've even used Twitter before a show to take requests.
You find out what songs have been let into peoples lives that way. If you have
a deep catalog, one way to *not* engage the crowd is to only play your new material. You may be very excited about your brand new record and want to share it
with the audience but this concert is not about you. The songs aren't even yours
anymore. Jeff Tweedy from WILCO says that when a musician releases a song
he gives it away. You and the writer don't have control over it anymore. So give up
only playing what you care about. When music is played live there is a sense of
shared ownership.

I compare it to a football team. When a you're from a big city and that city's
team wins, the fans use the proverbial *we*. "We won on Sunday—it was so great."
We? Where is the we? *You* weren't on the field on Sunday. *You* didn't get plastered
by the offensive line. *You* didn't kick that field goal. But in the end it is right to say
we because the team wouldn't exist if it wasn't for the fans. In the same way, in a
concert you're on stage performing and you are practicing a craft they appreciate or admire and you are creating a space where people can figure out issues of
identity. And the fans are part of it. It is out of your control, but there is now a
place, a space there for people. You are playing music that has somehow meant
something to the crowd. They are singing along. In this public space you have
created a place to share a common experience. You and the audience are making
a memory that draws you all together. I think that is why people go to concerts
instead of listening to a record in their living room. Because listening to a record
in your living room —you're still alone, while at the concert you are not.

Some say music can save your soul
Others say the devil loves rock and roll
All that boy sees is the girl in the second row

Can rock 'n' roll save your soul, or will it send you straight to Hell? The boy in my song doesn't care about cultural or theological debates. All he cares about is that the music at the concert tonight has created a space for him to meet a beautiful girl. Maybe he will have a chance to talk to her?

In spite of growing up in a conservative evangelical home, my parents were fully behind me being a musician. They had a few concerns about what impact the business might have on my character, but they kept a level head. When my father found out I wanted to do music in spite of receiving a good college education and having many good opportunities before me, he said, "Look son, I know you know how to work hard, I know you have integrity, so I'm behind you. Let's go downtown and I want to buy you the nicest guitar I can afford."

People have asked me if I am a Christian musician, why do I play at bars? The answer to me is fairly simple. Beginning at age seventeen until now I never listened to music made within the Christian music industry. I listened to folks like Radiohead, U2, Van Morrison, Bob Dylan, and Patti Griffin. In the subtlety of that music I found a more complex picture of God, a more honest identification of God. So much of contemporary Christian music felt one dimensional to me. Part of the cause for that flatness was because of commercial concerns and part was that in the '80s and '90s within broader evangelicalism there was not a lot of room for doubt and questions. The psalmist's frustration with God could be found in non-Christian music but not in the music that was being made for the church. So for me I never even thought about doing music for the Christian market. I wanted to be making music that could engage someone who didn't live in that one-dimensional reality.

My father-in-law, Brown Bannister, shares a similar point of view with me and feels like there is so much out of his hands in terms of what he started out to do in music and what it has turned into. And I don't even think that contemporary Christian music is wrong or horrible. I think there is a lot space in that world to affect a lot of hearts and move people to a greater understanding of the Gospel. And it has changed a great deal over the past decade. But I didn't want my music to be limited by JPMs (Jesus's-Per-Minute). As in, "Ahh, that song is great, but there's definitely not enough JPMs."

The way I think about it is that if I was a plumber and I was a Christian I wouldn't walk into someone's house and immediately tell them about their need for the redemption of the Cross. I would want to go in there and do a really great job fixing their plumbing. I see being a songwriter in a similar way. I want to do a really great job. I want promoters and sound men to walk away from the night and say, "What a pleasure to work with Drew Holcomb. He treated me with respect. He showed up on time. He asked me about my family. I want to be in community with that guy the next time he comes to town." At the end of the day I just want to be a faithful witness.

It's the first verse of the seventh song
All the under-agers are singing along
The drummer smiles and shouts out "Hallelujah"

The drummer is smiling, the high school kids are singing along, and there isn't a worry in the place. But the truth is that the music business is fairly cut throat. Few people are shouting out "Hallelujah." There is an assumption of self-interests most of the time. So people tend to be on edge. They assume you are going to try and take advantage of them. There are politics involved and there's leveraging of favors, but I think at the end of the day you can still work in the industry with integrity. I worked hard to glorify God in my music making when I started out and since it was just me back then—booking, mailing posters, fulfilling online orders, keeping up with social media, and such—I was able to stay on top of things. But as your career builds, a manager and booking agent needs to be added and you start to be able to take a more hands-off approach to that end of the business. Yet at the end of the day the artist is still responsible for the people working in your corner. That is one of the reasons I love my manager. Every time I hear about a conversation he had on my behalf I think to myself, "Wow, that is almost exactly how I would have said it if I had had that conversation." Integrity is hard but it is not impossible.

To keep my drummer happy and shouting out "Hallelujah" requires that I tour. Economics and art need to be in balance. It is true in any creative endeavor—music, writing, painting—if it is something you want to do full time you have to make it work financially. Touring is the way we create revenue and cash flow. One of my favorite things about touring is that it allows the three guys in my band to play music. All they want to do is play music. Touring makes a way for them to make money doing what they love. They are playing original music in new places every night. Because we tour we are able to do what we love for a living. Touring is how we make music work. Our website store sales, iTunes sales, and Amazon sales all go way up when we are on tour. When we are off the road everything goes flat. Touring provides that great payoff that transforms a hobby into a legitimate job.

You can look at the promoters and the booking as a necessary evil or you can look at them as a way more people get to do something unique and interesting with their lives. People don't get into the music business because they wanted to be rich. There are a lot quicker easier ways to get rich rather than trying to push

99¢ songs on the internet. There are so many spokes in the wheel of the music industry. It is a group effort. I try to give promoters the benefit of the doubt and assume that we are on the same team. And in the long run, if we are doing it right, they are.

After the show the girl from the second row is
At the merch booth buying a t-shirt
He says "hello," they talk about the band
They smile, they laugh and they flirt

The fascinating thing about the merchandise table is that somehow you convince your fans to write the name of your band across their chests. I sell t-shirts so I can pay my mortgage and get my name out there. They buy t-shirts because they want their friends to ask them about it so they get the chance to talk about their favorite band. Of all the things we do, it has the least philosophical grounding, but it has the most profit-margin! Like anything in our culture today, you identify yourself by what you wear. If you put on a Drew Holcomb t-shirt maybe it means you like to get in your car in the summer with the windows down and go driving with your girlfriend through a peaceful evening. If you are wearing a Black Sabbath t-shirt maybe it means you have some angst and you are trying to get it out there, and you are warning people not to mess with you.

What is interesting about this song is that it started out as true story that happened to me in tenth grade. In real life there was a beautiful girl at this concert I attended. I had seen her earlier at some high school event and was totally blown away. Then I saw her at this concert and she was two rows ahead of me. And I was like, "Go talk to her, go talk to her." Sadly, I never did. This song is about what should have been. That is what is great about song writing—you can change the whole trajectory of your life by telling the story from the perspective of "what if" instead of "what did."

Singing Hallelujah

One of the challenging aspects of touring is staying connected to the church, friends, and family. My church is very supportive of me. They meet on Sunday nights and therefore we are often able to get home in time to fellowship with them. And they have tried to create group phone calls for their musician members who are on the road. But I won't sugar coat it—it is difficult.

Everyone is different in how they handle this particular challenge of touring. I can only speak to what I have seen done by those closest to me. My friends in NeedtoBreathe will fly their spouses out every other week so that they can join them on the bus for the weekend. The Jars of Clay guys have made a commitment to be home Sunday through Wednesday morning. Certainly as your kids get older there is a pressure to be home. But if you make a commitment to be home you are inevitably going to be strangling your cash flow. My wife Ellie and I have made commitments to our families. The way that looks is that we plan things out with them six months ahead of time and no gig trumps those plans. When we are at home I have a group of men in my neighborhood I meet with weekly. We share life, encourage each other, and challenge each other. My bass player makes it a practice to call his wife immediately after every show and they will talk for 30–40 minutes. Everyone has different techniques to maintain sanity.

It is a very hard life. Touring is a sacrifice of both social and spiritual community. We have to be very intentional with our time. Being on the road for over 150 days a year has a impact on relationships. Ellie and I have realized we don't have time for new friends. We aren't avoiding people, but with only ten days a month to schedule time with people we know, we need to take care of the "house" we have already built and not add on any additions. I hope the longer we tour the less we will have to tour. And the longer we do this the more we realize we need to say no to things. When I first started out I'd say yes to every concert opportunity. But then I realized if I can't live in community with the people I love, then why am I doing this?

I want a normal life. I want it to be sustainable and not be always be about the odd, surreal world of making music. Being a touring musician can become its own sort of an Ivory Tower. And eventually you don't even need to build the Tower, it builds itself. Then the more attention you get, the more you believe your own hype. There is a guy here in Nashville named Al Andrews who has a ministry of counselling and support for recording artists and their families. He has been an incredible resource for Ellie and me, helping us think through our calling and our marriage. I asked him, based on his years of experience, what was his greatest insight into the life of a touring musician. Without missing a beat he shared his sagacity with me: *The human heart was not built for notoriety.* Isn't that great? And upon reflection you realize that it is so true. Believing your own publicity is a horrible road to take.

The inverse is also true. Believing your own negative evaluation of lack of success is also a dead end. The sooner I got the burden off of my mind of comparing my work to other people's work, the quicker I was able to enjoy the day-to-day successes, and have perspective on the day-to-day disappointments of trying to make it in music. I was able to get that perspective on my calling from time spent on the road with other artists. Hearing from musicians who were more successful than me that their frustrations and joys were mirror images of mine, regardless of the level of their success, was an epiphany.

I have been so encouraged by older artists who have called to encourage me when a record comes out or have had the courage to take me on the road as an unknown entity and "give me away" to their fans. I think that is the fun part of hanging out with NeedtoBreathe in the Green Room—talking about life, the South, and about being brothers. Just drinking the deep water of life with other artists and sharing the common struggle we have of trying to create something of value. And trying to do that out of the right state of being and the right heart, and not because we need to prove something to ourselves and to the world.

Some are sinners, some are saints
Singing the songs out loud
They all come for different reasons
They're not strangers in this crowd

None of us make our work in a vacuum. I tell guys all the time, if you're not happy now, you're not going to be happy when you make it. Bill Withers said, "It's okay to head to wonderful but on your way to wonderful you will have to pass through alright, and when you get to alright, take a good look around and get used to it because that may be as far as you gonna go." It is kind of a melodramatic, but I think it is true, we need to look around.

It is a weird thing. People pay money to go hear music being played live instead of playing it on their record player. The playing of that live music is my job. Concerts are a great equalizer, a musical melting pot. The soccer mom next to the goth-punk kid are working with me and the band to create a common experience. In a room full of strangers we are not alone. It is a strange and beautiful thing that there are not strangers in this crowd.

A Legend
in his time

Fame puts you there where things are hollow.
— David Bowie

Fame is a bee.
It has a song.
It has a sting.
Ah, too, it has a wing.
— Emily Dickinson

It was the 1980s, so we all can be forgiven. But in 1982 on Thursday nights we would change the channel (yes, get up and walk over to the TV and change the channel) to NBC just in time to catch the splashy theme song "Fame!" After all, who doesn't want to "live forever"? Who doesn't want to be remembered? Who doesn't want to "learn how to fly"? Then we were all treated to an hour of leg-warmer clad dancers with really big hair putting it all out there in hopes of attaining their "fifteen minutes of fame," as Andy Warhol had quipped. But the hands down best part of the show was the shadow voice that opened all 135 episodes of its six-year run, first at NBC then over at CBS: *You got big dreams? You want fame? Well, fame costs. And right here is where you start paying . . . in sweat.*

Fame does indeed cost, but maybe a bit more than mere sweat. Some might say it costs your humanity. Or, as Marilyn Monroe put it, it costs your soul: "Hollywood is a place where they'll pay you a thousand dollars for a kiss and fifty cents for your soul." Dan Haseltine of Jars of Clay, who quickly learned some-

thing about fame after the meteoric rise on the charts of the hit single "Flood,"
considers the cost of fame on another level, that of fame and the artist's craft. "It is
possible to be artistic, innovative, and famous," he concedes before adding, "but it
is difficult to be honest, vulnerable, transparent, and famous." And, again cycling
back to the cost of fame on the soul he says directly, "We cannot feed the giant,
fame, and continue to be vulnerable and human." One more thing, according to
Haseltine, who is also a songwriter, "Fame also seems to be a proponent of the
downfall of truthful writing."[1] Charlie Peacock adds another casualty, describing
an artistic apathy that sets in, "We can be so seduced by fame that we even stop
caring about what we are famous for."[2] Sweat, truth, honesty, vulnerability, good
writing, and humanity: the cost of fame.

MAN IN BLACK

Johnny Cash knew all too well the cost of fame. In the 1980s, that same
decade the dancers of "Fame" flashed across our TV sets, Johnny Cash considered himself "lost." Cash biographer Michael Streissguth picked the term "fizzled"
to assess Cash's endeavors in the late 1980s and early 1990s. *Examplia gratia* is
"Cash Country" in Branson, Missouri. This was to be "a sprawling entertainment
complex built around a twenty-five hundred seat theater."[3] And then it, well,
fizzled, leaving a lot of moved earth, hollow buildings, and a settlement for Cash
and his lawyers. He ended up at the Wayne Newton Theater, playing to crowds
at times a mere tenth of capacity. Then Cash met Rick Rubin on February 27,
1993 in Santa Ana, California. By May, Cash would be making songs in Rubin's
living room in Hollywood. Five decades after his first hits, Cash was on top again,
captivating yet another generation.

The Cash-Rubin meeting and all that resulted from it has assumed legendary
status, as well it should. Long-haired and scruffy, Rick Rubin lived in the world of
heavy metal and rap, far from the tourist bus-clogged highways slicing through
Branson, Missouri. But Rubin was exactly what Cash needed. Rosanne Cash puts
an extra-terrestrial spin on it, saying that Rubin "was like this angel that swooped
down into Cash's life."[4] Rubin, whether angelic or human, and Cash, who was
very much human in 1993 and all too clearly showing the wear of a few decades
of rather hard living, opened what is arguably Cash's most creative chapter in his
musical career. If awards are any indicator, from 1994–2004, Cash and Rubin
had quite a run. *American Recordings* (1994) won a Grammy for Best Folk Album,
while *Unchained* (1996), the second installment, took the honor for Best Country
Album. All five of the American Recordings hit the charts, with *American IV:
The Man Comes Around* (2002) climbing to the number two spot on the country
charts. Even *My Mother's Hymn Book* (2004) ranked number nine for Christian
albums. But it would take his death for one of the Rubin-Cash collaborations to
capture the coveted position. *American V: A Hundred Highways*, released posthu-

mously in 2006 took Billboard's number one position. Critics lauded the work, too. *Cash Unearthed* (2003), a box set seemed to appeal to them the most.

The American Recordings were original work, simple and stripped down. Cash had retired the show bands, which had trailed him through the previous two decades. Many cuts simply have Cash with aging voice and acoustic guitar before the microphone. Writing new songs, as well as combing through his own songs from the past, Rubin's songs, and seemingly any songs that had the sole quality of appealing to him, Cash recorded an impressive body of music. Veteran rockers and old-time members of the House of Cash and former sons-in-law joined in. And, of course, June was by his side.

The upshot of it all was that a thirty-something producer, with a long track record of adrenaline and testosterone charged hits, and a sixty-something singer songwriter, with decades of stardom behind him, passed through fame and on to the status of legend. Truth, honesty, vulnerability, good writing, and above all humanity remained intact.

The irony here, though, is that fame came along, too—if you can equate an MTV Award with fame. MTV revolutionized the music industry. Escaping no one's attention, the very first video played when MTV launched in 1981 was The Buggle's "Video Killed the Radio Star." As MTV is finishing up its third decade, you could almost make a case that it has killed the video star. Pander, pander, pander comes to mind. The artistry is about as thin as the clothing on the college-aged (dropped-out?) hard bodies glittering on the screens of its reality shows. But to this crowd Johnny Cash delivered his video, sending it right off to a Grammy, a Country Music award, and an MTV award. Artistic integrity and fame, too—Cash had accomplished the rare if not the impossible.

GUESS THINGS HAPPEN THAT WAY

This all came from the 1993 meeting of Cash and Rubin. What led up to the meeting is an equally worthwhile tale. Before he exited the stage for the last time in 2004 as a legend, he was just John R. Cash from the cotton fields of Dyess, Arkansas, born on February 26, 1932. Dyess was a colony created by the Works Project Administration on the flat plains and black soil of the Arkansas side of the Mississippi Delta, the home of the blues. Like so many, whether black or white, of his time and place coming of age in the pre-World War II Mississippi Delta, Cash learned to sing in the church. But he learned rhythm picking cotton. Few options beyond a lifetime of picking cotton were open to Cash so he joined the military. He enlisted in the Air Force and followed up his basic training with a regiment of courses to be an Intercept Operator. Next followed an assignment at Brooks Air Force Base in Texas. At a roller rink near San Antonio he met Vivian Libreto. A whirlwind courtship became a virtual letter writing campaign as Cash was stationed in Landsberg, Germany. Cash spent long shifts listening to, recording, and deciphering intercepted coded messages. He also bought a guitar, listened to records, and wrote letters to his "girl in San Anton," as their daughter Rosanne Cash's lyric puts it.

In July of 1954, three years after he met Vivian and in the same month Elvis recorded "That's All Right" for Sam Phillips at Memphis's Sun Studios, Johnny Cash completed his stint in the service. First stop was Memphis, to see his brother, Roy. Then Cash went to Texas, marrying Vivian Liberto on August 7. They stopped by Dyess so he could show off his new bride to the family before making their way to Memphis and their rented home and their new life together. Johnny tried quite unsuccessfully to sell appliances. Did Cash, without any gifts in the field of sales, have some intuitive sense that Memphis was about to give birth to rock-n-roll?[5]

Before TVs—the kind of TVs Johnny Cash failed to sell—people sat on their porches and visited with their neighbors. In the South, they also strummed on guitars while they sat and talked. This is what Marshall Grant and Luther Perkins, a couple of mechanics in Memphis, would do, neither one all that good at it. John R. Cash had strummed his guitar in Germany, singing with and, on just a few occasions, singing for his buddies. Once he got to Memphis, Roy Cash, John's older brother, thought it would be good for John to meet up with Marshall and Luther. They first met at the shop and quickly became friends. The three wives hit it off, too. They would play cards around the dining room table and John and Marshall and Luther would play on the porch serenading the streets with gospel tunes. Night after night, week after week, they played and sang.

There is a time, it seems, in most musician's lives when they have a decision to make. The old blues singers mythologized the "crossroads." The eerie, backwoods spot where, with guitar in hand and at the stroke of midnight, the would-be singer was prepared to trade all, even his own soul, for the craft. Here one would meet the devil, offer up his soul, and, if lucky, come away with "it." Fame and fortune, whiskey and women, the road and rambling, all and more lay ahead.

John R. Cash's crossroads ran along Union Avenue in Memphis, Tennessee, leading right up to the door of Sun Studios and Sun Records. John R. Cash didn't have much to lose. Sure he and Vivian were poor, barely able to pay the rent. But it wasn't as if his career as a salesman was about to take off. He was stuck. But he had determination, and perhaps from his mother, a little hope in his voice. He hounded, pestered Sam Phillips until Phillips relented and granted some studio time to John and Marshall and Luther. They pulled out their gospel, the only thing they had. Or at least, the only thing they thought they had. Phillips, who knew quite well what he wanted to hear and also knew quite well what people listening to their new radios and phonographs wanted to hear, told them sorry but it wouldn't work. Phillips sent him home and told him to come back when he had something worthwhile.

Here's where some myth has some in, thanks to *the* Cash movie, *Walk the Line.* The movie has Cash, having failed to impress Phillips with his gospel, on the spot offer up "Folsum Prison Blues." Not quite. Cash and crew actually went home and had to come back a few weeks later. And "Folsum Prison Blues" would come a few months later, his third recorded song.

On March 22, 1955, he recorded "Hey! Porter." But that's all he had. Sam Phillips needed a second song for the verso. They were called singles, but they had two sides. By May, Cash returned with number two, having written "Cry, Cry, Cry," a bluesy song that was exactly the thing Phillips was looking for. Perfect timing for Cash, since Vivian gave birth to their first child on May 24, Rosanne Cash, who would go on to rack up quite a few hits herself. Now Cash could support his family, as record sales and concerts followed. By 1956 he was on the charts.

What started in 1955 would roll on through six decades, most rare in the music industry. Even now, after Cash's death, he sells albums by the hundreds of thousands. In 1955 John R. Cash became Johnny Cash, and his fame would spread. As Cash recorded for Sun Studios and toured on the "Louisiana Hayride" with the likes of Roy Orbison, Carl Perkins, Jerry Lee Lewis, and Elvis Presley, Cash became known all around Mississippi, Arkansas, and Tennessee. His baritone voice and the boom-chick-a sound emanated from high school auditoriums to the receptive ears of teenagers gathered in the front rows and their parents in the back.

In the 1950s he was also on the road, a lot. There was only one way to get to the top of the music business, to sell records and garner the fans. You had to hit the road. For many that's still true. When a hit single takes, the record companies and the agents send the musicians out—families, if there are any, be damned. It's all about fame and getting out there, no matter what the cost.

In Cash's case, he first toured the South on the Louisiana Hayride. Next came the west coast and California, then north to Canada, further and further and for longer and longer periods of time away. Through the late 1950s more children were born—four daughters in all. Cash would send home the birthday cards from the road. And as one might come to expect he drifted away from his first love, the "girl in San Anton."

It was in the 1960s, however, that Cash's star truly rose. And as he took off, he left his family, his first family, behind. The later marriage of John and June Carter Cash has been well celebrated, and rightfully so. But as John took to setting his sights on June and the pursuit of his career it came at the cost of his marriage to Vivian and at the cost of pain to four young girls. The tribute song Rosanne wrote for her father, "Black Cadillac" has some chilling lines when you think of her as a little girl waiting at home for her daddy. Chilling lines like this one: "Now you were always rollin'/But these wheels burn up your life." Johnny off in his "Black Cadillac."

Marshall Grant blames it all on drugs. When Grant does speak on Cash at various Cash festivals he tells the same story, through tears, of how it was drugs that messed up Cash. "Only problem he had with his wife and kids," I heard him say, "was the amphetamines." Marshall concludes, "[Cash was a] great giant of a man killing himself with those little pills." Marshall Grant remembers the precise moment it began. Cash and the Tennessee Two were to open for Faron Young. But they were tired. They had been logging miles upon miles on the road, performing nightly. Gordon Terry, a fiddle player, offered John and Marshall two little pills. Marshall said no; Cash took them. Grant's voice drops as he fights back tears, "It was the beginning of the end for John," for his friend, for this "great giant of a man."[6]

By the end of the 1960s Johnny was in trouble, cancelling concerts and show-ing up stoned for recording sessions. The '60s was a curious decade for Cash, if not for all of America. He's recording albums of hymns, and getting arrested in turn for drunk driving and smuggling in pills from Mexico and, as we'll see later, picking flowers in Starkville, Mississippi.

Then June stepped in. Cash was detoxed and went back to church as 1967 was coming to a close. And by his side was June. By January of 1968, the divorce from Vivian Liberto was finalized, just days before the legendary Folsom Prison Concert. On March 1, he married June Carter Cash. Their honeymoon, of sorts, would come in May in Israel. Unlike the rest of most of America, Cash was leav-ing the '60s in much better shape than he entered them.

The 1960s were good for Cash's career, despite getting banned from the Grand Ole' Opry for kicking out the foot lights on the stage in what's been described as a "drug-induced fit." But the 1970s were even better. He had his television series on ABC on Saturday nights, he was playing the White House, making appearances at Billy Graham Crusades, and even starring alongside Kirk Douglas in a western. He's touring Australia, topping the charts, releasing his own movie, and being invited, rather ceremoniously, back to the Grand Ole' Opry. This time he's sober. (Marshall Grant says it was the birth of John Carter Cash that really sobered him up.)

Cars, houses, one in Jamaica, custom tour busses—Cash had it all. And amidst it all, Cash plugged away at correspondence courses in Bible and theology and even got ordained: The Rev. Johnny Cash, The Parson in Black. By the end of the decade, he cut the ribbon on the House of Cash Museum. Cash had come a long way from the cotton fields of Dyess, Arkansas. Fame was good to Cash.

The 1980s are a bit of a different story. For one, Cash's age caught up with him, depositing him in the hospital on numerous occasions for any variety of maladies. And the drugs came back, too, resulting in time at the Betty Ford Clinic. Cash himself called these the lost years.

Allan Messer, Nashville's premier music photographer, sees it differently. Acknowledging that this was a low period, Messer also challenges us to look at

John in the pictures from the 1980s, many of which were taken by Messer. "He looks happy, he looks good in those pictures," Messer claims. One type of photo you won't see is Johnny in the limo. "No shots in the limo" was the solitary ground rule Cash gave Messer as Messer shadowed Cash. Fans know of the luxuries their stars partake. Cash just didn't want his fans to see him indulging in them.[7]

As the 1980s gave way to the next decade Cash was closing the book on the lost years and about to enter into one of his most if not singularly the most creative period of his life. He was touring and recording with old music-making and drinking buddies Willie Nelson, Waylon Jennings, and Kris Kristofferson, dubbed the "Highwaymen." And he met Rick Rubin. Earlier in the same month that he met Rick Rubin, February 1993, Cash recorded with U2 in Dublin on their *Zooropa* album. That likely cultivated the soil for Cash's warm embrace of Rubin.

As for fame, in these years for the 1990s, he co-starred with supermodel Kate Moss in a video for his song "Delia's Gone." Even most younger rockers don't have that on their resume. In January of 1999 he received a Lifetime Achievement award at the Grammies. Cash limped through the early years of 2000 due to a litany of ailments. While all around him were concerned if not consumed with his health, June was hospitalized for a failing heart. Her death on May 15 caught them all, Johnny the most, by surprise. Devastated, Cash pressed on best he could, offering up one last concert at the Carter family fold, recording some final songs for Rubin, and taking an MTV award for the "Hurt" video in absentia, and sitting at the grave site of June. He died on September 12, 2003. He was buried next to June.

SAINT JOHNNY

Johnny Cash embodies so many things, complementary things, contradictory things. Like a tightly wound spring, he holds bound up within himself forces of explosive energy. He is simultaneously saint and sinner. As Kris Kristofferson's often-quoted lyric has it, "He's a walkin' contradiction/Partly truth and partly fiction." He's the embodiment of fame, the fame that gives and takes away. In fact, Johnny Cash makes for a good twentieth-century musical version of Job.[8]

As Job experienced not just loss but gracious restoration so too it is with Johnny Cash. He has passed from fame to legend, even to icon. Kris Kristofferson (and to a certain extent one could say that Kristofferson owes everything to Cash) called him "a true American hero." Dan Haseltine, no stranger to fame, called him "one of the icons of our time and culture." MTV's Kurt Yoder, spurred on by that Rubin/Cash collaboration, upped the ante a bit when he said, "Johnny Cash is a one man Mt. Rushmore of American rock/folk/country/whatever."[9] The gods of music give, take away, and, in Cash's case, give again.

Artists, be they painters, sculptors, writers, or musicians, desire and quest after the permanent. They desire to transcend their time and their place, to transcend the horizon of their own self and their own experience. Artists desire to create something that lasts beyond the boundaries, the limits, of the moment. Perhaps musicians face this challenge more poignantly than other artists. Music is so visceral, which makes it so vulnerable to the moment, to the temporary. Rarely do notes, tunes, lyrics, hover and stay. Instead, they escape into the ether. Having spent their force, they fade away. Musicians come and go, and so too their music, their creation. Like the hauntingly elusive train whistle in Cash's "Folsom Prison Blues," permanence exists beyond the bars that limit and proscribe the musician.

There is the rare artist who, however, passes through fame. Johnny Cash is one such artist.

THE MAN COMES AROUND

The question of the permanent, the creating of something that is beyond one's own horizon, is not merely a question for artists and musicians. Fame allures us all, with the glimmering offer of permanence.

Permanence does not belong to us. Charlie Peacock, who had one of his songs covered on an episode of "Fame," takes us to the Tower of Babel. But before that, to digress on Peacock's few minutes of fame on "Fame" may be worthwhile. A girl band, performing in the open air of downtown, sends Peacock's lyrics over a very happy and dancing crowd, punctuated by a guitar solo and the chorus, "If it's right it will stay/if it's wrong it will pass/Don't let yourself get fooled/only love will hold fast." It appeared in 1986, on season 6, episode 6. The band had a falling out and couldn't "hold fast." It must not have been right.

As for the series *Fame*, well it too passed on into the night. Its 135th and last episode offered a final plea in its title: "Baby, Remember My Name." Enter the shadow voice, "You got big dreams? You want fame? Well, fame costs."

How elusive fame seems to be. Emily Dickinson playfully said fame "has a wing."

Fame, it turns out, may best be reserved for God and not for us. Again, Charlie Peacock, "The only true hope for our chronic fame-seeking is to seek the fame above all names, Jesus."[10] Our work as artists, as musicians, as writers, as builders, as preachers, as parents becomes filled with meaning and with permanence when it moves beyond us and centers in God. Our work that leaves a lasting impression after the notes have floated off into the ether is that which concerns his name.

An ancient musician knew this all too well. In his song, written down for us in Psalm 115, he tells us not once but twice, "Not unto us." Instead, he says, "to your name give glory."

If fame is reserved for God, then the only songs that last are those that proclaim his name. It is the song of redemption that is remembered for eternity. The songs that last are the songs that sing of God's fame, God's glory. Perhaps it is this singular truth that Johnny Cash so profoundly grasped in the end as he and

Rubin churned out the American Recordings.

Cash sang the song of redemption throughout his life. Sometimes it was in hymns, at other times it was in his blues, or in his story songs of subversive factory workers, or in his ballads of Native Americans. It was even in his night in a Mississippi jail.

FOLSOM PRISON BLUES

Johnny Cash spent May 11, 1965 in the Starkville City Jail. He said it was for picking flowers. They said it was for public drunkenness. Since then, Starkville, and even its jail, has been good to Johnny Cash. His song "Starkville City Jail," performed at his San Quentin State Prison concert in 1969, and appearing on the live album, recouped many times over the $5 fine and forfeited $10 bond slapped on Cash that fateful night in May. When he returned to Starkville for a concert in 1970, Cash gave complimentary front row seats, and some flowers, to Starkville's police officers.

It took them awhile, but both the city of Starkville and the county of Oktibbeha, near the middle of Mississippi's eastern border, finally returned the favor. In November of 2007, with members of the Cash family present, Johnny Cash received a posthumous pardon for his crime. Past debts paid. All this came in the First Annual Johnny Cash Flower Pickin' Festival. The pardon, however, came with some fine print. It needs an annual renewal. And that came at the Second Annual Johnny Cash Flower Pickin' Festival held October 17–19, 2008. Members of the family and close friends were present once again, including daughters Kathy and Rosanne Cash, Johnny's original and longtime bassist Marshall Grant, and songwriter/singer Billy Joe Shaver among them. This fall it will happen again.

Like the whole of Cash's life, the Starkville episode is rife with mythology, a mythology that at times obscures or confuses the facts. It wasn't the Starkville City Jail. There is no such jail. It was actually the Oktibbeha County Jail. There's even a question if Cash actually picked the flowers. They weren't, it turns out, kept securely as evidence.

L. H. White, one of two of Starkville's finest charged with keeping the city safe overnight, met up with Cash as he was coming from the backyard of the Copeland house on state highway 182, on a stretch running through town then known as Lee Street. "I'm just pickin' flowers," Cash protested.

Johnny Cash was in town for a concert at the Animal Husbandry Service Building on the campus of Mississippi State University on Monday, May 10, 1965. (For $2 you could have heard him play.) His band, Marshall Grant on bass and Luther Perkins on guitar, drove home to Memphis after the concert. June Carter went to the University Motel, at the time named the Derby. But Johnny made some stops along the way, at a frat house, at a neighborhood house where the concert had spawned a party, and then to his motel room, drinking, and playing as he went along. He and June were in separate rooms—that night he was walking the line, at least for a little while. In his room Johnny shared some whiskey bottles with the Cleveland brothers, who owned a plumbing supply store next to the Derby. Then Johnny left his room shortly before 5 am.

The myth has it that Johnny and June had a fight, that he was fuming, and that he left to find some cigarettes. What can be known for sure is that he wandered along state highway 182 for a time before staggering up the Copeland driveway. Then he met up with Starkville's finest. "Do you know who I am?" he sounded off to deputy White. No. Now shut up and get in the car. So much for fame.

Cash was fairly agitated when he got tossed in the drunk tank. He kicked the steel door so hard he broke his toe. All totaled, Johnny Cash spent seven nights in jail in as many different towns.

Johnny Cash worked pretty hard on his outlaw image. "I shot a man in Reno, just to watch him die," he growls in "Folsom Prison Blues." Not quite. He was arrested for narcotics possession on a few occasions, issued fines for destroying property, mostly on or back stage, and then there's the notorious flower pickin' incident under consideration. Rebel and outlaw was more image than reality for Cash, more myth than truth. Symbols and mythology are, however, important.

June Carter Cash once said that his prison concerts were successful because prisoners knew he was the real thing. He never shot that man in Reno. Neither did he shoot his woman in "Cocaine Blues" for that matter. But Cash was the real thing in that he knew about guilt, the kind of guilt that comes from the outlaw in us all. "I keep a close watch on this heart of mine" can only be said of one who knows just what that heart is capable of.

Marshall Grant, carrying on with the theme of how drugs ruined his friend, treats the east Mississippi prison stint with gravity. This marks, for Grant, the low point, or maybe better to say the tipping point for Cash.

Getting drunk and failing to show up for concerts, that's a low point. Getting drunk and letting a flirting glance become a vow-breaking moment, that's a low point. But getting drunk and picking flowers? That's almost a Hallmark moment.

"So what are you in for?"

"Me? I ripped a flower right out of the ground. It never even saw me coming. Why I'll tell you . . ."

Even in his low point, Cash elicits sympathy, maybe even a smile, certainly not scorn. But picking flowers was not the low point in the 1960s for Cash. There were other moments from the 1960s worthy of scorn. It was the decade, as mentioned above, that he left his family, his first family, behind.

Two of those daughters were at the festival and one of them, Rosanne, headlined the festival. Redemption indeed.

Soon as Rosanne Cash, who has racked up an impressive string of number one hits, stepped on stage to close out the Starkville festival, she had the audience. "I don't usually visit the places where my dad spent eight hours in jail," she said before moving into "Sea of Heartbreak," one of the 100 songs her father told her she must learn in order to complete her education. Next followed some dark songs, her cover of "Billy Joe McAllister," and her own songs "Burn Down This Town" and "September When It Comes." There were fun songs too. Rosanne Cash's version of "Tennessee Flat Top Box," one of her father's own crowd pleasers, sounds just as good if not better than her father's. And she had to do "Starkville City Jail," throwing in "I've Got [Prison] Stripes" for good measure. Like her father, she knows what to do with an audience.

Sharing the stage at the festival with Rosanne Cash was longtime songwriting and music making buddy of Johnny Cash, Billy Joe Shaver, who knows a thing or two himself about punishment and pardon, guilt, and redemption. Shaver also knows how to put on a show. A year shy of seventy, Shaver held the audience of several thousand just like Cash used to. He did some Cash songs and some of his own songs. "You Just Can't Beat Jesus Christ," a song he originally recorded as a duet with Cash, was hands down the stand out of them all. "Well even though I'm a sinner, He will always be my friend." The song of redemption.

Yes, Johnny and Billy Joe will tell you, "Ain't no two ways about it, I owe it all to Jesus Christ." Harmonicas, guitars, basses, drums, daughters, and sons-in-law—all testifying to redemption on a cool fall night under Mississippi skies.

The City of Starkville and the County of Oktibbeha have pardoned Johnny Cash. The official proclamation declares, "Cash's contributions to humanity and struggles illustrate life's imperfections but also show the importance of making things right after making mistakes." But the pardon only lasts a year. The Johnny Cash Flower Pickin' Festival is a Mississippi version of Yom Kippur, the Day of Atonement.

As music festivals go, this one is not at the top of the list. Through most of the day, crowds mulling around numbered just a few hundred. Rosanne drew, but the number never got much past a couple of thousand. *The New York Times* dispatched a reporter, Dan Berry, one of their best. His story got buried, appearing on page 14 of the New York edition.

But the festival and that for which it stands, Cash in need of and seeking redemption, is the song of redemption, one of the many songs of redemption of the famous Johnny Cash.

CONCLUSION

Tom Douglas, a country songwriter with an impressive list of hits including Colin Raye's "Little Rock," Martina McBride's "God's Will," and Tim McGraw's "My Little Girl," met up with Waylon Jennings near the end of Jennings's life.

Waylon had teamed up with Johnny on the Highwaymen and back in 1965 they shared an apartment, both at a low ebb in life. Tom and Waylon took a lunch break from working on a song. Over tuna sandwiches Tom asked Waylon to use one word to describe the famous four Highwaymen. For Willie Nelson, Waylon said *laughter*. For Kristofferson, Walyon said *children*, which surprised Tom. Then Tom said to Waylon what about Waylon? Waylon replied *children*. Surprised yet again, Tom pressed for one more. Cash? Waylon said, "Sorry, hoss, [Cash is] larger than life, one word won't do."[11]

Waylon Jennings was right. When it comes to Cash, one word won't do. Famous doesn't quite capture it. Legend comes close. Outlaw could work, as long as you put outlaw in quotes. Penitent could also work. Redeemed seems to come the closest. The song of redemption pulses through Cash's music and his life. It's what makes for a good song, or a good novel or a good movie or a good painting for that matter.

Thinking of Cash and fame Tom Douglas himself said, "Johnny Cash didn't try to be famous. He just was." Cash was famous because, the rather circuitous route of his life notwithstanding, he knew the one to whom fame alone belongs. And it was to him and for him that Cash sang. We all had the privilege to listen in.

Endnotes

1   Dan Haseltine, personal correspondence, 4/14/2009. Jars of Clay released the album *The Long Fall back to Earth* on April 21, 2009.

2   Charlie Peacock, "The Fame Game."

3   Michael Streissguth, *Johnny Cash: The Biography* (Cambridge, MA: De Capo Press, 2006) 235.

4   Cited in Steve Turner, *The Man Called Cash: The Life, Love, and Faith of an American Legend* (Nashville: W/Thomas Nelson, 2004) 196.

5   I am indebted to Steve Turner, *The Man Called Cash*, for the chronology here and what follows.

6   Marshall Grant, *I Was There When It Happened: My Life with Johnny Cash* (Nashville: Cumberland House, 2006); Marshall Grant, presentation at Johnny Cash Flower Pickin' Festival, Starkville, Mississippi, October 18, 2008.

7   Interview with Allen Messer, October 17, 2008.

8   See Rodney Clapp, *Johnny Cash and the Great American Contradiction: Christianity and the Battle for the Soul of a Nation* (Louisville: Westminster John Knox Press, 2008), for a trenchant and profound analysis of the contradictory Cash.

9   All three quotations in Dave Urbanski, *The Man Comes Around: The Spiritual Journey of Johnny Cash* (Lake Mary, FL: Relevant, 2003) vii, xii.

10   Charlie Peacock, "The Fame Game."

11   Personal correspondence from Tom Douglas 5/01/2009.

RESOURCES
and bios

In the back of Calvin Seerveld's book *A Christian Critique of Art and Literature* there is a booklist section entitled, "Kindred Readings Behind, Around, and Beyond the Text." This appendix works in a similar way. Following is a list of books distilled from a huge list of recommendations provided by contributors to this project.

Jeremy S. Begbie, ed.: *Beholding the Glory: Incarnation through the Arts* (Grand Rapids: Baker, 2000).

Jeremy S. Begbie, *Resounding Truth: Christian Wisdom in the World of Music* (Baker Academic, 2007).

Jeremy S. Begbie, *Theology, Music and Time* (Cambridge, Cambridge U. P., 2000)

Jeremy S. Begbie, *Voicing Creation's Praise: Towards a Theology of the Arts,* (Edinburgh: T & T Clark, 1991).

Harold Best, *Music through the Eyes of Faith* (HarperSanFransico, 1993).

Daniel K. L. Chua, *Absolute Music and the Construction of Meaning* (Cambridge, Cambridge U. P., 1999).

Nicholas Cook, *Music, Imagination & Culture* (Oxford: Oxford U. P., 1990).

William Edgar, *Taking Note of Music* (London: S.P.C.K., 1986).

Gaines, James R., *Evening in the Palace of Reason: Bach Meets Frederick the Great in the Age of Enlightenment* (Harper, 2005)

Giles Oakley, *The Devil's Music: a History of the Blues,* 2nd ed. (New York: Da Capo, 1997).

Donald Jay Grout & Claude V. Palisca, *A History of Western Music,* 4th ed. (New York: W. W. Norton, n.d.).

Jamie Howison, *God's Mind in That Music: Theological Explorations through the Music of John Coltrane* (Eugene, OR: Cascade, 2012).

Image: A Journal of the Arts and Religion (Seattle, WA).

Jamie James, *The Music of the Spheres: Music, Science and the Natural Order of the Universe* (Springer, 1995).

Paul Jones, *Singing and Making Music* (Phillipsburg: P & R Publishing, 2006).

Bob Kauflin, *Worship Matters* (Crossway, 2008).

Bryan Magee, *The Tristan Chord: Wagner and Philosophy* (New York: Henry Holt, 2000).

Ingrid Monson, *Saying Something: Jazz Improvisation and Interaction* (Chicago: U of Chicago Press, 1996).

Ken Myers, *Mars Hill Audio Journal.*

Stephen J. Nichols, *Getting the Blues: What Blues Music Teaches Us about Suffering & Salvation* (Brazos, 2008).

Flannery O'Connor, *Mystery and Manners* (New York: Farrar, Straus & Giroux, 1962).

Alice Parker, *The Anatomy of Melody: Exploring the Single Line of Song* (GIA Publications, 1997)

Charlie Peacock, *At the Crossroads: An Insider's Look at the Past, Present, and Future of Contemporary Christian Music* (Nashville: Broadman & Holman, 1999).

Rebecca Rischin, *For the End of Time: The Story of the Messiaen Quartet* (Ithaca: Cornell U. P., 2003).

H. R. Rookmaaker, *The Creative Gift* (Westchester: Cornerstone, 1981).

H. R. Rookmaaker, *Modern Art and the Death of a Culture* (Downers Grove, IL: Inter-Varsity Press, 1970).

H. R. Rookmaaker, *New Orleans Jazz, Mahalia Jackson and the Philosophy of Art* (Carlisle, U.K., Piquant, 2002).

Philip Ryken, *Art for God's Sake: A Call to Recover the Arts* (P & R Publishing, 2006).

Francis A. Schaeffer, *Art and the Bible* (IVP, 1973).

Christian Scharen, *Broken Hallelujahs: Why Popular Music Matters to Those Seeking God* (Brazos, 2011).

Calvin Seerveld, *Bearing Fresh Olive Leaves,* (Toronto: Tuppence, 2000).

Calvin Seerveld, *Rainbows for the Fallen World,* (Toronto: I.R.S.S., 1980).

Jon Michael Spencer, *Blues and Evil* (Knoxville: University of Tennessee Press, 1993).

Calvin R. Stapert, *My Only Comfort: Death, Deliverance and Discipleship in the Music of Bach* (Grand Rapids & Cambridge: Eerdmans, 2000).

Igor Stravinsky, *Poetics Of Music In The Form Of Six Lessons* (Harvard University Press, revised edition, 1993).

John Tavener, *The Music of Silence* (NY & London: Faber & Faber, 1999).

Janna Tull Steed, *Duke Ellington: A Spiritual Biography* (New York: Crossroad, 1999).

Steve Turner, *Hungry for Heaven: Rock 'n' Roll and the Search for Redemption,* Revised Edition (Downers Grove: Inter-Varsity Press, 1995).

Steve Turner, *The Man Called Cash: The Life, Love, and Faith of an American Legend* (Thomas Nelson, 2005).

Peter van der Merwe, *Origins of the Popular Style: the Antecedents of Twentieth-Century Popular Music* (New York, Oxford: Oxford University Press, 1989).

Paul Westermeyer, *Te Deum: The Church and Music* (Augsburg Fortress Publishing, 1998).

CONTRIBUTORS

Vito Aiuto is the senior pastor of Resurrection Williamsburg, a church in Brooklyn, NY (ResurrectionWilliamsburg.com). He also makes music with his wife, Monique, as The Welcome Wagon. Their most recent record, *Precious Remedies Against Satan's Devices,* was released by Asthmatic Kitty Records in 2012. *asthmatickitty. com/artists/The-Welcome-Wagon*

Diana DiPasqaule Bauer characterizes herself as an Eastside City girl growing up as one of the few Presbyterians in a densely populated Italian Roman Catholic neighborhood. She began her love for art and music on those mysterious visits to Pompeii Roman Catholic Church for weddings, christenings and funerals. Diana authored a book titled, *Lexei's Hope* published by Veritas Press. Currently, Diana is president of Square Halo Books and is a certified CCEF counselor in the Baltimore-Washington Metro area. She is mother to Maya, William, Suzannah and Chara, mommy-in-law to Brad and Ryan and grandmother to Lyric, Lexei, Isabella, Isaac and one on the way.

But mostly she is a proficient sinner sold out to the only lover of her soul and happily married to her one and only Alan Dean, who loves her killer lasagna and thinks she is the best companion as they travel the world.

Bethany Brooks teaches and plays piano. She holds the MMus in piano performance from the Royal Academy of Music in London and has performed in Philadelphia, New York, London, Mexico City, Odessa, and Istanbul. Most summers, she serves as staff pianist at the Crescendo Summer Institute of the Arts in Sárospatak, Hungary. In her not-so-classical moments, Bethany is keyboard player and vocalist for numerous bands in Philadelphia's roots music scene. Her recording project of 'retuned' hymns, *Quarry Street Hymnal*, was released in November, 2012. Bethany directs music at City Church in west Philadelphia. She lives nearby in an old row-home with a few friends, on a tree-lined block in a crunchy-granola neighborhood, surrounded by cafes that she wishes she had time to frequent with a good book. *QuarryStreetHymnal.com*

Paul Buckley is director of worship and music at Grace Presbyterian Church (Presbyterian Church in America) in Ocala, Florida. Previously, he was a copy editor for *The Dallas Morning News* and an assistant editor for the paper's award-winning religion section. He has won several writing awards in a national contest. He is a graduate of Westminster Theological Seminary in Dallas (now Redeemer Seminary) and Philadelphia. He's single, and any wifely prospects will need to like a little Psalm chanting.

Ned Bustard is the owner of a graphic design firm called World's End Images and was the art director for the late, great, alternative Christian music publication, *Notebored Magazine.* He has written a number of books for children including *Legends & Leagues, Ella Sings Jazz,* and a historic novel *Squalls Before War: His Majesty's Schooner Sultana.* His most recent book was a collaboration with Steve Nichols, *The Church History ABCs.* In his spare time, he is the creative director for Square Halo Books, for whom he edited the book *It Was Good: Making Art to the Glory of God.* He currently is living in Lancaster, Pennsylvania with his wife, Leslie, and three daughters, Carey, Maggie, and Ellie. *www.NedBustard.com*

Mark Chambers is a composer and church musician. His concert music displays both intuitive and rational qualities while exploring spiritual and theological concerns. His music has been performed across the U.S. and Europe by ensembles and performers such as Hugh Sung, Sato Moughalian, Carla Rees, and rarescale, Duo Aksak, and Craig Hultgren. In addition to regular concert performances his music has been presented at international festivals such as the International Arts Movement, Spark, SEAMUS, MAXIS II (UK), and Pulsefield Soundscape. He was selected as a finalist in the 1st Annual Concurso Minaturas (Spain), and other musical awards include the Victor Herbert / ASCAP award and a College Music Society Composition Award. He holds degrees from The University of Alabama, The University of Tennessee, and Samford University. He currently resides in Virginia with his wife Jennifer and their three children, as well as their black lab, Ruby. *MarkChambersMusic.com*

William Edgar is currently Professor of Apologetics at Westminster Theological Seminary. He studied musicology at Harvard and Columbia. He holds the Docteur en Theologie from the University of Geneva (Switzerland). He has taught at the Reformed Theological seminary in Aix-en-Provence. His books include *Taking Note of Music* (SPCK), *La Carte Protestante* (Labor et Fides), and *Reasons of the Heart* (Baker). He has written numerous articles on such subjects as cultural apologetics, the City of Geneva, and African-American music. His favorite avocation is jazz piano. He plays part-time with a professional jazz band. His wife Barbara is Administrative Secretary for the Huguenot Fellowship. They have two children, Keyes, a lawyer in New York, and Deborah, a campus chaplain at Harvard, and three grandchildren.

Julius Fischer, Jr. earned his B.S. degree in Music Education with a piano major from Towson University. As a young teenager, his music interests set him on a divergent path as he both studied bassoon at the Peabody Conservatory Prep and played keyboard in a pop variety band that performed a Kiss tribute show. Before entering Music Ministry on a full-time basis, he taught piano at Dundalk Community College and worked as a freelance musician in the Baltimore/Washington area, doing everything from musical theater to Klezmer. At the same time, he worked as an organist at Seventh Baptist Church in Baltimore City. Since 2000, he has been serving as Minister of Music at Abbott Memorial Presbyterian Church, also in Baltimore City. There, he particularly enjoys encouraging children in their musical endeavors through lessons offered by the Abbott Center for Arts, a music ministry for local children. His wife Angela is a Latin teacher, and he has two teenaged daughters whose current interests include volleyball and music.

Ruth Naomi Floyd, Vocalist and Composer, has been at the forefront of creating vocal jazz settings that express Christian theology for 20 years. Critics have praised Ruth's discography for its distinctive sound of progressive ensemble jazz that is seamlessly blended with explicit Biblical messages of unwavering faith in God. Ruth leads her own multi-faceted ensemble and her music consists primarily of original compositions. Ruth is Adjunct Professor of Vocals in the Church Music Program at Cairn University. For almost two decades, Ruth has been devoted and active in providing compassionate care and spiritual support to people infected and affected by HIV/AIDS in United States and Africa. Ruth is also a noted fine art photographer (the photos on the cover were taken by her—*www.RNFimages.com*). She is married to Kenyatta, an ordained minister, and they have two children, Isaiah and Grace. *www.RuthNaomiFloyd.com*

Mark and Jan Foreman Mark is the Lead Pastor at North Coast Calvary Chapel (NCCC) in Carlsbad, California, known for its unique, borderless philosophy of being "a church without walls." He is the author of *Wholly Jesus*, which champions the concepts of both personal and cultural transformation. Jan Foreman serves as the Women's Teaching Director at NCCC. She also directs women's outreach into the local and global communities. Mark and Jan have been married for 40 years and together they've been parents to two grown sons, Jon and Tim, who are part of the band Switchfoot.

David Fuentes is Professor of Composition and Theory at Calvin College in Grand Rapids, Michigan where he composes concert and liturgical music for chamber ensembles, solo instruments, orchestra, and chorus. He also writes music for film, dance, television, theater, and integrative collaborations with visual artists, here and abroad. The recipient of numerous commissions, grants, and prizes, Fuentes also lectures on contemporary composers, film music, music and faith, and music and vocation. His book, *Figuring Out Melody* is a step-by-step manual for composition, valuable for novices and experts alike. He is currently writing two interrelated books: *Ears To Hear,* which looks at general ways in which people throughout human history have considered music "spiritual" and demonstrates how Christians might use these to cultivate the fruit of the Spirit, and Music Making as Christian Service, which investigates new perspectives and questions about faith and music that help professional musicians see their art as Christian Service.

Keith Getty and his wife, Kristyn, have been writing hymns for more than a decade, bridging the gap between traditional and contemporary, and creating what is described as singable theology. Their songs, many co-written with Stuart Townend, have pioneered a new generation of modern hymns that are sung in small churches, large cathedrals and concert halls around the world. In particular, the renowned Getty/Townend hymn, "In Christ Alone," is among the most-sung hymns in churches throughout North America, Europe, Australia, and Africa. Under the Getty Music label, Keith and Kristyn have recorded multiple albums: *In Christ Alone* (2007), *Awaken the Dawn* (2009), *Joy-An Irish Christmas* (2011), *Hymns for the Christian Life* (2012), and *Live at The Gospel Coalition* (2013). In addition to their *Hymns for the Christian Life* hymn tours and annual *Joy-An Irish Christmas* tours, the Gettys have shared their music at the United States Pentagon, the GMA Dove Awards, Franklin Graham crusades, at the Grand Ole Opry in Nashville, for President George W. Bush, and on the stage of London's Royal Albert Hall. They have spoken at universities from Harvard to Wheaton and remain involved in conferences including the Lausanne Congress and The Gospel Coalition. Keith and Kristyn divide their time between Northern Ireland and their home in Nashville where they write, tour and oversee the work of Getty Music.

Steve Guthrie is Associate Professor of Theology at Belmont University, where he directs the Religion and the Arts program. He holds a PhD in theology from the University of St. Andrews, and served as Postdoctoral Research Fellow at the

Institute for Theology Imagination and the Arts, and Lecturer in Theology at the University of St. Andrews. He is the author of *Creator Spirit: The Holy Spirit and the Art of Becoming Human*, and is the co-editor (with Jeremy Begbie) of *Resonant Witness: Conversations between Music and Theology*. He earned a degree in music theory from the University of Michigan School of Music, and before studying theology spent several years as a minister of music and performing musician. He continues to perform music regularly in the Nashville area.

Drew Holcomb, releasing his first solo album in 2005, was later joined by The Neighbors (Ellie Holcomb, Nathan Dugger, and Rich Brinsfield). Selling more than 80,000 records, his band has established itself as a formidable indie act, playing more than 1,500 live dates, selling-out headline shows, and touring alongside such varied acts as The Avett Brothers, Ryan Adams, NeedToBreathe, and more. The band's songs have been used in countless television shows and commercials, most notably in TNT's Emmy Award winning 2011 NBA Forever spot (called "possibly the greatest sports commercial of all time" by Rick Reilly of *Sports Illustrated*). In addition to his musical talents, Drew also studied Divinity at St Andrews University in Scotland, where he received an M.Litt with his thesis, "Bruce Springsteen and the American Redemptive Imagination." Originally from Memphis, Drew, his wife Ellie, and their newborn daughter, Emmylou, call East Nashville home.

Joy Ike is a full-time singer-songwriter based out of Pittsburgh, PA. Her music has turned up on *Relevant Magazine's* The Drop, and various NPR affiliates in the Northeast. Her music has continually been noted for its lyrical depth—addressing the human condition, thoughts on love, and the search for God in a very tangible way. A write-up on NPR's All Things Considered says "The depth of subjects she tackles in her poetic lyrics are perfectly complemented by a unique blend of neo-soul, with just the right dash of pop . . . a truly compelling act to watch in person, with the ability to create an intimate setting in locations big and small." As a former publicist Ike is also the founder of *Grassrootsy.com*, a music marketing blog for independent artists. She believes the greatest tragedy in the world is having a talent and keeping it to yourself. *www.JoyIke.com*

Tom Jennings is a pianist and composer who has served since 1995 as Music Director at Redeemer Presbyterian Church in New York City. His innovative work among the 300 professional musicians who attend Redeemer has been featured in publications such as *JazzTimes, Worship Leader, byFaith, Charisma,* and a documentary for Anglican Media Sydney. He holds the Doctor of Musical Arts degree in classical piano from Manhattan School of Music. Hailed by the Boston Globe as a "thoughtfully attuned pianist," he has performed in a remarkably diverse array of settings—as recitalist, orchestral soloist, accompanying opera stars such as Jerome Hines and Ben Heppner, in Broadway shows, and performing with cabaret luminaries such as Leslie Uggams and Steve Ross. His wife Michelle is an opera singer. They have two children, Daniel and Leah, aspiring basketball and theater stars.

Shai Linne is a recording artist with Lamp Mode Recordings, an independent Christian hip-hop record label whose mission is to highlight the character of God while presenting the gospel of Jesus Christ and a biblical worldview through hip-hop culture. Shai is a theologian, poet, and pastor-in-training, having recently completed a pastoral internship at Capitol Hill Baptist Church in Washington D.C., where he is a member. Shai has appeared on numerous independent and national Christian hip-hop releases and has released four solo projects of his own: *The Solus Christus Project* (2005), *The Atonement* (2008), *Storiez* (2008) and *The Attributes of God* (2011). Shai lives in Washington, D.C. with his wife Blair. They have a son named Sage. Visit Shai on Twitter at *twitter.com/shailinne*

Sandra McCracken is an independent singer-songwriter whose smart, soulful blend of folk, pop, and gospel is as progressive as it is timeless. A founding contributor of the Indelible Grace projects, McCracken's contemporary settings of classic hymns are sung in congregations across the country. Drawing inspiration from Bob Dylan, Johnny Cash, Emmylou Harris, and U2, McCracken crafts songs wedding razor-sharp hooks to incisive, confessional lyrics to create a transcendent portrait of the human spirit. McCracken currently lives, writes, and records at her home in East Nashville, Tennessee with her husband, Derek Webb, and their two children. *www.SandraMcCracken.com*

Brian Moss is a pastor, musician, songwriter, and worship leader. Currently serving as Associate Pastor at Maple Valley Presbyterian Church in Maple Valley, WA, Brian has a Master of Divinity from Regent College in Vancouver, BC and a Bachelor of Music from Belmont University in Nashville, TN. Brian has recorded several albums including a collection of new songs inspired by the Psalms. Brian and his wife, Stephanie, have five children. *www.PrayerbookProject.com*

Stephen J. Nichols is research professor of Christianity and Culture at Lancaster Bible College in Pennsylvania. He earned master's degrees in theology and philosophy and a PhD from Westminster Theological Seminary. He has written fifteen books on such topics as the Reformation, Jonathan Edwards, American evangelicalism, and blues music. Among his books are *Jesus Made in America* (IVP) and *Getting the Blues: What Blues Music Teaches Us about Suffering and Salvation* (Brazos). With artist Ned Bustard, he's also the author of *Church History ABCs*. Steve is a visiting lecturer at London Theological Seminary in the UK and an adjunct professor with Reformed Theological Seminary at the Washington, D.C., Charlotte, NC, and Jackson, MS, campuses. Steve and his wife Heidi live in Lancaster with their three children.

John Patitucci has been at the forefront of the jazz world for the last 30 years and active in all styles of music. He is a three-time Grammy award winner, has been nominated over fourteen times, and has played on many other Grammy award-winning recordings. John's two latest cds, *Remembrance* and *Line by Line* were both nominated for Grammys for Best Instrumental Jazz Album. In 2005, as a member of The Wayne Shorter Quartet, John won a Grammy for Best Instrumental Jazz Album. He has performed and/or recorded with jazz giants such as Dizzy Gillespie, Wayne Shorter, Herbie Hancock, Chick Corea, Stan Getz, Freddie Hubbard, Roy Haynes, Wynton Marsalis, Michael Brecker, Kenny Garrett, Victor Feldman, Nancy Wilson, and countless others. In 2012, John also launched his interactive online bass school through ArtistWorks (artistworks.com). John is currently Artist in Residence at Berklee College of Music's Global Jazz Institute. *www.JohnPatitucci.com*

Charlie Peacock is Grammy Award-winning, multi-format performer, songwriter, and record producer has excelled in pop, gospel, country, Folk-Americana, and jazz. In addition to recording his own albums (most recently, *No Man's Land*), he has produced and written for numerous artists ranging from Amy Grant to Switchfoot and The Civil Wars. Named by Billboard's Encyclopedia of Record Producers as one of the 500 most important record producers in music history, his main passion is for fishing. His wife, Andi, is a master gardener and a writer. They live in Nashville in a remodeled turn-of-the-century country church and have two grown children, Molly and Sam. *www.CharliePeacock.com*

Doug Plank is a singer, songwriter, and a pastor overseeing worship and singles at Crossway Church (crosswaypa.org), and is married with five children in Millersville, Pennsylvania. He has been a lifetime musician and a songwriter for Sovereign Grace Music (sovereigngracemusic.org) and worship leader for the past ten years. His most recent musical efforts have been the recording of an album with Crossway Collective and he continues to write songs and discover and rearrange old hymns for corporate worship as well as for the sheer joy of it. He has written no books, but tends to read a lot of them. Aside from making music, his favorite avocation is a Tolkien book, a good biography, or lately, televised British dramas with wife Brenda by his side.

Hiram Ring is a songwriter, musician and linguist currently residing in Singapore, pursuing a PhD in Language Documentation and Grammatical Description with a focus on an unwritten language in a remote part of India. He was born and raised in Ghana, West Africa, where his parents are Bible translators with Wycliffe. He speaks seven languages and has lived on five continents. His second solo album *Home* explores life from the eyes of a world traveler and spiritual sojourner, consistent themes in his previous music. He enjoys collaboration with church friends and his hymn and sacred compositions can be heard on Pageant Music (Matthew Monticchio) and Cardiphonia (Bruce Benedict) releases. *www.HiramRing.com*

Michael Roe is a session guitarist, record producer, songwriter, and singer. He began his career in the late '70s as producer and host of the nationally syndicated radio program Rock & Religion, which featured music and interviews with a wide range of artists including T-Bone Burnett, Pete Townsend, The Doors, and Mark Heard. He has recorded several solo albums, instrumental albums, and is part of the Lost Dogs. But he is best known as frontman for the critically acclaimed band, The 77s. Regardless of the hat he is wearing, Roe desires not only to put forth finely crafted songs but also to show himself real—writing from the experience of life's difficulty and struggle as well as its joy and promise. A self-described "jazz hound," Michael is married with one daughter and lives in Northern California. *www.MichaelRoe.com*

Chelle Stearns is currently an Assistant Professor of Theology at The Seattle School of Theology & Psychology in Seattle, Washington. Her academic work focuses on the intersection of theology and music, especially in how music is able to open up and deepen our exploration and understanding of the Trinity. Her Ph.D. dissertation explored the compositional philosophy of Arnold Schoenberg and the nature of unity within musical space. Her published writing looks at how music and the other arts function theologically in the church, and she is currently researching how a theology of music and worship can help us reimagine a theology of reconciliation for the church today. Chelle has a long history of serving in the Church as a musician, teacher, and worship leader. Over the years, she has remained an active amateur musician, believing that performance both enhances and informs her academic work.

Gregg Strawbridge, PhD, is the pastor of All Saints Church (CREC) in Lancaster, Pennsylvania (since 2001). He studied music and classical guitar at the University of Southern Mississippi. His written publications include *The Case for Covenantal Infant Baptism* (ed.), *The Case for Covenant Communion* (ed.), and the booklet, *Classical and Christian Education: Recapturing the Educational Approach of the Past.* Along with loving sailing, motorcycling, and swimming, he is an avid musician. His latest recording is named for his sixth great grandfather, the first Methodist preacher in America (Robert Allen Strawbridge d. 1781) *Strawbridge House—Roadside Hymns* (available through WordMp3.com and iTunes) which features his daughters (Joy, Jenna, and Julie). Gregg and his wife Sharon live in Brownstown, PA. His lectures and articles are available at *www.WordMp3.com*

Kirstin Vander Giessen-Reitsma is the editor of *catapult magazine*, a bi-weekly online publication of *culture is not optional (*cino). *cino's work also includes community gardening, art, and play at the Huss Project in Three Rivers, Michigan. In addition to working with *cino, Kirstin and her husband Rob helped found a fair trade store in Three Rivers in 2003. By way of tentmaking, they do freelance writing, teaching, and design. Kirstin refreshes her body and mind by gardening, biking, singing, camping, reading fiction, cooking prolifically, and gathering combinations of wonderful people around tables and bonfires. *www.CultureIsNotOptional.com*

Gregory Wilbur is currently Chief Musician at Cornerstone Presbyterian Church in Franklin, TN, as well as Dean and Senior Fellow of New College Franklin—a Christian liberal arts college that he helped to start. He earned his Masters in Music Composition at the University of Alabama. He is the author of *Glory and Honor: The Music and Artistic Legacy of Johann Sebastian Bach* and has released two CDs of his compositions of congregational psalms, hymns, and service music. In addition, he writes for choir, orchestra, film, and chamber ensembles. His wife, Sophia, home-schools their young daughter, Eleanor, and they all enjoy reading, cooking, taking walks, and enjoying life in middle Tennessee. *www.GreyFriarsPress.com*

ACKNOWLEDGMENTS

It Was Good was and is a collaborative effort. Special thanks must be extended first of all to the talented contributors—without them there would be no book. Thanks as well to my friend (and collaborator) Rob Bigley for the technical assistance he gave on early drafts of the book.

Recognition needs to be made of the following for bringing good music into my life: EDB, Sr., David Giardinere, Bob Kauflin, Charlie Peacock, Matt Monticchio, George Yellak, WFLN, WZZD, WJTL, WIXQ, WHFS, WXPN, Bill Myers, Jeff Deacon, Erik Arneson, Arvo Pärt, Camelot Music, XYZed Music, Exit Records, Broken/BAI, Re:think, Cornerstone Festival, Indelible Grace, Noisetrade, and the late, great *Notebored Magazine.*

Lastly, unending thanks must be given to my favorite concert companion, Leslie Bustard—for sacrificing our time and money for the greater good of this work, and joining in with prayer and encouragement to see it develop into an acceptable service.

FREE MUSIC

NoiseTrade is a service that helps artists connect to music fans. Artists and fans can work together, exchanging music for a little information and giving fans ways to share music from artists they like. It began in 2006 when Sandra McCracken's husband, Derek Webb, gave away one of his albums for free online. It was the massive success of this experiment that inspired him, with the help of a few trusted friends, to start NoiseTrade. Several of the contributors to this book have used NoiseTrade, so it seemed appropriate to share music from *It Was Good: Making Music to the Glory of God* with our readers through this means. Follow this link (http://www.Noisetrade/ItWasGood) to download the following music for free. And while you are there, spend time browsing through the NoiseTrade site to discover other great music that you can download as well.

Track Listing

ARTIST	SONG
Rob Bigley	Deo Gloria
Brian Moss	This Is All My Joy (Psalm 16)
Sandra McCracken	Dynamite
Bethany Brooks	My Song is Love Unknown
Charlie Peacock	Death Trap
Coal Train Railroad	Belly Button Stays the Same
The Welcome Wagon	Sold! To The Nice Rich Man
Gregory Wilbur	Glory Be to God the Father
Mark Chambers	… glass darkly … (mvt. 1)
Brian LoPiccolo	Death Swallowed in Victory
Doug Plank	Shadow of Your Wings
William Edgar, Ruth Naomi Floyd, John Patitucci	Lord, Don't Move That Mountain
Ruth Naomi Floyd	Open The Door To Him
Hiram Ring	Two Trees
Gregg Strawbridge	Wisdom
Julius Fischer	I Saw Three Ships
Joy Ike	Time
Drew Holcomb & The Neighbors	Hallelujah

A FEW OTHER
good books . . .

It Was Good: Making Art to the Glory of God
"Artists show how we can be the creators—not just critics—of culture. Thoughtful, insightful essays wrestle with theology and practice of the creative enterprise. You'll see hints of classics from Madeleine L'Engle (*Walking on Water*), Hans Rookmaaker (*Art Needs No Justification*), and Richard Niebuhr (*Christ and Culture*)."
—*Christianity Today*

"This has proved to be a valuable, insightful and penetrating collection: a very fine "gateway" into a growing field."—Jeremy Begbie, Duke University

The Beginning: A Second Look at the First Sin
"Bauer's work demonstrates a strong commitment to the authority of Scripture as well as a creative approach to the theology of the fall into sin. His efforts will stimulate much helpful discussion about the nature of good and evil on very practical levels."—Richard Pratt, Reformed Theological Seminary

Objects of Grace: Conversations on Creativity and Faith
"[A] colorful and concise collection of interviews and art from some of America's most intriguing Christian artists. [James] Romaine interviews ten artists, presenting color reproductions of the artists' work along with the text of the interviews. Each artist dialogues on what it means for a Christian to engage in the creating process."—*Image: A Journal of the Arts & Religion*

C.S. Lewis and the Arts: Creativity in the Shadowlands
"This thought-provoking collection of essays refreshes and refocuses our understanding of C.S. Lewis's work. It does this by re-establishing the importance of the relationship of art and aesthetics to Lewis's moral and ethical writings while providing fresh insight into some of his own artistic endeavors. It is a brilliant book that needs to be on the shelf of every Lewis fan or scholar."—Dr. Melody Green, Urbana Theological Seminary

To learn more about these books as well as the entire Square Halo Books catalog, visit:

SQUAREHALOBOOKS.COM